COOPERATIVE LEARNING, COOPERATIVE LIVES

A Sourcebook of
Learning Activities for
Building a Peaceful World

Nancy Schniedewind
and
Ellen Davidson

DISTRIBUTED BY:
CIRCLE OOKS
30 WALNUT STREET
SOMERVILLE, MASS. 02143

Wm. C. Brown Company Publishers
Dubuque, Iowa

Book Team

Publisher—Ernest T. Nedder
Editorial Director—Sandra Hirstein
Production Editor—Marilyn Bowers Gorun
Production Coordinator—Marilyn Rothenberger
Art Director—Cathy Frantz
Illustrators—Susan Jones
           Noelle Porter

ISBN 0–697–02274–9

10 9 8 7 6 5 4

CONTENTS

ACKNOWLEDGMENTS

Cooperative Learning, Cooperative Lives is truly a work enriched by collaboration! The energy and dedication of many people are reflected in its pages.

The creative and life-filled art work was done by Susan Jones, with several pictures by Noelle Porter. The cartoonist whose work appears most frequently is Bulbul. Several New York teachers have spent many hours with us sharing feedback and ideas based on their own teaching expertise. They include Mary Travis, David Bloom, Marie Turowski, Mary Pezzo, Jacques Chaput and Marni Panuska. Their input has been invaluable. Thanks also to Nancy and Ted Graves and Mara Sapon-Shevin of the International Association for the Study of Cooperation in Education (IASCE) for reviewing the manuscript and offering very useful suggestions and support. Our dedicated typists were Marni Panuska and Ed Seliger.

Nancy owes special thanks to Hank Kopple of the Philadelphia Affective Education Program for introducing her to cooperative learning and to David and Roger Johnson for initial training in the field. To teachers working with her in the Poughkeepsie, New York Public Schools Cooperative Learning Project, the Cooperative Learning Project at the Evans School in Wappingers Falls, New York, the Human Rights Education Program of the Shoreham-Wading River Schools, New York, and to graduate students in her course "Cooperative Structured Learning," Nancy gives particular appreciation for their willingness to implement so much of what they learned about cooperation in their classrooms and for their generosity in sharing inspiring anecdotes and enriching feedback. Various members of IASCE have offered plentiful knowledge and inspiration. Her very special thanks goes to family and friends, especially Dave, Jesse, Mom, Carol and Lee, for renewing her energy day to day over the years.

This book is dedicated to David Porter and Jim Hammerman whose commitment to cooperation in their values, ideas and life practice has sustained and nurtured the vision in this book. It is also for Jesse whose creativity, effervescence, and zest for life affirms our hope for the future.

INTRODUCTION

"We did it!" Think of the high level of energy and the proud feelings students express when they successfully accomplish an academic task or class project together with their peers. Whether it's performing a play, solving a complicated math puzzle, running a relay, figuring out a scientific experiment, presenting a concert, or creating change through a community action project, students experience not only shared accomplishment, but also positive feelings toward each other. The aim of this book is to enable you to create this constructive experience of cooperation in both student learning and student interaction in your classroom.

Cooperative Learning, Cooperative Lives: A Sourcebook of Activities for Building a Peaceful World is a resource book for teachers. It will help make your classes places of increased learning, caring, and cooperation. It provides a teaching methodology to enable your students to improve individual mastery of academic skills, successfully reach academic goals together, and relate to each other with more respect, concern, and liking. Its lessons help students see how cooperation offers the potential for fulfilling interaction with others, enriched lives in our communities, equity in our nation, and peace in the world.

This volume is a handbook for learning cooperation. This phrase has two meanings. First, this book enables students to learn together cooperatively in the classroom. Lessons employ an innovative, but very well-tested, teaching methodology—cooperatively-structured learning. When learning is structured cooperatively, students work on an academic task with each other, rather than competitively or individually. They help each other learn, are accountable for the task as a group, and are responsible for their own and each other's progress. Young people work together so **everyone** succeeds. In the process, your classroom can become a learning laboratory of cooperation.

Second, the learning activities in this book help students explore the idea of cooperation itself as it affects them, their classroom, friends, communities, and the broader society. Through both interdisciplinary and content-area lessons, they consider the price we sometimes pay for competition and they become aware of the potential benefits of cooperative alternatives. They explore how cooperation among people can bring greater equality for all and can reduce the harmful effects sometimes caused by competition.

Cooperation is important not only for schools, but for society as well. If we are to survive as human beings and transform a world of inequality, international conflict, and potential nuclear disaster, young people must develop cooperative skills and values more fully than their elders have. Since we live in an increasingly interdependent society, we must teach collaboration. For with it comes the possibility of survival, justice and peace.

TEACHERS AND COOPERATION

A focus on cooperation can meet many of the needs you currently face as a teacher. Cooperatively-structured learning has proven to be very effective in dealing with two major expectations that teachers, parents, and societies have for students: academic achievement and the development of constructive patterns of social interaction.

A commitment many teachers make is to promote academic excellence for **all** their students. Given the heterogeneous nature of our classrooms—with students mixed by academic skill levels, race, class background or handicap—this is difficult. Cooperatively-structured learning is one of the best methods of ensuring academic achievement for all students, while also enhancing respect for diversity and decreasing prejudice, competition, and aggression. Most teachers seek to improve students' higher order cognitive abilities. Cooperatively-structured learning becomes even more appropriate when that goal is considered. More than most other approaches, cooperatively-structured learning increases students' ability to comprehend, analyze, interpret, and evaluate material, and to solve problems and draw conclusions.

Cooperatively-structured learning also engages students in learning with each other. Students learn skills and information that they can use—to affect their lives, improve their interaction with others, and benefit society. They learn to interact constructively with their peers, both those like and those different from themselves. Recent studies show that what teachers and parents most want for children is that they develop intellectually, personally, and socially. Cooperatively-structured learning can be extremely effective in helping children reach these goals.

We expect, as well, that *Cooperative Learning, Cooperative Lives* may meet some of your personal needs as an educator by stimulating your thinking and renewing your commitment to teaching. Your thoughtful exploration of the issues raised in this book will provide a chance for you to examine how we are socialized in school and society with regard to cooperation and competition. You may be challenged to examine your own assumptions, values, and classroom practices. While some examples and situations in the lessons may be different from those in your own life experience, we hope you'll be open to exploring these cooperative models of interaction and living. In addition, cooperatively-structured learning provides a new teaching approach that can enliven and freshen you as a teacher. It will support **you** in making your classroom a more supportive and enjoyable one. Finally, by helping students better understand cooperation, and offering a vision of a cooperative society and world, you are making an important contribution to our collective hope for justice and peace.

As individuals and educators we fully support appropriate competition. There are many times in both learning situations and in life that competition can be valuable, equitable, and fun. However, since in our society and schools competition is more pervasive than cooperation, and since students have fewer opportunities to learn and practice cooperation, this book focuses particularly on cooperation.

APPROACH TO LEARNING

The activities in *Cooperative Learning, Cooperative Lives* reflect a humanistic approach to education. Cognitive and affective learning is integrated so that students not only gain knowledge about cooperation, but also learn how to cooperate. By its nature, cooperative learning is participatory and experiential. Students become engaged with each other and, with your guidance, are able to analyze how well they collaborate and then practice ways to improve their skills. Some activities employ an inquiry approach where the outcome of student investigation may be different from group to group and school to school. We believe this is as it should be.

Activities in *Cooperative Learning, Cooperative Lives* combine standard academic subject matter with knowledge about, and skills for, collaboration. While many lessons are interdisciplinary, others focus on particular subject areas such as social studies, language arts, math, science, art, and physical education. While participating in a language arts lesson, for example, students learn about cooperation and how to cooperate. Both the content and process of this resource book create positive interdependence among students. While written for upper elementary and middle/junior high school students, many of the activities, especially those in Chapters 6 and 7, are appropriate for high school students as well.

FORMAT AND SEQUENCE

The foundation of *Cooperative Learning, Cooperative Lives* is a thoughtful developmental plan. Through carefully-sequenced chapters and lessons focused on various content areas, students slowly build cognitive understandings about cooperation and process skills for working together.

Chapter 1 provides the rationale for *Cooperative Learning, Cooperative Lives.* Detailing the effects of competition on schools and society, it illustrates the positive changes that are possible from more cooperative approaches to learning and living. Chapter 2 contains more concrete information about cooperative learning in schools. It offers teachers practical strategies, learning formats, and solutions to problems common to cooperative methods.

Learning activities that are structured cooperatively comprise the remaining chapters. Students will develop skills for working together interdependently through the **process** of doing the activities. Similarly, through the **content** of the activities, students will learn about ways people have cooperated, do cooperate, and can cooperate in their lives, communities, and society. In other words, students will examine how the cooperation they experience in cooperative learning groups can be transposed to their school, communities, the nation, and the world. Values implicit in cooperative learning are a democratic sharing of responsibility and power, appreciation of diversity, and responsibility for self **and** others. Examples of cooperation beyond the classroom that reflect these values will be highlighted in the learning activities.

Chapters are arranged sequentially from more simple to advanced levels of cooperation, both in terms of process and content. It is crucial that students develop a core of fundamental skills to work efficiently in cooperative groups. Various lessons in the first two activity chapters teach these skills. In Chapter 3, students can practice basic communication skills—sharing feelings, giving feedback, and listening. Activities in Chapter 4 provide opportunities to learn more advanced skills—among them brainstorming, group process skills, role play and conflict-resolution methods.

Also introduced sequentially are cooperative learning formats—the forms in which students work together. Activities in Chapter 3 provide opportunities for students to use Partner and Group Project formats. Through lessons in Chapter 4 these are reinforced while students are also introduced to the Jigsaw, Peer Teaching and Cross-age Project formats. To increase both the variety and complexity of interdependence, students may participate in Learning Center, Cooperative Card Game, Cooperative Board Game, and Research Project formats in Chapter 5. Finally, in Chapter 6, a Cooperative Treasure Hunt is presented. In this way, students engage in a repertoire of cooperative learning formats as the year progresses. Thereby learning remains challenging and engaging and, by the end of the year, students are skilled at learning together in a variety of mutually-supportive ways. A few lessons in each chapter are not structured cooperatively. These lessons either teach a skill or provide an experience to highlight possible prices of competition. The key to these lessons does not indicate a format.

The development of the theme of cooperation in the content of the activities is also sequential. Lessons in Chapter 3, "Finding and Appreciating Strengths in Ourselves and Others," focus on cooperation and competition in the lives of your students. Activities help students develop or reaffirm a positive self-image, so that their needs to be competitive, aggressive, and superior are reduced, and their potential for collaboration enhanced. Rather than being threatened by differences, students realize how they can learn from these differences and therefore are attracted to cooperation rather than to competition.

Chapter 4, "Joining Together at School," contains lessons that enable students to see how competition can hinder friendships. These lessons teach students better to cooperate with their peers. Also explored are ways in which peer groups can be a source of positive influence, ways to learn from group diversity, and alternatives to violence—through conflict resolution. Creative projects that students can carry out independently to enrich the school are highlighted.

Chapter 5, "Pulling Together in Families, Communities, and Workplaces," provides lessons that explore how competition can affect those various settings in students' immediate environments and presents cooperative alternatives. The focus is on concrete examples of people in families, communities and jobs joining together toward mutually-beneficial goals.

Activities in Chapter 6, "Making Everyone Winners Across the Land," provide opportunities for students to examine how competitive individualism and competitive policies and practices of social institutions can negatively affect groups of people in our country and serve to divide Americans. Through examples from past and present, students learn ways in which people can work interdependently toward goals which unite all of us for the good of us all.

"Working Together for Worldwide Interdependence and Peace," Chapter 7, contains lessons that offer a vision of a cooperative and peaceful world and strategies for its realization. Again using historical and current examples, students examine how nations' dependence on force and violence, extreme nationalism, and international one-up-manship affect global relations. Students are then exposed to both collaborative alternatives within nations and models for peace among nations of the world. Student initiatives that can contribute to worldwide understanding and peace conclude the chapter. Thus, over the course of the year, students expand their awareness of cooperation—from self to society.

The Resources section of *Cooperative Learning, Cooperative Lives* contains practical information to assist you in making cooperative learning work in your classroom. Initially, ten different Teaching Formats to structure learning cooperatively are described, with advantages and disadvantages of each. A variety of Evaluation Formats are listed. From these, you may choose appropriate ones to use in evaluating both the content of what students learn and the process of their cooperative work. Each description includes an example and details of the respective advantages and disadvantages of the format. The "What Would You Do If . . . ?" section suggests alternative strategies for dealing with common problems that may arise when you start transforming your class into an experience in cooperation. Concluding the Resources section are supportive statements from teachers and students, veterans of cooperative learning.

The annotated Bibliography includes books and articles on cooperative learning, children's stories and resources about cooperation, background reading for teachers about interdependence in learning and living, and relevant media resources.

USING THE BOOK

Cooperative Learning, Cooperative Lives fits easily into your standard curriculum. While it's important to follow the chapters and subsections sequentially, you may choose those lessons from each chapter section that will be most appropriate for your students. Most teachers of the middle grades will choose to use *Cooperative Learning,*

Cooperative Lives over the course of a year. Others will choose to use only segments of the book at a given grade level. Since the concepts and cooperative learning formats are most basic in Chapters 3 and 4, a fourth-grade teacher in one school district might choose to use only those activities with her class. In another district, an eighth-grade social studies teacher might find the activities in Chapter 7 ideal for his students and curriculum. While the activities have been developed to be integrated throughout the school year, such adaptations are certainly appropriate.

First read Chapters 1 and 2, and then the materials in the Resources section of the book. Skim the activity chapters. Then go back and work slowly through the lessons you select to use. Lessons include helpful guidelines for implementation. The subject matter and type of cooperative learning format are each coded in the right hand corner. Objectives are spelled out, as are materials needed. Implementation steps follow. Most lessons include a section called "Completion." This describes what the group must complete in order for each student to receive credit for the activity. If you need or want to grade students for lessons, or want to further assess content learning of individual students, choose one of the evaluation methods described in the Resources.

It is ideal if you can form a support group with other teachers who will work together to implement cooperative learning. If there aren't enough teachers in your school, create a group with teachers from other schools. You can provide suggestions, feedback, and encouragement for each other. Take inservice training when possible. Try to arrange released-time to visit each others' classrooms to provide ideas and support. Try to structure opportunity for team teaching. Don't underestimate the power of cooperation among teachers!

This book is a resource of cooperatively-structured learning activities. While Chapter 2 and the Resources section provide a solid overview of cooperative methods, this book is not a comprehensive introduction to cooperative learning *per se.* The many teachers who have had courses or inservice training in cooperative learning, or who have read books about this approach and have implemented cooperative learning in their classrooms, will be ready to use the activities in this book. Educators without background in cooperative learning would be advised also to read materials devoted to cooperative learning as a teaching methodology, such as *Learning Together and Alone* by David and Roger Johnson or other books described in Chapter 2. For teachers unfamiliar with the use of small groups in the classroom, a book such as *Developing Effective Classroom Groups* by Gene Stanford would also be useful.

Cooperatively-structured learning is not for everyone. At first, cooperative learning is difficult to implement because it takes careful thought relative to structuring your classroom and your preparation time. While cooperative learning makes teaching much easier and more enjoyable, it is a method for those teachers willing to put thoughtful time into planning. A teacher using cooperative learning needs to feel comfortable having students work in small classroom groups. An educator using this approach will want to feel secure enough in the classroom to be able to delegate some responsibility, decision making, and power to students. One veteran teacher might excitedly jump into the activities in this book, another might decide it's not for him, while a beginning teacher might wait a year to solidify classroom management techniques and gain self confidence before trying cooperative learning. All are fine decisions!

By asking students to examine the ideas of cooperation and competition, *Cooperative Learning, Cooperative Lives* encourages critical thinking. Young people and adults alike are seldom challenged to assess these modes of interaction which are the underpinnings of all aspects of society, from the personal to the social. Just as the pedagogy of cooperatively-structured learning sometimes raises eyebrows in a school district, so too might the questioning of assumptions about competition and cooperation. Though it is not encouraged in all school districts, such critical thinking is, we feel, essential to meaningful education. Only when students are exposed to all points of view about various ideas and values can they make thoughtful decisions about their lives and about their participation in society. That, we believe, is what education in a democratic society is all about.

It is our experience that activities in *Cooperative Learning, Cooperative Lives* can be taught in most school districts. That is not to say that you shouldn't be prepared for resistance. Some teachers, administrators, and parents, because of misinformation, closed value systems, or political viewpoints, oppose the teaching of critical thinking. Your commitment to providing all students with skills and knowledge for developing a critical awareness about competition and cooperation, and with skills for critical thinking as well, will be important in meeting any resistance. Other educators and parents who share your aims can be enlisted to support these goals.

In fact, many teachers who use cooperatively-structured learning and teach about cooperation involve parents from the beginning of the school year. They write parents explaining: that their child will be in a cooperative classroom where he or she will be sharing the responsibility for learning with peers; that some lessons will be structured cooperatively; and that children will be examining the implications of cooperation for their own lives and for society. Some teachers even structure parents' nights cooperatively so parents can *experience* cooperative learning and thus understand it and support it. Teachers encourage parents to be involved in cooperative classroom projects throughout the year. Why not try some of these, or other, approaches to parental involvement appropriate to your situation!

TEACHING FOR EACH AND ALL

We write this book with the hope that by teaching for each and all, educators across America will become part of a strong and intricate web of educational and social change. Our classrooms will become more cooperative ones, where all students will learn to value and respect each other, support and be supported in academic development and learn cooperative skills for lifelong use. Moreover, by proposing cooperative models for learning and living, we will contribute to the longer-range goal many of us share—an equitable society and a peaceful world.

1 WHY COOPERATIVE LEARNING AND LIVING

The effects of cooperation or competition on our learning and our lives are extremely powerful, whether or not we have stopped to think about that. Our early school memories often trigger recognition of the influence of competition or cooperation. For most of us, products of standard classrooms and a competitive society, competitive experiences dominate. Scan your memory to see if any of these following scenarios were real to you as a child. Since this is a book on cooperation, why not read aloud with a friend, one reading "one-up" and the other "one-down." Share the memories these experiences trigger.

a. **"One-up"**

You raise your hand wildly, wanting the teacher to call on you. She calls on someone else. You're happy when he gets the answer wrong. Before he finishes, you wave more wildly, with the hope that now you can get a chance to show the teacher and other students how smart you are.

"One-down"

You go out to recess and the teacher picks two captains who will choose teams. You wait and wait to be picked until you're almost alone. You feel worse and worse. . . .

b. **"One-up"**

You develop a passionate jealousy toward a student in your class who does as well as you academically. You're ostensibly friendly to her, but inside you feel hostile, especially when you lean over toward her desk to see what grade she got, and it's higher than yours.

"One-down"

You cheat. You know it's not right, but feel you can't get a high grade without resorting to that crib sheet or wandering eye syndrome. The day of the test you make sure to sit next to someone who "knows it."

c. **"One-up"**

You're walking home from school and come up behind some students in a lower grade. You and your friends threaten, "Clear the sidewalks, you squirts, or we'll clear it ourselves!" As they step aside, you feel powerful and strong.

"One-down"

At recess, a group of students pick on you and grab your hat. "Catch us if you can!" When you don't go after them, they taunt, "Scairdy cat, scairdy cat! Com'on, you sissy!" You retort, "Sticks and stones can break my bones, but names can never hurt me," but inside you're hurt, embarrassed, and afraid. You vow to get your big brother to teach you how to fight so you can "get even."

d. **"One-up"**

You come to believe that some kids in your class can't learn a thing. You call them dumb—or at least think that. You avoid the "slow" kids at recess, in the lunchroom, and on the bus.

"One-down"

You feel very inadequate when put in a low group. From then on, you believe you'll never be "good" in that subject.

My first grade teacher divided my class into three singing groups—the Robins, Bluebirds and Frogs. Yes! And I was in the Frogs. Not only did we sit closest to the teacher—so she could interrupt easily to correct our pitch with her round "harmonica"—but we were allowed to sing only a fraction of the songs. Most of the time we sat quietly listening to the sweet intonations of Bluebirds and Robins. Despite encouragement and prodding from upper grade teachers, I would never try out for elementary chorus. I was sure a "frog" could never "make it."

Nancy

e. **"One-up"**

You tell friends you really didn't study much for the upcoming test, even though you did. You don't want to seem too eager to learn. Yet when papers are given back, you privately squabble with the teacher over two points, which would make the difference between an A− and a B+.

"One-down"

You don't understand the math problem that the teacher has done on the board, but you're afraid to raise your hand in front of the whole class for fear of being embarrassed and looking stupid. (Little do you know that half the class feels the same way!)

Now try to imagine yourself as a child in a different kind of classroom—one structured cooperatively. Seldom do you feel one-up or one-down, but usually "one-with" others. You do a significant amount of work in small groups. Because group members are responsible for each other and accountable as a group, you want others to learn, and are happy when they can have a right answer. You feel pride if other students do well.

There is little need to cheat, for you're encouraged to ask other students for help. You're more comfortable taking tests or writing papers because you've been helped by your peers to learn the material. They've made sure you understand it. Since you'll be evaluated as a group, you're not in it alone. All do their best for the sake of the group.

Even though you used to classify some kids as "dummies," doing that doesn't make you feel one-up any more. You've helped "slow" kids study and seen that they learn well, only sometimes in different ways and at a different pace than you. In fact, in some cases they have skills that you don't have. Furthermore, by working in groups, you've found that you have much in common with students you put down before. Now you play soccer together after school. You don't put-down and others don't put you down. There's no need to. Your self-concept is just fine without having to bolster it at the expense of someone else.

Since groups are heterogeneous, you're not placed in a "low group." Even though there are differences in how quickly students learn certain things, you talk about that and accept the differences. While you do some things very well, in different subject areas other students are more advanced than you.

You don't mind admitting that you know the material. This gives your group confidence and enables you to help others. In turn, you feel comfortable admitting that you're confused, since now you can easily ask another group member for assistance. You've learned that to admit you don't understand something is the best way to get help and your group can succeed. Your own self-confidence as a group has been bolstered because you've been able to complete marvelous projects as a group that you never could have done yourself.

At recess, and to-and-from school, you don't feel the need to use your physical strength, age or status to bully others. While you used to feel "might makes right," you no longer experience the need to threaten or pick on others. When conflicts do occur, you know there are alternatives to fists, taunts, and powerplays for settling them.

And on the playground, when a game requires teams, you are divided up in creative ways, not on the basis of skill. Lots of games are cooperative, so it's not a matter of how good you are as an individual but how well you play together as a group.

You like the other students in your class and feel confident in your skills and abilities. The academic involvement of your whole class is high. You know that others care that you learn just as you care that they learn. You feel accepted, you are part of a community.

The second classroom is not a "pie-in-the-sky" fantasy. It is an example of many cooperatively-structured classrooms fostering increased achievement, positive self-concept, and positive peer interaction. While developing such a classroom does take hard work over a long period of time, and while initially some students may be resistant, it is do-able! *Cooperative Learning, Cooperative Lives* is a resource for creating such a classroom.

Before describing the practicalities of creating this classroom, let's examine competition and cooperation and their implications for both learning and living. How do we define these two modes of interaction? Competition implies that people learn or work as individuals **against** each other, most often with inequitable resources and opportunities, toward goals that benefit themselves. Policies of competitively-structured institutions reinforce such individualism. Cooperation suggests people working **together** toward **common** goals that benefit *all*. Norms and values of institutions, in this case, are those which reinforce collaboration. The following chart provides more detail . . . and food for thought.

Competition	Cooperation
My goal is most important.	Both the common goal and my goal are important.
I work and learn alone.	I work and learn with others.
I work and live to benefit myself.	I work and live to benefit both myself and others.
Protecting my own information and ideas is important.	Trust and sharing with others is important.
I consider my needs first.	I consider both my needs and others' needs as important.
I have positive feelings when I succeed or win over others.	I have positive feelings when all succeed, together.
I feel good about myself when I top others.	I feel good about myself when I accomplish something in collaboration with others.
A positive value is to support myself; others are unimportant unless I need them to help me.	A positive value is to support and help others as well as myself.
I am responsible and accountable only to myself.	I am responsible and accountable to myself and to others.
Others refer not merely to family, friends, or peer group, but to people different from ourselves—low-skilled students if we are highly skilled, low-income people if we are middle-class, and so forth.	

While the chart sets up competition and cooperation as two poles, most likely you thought of many ways they overlap in your daily life and work. Clearly the reality of our lives is complex. Also, as we discuss later, there are many situations where cooperation is appropriate, just as in others competition is—especially in situations that produce minimal anxiety and in which everyone has an equal chance of winning. Nevertheless, it is important to be clear about those concepts and the values implicit in each.

As authors, we value both appropriate competition and cooperation. Yet we believe that cooperative ideas and values have the potential of offering us so much more in our lives, schools, and society than we currently allow them to.

Our approach to cooperatively-structured learning reflects a particular teaching philosophy as well as a commitment to cooperation as a positive idea in learning and living. While you may not agree with all the value implications of cooperation, you can still use the teaching philosophy and strategies in your classroom, and with great success. While we hope you will utilize what you're comfortable with, we also urge you to keep an open mind to the possibilities for cooperation that you may never have considered before!

THE EFFECTS OF COMPETITION IN SCHOOLS

Our nation's schools, by and large, foster more competition than cooperation. Students learn well that success in school means getting a gold star, achieving the best grade, or attaining a high class ranking. Students learn less well how to work cooperatively with others, how to help others toward their goals, and how to create situations where everyone can succeed. While it is important that students learn healthy and productive ways to compete, an overemphasis on competition can be harmful.

On the preschool level achievement orientations are primed with stars, stickers, and other symbols of scholarly success. The elementary years extend the symbols to include badges, certificates, and report cards. Formal arenas for besting are provided in the form of spelling bees and other pupil contests. By junior high at the latest the competition has stopped being fun and games. The pace is now stepped up to include marking on the curve, honor rolls, and the ever-present goading of grades as the key to college admission. The system reaches its apex in the senior year with specifications of class rank, merit scholarship, a plethora of awards for achievement in a variety of subjects and a constant shadow of college board scores cast over high achievers.

The system continues. High achievers are considered, and ironically consider themselves, even more fortunate in overcoming standardized examinations for graduate schools with hardly a respite for yet other hurdles to come. Competition becomes more painful and the stakes become higher; the fun and games of early childhood often turn to deadly contests. By definition, where rewards are limited, some must be losers.

Emmy A. Pepitone,
Children in Cooperation and Competition,
Lexington, MA: D.C. Heath, 1980, xxii-iii.

Students' learning, self-concept, and ability and inclination to work with others can be impeded in a school where there is a major stress on competition. This can be explicit in practices such as posting an Honor Roll or in the spelling baseball example described below, or implicit such as individual students getting praise for doing better than someone else. Jules Henry describes a typical competitive scenario—a game of spelling baseball. In an effort to take the boredom out of learning spelling, the teacher has, consciously or not, set up four layers of competition. Children compete with each other to get the words right, compete with peers for status and approval, compete for approval of the teacher, and compete as members of a team. Two children are chosen captains and the teacher gives out words to learn. In the game, each word is a pitched ball and each spelled correctly a base hit. As the outs increase, so does the pressure on the students.

> The child who is now writing "Thursday" stops to think after the first letter and the children snicker. He stops after another letter. More snickers. He gets the word wrong. There are frequent signs of joy from the children when their side is right. . . . Although the children may never learn to spell "success" . . ., they know what it is, how to go after it, and how it feels not to have it.
>
> Jules Henry,
> "In Suburban Classrooms" (86,87).

Think about both your school experiences as a student and your current teaching situation. Are any of the following effects of an overemphasis on competition familiar to you? When students consistently evaluate their academic potential in comparison to others, academic learning often suffers. Slow learners begin a cycle of failure. Some do anything—act out in class, feign understanding, cut class—to avoid admitting failure. Others pretend to understand nothing in order to get the teacher to leave them alone and never question them. Others give up entirely, believing that they are stupid and can't learn. A fourth-grade student in a resource room, when recently given the task of drawing an animal, drew a rhinocerous. He reported, "I wanted to make something ugly. Everything I do turns out ugly, so I wanted to start out with something ugly." This child had not only internalized low self-expectations, but had begun to protect himself accordingly. In a cooperative environment, that protective energy might be transformed into successful academic experiences!

Fast learners too are hurt by excessive competition. These students often develop a psychic investment in "being best," and then have trouble dealing with failure, or experiencing equality with others. They judge their successes by extrinsic motives, rather than intrinsic ones, and sometimes lose the joy of learning. Learning becomes a means to an end—and the end is winning. If their priority is doing better than others, cheating often becomes acceptable. Even when students understand something, they may be unwilling to help others, for such would threaten their status. For example, in our local gifted program there was only enough room for six children from each grade; therefore, advanced students wouldn't help each other, for those "others" were a threat to their status in the special program. Furthermore, fast learners often put down slower learners, reinforcing their own sense of superiority, and sometimes creating tension or conflict in the class. High achievers also can shy away from risk-taking, declining participation in new types of activities because they want to be sure to succeed.

Perhaps you've seen how students' self-worth suffers as well. In a competitive environment students often learn to feel good about themselves by putting other people down. How many put-downs do you hear each day in your school? The playground and bus are often worse. On the elementary-middle school bus that travels one of the author's roads, a constant taunt to the day's outcast is commonly heard through the open windows—"You're the stupidest kid in the schoool. You're the stupidest kid in the schoool. . . . "

Overly competitive environments thwart young people's skills and inclinations to help each other. Many students come to dislike behaviors that enhance another's success and have angry feelings toward themselves, winners, and school. In a classic study by Linden Nelson and Spencer Kagan, ten-year-olds in Los Angeles sacrificed their own rewards in a marble pull game in order to reduce the rewards of their peers. Students are losing out not only on the knowledge that our success doesn't have to be at the expense of someone else, but also that in helping others we often help ourselves.

Conclusions: The Kagan and Masden Study

Anglo-American children took toys away from peers 75% of the time if they couldn't have one. The research shows environments provided kids are barren of experiences that sensitize them to the possibilities of cooperation. Anglo-American children fail to realize what they get in a situation is a function of what others do as well as their efforts.

Linden Nelson and Spencer Kagan,
Psychology Today (9/72): 53–56, 90–91.

The development of self-centered personalities in competitive classrooms and schools ultimately has negative effects on society as a whole. Emmy Pepitone conducted an experiment with second graders where there was a scarcity of materials. **Not one** of the children thought of helping others. The development of such a strong sense of personal deservedness in people doesn't lend itself to a society of cooperation and peace. However, anthropologists tell us that scarcity conditions don't have to lead to competition; in many cultures they lead to sharing. In fact, in the Phoenix School in Cambridge, Massachusetts, where classes are structured cooperatively, scarcity of material produces the opposite effect from Pepitone's study. It produces sharing.

Unless faced with a dissonant experience, a child growing up in a world where much is given and little is asked will come to believe she is entitled to such treatment and will see a just world as one where objects can be had for the asking or taking.

Emmy A. Pepitone,
Children in Cooperation and Competition,
Lexington, MA: D.C. Heath, 1980, 317.

You might think. . . . But wait, we talk with children about cooperation, we encourage them to work with each other. . . . Yes, educators talk a lot about cooperation. However, when we take a closer look and compare our practices to our words, there is often a stark discrepancy. In the 1930s, in a classic study of cooperation and competition in schools, M. May and L. Doob pointed out how the ideology of American education supports cooperation, but how the practical reality does just the opposite. How different is the situation today?

> The state of affairs in American culture then is that, while paying respectful homage to cooperative ideals, we go right on with our competitive system and justify it on the ground that "human nature" is basically and fundamentally competitive and always will be so. . . . In the public school . . . we thus find this curious paradox: the basic structure of the system is competitive; but the ideals of cooperation are emphasized. . . . The set up of the school is such that a large portion of daily activities of the pupils is more competitive than cooperative. At the same time, all of the human virtues and attitudes that are favorable to cooperation are stressed.
>
> M. May and L. Doob,
> *Competition and Cooperation.*

We encourage you to look again at your classroom and school. What effect is competition having on the students you teach?

OUR SOCIETY: SOME PRICES OF COMPETITION

While as an educator you are perhaps largely concerned about what you can change in your classroom and school, what happens there is reflective of, and has impact upon, how we live together in society. After all, conditions in society affect our feelings, opportunities, and options as educators, just as they profoundly affect the lives of our students.

> Individualism finds its roots in an attempt to deny the reality and importance of human interdependence. One of the major goals of technology in America is to "free us" from the necessity of relating to, submitting to, depending on, or controlling other people. Unfortunately the more we have succeeded in doing this the more we have felt disconnected, bored, lonely, unprotected, unnecessary and unsafe.
>
> Philip Slater,
> *The Pursuit of Loneliness.*

> No one is ever good enough in a competitive situation. Each success is temporary. Immediately upon achieving success the competition begins for the next prize. Competition encourages separateness.
>
> Ruth Salo, preschool teacher,
> Pearl River, NY.

Consider the impact of an overemphasis of competition in society. Many people feel very much alone or "on their own" in the world. Some are very reticent to ask others for help and to interact or work with people different from themselves. Many profess and live by the value, "I'm out for Number One." Examples come quickly to mind. In your daily life you probably see people out for their own ends, with no concern for how their actions affect others. Examples cross all class and professional lines, such as medical students who deliberately and secretly ruin their classmates' cadavers. The nightly news brings into our homes accounts of worldwide conflict, war and human suffering precipitated by international competition. Today excessive competition brings with it the potential of the annihilation of human life itself. National self-interest, comparable to individualism in personal life, usually blocks more cooperative alternatives to the resolution of conflict.

Think about the very real and very high cost of an overemphasis on competition. Have you ever physically hurt yourself moving or lifting something because you were reticent to ask a friend or neighbor for help? Competition can cost money too! In some communities each family owns items that neighbors could share, for example—lawn mowers, power drills, ladders and so forth. Nor do we make life as easy for ourselves as we could—financially and psychologically. Some household members, in areas of high crime rate, either worry excessively, curtail their movement in their neighborhood, or invest in elaborate and expensive crime prevention devices. Cooperative, neighborhood safety watches, as already organized in some communities, are not only cheaper and more effective, but build neighborhood solidarity as well.

No Contest

For a superb analysis of the prices we pay for competition in our society, see *No Contest: The Case Against Competition* by Alfie Kohn. It carefully documents why we lose in our race to win.

Look at typical work situations. Overemphasis on competition fosters the "struggle to get to the top at any cost" mentality. How often do people stop to think about the prices of such a race and the "rewards" of heart attacks and death in the prime of life? Structural competition also reinforces hierarchical work situations where a few people in top positions do excessive amounts of work, often for disproportionate salaries. At the same time, other people with comparable skills or potential are out of work. More egalitarian, cooperatively-structured institutions could include more people and better use the talents of many competent people. More broadly-based decision making would result from such changes. Too often those at the top of institutional hierarchies fail to consult others for fear of looking inept or indecisive, while the most creative solutions to problems usually result from lots of heads, not just one.

Our society's expectation that we should compete rather than cooperate keeps us from seeing the ways our lives are connected with others. Our privileges and goods for daily living come to us from the shared labor of others. For example, the food bought at the supermarket has been grown, picked, packaged, transported, and shelved by the work of others. When you stop at a traffic light, do you think of the labor of the following people: the inventor (a black man, Garrett Morgan), the constructors, installers, repairers? Their ingenuity and skill prevents you from getting hurt. When you give in to the temptation of throwing a piece of paper on the floor of a public building or highway, do you remember that someone—even if it's not you—will have to pick it up?

Friendship and Competition

Michael Spino describes his reaction to an early basketball practice session when his friend broke his ankle. "I was glad—happy that the competition for community love was lessened."

Michael Spino,
"Athletes: The Competition for Community Love."

Many people have a hard time understanding the life experiences and needs of those different from themselves. The competitive norms in our society and the practices of its institutions contribute to this. When people strive to get ahead at the expense of other people, it is counterproductive to look at the feelings or viewpoints of others. To do so would likely impede personal progress, or cause rethinking of priorities—which, we fear, would result in self-defeat. This fear is false.

Societal values and institutional practices bolster competitive individualism, the notion that each person's success or failure in life depends solely on her efforts and merit, and that each person has an equal chance to compete and succeed. This contrasts with the growing awareness among Americans that one's race, sex, class or age is often a powerful determining factor in one's chances for success. Many people, accepting the ideology of competitive individualism, still believe that if they succeed it's because of their goodness. They must compete with others to feel successful and must feel better than others in order to feel good about themselves. With this thinking, people feel they've "made it" on their own and so deserve their position. If others haven't "made it," it's their fault and the "winner" has no responsibility for the "loser." This blaming-the-victim mentality allows people to justify their privilege and others' lack of it without examining the pervasiveness of institutional and societal discrimination. This fosters continued diversion, conflict, and inequality in society.

DO YOU HAVE A GAME WHERE EVERYBODY CHEERS
... FOR PEACE AND JUSTICE !

Competition can encourage individuals, groups, and nations to resolve conflict through use of power, force or violence and to compensate for weakness with physical might. In our personal lives this can take the form of anything from manipulation and subtle power plays that undermine relationships to overt wife battering and child abuse. Young people learn through toys, comics, books, television, and video games that violence is a legitimate means for gaining power and settling conflict. From the supposedly-benign clashing of bodies during the annual Super Bowl to the official sanctioning of war (or the threat of it) as the key to solving international problems, the values, institutions and policies of our nation reinforce the use of power and aggression in order to "win." Such conditioning threatens not only the quality of personal relationships and the potential for a humane society, but the very existence of life on our planet.

As you go through a typical day, look around and think about the impact that an overemphasis on competition has on you, your peers, and our society. Are we learning and living in the most constructive and human way possible? Talk with your friends and colleagues about your observations and thoughts.

COOPERATION IN SCHOOLS: THE POSSIBILITIES AND POTENTIAL

Why, you might ask, should a teacher consider developing a learning situation where cooperative norms, values, and teaching strategies are stressed? And if I'm convinced about the why, what would such a learning situation look like?

The whys of cooperative learning are answered not only by many educational researchers, but by classroom teachers as well. In their excellent book, *Learning Together and Alone: Cooperation, Competition, and Individualization,* David and Roger Johnson provide a very convincing rationale for cooperative learning and a thorough review of research.

In outlining the way learning is structured for student interaction, the Johnsons define three goal structures. These goal structures are described in the box below.

Goal Structures

A competitive goal structure: students perceive that they can obtain their goal if, and only if, certain others fail to obtain theirs.

An individualistic goal structure: the achievement of the goal by one student is unrelated to the goal achievement of others.

A cooperative goal structure: students perceive that they can obtain their goal if, and only if, the other students with whom they are linked can obtain their goal.

New research shows that different goal structures are more conducive than others to particular cognitive outcomes in student learning. Teachers will best teach simple drill activities and competitive skills by structuring learning competitively. For example, speed drills using math flash cards to reinforce tables is highly appropriate. Simple mechanical skills and individualistic skills are most successfully taught by using an individual goal structure. Thus an industrial arts teacher would most effectively structure a lesson on use of the power drill individually. For a wider range of higher-order cognitive skills, such as problem solving, mastery of factual information, mastery of concepts and principles, cooperatively-structured learning is most appropriate.

A cooperative goal structure is more effective than a competitive or individualistic one for producing a wide variety of affective learning outcomes in students. These include pluralistic, democratic values; enjoyment of learning; positive self attitudes; and acceptance of cultural, ethnic, and individual differences.

A summary of the Johnson research is in the next box. Cooperation is the most appropriate goal structure for much of the cognitive and affective learning that teachers desire for their students.

Goal Structures and Cognitive and Affective Outcomes

Cognitive	Coop	Comp	Indiv
Mastery/factual information	x		
Retention, application, transfer of factual information, concepts, principles	x		
Mastery/concepts, principles	x		
Verbal abilities	x		
Problem-solving ability/success	x		
Cooperative skills	x		
Creative ability: divergent and risk-taking thinking, productive controversy	x		
Awareness/utilization of one's capabilities	x		
Perspective- (role-) taking abilities	x		
Speed/quantity of work—drill activities		x	
Competitive skills		x	
Individualistic skills			x
Mechanical skills			x

Affective	Coop	Comp	Indiv
Interpersonal skills for humanness	x		
Group skills for humanness	x		
Pluralistic, democratic values	x		
Acceptance/appreciation of cultural, ethnic, individual differences	x		
Reduction of prejudice/bias	x		
Valuing education	x		
Positive attitudes toward school, subject area, instructional activities, school personnel, other students	x		
Learning enjoyment/satisfaction	x		
Moderate anxiety levels to promote learning	x		
Positive self attitudes	x		
Emotional capacity	x		

Key Coop—Cooperative Goal Structure
Comp—Competitive Goal Structure
Indiv—Individualistic Goal Structure

Now picture a classroom where learning is structured cooperatively. Students work together on a common academic task and when finished exclaim, "**We** did it!" and feel pride in their group accomplishment. You hear, "Maria, I didn't know you spoke Spanish! Can you teach me some words?" In heterogeneous cooperative groups students learn about each others' unique skills and grow in respect for others' life experiences. From another corner comes, "I can help you with that, Raymond." Students not only gain skills in assisting others, they also learn that they are cared about. Cooperation often becomes second nature.

Cooperatively-structured learning positively affects both self-concept and academic learning. Students build confidence working together. They help each other remember multiplication tables using flash cards; they work as a group to plot a journey with an atlas, or use dictionaries to define and help each other learn vocabulary words. Students also accomplish unique projects impossible to do alone. One class programmed a daily news show for the whole school. Only because work was divided and each student did one thing could they create and maintain their exciting program.

Another class created a baby quilt for a teacher who was going to have a baby. Each child designed a square. When the squares were sewn together, they had an incredible quilt—much more striking and exciting, the children felt, than any one square had been. Such spectacular projects not only develop very positive expectations in children about what they can do, the projects also build community!

Students from all achievement levels make gains in cooperatively-structured classrooms. When they help others learn, high achievers develop advanced cognitive skills through teaching. You've probably seen that some high achievers tend to be isolates and often do independent work appropriate to their academic level. For their psychological development, these students need also to work **with** others on stimulating tasks. Cooperatively-structured groups meet that need.

Most assuredly, you've also had slow learners who are so frustrated by a history of failure that they are unwilling to try. In cooperative groups these students usually become willing to take what to them is an academic risk. Because the talents they do have are utilized and appreciated, they become more willing to accept more difficult challenges. For example, a group was assigned to write and illustrate a story cooperatively. Richard didn't write well, but he had a very creative mind and contributed humorous ideas for the plot. His skills were needed, so group members didn't put him down. Richard took pride in the finished project. Later, in a written assignment, Richard was willing to try writing because of the successful cooperative language arts project behind him.

When practicing to function in cooperatively-structured groups, students learn skills that they can use both in and out of school. (You'll gain strategies for teaching these skills to students in Chapters 3 and 4.) Here are just a few examples. Since cooperatively-structured groups demand the constructive involvement of all students, and since teachers set firm norms against put-downs in cooperative classrooms, students develop skills in giving constructive criticism to each other. Students certainly don't learn these skills overnight. They come with practice. And they do come! For example, "Jose, when you don't do your homework I feel let down, because that hurts our project." These "I-messages" are frequently heard not only in the cooperative classrooms, but often on the playground and at home. The box below describes how conflict-resolution skills, taught in a cooperative classroom, were transferred to the playground.

A Principal's Report

Mr. Morrell noticed a fight brewing on the playground. He walked toward it, with plans to break it up. But there was Georgie, a student in a cooperative classroom, mediating the disagreement with cooperative strategies. In several minutes the conflict was resolved, nonviolently and by peers. Mr. Morrell's authority wasn't needed!

Report to Rosemary Tanner, teacher,
by Timothy Morrell, principal,
Columbus School, Poughkeepsie, NY.

The positive effects of cooperative learning in academic subjects apply to physical education and extra-curricular activities as well. For example, Jim Lignori, a teacher in Montgomery, New York, taught a cooperatively-structured soccer team of elementary students. He used cooperative group activities to build cohesion, gave much praise, encouraged peers training peers, did not tolerate verbal abuse of players, and rotated positions during games. During the final championship game, this team played cooperatively as a team and afterward received no negative and blaming criticism from children or parents. In a comparable competitively-oriented team, however, there was much blaming and one child cried from the negative criticism received. All the players on the cooperative team wanted to play again and had confidence they could play. In the competitive team, four wanted no further involvement and three expressed the feeling that they lacked the ability to play successfully.

Creating Winning Children

If the aim of sports is to create a constructive, self-rewarding pastime for children, then the results of this study would suggest that while a cooperative system does not always create a **winning team** it does create **winning children**—boys and girls who have a compassionate understanding of themselves and their friends, and who are anxious to continue having fun **with** people, rather than **for** people.

Jim Lignori,
Montgomery, NY.

Finally, by collaborating, students learn that they can work together to create change. Many young people today feel alienation and powerlessness in their lives. As they grow older, antisocial behaviors can result. However, if students learn that they can collaborate to act upon their world, solve problems, and change that which is unfair, they become more personally powerful and gain confidence to work for constructive changes throughout their lives.

Students learn more than subject matter in these classrooms. They learn basic cooperative skills and attitudes which are vital for people to make change. It is one thing to get a Title I kid to do splendidly and get into Harvard. It is another for a group to know how to bring pressure so that quota systems are dropped and the law changed.

Hank Kopple, Philadelphia Public Schools,
The Interdependence Journal.

IDEALS AND REALITIES: A COOPERATIVE SOCIETY

As we broaden our vision and picture schools where cooperation is valued, let us place this in the context of a more cooperative society. Fortunately, it's not necessary to rely only upon our imaginations to do this. There are many past and current examples of people living and working cooperatively to create better lives for themselves and to foster a more fair society for all.

In early America, colonists collaborated for survival and community. Barn-raisings and quilting bees not only enabled people to accomplish together what they couldn't alone, but provided an opportunity for socializing and festivity. Many cooperative communities, such as those of the Shakers, have existed throughout American history and exist today.

From past to present, various groups who might not ordinarily have interacted came together for common goals. Before the Civil War, blacks and whites, slaves and citizens, Northerners, Southerners and Canadians worked together to sustain the Underground Railroad. Thousands of lives depended on the intricate cooperative network these strangers developed to bring slaves to freedom.

During World War I, scientists from many different countries put aside national self-interest in order to pool their knowledge. Among other successes, they developed penicillin, which ultimately saved thousands of soldiers' lives. More recently, tenant farmers and lawyers, blacks and whites, turn-of-the-century graduates of Tuskegee and contemporary college students joined to participate in sit-ins, voter registration, and marches during the Civil Rights Movement. Significant changes were made in the lives of the oppressed and in the structures perpetuating racism.

Historically and today, creative and cooperative approaches to dealing with conflict and force pose alternatives to the violence that competition breeds. For example, a jail cell full of wives of striking coal miners, inspired by the tireless labor organizer Mother Jones, creatively confronted institutional power by singing loudly to their crying babies throughout the night until released by their frazzled jailkeepers. Today women, men, and children are learning mediation skills. They use these skills to help themselves and others resolve conflicts with friends or family, conflicts in school, and conflicts between groups in large institutions.

Look at our nation's communities today and you will see examples of people improving their lives through cooperation. In a school in one of our communities, a teacher of children with disabilities developed a peer-assistance program including the disabled and the abled-bodied. It was a magnificent success! Handicapped children receive friendship and special attention and are included with other children on the playground, in the lunchroom and on outings. Able-bodied children experientially learn the realities of being disabled and develop an appreciation not only of their friends' perseverance and courage, but also of their own privilege and responsibility as able-bodied. Such a cooperative school-based program brings lifelong learning for all.

In the school in which one of the authors teaches, there is no hierarchical structure among the five-member staff. Each teacher has two areas of general responsibility and all share equally in the decision making that affects the school. The second author formerly taught in a public high school that was organized similarly. In many schools, students are being taught conflict-resolution skills as a model of creative alternatives to violence. As more and more children grow up knowing that they don't have to cope with the "might-is-right" axiom, we have the hope of a more cooperative society and a more peaceful world.

In many communities today there are creative examples of cooperative living. You may belong to a food co-op where, in exchange for a few hours of work a month, members buy healthy food at close to wholesale prices. Other communities have barter banks where, in a local office, people list what they have to exchange and the services or items they want in return. For example, you might list household carpentry work as a skill and, in return, want a cord of wood or a used sewing machine. Without exchange of money, people share skills and goods with others.

These and other examples of cooperative community endeavors can be expanded even more. Cooperative parent-run child-care centers offer parents decision-making power and teaching responsibility in their child's preschool education. Block-based safety watch networks, discussed earlier, could transform many more of our neighborhoods. In these examples, people are working creatively at a grassroots level, demonstrating that collaborative alternatives **are** do-able. At the same time, *broader* structural changes are needed to make the whole framework of our society more cooperative.

Cross-cultural studies by anthropologist Ruth Benedict show that the overall structure of a society accounts for the relative degrees of aggression and competition, or nonviolence and cooperation—in that society. Societies that are organized so that individuals get ahead at the expense of others—that is, competitively-structured societies—are more likely to produce aggression. Benedict discovered that aggression is lowest in social orders where the individual, by the same act and at the same time, serves his own advantage **and** that of the group. These societies are organized so that the group values and rewards the individual for doing what benefits the group. For example, in Eskimo society men prove their individual prowess by bringing back a seal and they help the community by distributing seal meat to everyone in the community. The hunter receives praise and all are fed. Benedict calls such societies high on synergy, the combination of actions of a number of things or people providing results greater than the sum of the separate actions.

Synergy

Synergy is a process by which the whole becomes more than the sum of the parts, while at the same time the parts retain their individuality. You can move a calf or thigh muscle separately, for instance, but when you move them together you can walk—but as you walk the separateness of the muscles is retained.

Journal of Interdependence:
Philadelphia Affective Education Project.

Can our society become more synergistic? We believe it can, but only through a process that is itself cooperative and synergistic. It is people—working together across lines of sex, race, class, and sexual orientation—who can provide the impetus for such changes. Historically, unions have brought workers together to improve conditions for all. Today the United Farm Workers Union, for example, still coalesces not only Chicano agricultural workers, but religious leaders, middle-class consumers, and people of all races in a movement for humane working conditions for those who pick our fruits and vegetables. The disarmament movement has produced living statements of collaboration and synergy. For example, months of cooperation among a diverse and hard-working group of people brought a million people to New York City in June 1982 to demonstrate for disarmament. Trade unionists and clergy, artists and educators, people of color and whites, grandparents and infants marched together for "bread not bombs." As we understand and appreciate the differences among us, we can take the next step—collaboration—the pathway to those changes that can create a more cooperative and just society.

ADDRESSING "THE BUTS"

BUT! As you've been reading about cooperative learning and living, numbers of "buts" have probably flashed through your mind. That's only natural. We've been raised in competitively-oriented schools and a competitively-oriented society. Cooperative alternatives are often less familiar in our thinking and experience.

Let's examine some of the "buts" regarding cooperation in school. "But, are you implying that students will be working cooperatively all the time?" No, not at all. In a cooperative classroom, students will still work competitively and individualistically, as well as in collaboration.

As discussed earlier in this chapter, different goal structures are most appropriate for various cognitive and affective learning outcomes that you want from academic tasks. Therefore, in a cooperative classroom students will be learning in all three goal structures. Rather than this being a hit-or-miss operation, proper goal structures will be used for each learning activity. In Chapter 2 are more guidelines for this use of goal structures.

"But won't cooperation thwart students' individuality?" Experiences of teachers using cooperative goal-structuring claim it does just the opposite. It teaches individuality. Why? Individuality is the development of the full and unique potential of each human being. Unfortunately, the competitive norms and practices in schools encourage students to compare themselves to others over and over again. Many students think less about what they want to do or how they can best use their abilities than what others think about them or how they compare to others. Cooperative classrooms encourage respect for diversity and individuality. Each student's unique strengths are appreciated and used in cooperatively-structured learning. You'll see more specifically how to build this into your classroom in later chapters in *Cooperative Learning, Cooperative Lives*.

"But . . . won't the potential of the most skilled students in the class be thwarted if they're always helping others?" First, they certainly aren't always helping others, though sometimes they do just that. Both teacher-experience and educational research show that in teaching others, higher cognitive abilities are developed and learning becomes more thoroughly internalized. Consistently the research shows that highly-skilled students do as well or better in cooperatively-structured learning as they do in learning that is structured individually or competitively. Teaching is one of the best forms of learning! Secondly, in many cooperatively-structured learning activities students work on academic tasks at their own level, even though the total group project is a collaborative one. Making sure academically-advanced students are being stretched to their potential in cooperative groups is not always easy—**and** it's very possible. Strategies for doing this are described in Chapter 2.

"But . . . students won't work as hard, learn as much, or learn as well in cooperative groups." In fact, most teachers using cooperative learning have found that their class as a whole works harder and learns more. This is especially true because low-skilled or poorly-motivated students become an active part of the learning process. When a middle-school math teacher in Philadelphia, Pennsylvania, structured her class cooperatively, achievement test scores rose three grade levels by the end of the year. In their major study of cooperative learning in the Austin, Texas, Public Schools, Elliot Aronson and his colleagues point out that high achievers did just as well in cooperative groups as others did in control groups, and that low achievers improved significantly.

More Than Academic Benefits. . .

In a very comprehensive evaluation of cooperatively-structured classrooms in Austin, Texas, Elliot Aronson compared these classes to similar competitively-structured classes. His study found that in cooperative classes:

1. Students liked their groupmates and classmates better.
2. Self-esteem was higher.
3. Students increased in their belief that they could learn from other students.
4. Academic achievement was higher.
5. Students liked school better.

Elliot Aronson, *The Jigsaw Classroom*.
Copyright © 1978 by Sage Publications.
Reprinted by permission of Sage Publications, Inc.

You might also wonder if being accountable as a group will affect student learning. In a classic experiment, Martin Deutsch evaluated two classes who were learning similar subject matter. One class's grade for the course was based on the overall quality of written work and class discussion of all members, and all were given the same grade. Grades for students in the other group were based on each individual's contributions and work. Deutsch found that the cooperatively-structured class produced higher quality work and that the ideas and communication were more stimulating. Students felt better about that experience and they liked and encouraged each other more. Cooperative learning doesn't imply lowering our academic standards and expectations! In fact, it's much less threatening for students to be accountable as a group. They often risk more—and learn more.

"But . . . won't classroom management be a problem? Won't there be confusion, noise, and disorder?" Let's be honest. When students are talking with each other about ideas that stimulate them, there will be more noise than when they are working on their own. Remember, however, noise can also be a sign of learning! Strategies to keep your class from being too noisy are discussed in Chapter 2. Cooperative classrooms are not, however, confusing and disorderly—there is much more structure than in many classrooms. In addition, during the first part of the year you'll be teaching students the skills to work cooperatively. These skills help students learn self-discipline and take responsibility for management. In the long run, you'll find that classroom management will become less of a concern for you, and more the responsibility of **everyone.**

A final but! "But . . . if we teach children to work cooperatively, we're not training them for the real world." While it's true that our society emphasizes competition, students have already learned and will continue to learn, competition. What they haven't practiced enough is cooperation. Cooperative learning is compensatory learning, given the powerful effect competition has already had on children. A foundation in cooperative skills will enable students to cope better with different life experiences, since the students will have alternatives for handling these experiences. Such choice empowers people. In addition, cooperative experiences help students learn how to work together to create change. Such change can ultimately transform our society into a more cooperative one.

The questions you may have about cooperative learning are legitimate. We hope by reading further, and working with your students, any "buts" you may have will become "why nots," as they have for many of us here.

A Summary:
Responses to "The BUTS"

A principal, parent or colleague says . . .

You say . . .

1. But if your students work cooperatively, they won't learn how to compete or work individually.

1. Students work cooperatively on some tasks, on others they work competitively or individually. Different goal structures are more effective for different learning outcomes. From their previous school experience most know well how to compete and to work on their own.

2. But cooperation thwarts individuality.

2. Cooperatively-structured groups enhance individuality because each student's strengths and competencies are respected and used in a group task.

3. But won't the advanced students be held back by helping others?

3. Research studies show that advanced students are not held back by cooperative learning. Higher cognitive abilities are developed by such teaching. Advanced students help others sometimes—not all the time. Cooperative tasks can be structured so some students do advanced work and are still part of the group task.

4. But students goof off and learn less in groups.

4. Teachers and researchers have found that students are more motivated and learn as much or more in well-structured cooperative groups as compared to standard classrooms.

5. But if students are accountable as a group the quality of the work will lessen.

5. Researchers and teachers have found that the quality of both individual work and a final group product increases.

6. But cooperative groups are unmanageable.

6. Cooperative groups are very well-structured. Once students learn cooperative skills, management is significantly easier.

7. But cooperation doesn't prepare students for the real world.

7. Students have already learned how to compete well. They need to learn how to cooperate so they will have alternatives available to them as they deal with life and potentially change society.

ROADBLOCKS TO COOPERATION

We hope your commitment to cooperation in learning and living is growing. Why then don't we see more cooperation around us? Competitive individualism, inequalities in society, and dependence on violence to solve interpersonal and international problems can block cooperation. Just as any attitude, norm, or policy that assumes that certain groups or certain people are superior to others can thwart cooperation, so can unequal power situations. All of us are complex, interesting, and important people. Our judicial foundation, our spiritual heritage, and our Constitution tell us that all people are equal. Yet, in our effort to survive in a competitive society, we learn to see ourselves as better than others. This difficulty in **feeling** equal to others is a result of our training in competitive individualism. Individualism gives people the impression that when they achieve, or don't achieve, it's only because of their merits. It obscures institutional discrimination that gives some groups of people more advantages than others, and it also obscures the ways in which human beings are connected to and responsible for each other. Therefore, people can easily distance themselves from others. You see this clearly in school when students bicker, name-call, and put each other down and when they compete for grades, teacher attention, or peer approval. You see it when students sink into a syndrome of failure or when they disregard others and look out only for themselves.

> Competitive individualism thwarts our potential for living with ourselves, each other and nature. In the scramble to get to the top we forget how to love, to think, and we lose track of who we are and what we want.
>
> Claude Steiner,
> *Scripts People Live.*

A camp situation was the setting for an experiment that demonstrated the power adults have in catalyzing competitive individualism through the structure of a learning or living environment. Muzafer Sherif divided the campers into two teams and instituted a competitive tournament of games. Boys started calling each other names and turning against their buddies. Even bringing campers together for social events didn't lessen the high level of hostility present. When interpersonal tension was intense, Sherif created two serious problems that threatened the well-being of everyone in the camp. The water pipe in the camp burst and the food truck engine died. Boys had to work together to try to fix these. Hostility gave way when the group pulled together to achieve an overriding goal which was compelling for all. Feelings remained positive afterward. Think of this example as you look again at the alternatives for structuring your classroom and the predictable student reactions from competition, individualism, or cooperation.

In addition to competitive individualism, other forms of inequality can hinder cooperation. In situations where children of one sex have culturally-conditioned expectations about female or male abilities, sexism blocks cooperation. The example of fifth graders in a mixed ball-throwing game reported by Helen Solomons is typical of the subtle sexism active in many situations. Boys perceived the girls to be less competent than the girls actually were. High-ability girls gave away two times as many passes as high-ability boys. Girls were persuaded by the team to sacrifice their turn at throws, while boys were not. None of this leads to strong interdependent teams or to the development of the girls' fullest capabilities.

During one game, a girl in the second highest-ability group had the ball. Her team-mates hissed at her to, "Pass to Bobby." Bobby, meanwhile, was jumping up and down at her elbow chanting, "Pass it to me. Come on, pass it to me." The girl was obviously very uncomfortable. What if she threw and did not do well? What would her teammates say then? Maybe Bobby could do better than she, even though he had not done as well as she so far in the game. But maybe that was just luck. How could she be sure that she could do it again? This was not the kind of situation in which she could relax and be free to concentrate on doing her best. Very red in the face, she gritted her teeth and threw the ball, to a chorus of complaints from her teammates. It was not a perfect shot, but it was well above average, and the children did not make any further comments. When it was this girl's turn to throw once more, the other children again shouted at her to pass. This time she shrugged and with a gesture of obvious disgust passed the ball to Bobby, who had missed the target completely his previous two shots. The other children were very pleased; the other girl on the team even patted her on the arm as if to assure her she had done the right thing.

One of the interactions between two boys contrasts starkly. During one game, the lowest-ability player on the team (a boy) passed the ball to the second highest-ability player (a boy), saying that he believed the other could do better. The better player returned the ball with the comment, "No, you ought to try it yourself. You need the practice." The low-ability boy passed the ball back, saying he was not very good. The higher-ability boy returned it again, with an encouraging, "Go on, Jimmy, you can do it. Just do your best." Meanwhile standing beside them were the two girl members of the team, one the highest-ability player and the other the third highest. Both passed several times to the better of the two boys; he never returned it to them the way he had to the other boy, nor did anyone suggest that he ought to.

Helen Solomons,
in *Children in Cooperation and Competition*,
Lexington, MA: D.C. Heath, 1980.

Inequality based on age, class, and race can similarly block cooperation. You've seen upper-grade students discriminate against younger students by name-calling, playing tricks, and taking advantage—all because of their age superiority. Here ageism takes its toll. Comparably, when middle-class students put down and distance themselves from lower-class students, class bias gets in the way of cooperation. One of the many ways middle-class students use to convince themselves of their superiority is in flaunting their possessions and opportunities—computers, bikes, records, lessons they take or places they've travelled to. Lower-class children, reinforced in their feeling of being "not O.K.", sometimes react defensively. Cooperation is thwarted at both ends.

Racial discrimination in students' attitudes, in teachers' attitudes or in school policies can thwart cooperation. Often white students feel superior to minority students and name-call, put down, and exclude them. Sometimes students use such distancing behaviors to cover feelings of confusion or a threat. Students of color then react, often by testing or ganging up on white students.

Schools often inadvertently give the message that "white-is-right" by under-representation of minority people in texts, in curriculum materials, on bulletin boards, and in the celebration of holidays. Such attitudes and policies reinforce feelings of inferiority in minority students and may also trigger hostility. As an educator, if you consciously promote greater equality in your classroom and school, you'll pave the way for greater cooperation as well. While the lessons in this book reflect this commitment, a more focused resource for such an endeavor is *Open Minds to Equality: Learning Activities to Promote Race, Sex, Class and Age Equity* (Englewood Cliffs, NJ: Prentice-Hall, 1983).

Remember, too, that in our broader society, equal power relations are important for cooperation. "Second-class" or less powerful people can't be expected to cooperate with those who keep them in their place. An important part of fostering cooperation is to struggle for greater equality in social institutions.

What's equally hopeful is that a cooperatively-structured classroom can reduce prejudicial and stereotyped attitudes that students bring into the classroom. A solid body of literature points to the positive effects of cooperative groups on people's acceptance and liking of each other. For example, many researchers including Russell Weigel, Robert Slavin and others, have found that cooperative interracial groups lead to more interracial acceptance. In such groups, goals are cooperative, students interact over time, and members have equal status. Further, a link exists between the development of social perspective-taking—the ability to see another's point of view—and interaction in cooperative groups. Therefore, by providing opportunities for students to work in heterogeneous cooperative groups, you will enable the students to "get into others' shoes" and bridge the distances between people—distances that inequality fosters. Cooperative teaching and cooperative learning are synergistic. Cooperative processes foster greater equality and teaching toward equality catalyzes greater cooperation.

Nations today use force, or the threat of force, to control society. Such an emphasis on violence can block cooperation by assuming that "human nature" is inherently competitive and aggressive and that organized military might is needed to control people and nations. Reliance on force and might are learned by children at impressionable ages through movies, television, competitive sports, cultural values, computer games, and many educational materials. The impact of this learning emerges in student behavior in the verbal or physical use of force to "get my way." Think of how students with more power pick on their "weaker" counterparts whether the "power" be advantage of age, strength, self-confidence, lack of disability, or whatever.

How spontaneous is the child's readiness to use force to solve classroom disputes and how spontaneous is the readiness to run to the source of ultimate power—you, the teacher? How much do rules that "control" children and regulate behavior take the place of teaching skills which provide students with the ability to solve problems, develop self-discipline, and peacefully resolve conflicts themselves? Reliance on power and force can block cooperation in the classroom. Providing student opportunities for developing personal and collective responsibility and for sharing power, rather than relying on domination and force, can enhance peaceful resolution of conflict in the classroom and in the world.

Whether among individuals, groups of people in society, or nations, equal power and resources are vital to true cooperation. Genuine cooperation is difficult in situations of unequal power. Therefore, important in working toward cooperative personal, school, national or international relationships is the struggle for equity and justice. Cooperative skills can be and have been used for anti-democratic goals. After all, KKK members can cooperate to terrorize those different from themselves just as some citizens can collaborate with a fascist regime. As educators in a democratic society we must link cooperative skills with equalitarian goals achieved through democratic means. Cooperative skills can, in this way, be very powerful tools in struggling to create a more cooperative and just society. The activities in this book reflect this linkage between cooperative skills and the goals of bringing greater equity to power relationships at all levels of our lives, from the personal to social.

CONCLUSION

We hope you are now even more curious and stimulated about the potential for creating a cooperative classroom. *Cooperative Learning, Cooperative Lives* offers you two important ingredients for reaching this goal. First, it provides strategies for teaching students to work effectively in heterogeneous cooperative groups. Secondly, it contains many activities in various subject matter areas that focus on cooperation. Thus students are learning about cooperation, cooperatively.

Most learning regarding cooperation occurs when both the **process** and **content** of activities focus on cooperation. *Cooperative Learning, Cooperative Lives* is a book for teachers that provides insights and guidance in both process and content. Much research and public school practice have focused solely on teaching traditional subject matter cooperatively. While students learned how better to work interdependently and grow in liking of those with whom they work, they did not necessarily acquire a broader understanding of cooperation in their lives and society. For example, one recommendation from the Austin, Texas, Cooperative-Teaching Project is that to enhance student cross-racial learning and liking an educator needs not only to mix groups racially, but should focus on **content** dealing with stereotypes. So, too, in Weigel's comparable attempts to affect biased attitudes through cooperative learning, researchers found a change in attitude toward individual Mexican Americans, but not Mexican Americans as a group. Teaching content about Mexican Americans—their history, culture, contributions and the discrimination faced—would most likely have created broader results. Similarly, cooperation among students will be most effective when the process *and* content of learning activities is based on cooperation. This can be accomplished while teaching required, important academic skills in standard content areas.

Our goals for *Cooperative Learning, Cooperative Lives* are not only to have students learn to cooperate among themselves, but to see the broader possibility for cooperation in their lives, schools, communities, and society in general. To learn and to live cooperatively necessitates not only having the capacity to cooperate but an understanding of social factors that can thwart cooperation, a knowledge of strategies to change those, the vision of a more just and cooperative society, and the courage and patience to work toward the realization of that society. This book provides the tools toward these ends.

We're pleased you've joined us in this challenging endeavor!

Vietnamese Saying

In hell, people starve because their hands are chained to six-foot long chopsticks, too long to bring rice to their mouths.
Heaven is the same.
Only there, people feed each other.

Quoted in *Women of Vietnam* by Arlene Eisen-Bergman.

---

2 THE NUTS AND BOLTS OF IMPLEMENTING COOPERATIVE LEARNING

> It would be valuable if the basic process could be changed so that children could learn to like and trust each other not as an extra curricular activity but in the course of learning their reading, writing, and arithmetic.
>
> Elliot Aronson, *The Jigsaw Classroom*, 23.
> Copyright © 1978 by Sage Publications.
> Reprinted by permission of Sage Publications, Inc.

COOPERATIVE LEARNING IN A NUTSHELL

When your principal, a colleague, or a parent asks, "Now what is this cooperatively-structured learning?", what can you say? Below we sum up in a nutshell what's been proposed.

First, point out that cooperatively-structured learning is a distinct pedagogical approach because collaboration is required among students for success. In the words of the Johnson brothers, students "sink or swim together." Academic success can occur only when students work interdependently. Like a recipe where every ingredient is needed for a tasty outcome, in cooperative learning everyones contribution is necessary for group success. Learning is structured so individual competitiveness is incompatible with success.

In cooperative classrooms, students help each other learn as they work together toward a common goal. Students' varied skills are respected and used. It is assumed that everyone has something to contribute to the group, and the teacher structures the task so that this happens. Students realize that it's not only the teacher who is the expert, but that they too are experts. They learn to rely on each other for support and knowledge.

What makes cooperative learning different from "working together in groups" (something that many teachers already stress) is that cooperative learning is structured in such a way that students become accountable to each other. In many typical classroom groups, some students automatically take a leadership role while others fail to do their fair share of work. In cooperative groups, because students sink or swim together, if one student doesn't do her part, the whole group suffers. Just as with a jigsaw puzzle, if one piece is missing, the whole isn't complete. A combination of positive peer pressure and support can draw the recalcitrant student into the group and encourage her academic success along with that of the group.

Group Work—Standard and Cooperative

Working in Groups	Cooperatively-Structured Groups
1. The task is usually a project.	1. The task can be one of many academic tasks—a project, the study of spelling words, the completion of work at a learning center, and so forth.
2. Sometimes some students do more work and take more responsibility than others.	2. Students do a fair share of work and take responsibility for that work.
3. Slower learners may feel less able to do the assignment and may participate less.	3. Slower learners participate actively because the assignment is structured so they can readily handle their responsibility.
4. Some students are ignored by others.	4. Each student's participation is encouraged by others since it is needed for group progress.
5. Active group members resent "do-nothings." "Do-nothings" feel even less motivated and capable at the end of the task.	5. Since each student's work is necessary and valuable, self-confidence and academic competence increase for all.
6. Each student cares most about what he learns and what grade he gets.	6. Each student cares about what he learns, what others learn, and what grade they together receive.
7. The group is evaluated either as a group with no individual accountability, or each student's part of the work is evaluated individually.	7. The group is evaluated as a group and each student's individual learning affects the group grade.
8. Students, expected to know how to work in groups, *sometimes* work together cooperatively, but there is great inconsistency in this.	8. Students, not being expected to know how to work cooperatively, are taught skills for doing so.

For example, Elliot Aronson tells the story of Carlos, a Chicano student in Austin, Texas. Carlos had trouble with English because it wasn't his native language. In order not to embarrass him, the teacher wouldn't call on him. In fact, she wrote him off. In small cooperative groups students drew him out. His communication improved. After a while, other students realized that Carlos wasn't "dumb" at all!

Teachers structure cooperative groups more carefully than they structure for "typical group work." They make sure that the task is appropriate for the cognitive and affective abilities of each of the students in the group. They structure the task so that students are required to work cooperatively. Students are taught skills—such as listening, effective communication, problem-solving—so they can work together well.

You could conclude your discussion with the point that cooperative learning is a distinctive teaching methodology that is deliberate and well-planned. While it takes more thought and organization than the usual "working in groups," the rewards are much greater. Students feel less frustrated and more successful; they are connected to and responsible for each other; and their academic achievement increases.

MODELS OF COOPERATIVE LEARNING

There are many ways to set up a cooperative classroom and we suspect that after reading this book, you'll create the unique model that's best for you and your students. In his book, *Cooperative Learning: Resources for Teachers,* Spencer Kagan presents an overview of many varied approaches to cooperative learning. Here, we briefly describe the work of three sets of educators, among many, who have developed models for cooperative learning—models that are representative and that have proven to be effective in our nation's schools.

David and Roger Johnson's method of cooperative-goal structuring is described in detail in *Learning Together and Alone* and *Circles of Learning.* In the Johnsons' model, students work together in cooperative groups toward a common academic goal. They are positively interdependent because they have a common goal, each completes a part of the task, and they are rewarded as a group. Students are individually accountable for mastering the material and are evaluated as a group. The teacher intervenes as needed, to teach or reinforce cooperative skills. Especially useful in the Johnsons' work are the very practical guidelines they provide for setting up, monitoring, and evaluating cooperative classrooms.

To Introduce a Cooperative Lesson

Today we will work on this project cooperatively. What this means is:

1. There will be one paper per group.
2. Each member agrees with the group answer, and may indicate by signing.
3. Make sure each group member has a say.
4. Assist all group members in understanding the material.
5. Express your ideas and don't change them unless you're logically persuaded to do so.

Adapted from *Learning Together and Alone.*

The Johnsons focus on the importance of the **process** of student interaction. They stress the whys and hows of teaching students cooperation, communication, and controversy skills, and of building a trusting environment. (Chapters 3 and 4 in *Cooperative Learning, Cooperative Lives* contain activities that teach these and other skills.) The Johnsons also provide diversified methods for evaluating the process and outcome of collaborative group learning. They advocate a full network of cooperation in the classroom—cooperation within groups and among groups. Dee Dishon and Patricia O'Leary's *A Guidebook for Cooperative Learning* provides sequential and practical materials to implement this approach to cooperative learning.

Another model, Student Team Learning, involves use of student teams in which students tutor each other. Students are evaluated individually and high-achieving teams are given public recognition. Originally developed by Robert Slavin, David DeVries, and Keith Edwards at Johns Hopkins University, this model is described in the Student Team Learning material and curricula available directly from the Center for Social Organization of Schools at Johns Hopkins.

A number of approaches to Student Team Learning exist. In Student Teams-Achievement Divisions (STAD) students are assigned to four or five-member heterogeneous teams. The teacher introduces new material each week and during the week team members study worksheets on the materials. They make sure all their teammates understand the material. Students then take individual quizzes. Each student's contribution to the team score is determined by the degree to which the student's quiz score exceeds the student's own past quiz average. Teams with the highest exam scores are recognized each week in a class newsletter or other public forum.

Another approach to Student Team Learning is Teams-Games-Tournaments (TGT). TGT uses the same teams, instructional format, and worksheets as STAD; however, students play academic games to show their individual mastery of subject matter. This is an example of mixed goal-structuring, in that peer teaching is cooperative, but the teams compete with each other.

Another model developed by Elliot Aronson and his colleagues in a cooperative learning project in the Austin, Texas, public schools is described in their book, *The Jigsaw Classroom*. In a jigsaw classroom, each student in a heterogeneous group is assigned certain information that she must learn and then teach to other members of the group. Each student's information is essential to the whole task. For example, if a group is studying the life of Sojourner Truth, the black abolitionist and women's rights activist, each student is given material on a segment of Sojourner's life. The group won't learn the total account unless all students teach their parts. In Aronson's jigsaw model, students stay in the same group for six to eight weeks. While they work to learn material as a group, they are graded individually.

To foster greater effectiveness, Aronson suggests the use of a reliable student leader selected and trained by the teacher. Leaders receive two or three periods of training each week, learning through role play how to intervene to solve problems that may arise in their group. Their role is: to help the group get organized, to help the group stay on task, to be a liaison with the teacher, to model productive member behavior, to ask questions, to ask people to do things, to deal with disagreement, and to encourage feedback.

In a model jigsaw classroom, a group assembles and the group recorder gets their folder. The leader reads where they are in the task and they develop an agenda for the day. She reads the previous day's notes on how the group functioned. The teacher gives out materials and aides for teaching the materials, and explains the responsibilities of the groups. The group works until five minutes before the ending time, then evaluates the work and the quality of cooperation.

Educators working with the jigsaw model have developed modifications, some of which are described in the Johns Hopkins publications as Jigsaw II. Here all students get the same body of material to read and study. In addition, each student is assigned to concentrate on one topic, section, or series of questions. The student becomes an expert on that material. Experts from different groups meet with each other to review material before returning to their group to reinforce key points with other members. In this approach, individual assessments of student learning are averaged into a group evaluation.

A fourth model, coordinated teamwork, is represented in Spencer Kagan's Co-op Co-op methods and Shlomo Sharan's Group Investigation approach. These models involve more complex organization of groups, including division of labor, a high degree of individual initiative, and group integration. These methods often involve significant division of labor between groups and encourage more self-direction from students.

All of these models for cooperative learning have increased academic learning as well as social growth and human community. The resources cited above provide further information on all three variations of cooperative learning. You can choose any one of these, or elements of those you think will be most effective with your students.

Cooperative Learning, Cooperative Lives draws, to greater or lesser degrees, on all models. It reflects most directly the philosophy of the Johnsons' in that formats are purely cooperative and students, while individually accountable for mastering material, are evaluated as a group. We have branched out from these models to provide a variety of cooperative activity formats, strategies for cooperative skill-development, and methods of evaluation that may make the implementation of cooperative learning even smoother for you. Further, *Cooperative Learning, Cooperative Lives* provides a well-sequenced series of cooperatively-structured activities. These lessons are not only cooperative in form, they also teach **about** cooperation.

TEACHING FORMATS FOR COOPERATIVE LESSONS

There are a number of useful and creative ways for a teacher to structure lessons cooperatively. Below, we define ten such formats that are purely cooperative. They don't utilize individual rewards or reward one group over another. There is no intergroup competition. More detailed descriptions of the formats, advantages and disadvantages of each, and information on teacher preparation are described under Teaching Formats in the Resources section of this book (page 505). Lessons using each of the formats can be found in the activity chapters. By becoming familiar with the variety of formats, you can teach those cooperative lessons which are appropriate for your students and your educational goals. You can also create your own lessons using these formats and the content you regularly teach. These formats are to be distinguished from the four broad models described in the previous section. These more specific approaches for structuring a lesson, delineated by the authors, are often used within the frameworks of several of the more generic models.

Cooperative teaching formats range in complexity. The formats are described in order of difficulty and lessons in the activity chapters reflect this developmental sequence. For example, you should start the year with partners or simple group projects and, once students are used to this, move into the more complex formats.

A **Partner** format is one in which two students work together to accomplish a task. The use of partners is a very effective way to introduce students to cooperative learning. The **Peer Teaching** format is similar. Here, one student who is more skilled in a certain area works with another to teach the skill or review material. This format may also be used with small groups.

Students work cooperatively to create a project or complete a task by pooling their skills and knowledge in a **Group Project** format. All must participate and agree. The **Jigsaw** format is a carefully-structured format that assures that all students participate actively in the task. In a jigsaw, students are divided into groups and each is assigned information necessary for the group to complete its task. Everyone must contribute for the group to be successful. The jigsaw is particularly appropriate to heterogeneous classes. It also necessitates the involvement of shy students and assures that dominant students won't take control.

A **Cross-Grade Project** format provides upper-grade students an opportunity to teach skills or implement projects with those in younger grades. The **Learning Center** format is comparable to a standard learning center except that here students work cooperatively to complete tasks at various centers. There is an obvious advantage in having a variety of activities reflecting different learning styles and subjects.

Educational games can be structured so students work interdependently. When using the **Cooperative Board Game** format, students work collectively to play a cooperative board game dealing with subject matter they are studying. They win or lose as a group. In the Cooperative Board Game format, rules for familiar card games are adapted to various subjects and the games are structured cooperatively. Games include Rummy, Concentration, and Double Solitaire.

The **Treasure Hunt** format enables students to be active and moving while working together. Teams work independently of each other as they follow a series of clues involving the subject matter being studied. The final clues of each team are pooled, or a puzzle using each group's final clue is solved, to gain a "treasure" for all. This format is highly-motivating for individuals, teams, and whole classes.

In a **Research Project** format, students work cooperatively on a project or problem, using either the library or human resources or both. Tasks are sometimes assigned in a jigsaw manner. The compilation of results is a comprehensive group effort. When designed well, research projects can appeal to students with different skill levels.

These teaching formats provide a variety of ways of structuring cooperative learning. After examining the advantages and disadvantages listed in the Resource section and trying these formats, you'll determine which are most appropriate for your class.

At the beginning of each lesson plan you will see one or more of the following abbreviations: M–mathematics; LA–language arts; R–reading; C–communication; SS–social studies; S–science; A–art; PE–physical education. By using these you can glance through each chapter to find lessons in appropriate curriculum areas.

STRUCTURING COOPERATIVE LEARNING IN THE CLASSROOM

SETTING UP YOUR ROOM

Setting up your classroom is the first step in preparing for cooperative learning. One way is to arrange the room permanently so that it is conducive to cooperation. Other work can be done in such a setting as well. Arrange desks or tables in clustered groups or arrange individual desks in pairs. Use bookshelves, screens, and dividers to enclose a carpeted corner with pillows where students can work apart from the large classroom when this is needed. Set up a small, safe area for "in-process projects" so students don't unintentionally ruin others' work. A second alternative is to keep your room in your standard arrangement and move desks into clustered groups only for cooperative work. Set clear norms for moving desks quickly and quietly.

Cooperative Convincer

At the beginning of the school year, plan a big classroom project that a student just couldn't do alone. For example, the class could create a huge mural, write a class recipe book, or create potato block T-shirts with each students' potato block symbol stamped on each person's T-shirt. Such inherently cooperative projects that result in unique products often convince students of the exciting benefits of cooperation.

SCHEDULING TIME

At first, it takes longer to cover material when learning is structured cooperatively. As the weeks go on and students become skilled in this new format, cooperative lessons take no more time than other methods. The advantage is that more students are learning and retaining the material. Also, they'll keep these cooperative skills from one year to the next!

When introducing a cooperative lesson, be sure to set a time limit for the activity. Make this limit clear. There is no reward for finishing first; the point is to complete the activity and do it well. On short activities that have a worksheet, make the last question on the worksheet an open-ended one so those groups that finish first have a challenging question to work on while others finish. For longer-term lessons, provide short activities, or mini-projects, to keep students involved until all finish. Appropriate mini-projects can entail work on class projects, like a class newspaper. Mini-projects should be educationally-useful and motivating, but not so special that other students rush with their lessons in order to work on the mini-projects. Also include in your weekly schedule some "catch-up times" for groups that need that extra bit of time to finish their work.

A Beginning List of Mini-Projects

Begin these types of projects in your room and students can contribute to them when their group finishes other assigned work.

- group mural
- jigsaw puzzle
- time line
- large crossword puzzle on bulletin board
- bulletin board headed COOPERATION—students make as many words from it as possible

Put these activities on dittos, ready to give to individuals, partners, or small groups.

- math games
- word finds
- brain teasers
- scrambled words

STRUCTURING AND ASSIGNING A COOPERATIVE LESSON

When designing a cooperative lesson, be sure that each student in a group is able to do the work assigned. Nothing hinders a student's willingness to work collaboratively than facing work far beyond his skill level. Next, assign students to heterogeneous groups. Initially, you should create the groups, but later this may be done randomly. On other occasions, you may want to assign students to groups with more intentionality, based on your knowledge of skills in various subject areas or personalities. Assign small groups of two or three students at first. Once students are comfortable with cooperative learning, four or five students can work in a group.

Introduce the activity by telling students that they will work cooperatively. Remind them that this means that there will be one paper or product per group and that each student's information, contribution, and learning will be necessary to the successful completion of the task. Remind students to assist each other in learning the material and that each individual member will be held responsible for that material. Give clear directions. Often it helps to write the directions on the board and have someone copy them for each group. The end-product and the criteria for evaluation should be clearly specified. Move around from group to group as students are working. Help them solve those problems they can't solve themselves.

Strongly encourage students to ask for help from each other when they need it. Repeatedly impress upon them that it's okay to say they don't know or don't understand something. Make this a class norm. Since it is crucial that students receive help when they need it, give all students practice and encouragement in responding to others' requests for help. Be alert for students who may not be getting the help they need from their peers. Helpers are instructed not to do the work for someone else, but to assist each other in learning.

To discourage competition between groups, avoid exclusive use of identical class assignments. When students all work on the same topic, vary the activity slightly, when possible. This is even easier in the kind of classroom where students are working on different activities simultaneously. With such variety, competition is lessened. For example, in a self-contained classroom, post a social studies and a science assignment. Half of the groups do the science and half do social studies on Monday at 11:00. They reverse on Tuesday at 11:00. Such an arrangement often helps cut down noise level as well.

To Set Up a Cooperative Goal Structure

1. Choose specific instructional goals.
2. Select the most appropriate group size for the lesson.
3. Assign heterogeneous groups (remember: heterogeneity is not only defined by academic level).
4. Arrange classroom for "clustered separateness."
5. Prepare materials for lessons, record information about cooperative skills.
6. Explain the cooperative goal structure; present the lesson.
7. Observe student interaction; help solve problems.
8. Evaluate group results in terms of lesson criteria.

For further information, see David and Roger Johnson,
Learning Together and Alone,
Englewood Cliffs, NJ: Prentice-Hall, 1975.

TEACHING COOPERATIVE SKILLS

It is unrealistic to assume that students know how to work together effectively in groups. Therefore, it is important to teach cooperative skills throughout the year.

Begin with easy skills like giving praise or asking for others' ideas. As the year progresses, students can practice more difficult skills such as giving constructive criticism and arbitrating a conflict. Consult *Circles of Learning* and *Guidebook of Cooperative Learning* for examples of many cooperative skills, there called "social skills," and a suggested sequence for teaching them.

When assigning the lesson, present not only an academic goal, but a cooperative skill goal as well. For example, tell students that this week they will practice giving praise. Ask students for examples of what they might say if they like another group member's idea or appreciate something she is doing to help the group. Tell students you will be observing them and will be watching for use of this skill. Indicate you will provide worksheets or checklists for the group to use in evaluating their progress.

PROCESSING

Processing a cooperative activity is as important as planning and implementing it. "Processing" is the asking of questions about what happened. It serves to help students make generalizations about both the process (how they worked together) and the task (the academic project or assignment). By responding to clear processing questions, students reflect on their cooperative group experience. They step out of it to determine, for example, what helped or hindered their group in accomplishing the task.

Leave plenty of time for processing cooperative activities, so students can appreciate what they did well, learn from their mistakes, and improve their cooperative skills for the future. Help them generalize and use what they learn from one group session to the next. As a rule of thumb, ask questions about students' feelings and the group process first. Follow those up by questions about the task or content.

Examples of General Processing Questions

Process

1. What were some of your feelings as you did this activity?
2. Did anyone do anything that made you feel especially positive about your group or project? Especially negative? How did the group try to change that?
3. What did group members do to help the group accomplish its goal? What did they do to hinder it?
4. What will you do differently next time you work together?

Content—Listed here are general questions. Make yours more specific according to the content of your lesson.

1. What were the most important ideas that you learned from this lesson?
2. What did you discover that surprised you?
3. What more would you like to learn on this topic?

It's important to process student progress on the cooperative skill they are working on each week. As in the situation cited above, students may be working on giving praise. Each day, give students five minutes to evaluate their success at giving praise either with a short discussion, worksheet, or checklist. At the week's end it's possible to tie effectiveness in giving praise to their group's evaluation.

Draw Learning from Frustration

Below is an abbreviated segment of processing following a lesson in which students bickered among themselves, didn't start right away, and failed to complete the task.

Teacher: How do you feel about what happened today?

Tom: I feel lousy. We didn't finish our assignment.

Juanita: I'm angry. Some people in my group wouldn't get to work.

Teacher: Do others see what happened the same way that Tom and Juanita do?

Jane: I agree. I didn't want to get started because someone took my pencil. That makes me so mad.

LeRoi: I tried to get our group going, but no one would listen to me.

Teacher: OK. It sounds like you had serious problems getting started. Let's think about what you could do differently so we don't repeat this. Jane, what could you have done about your pencil?

Jane: I could have asked for another one.

Teacher: Yes. What else could Jane have done first?

Becky: She could have asked people in her group if anyone took it by mistake. She could have told them how upset she was about it.

Josh: Yes, and then the group could have made an announcement to the whole class. Someone might have it or someone would lend her one.

Teacher: Fine ideas! So let's write this on the board. *If anyone has an individual problem that keeps him or her from being helpful in the group, tell the group. The group can help you solve the problem.* Let's remember that! Now what could you do differently so you get started on your task right away?

Latisha: We could talk seriously to the people who won't get going and tell them how they are hurting our group.

Ralph: We could set a time limit—say three minutes—and one person would keep time. If we aren't busy on the assignment by then, the time-keeper calls time and we then **must** get started.

Teacher: Again, very workable ideas! Let's write these down. . . .

FREQUENCY OF COOPERATIVE LEARNING

How often, you might wonder, do teachers use cooperative learning? Some teachers choose to ease into cooperative learning by first teaching basic cooperative skills for communication and listening, then structuring a few activities cooperatively, building more in as the year progresses. Most begin cooperative activities on the first day of school and teach cooperative skills in conjunction with teaching cooperative lessons.

Most educators intermix cooperative activities with those that are structured competitively and individualistically. The Johnsons suggest that if a teacher matches the optimum goal structure with the learning outcomes they want for students, cooperation will be used 70 percent of the time, competition 10 percent, and individualization 20 percent. Many teachers find this formula appropriate, while others tend to use the three goal structures in more equal proportions.

Some educators structure their entire educational program cooperatively. For example, Daniel Fader, author of *Hooked on Books,* ranked his students according to their reading preparedness. He formed triads composed of students of high, medium, and low reading levels, and made a nonnegotiable rule that the triad was responsible for learning together. He provided structure, methods and opportunities for learning in this triad. This totally-cooperative structure resulted in significant progress for all. The choice, of course, is yours regarding the extent of cooperative learning you incorporate into your class.

Remember also that students can work cooperatively in partners or small groups even if the whole class isn't doing so. Encourage students to read to each other or help each other with difficult assignments. For teachers who teach in a self-contained classroom, set up a cooperative game corner. Once students have learned to play some cooperative board games, they can use that space to play together quietly. Maybe once a week upper-elementary students can go to the library to read books to first graders. Cooperative learning takes many forms!

Cooperative projects also build positive interdependence among teachers. Plans can range from monthly potluck suppers for personal sharing to teacher-initiated and implemented projects for the school. For example, teachers from a number of classes might work together to organize a monthly video show for the school. Students in each participating class take a segment to produce and then the entire show is played for the school. In this case, teacher cooperation then involves the students.

TEACHER SUPPORT

Encourage several teachers from your school or district to develop cooperative learning in their classrooms as you are doing this. In this way, you and other teachers can work cooperatively to share experiences and solve problems. A monthly after-school support group is an ideal format for such sharing. Not only will you get new ideas and advice, you'll be experiencing the very cooperation you want for your students.

The How To's of Cooperative Learning

Cooperative Learning, Cooperative Lives provides learning activities for classroom use. There are a number of fine resources that focus exclusively on the process of structuring learning cooperatively. Order these for your own professional library or for your school and refer to them often!

Learning Together and Alone, David and Roger Johnson.

Circles of Learning, David and Roger Johnson, Edythe Holubec, Patricia Roy.

Cooperative Learning—Resources for Teachers, Spencer Kagan.

A Guidebook for Cooperative Learning: A Technique for Creating More Effective Schools, Dee Dishon and Pat Wilson O'Leary.

Using Student Team Learning, Robert Slavin.

Jigsaw Classroom, Elliot Aronson, *et al.*

POTENTIAL PROBLEMS AND SOLUTIONS

GETTING STUDENTS USED TO COOPERATIVE LEARNING

It's difficult for some students to get used to working in cooperative groups. This may be the case for your students. If so, assign a short, well-defined task with a clear goal. Give them a fixed amount of time—for example, say, "In twenty minutes, I expect you to turn in your papers." Take a serious attitude. Tell them, for example, that their group work must be done before they move on to a new task.

You can begin cooperative learning by setting up small groups with whom you work periodically. In these groups, students can learn cooperative skills under your supervision, or you might find it helpful to begin with a task in which students work on an individual project that is then combined with the work of others to create a cooperative project. For example, each student makes a block print that represents herself. Students bring in T-shirts and block their print on each others' shirts—creating cooperative T-shirts for all.

Don't get discouraged if students find cooperative groups difficult at first. Remember that learning to work cooperatively involves the gradual development of skills and concepts.

DEALING WITH HETEROGENEITY

In heterogeneity is strength! In mixed groups, students have the chance to learn from others with diverse life experiences, perspectives, and skills. Heterogeneity is basic to cooperative learning. At the same time, it's important that you structure heterogeneous groups in such a way that everybody learns!

It is a reality that students have different levels and types of ability and skills. Often in classrooms, teachers avoid talking about differences, but students know well that they exist. In a cooperative classroom, talk honestly about these differences so they are neither a cause for shame nor conceit. Help students pinpoint and avoid a "blaming-the-victim" mentality—that is, it's slow learners' fault that they learn at a different pace. Rather, encourage objectivity and support.

There are things both you and your students can do to help heterogeneous groups work well. Assign group tasks that call for different kinds of abilities. For example, a group project might need reading, research, writing, art work and interviewing. Be sure, however, not to put an academically-unskilled student who is good in art with a high achiever who is also good in art. In that case, the former student's skill will not be unique. In such a multi-faceted task, a student who might not be strong in art may be a good researcher, and so forth. If many different abilities and skills are needed, all students can use their competencies. Assign tasks with different levels or amounts of work. In reading, for example, assignments might look similar, but the reading levels would be different. It is crucial to provide material that students **can** handle. Students may prefer to work individually on a task before they begin interacting cooperatively. This often bolsters confidence. In assigning groups, it is usually wise to disperse students with the most serious learning problems and group them with students who will be supportive helpers.

Students, too, can make heterogeneity work. After you've taught them skills and strategies for effective peer tutoring, they become wonderful resources for each other. Once they learn cooperative skills and become more aware of their group process and more able to modify it, they will take more and more responsibility for seeing that heterogeneous groups function effectively. In nonjudgmental, cooperative classrooms, slower students learn to ask for help and to give it as they are able.

Elliot Aronson's "counterpart groups" or Robert Slavin's "expert groups" are options to add to the jigsaw approach to cooperative learning. In this case, each jigsaw group studies the same material. After each group has been assigned work, the teacher temporarily regroups students who are responsible for the same piece of information into counterpart groups to study together. When regular jigsaw groups are reconstituted even the student with more limited skills has confidence that she knows the information and can teach it.

What about the effects of heterogeneous groups on the student who learns rapidly? As noted above, with well-designed cooperative activities, the fast learner will do challenging work at her level. Even in activities that involve peer teaching, experience and research show that advanced students gain both socially and academically.

High Achievers and Cooperative Learning

A research team headed by Ronald Lippitt studied several peer teaching programs and found that tutor and pupil are helped by peer teaching. Tutors show improved attitudes and interest in school, increased ability to work cooperatively with other children, increased self respect and belief in their own ability. Both tutors and pupils showed academic gains.

Reported by Elliot Aronson, *The Jigsaw Classroom*.
Copyright © 1978 by Sage Publications.
Reprinted by permission of Sage Publications, Inc.

As teachers we know that we continually learn more about the topics we teach in the process of teaching others. . . . There is no evidence that the experience of tutoring is detrimental to learning. On the contrary: studies of peer tutoring reveal substantial gains for tutors. In cooperative learning the high achievers gain as much or more than high achievers in traditional classrooms.

Spencer Kagan,
Cooperative Learning: Resources for Teachers.

High achieving students working in heterogeneous learning groups score higher on retention tests than do high achievers who participate in competitive or individualistic learning situations. The quality of reasoning strategies used by the high achievers was higher when they were in cooperative learning situations. . . . While bright students are often resented and sometimes ostracized in a competitive setting, they are seen as desirable partners in a cooperative setting.

David and Roger Johnson, Edythe Holubec, Patricia Roy,
Circles of Learning.

KEEPING ADVANCED STUDENTS CHALLENGED

A cooperative classroom can provide the setting for challenging advanced students more effectively than can a traditional classroom. For example, by having heterogeneous spelling or math fact groups with a range of work to be mastered, the students who learn more quickly are challenged to help others learn simpler content as well as to learn the more difficult content themselves. By having heterogeneous groups researching information on a specific topic, the more advanced students are challenged to use more difficult and more complex research materials and then to share this information with their groups.

Cooperative learning does promote the academic achievement of faster learners. You can also use particular strategies to assure yourself that these students are indeed being challenged. As noted earlier, a well-planned cooperative activity—especially with the jigsaw format—can include segments geared for advanced students at their level of ability. Similarly in a contract-grading system (see pages 509–511), advanced students complete more difficult work in order to receive the grade for which they contracted. Consider setting up an in-class or cross-grade peer-tutoring program where advanced students are assigned coordinating and organizing responsibilities. Since faster students aren't always high achievers in every area, provide group projects in which these students are assigned tasks where they aren't most advanced. For example, give a creative writing segment of a project to the math whiz and a data-gathering and statistical segment to a verbal pupil. In all these ways, fast learners can gain the experience of learning together cooperatively and, at the same time, be challenged and motivated.

HELPING STUDENTS HELP EACH OTHER

Students don't come into your classroom automatically knowing how to help each other learn. As previously noted, they need to be taught skills for helping. Provide role plays where students can practice teaching, and being taught, cooperative skills. From this, they can generate guidelines for helpful and not-so-helpful forms of tutoring. For example, they might discover that hurriedly telling someone an answer is not a good way to nurture learning. Activities in Chapters 3 and 4 provide ideas for teaching these helping skills.

Sometimes students are overeager to help. Therefore it's useful to have a class discussion about how to ask for help and how to decline when help is not wanted. Students can practice phrases like, "If you'd like help, I'd be happy to give it to you, but if you don't I won't be offended. If you decide later you want help, just let me know."

The strategy of "specialist" is a creative one for dealing with heterogeneity and for building helping skills. In a given cooperative activity, each student is assigned to be a specialist in an area of his competence. For example, in a language arts activity, one might be a specialist on punctuation, another capitalization, another verb agreement and so forth. As students write papers or stories, they consult the specialist when in doubt about a particular area. The papers are cooperatively proofread, with each specialist checking for his area of expertise. In this way students are on equal footing, assisting each other in a cooperative activity.

DEVELOPING SHARED GROUP LEADERSHIP

How often teachers watch one student take over a group! The structure of cooperative learning, especially the jigsaw method, helps avoid this. In addition, there are other strategies (many of which are included in Chapters 3 and 4) to encourage equal participation in cooperative groups.

Teaching cooperative skills and careful processing of cooperative activities help students pinpoint and change domineering or withdrawn behavior. When students answer a processing question, like "To what extent did people participate equally?," they must discuss levels of involvement, and can pinpoint behavior changes in preparation for the next time they work together. After they learn I-messages—a statement about how another person's behavior makes them feel—they can give direct feedback to the "boss." (See pages 166–167.) Verbalizing about successful group behavior helps them apply those behaviors to other situations.

The token method is also effective. All students are given an equal number of tokens (for example, ten) for a cooperative activity. Each time a student speaks, she uses a token. Once a student's tokens are gone, she can't speak any more. This makes students judicious regarding the frequency of their verbalization and the value of their contribution.

Try assigning students function-roles during a cooperative activity. For example, in one group each student takes one of the following roles—an organizer, clarifier, peacekeeper, recorder, and includer. Consciously assign roles in which students need practice and can carry out successfully. For example, give an overly domineering student a more process-oriented role, such as includer—one who invites others' participation in the task. Taking on roles provides students a structured opportunity to try new behaviors. To reinforce student commitment, grade cooperative groups **both** on content—how well they accomplished the task, and process—how well they worked together. Methods for doing that are discussed later in this chapter.

Task-Oriented Group Roles

Fifth grade teacher Mary Travis had particular success with assigning students the very practical task-oriented roles suggested by the Johnsons.

Checker—Checks to make sure everyone else in the group knows how to get the correct answer.

Observer—Checks students on cooperative skill being practiced.

Reader—Reads the assignment, task, or problem to the group.

Recorder—Records the group's answers to be handed in.

DEALING WITH NAME-CALLING

Trust, respect, and a willingness to admit you don't know are essential ingredients of a cooperative classroom. Name-calling undermines all three. Therefore, it's essential to set a nonnegotiable norm: no put-downs. Plan affirmation activities so students develop strong positive self-concepts. Use activities in which students find those things they have in common. The more like others they feel, the harder it is to put them down. It is very important, of course, for you to treat students with respect and understanding thus creating classroom climate that is affirming and positive.

Students often resort to name-calling because of their own feelings of inferiority and anxiety and because of peer pressure. Other reasons for name-calling include: societal pressure, role modeling by adults, attempts to be "cool," and attempts to establish identity. While name-calling is one of the most difficult things for a teacher to deal with, there are some approaches that help. Work with name callers so they feel more secure and less afraid, decreasing their need to name-call. Role-play alternatives to name-calling. For example, when faced with a troublesome situation, students can learn to say, "We have a problem, what are we going to do about it?" As a teacher, work with the feelings that underlie name-calling.

Cultural Norms and Put-Downs

Some children may say that, in their culture, put-downs are considered funny and cool. You may want to use this as an opportunity to encourage students to explore their own cultural norms and values and to think about whether there are some which they don't want to keep. You can explore the idea that one can be proud of one's ethnic heritage but still choose to give up a particular piece of it which is not productive. That does not mean rejecting one's background, but simply understanding that all cultures have developed over time and some patterns, which at one point may have been useful, are no longer good for us.

CONCENTRATION ON TASK

While cooperative activities are conducive to keeping students on task, there are additional things you can do to encourage concentration. Make time limits clear for a particular assignment. If an activity has different parts, intervene to indicate the end of certain sections. For example, "The three minutes for brainstorming are over. Move on to making your list." Structure large projects into parts, and have students sign as they get each section done.

INTERPERSONAL PROBLEMS AMONG STUDENTS

Student behavior problems have the potential for disrupting cooperative groups. Chapters 3 and 4 are filled with lessons that help students develop skills for understanding and dealing with these problems. In many cases, these skills enable group members, with your support, to take responsibility for working out these problems in their groups.

Sometimes other measures are appropriate. Mary Travis, fifth grade teacher in Arlington, New York, has set up a procedure that keeps an interpersonal conflict between two students from disrupting the whole group. She sets a norm that the back table is the place where two students who are in conflict go to work it out. She asks those students to go to the back table, talk about what's bothering them, try to resolve the problem, and return to their group in five minutes. She intervenes only as necessary.

Another potential problem is the shy student or the overly-aggressive student. These students sometimes don't want to work in a cooperative group. Often if you let that student sit out, he will be eager to participate constructively next time because everyone else was so energized and so involved. On occasion, a student is too destructive to be assigned to a group. Have that student work with you on a special project. Present the opportunity of joining a cooperative group as a privilege to be earned. With your support and with well-planned independent work, such a student often makes gains rather quickly and can join the group.

Other students can take responsibility for the withdrawn student. Eric Perlberg, a teacher in Accord, New York, approaches another group member this way. "John, it's part of your job as a group member to get Laverne to participate. Now let's think about how you could do it." When group members get angry at a student for withdrawing or goofing off, Mr. Perlberg helps them redirect their anger by telling the person how they feel. For example, a productive student said to another, "Sue, this is part of your job as a group member and we have to accomplish it together." Soon students take more of this responsibility on their own.

A NEW STUDENT

As the year progresses, cohesion is strong in a cooperative class. Procedures and norms have been developed that are unknown to a new student who joins in mid-year. Have your students develop creative tasks that acquaint a new student with cooperative procedures. Some of your students undoubtedly like to befriend new students. Encourage them to take on that responsibility. Find out what the new student is particularly good at or interested in. Develop a few activities that focus on those strengths, helping the student feel competent and needed.

NOISE

Noise in a cooperative classroom is usually the sign of active learning. At the same time, a classroom can sometimes get too noisy for your students or for those in neighboring classrooms. Explain to the teachers next door what you're doing and invite them to contact you if it gets too noisy. To deal with noise, use a signal to quiet students down. Play a few notes on a harmonica or flip the light switch. (When things really get desperate, let loose a barking dog!) Ask one person in each group to be responsible for keeping the noise level down, or include this as part of process evaluation. Whenever possible, have only some of the students work in cooperative groups at a given time, and others work individually. Students working individually can often go to the library. Use process intervention. For example, in the middle of a group project interrupt work **briefly** to ask each student this question: "How necessary to the successful completion of the task is your group's noise level?" Each person checks off a spot on a continuum.

1	2	3	4	5	6	7	8	9	10
noise level very necessary									noise level not necessary

Group members discuss responses for two or three minutes and then move right back into the task. Have your class work cooperatively to cut down on noise. Make a large noise barometer out of poster board. The class sets a goal and tries to keep the noise level at or below that point for the week. This becomes a cooperative challenge!

EVALUATION

Evaluation of student learning is essential to any teaching approach. What, you may ask, are the most effective ways to evaluate cooperative learning?

For many teachers cooperative lessons will be only part of a teaching approach that also includes competitive activities and tasks oriented to the individual student. Each type of activity should be evaluated differently and each evaluation recorded. At report card time, all results are combined for an overall average. Thus, evaluation of cooperative projects would be only part of an individual mark on a report card.

In accurately evaluating student learning, be sure to evaluate the way **you** have structured your class for cooperative learning. In *Learning Together and Alone,* the Johnsons provide observation forms for teachers to check their classrooms. In addition, student-perception questionnaires can give accurate feedback indicating how well you have communicated the concepts and process of cooperative learning to students.

Sample Questions for a Student-Perception Questionnaire

On this assignment we were supposed to:

_____ a. Work with others to create a group product.

_____ b. Work independently to create individual products, without paying any attention to other students.

_____ c. Work independently to create individual products better than anyone else's.

Check one:

_____ a. I am happy when the teacher praises the work of one person in my group since it means we are all doing well.

_____ b. It makes no difference to me one way or the other when the teacher praises the work of someone else, since this is irrelevant to my own accomplishment.

_____ c. I am unhappy when the teacher praises the work of another student because it must mean that my work is inferior.

Adapted from *Learning Together and Alone.*

First a word about grades. . . . Grades are used in American education both as incentives for students to learn and as ways to measure that learning. While most teachers must give grades, it is important to note that there are alternatives to grades, both as incentives and as evaluation tools.

Cooperative learning means that there is both a cooperative **task** and a cooperative **incentive** to work together to learn. Lessons in *Cooperative Learning, Cooperative Lives* contain activities in which students work together to accomplish a shared goal. Also, there are cooperative incentives that encourage students to work together to learn and to be accountable for each other's progress. Grades are the most common incentives used in schools. You may use grades for incentives and choose one of the evaluation formats described in the Resource section of this book. Other incentives include exciting material and the feeling of mastery in learning. Incentives in cooperative learning also take other forms: the desire to help others learn and the concern for their progress, the satisfaction of being part of an effective group, and the feeling of competence in helping others learn. Activities in *Cooperative Learning, Cooperative Lives* include skill training for students so that they develop the competencies for such effective group interaction. Rewards in cooperative learning can be grades, but also successful group products, the learning itself, the positive experience of cooperating, competence in helping, appreciation at being helped, and peer approval. The content and methods used in lessons in *Cooperative Learning, Cooperative Lives,* are designed to stimulate students' motivation to learn. The positive value placed on cooperation contributes to increased student incentive to help each other learn. An ultimate goal of this approach is that a cooperative goal structure could become unnecessary. Students would develop the intrinsic desire and practical skills to be accountable for both their and others' learning.

Evaluation of student learning can be accomplished in a variety of ways. Informal methods are often useful. If cognitive objectives for lessons are clear, for example, teachers can evaluate much through observation. The Johnsons provide useful checklists to help you with this type of evaluation. Students themselves can evaluate their progress. For example, one of the authors had students tape-record their reading. Group members practiced together and later re-taped their reading. By using the pre- and post-tape, they assessed their own progress. Students can set group goals and attempt to improve their own record. For example, if they have been studying spelling as a group, when ready for evaluation, members take turns spelling words. They count the number of words spelled correctly before any word is spelled incorrectly. This is their record. They work to improve that on the next spelling assignment.

More Student-Student Evaluation

In Spencer Kagan's model of cooperative learning, Co-op Co-op, evaluation is made at three levels: (1) Teammates evaluate individual mini-topic presentations; (2) Classmates evaluate team presentations; and (3) The teacher evaluates individual mini-topic papers or projects. Students participate in the construction of evaluation forms; they are evaluating the extent to which individuals and teams helped the class in reaching its learning goals.

Cooperative Learning: Resources for Teachers

More formal methods of evaluation are often needed, especially when cooperative-learning activities must be graded. The Resource section of this book outlines a variety of evaluation formats that can be used to evaluate student learning and, when desired, assign grades. These evaluation formats are only some of many possibilities. The first set, **Content Formats,** describes alternatives for assessing cognitive learning—subject matter material. The second set, **Process Formats,** provides methods for evaluating the way students work together. If we value cooperative skills and want students to work hard on these, we will want to evaluate the process of student interaction. In situations where grades are important to students, the knowledge that their interaction as a group will be graded is a very positive incentive for effective group work. Once students become used to both kinds of evaluation, they understand that a learning activity can be graded both for content and process and the average taken as the overall group grade. Both advantages and disadvantages of each evaluation format are described. This enables you to determine which is best for a particular lesson, class, or time of the year.

And the Next Year

Children who spent a year in a jigsaw classroom where cooperation was the dominant mode of interaction performed as well as ever when moved next year to a classroom where competition dominated.

Elliot Aronson, *The Jigsaw Classroom.*
Copyright © 1978 by Sage Publications.
Reprinted by permission of Sage Publications, Inc.

CONTENT FORMATS

Different forms of evaluation serve various educational goals and needs of students. The Resource section includes descriptions and examples of three categories of content-evaluation formats. When utilizing the first, "Group Project-Group Grade," each student receives the grade of the group. It is very important when using this evaluation format that a mechanism for positive interdependence be structured into the test; otherwise, one student will do the work and others get credit. For example a teacher would have structured tasks for all students into the lesson or taught enough cooperative skills to make students accountable for involving everyone and helping everyone learn the material. Process evaluations, discussed below better guarantee participation by all students.

The second category of content formats, "Contract Grading," includes formats through which students receive grades according to the amount of work their group completes. Within the group, students can do work at different levels or in varying amounts. These formats are particularly useful for projects or learning centers.

The last category provides the greatest accountability of students for each other's learning. Formats providing "Individual Accountability for the Group Result" build in strong incentives for each group member to make sure that all others know the material. One example is "Group Average," in which each individual's grade is averaged into a group grade. Each individual receives the grade of the group. Such formats are useful for careful assessment of the learning of specific content material and of individual students.

Student Opinion of Group Grade

Fifth graders in Mary Travis's cooperative classroom like the group grade very much—as early as November of the school year. They very much enjoy helping each other and seeing their effort reflected in a grade.

In choosing a format to evaluate content-learning, consider the amount of academic pressure generated by peer accountability. For example, when students work together on a project and are evaluated as a group, accountability for each other's learning is limited, but the level of threat is also low. This format might be appropriate in a heterogeneous group with one or more low-skilled students who want to learn but become blocked by pressure. In a situation involving students of more or less equal skills, for whom academic pressure is not a deterent, a format necessitating a high level of accountability, that generates strong peer pressure to learn the material, might be appropriate. An example is the "Lowest Grade Format." Students work together to learn common material. The grade of all individuals in the group is the lowest grade received by any member on an individual quiz.

The degree of motivation students have to help each other is another consideration in choosing an evaluation format. If such motivation is needed, a group can work together on a task knowing that the group will be evaluated on the basis of the learning of one member, chosen at random by the teacher. This means that students must make sure everyone understands the lesson well. It encourages students to ask for clarification or help when they don't understand.

The span of student ability level is another factor to consider in the choice of evaluation format. If there is a wide range of abilities in a group, a contract-grading format would be appropriate. Students work on a group project but, within it, on individualized or "partnered" tasks. The students are evaluated as a group. In this case, use of diverse ability-levels in the improvement score system would be helpful. Consult the Resources section for details on all methods.

Creative Learning Activities: A Key to Student Motivation

Student motivation depends, in large measure, on how the content is presented and on the degree to which it respects student skill level. Grades motivate some students, but your creativity in presenting material is of prime importance to **all** students!

PROCESS FORMATS

The Resources section of this book also contains descriptions and examples of three categories of process formats. These are for evaluating, and, when desired, grading student progress on particular cooperative skills important for effective group process. As with content formats, the choice of process formats requires consideration of the variables.

In the first category, "Process Observer," are formats that use a student observer's notes of member behavior to evaluate group improvement on a designated cooperative skill. Student observers gain skills at watching for particular behaviors that help or hinder the group. The observer watches the process rather than participating in it. These formats are particularly useful at the beginning of the year when students are first becoming conscious of group process and are learning to pinpoint particular cooperative skills.

The second category, "Teacher Assessment," includes a format for teacher evaluation of improvement in cooperative skills. This is especially appropriate in classes where students have not yet learned to be objective and fair when observing others' behavior.

The final category of process formats, "Student Self-Assessment," provides methods for the students to assume responsibility for pinpointing and evaluating progress on specific cooperative skills in other group members or in themselves. Here, students develop the not-so-simple skill of participating in a group task and watching for cooperative skills at the same time. These formats are most useful at that point in the school year when students have become skilled at identifying particular cooperative skills. These formats have the advantage of giving students responsibility for choosing skills to work on and for building confidence and changing behavior.

Thus, all methods are similar in that students are evaluated as a group, but the choice of format will vary greatly depending on the needs of your class and on your goals for cognitive and affective learning.

Such are the "nuts and bolts" of cooperatively-structured learning! While this approach may seem complex at first, it becomes surprisingly comfortable for most teachers once they try it. The activities in the remainder of the book contain a carefully-sequenced series of activities. These are the resources which help make cooperative learning successful for you and your students.

3 FINDING AND APPRECIATING STRENGTHS IN OURSELVES AND OTHERS

"Finding and Appreciating Strengths in Ourselves and Others" begins the activity chapters of *Cooperative Learning, Cooperative Lives*. These chapters contain lessons which will enable students to learn academic content, develop cooperative skills, and discover how people cooperate in their lives, communities, and society.

Section A, "Celebrating My Uniqueness and Finding Similarities with Others" contains lessons that enable students to identify and share special qualities or skills they have. It helps them discover, despite outward differences, what they have in common with others. The more positive self-concepts that students develop, the less need they'll have to compete. Feeling good about themselves won't depend on being better than someone else. Students can learn that each is uniquely skilled and worthwhile. No one need feel compelled to be the best. Activities also encourage students to look beneath surface differences to find feelings, experiences, and interests which they share with others. The more able they are to recognize such human bonds, the more able and willing they'll be to cooperate with others.

When students feel bad about themselves, they have several choices. They can turn these negative feelings on themselves, push them out onto other people, or try to change the situation. "Getting Rid of Those Put-Downs," Section B, is comprised of lessons that help students pay attention to put-downs and find alternatives to them. As all teachers know, put-downs can be among the most negative and devisive forms of competition in a classroom. Students can learn to see why they put others down. They can learn alternative ways to meet their needs. Activities provide students with skills for giving both positive and constructively-critical feedback. Examples are given to help students positively reinforce each other, forming the basis of a cooperative class spirit. Students also learn that helping others is an alternative to put-downs and they practice such helping.

Often, perceived differences among people scare and threaten students and therefore hinder potential cooperation. Section C, "Respecting and Learning from Differences," contains lessons in which students discover what they can learn from these differences. They consider how boring life would be if everyone were alike. Students examine their commonly-held notion that if others aren't the same as themselves and their friends, those others are "weird" and unacceptable. They learn the value of differences and are motivated to cooperate with all people toward the common good.

The formats in this chapter are primarily for activities involving partners and small groups. These structures are most effective in helping students become used to cooperative learning. More complex cooperative-formats are introduced in later chapters.

Communication skills are taught in both Chapters 3 and 4. In this chapter, through certain lessons in each section, students learn specific skills: section A—sharing feelings; section B—giving positive and constructively-critical feedback; section C—listening. Once introduced, these skills should be reinforced throughout the year.

The lessons in this chapter, and throughout the book, can be adopted to higher or lower-grade levels. The skills and ideas taught in this chapter are relevant to all. If the context or examples are too basic for your students, revise the lesson accordingly.

A. CELEBRATING MY UNIQUENESS AND FINDING SIMILARITIES WITH OTHERS

SUBJECT—LA, A
FORMAT—PARTNERS
AND GROUP
PROJECT

People Posters

OBJECTIVES

To encourage students to identify, share and appreciate positive qualities about themselves

To enable students to learn about and appreciate their classmates' abilities and strengths

MATERIALS

Paper—either large oaktag, butcher paper, or poster paper, depending on the project chosen—magic markers or crayons, worksheet "About Me" (see end of chapter, page 72)

IMPLEMENTATION

Tell students that, with the help of their classmates, they will design People Posters, posters that describe the positive qualities, strengths, and abilities of people in the class. Seat students in partnerships to share materials and ideas.

STEP 1

Option 1—Body Posters, for younger students

Give partners large pieces of newsprint. One child's partner traces the outline of the other's body on newsprint. The partner does the same. They can draw a face and hair if they wish. In big letters they write their name under the body. Set aside.

Option 2—Name Design, for older students

Give students pieces of poster board or large pieces of heavy paper. Students creatively design big block letters that spell their first name. They design the letters colorfully, if they wish. Set aside.

STEP 2

Tell students they will be thinking about things they like about themselves and will have a chance to find out things others like about them.

Distribute "About Me" worksheets. Read over the first section and solicit examples from the whole class so students get the idea. Each student fills out the first part of the worksheet. If they're stuck, their partner helps them think of ideas. Partners proofread each other's papers for spelling.

Students take the worksheet home for other people to fill out the bottom part. They return it the next day.

STEP 3 Pair two sets of partners together. Students read their "About Me" worksheets to each other. Tell students to ask questions of each other and encourage those who are shy or modest. Remind them that we all have many positive qualities and talents and their job is to find out about these qualities and talents from others in the group.

STEP 4 Students stay in groups of four. One at a time, they lay out their People Poster. Taking information from the "About Me" worksheet and from their experience of one another, they draw pictures that depict strengths, skills, and positive qualities about that student. The pictures are drawn inside the body of the body poster or around the letters in the name design. A few written statements can also be included. Then students work on the poster of a second student, and so on. . . .

When groups are finished, have all group members sign each poster. Put the People Posters around the room or in the halls or the cafeteria. Collect "About Me" worksheets. Gather into a large group for discussion.

DISCUSSION

1. Partners, what are some of the positive qualities, skills, or strengths you learned about your partners?
2. What are some of the special qualities you shared about yourself?
3. What are some of the unusual aspects of yourself that others appreciate in you?
4. How hard, or how easy, was it to recognize and talk about your strengths? Why is that?
5. What can other people in the class do to make us feel good about our uniqueness and skills?
6. What do some people do to make us feel bad about, or forget, our strengths? How can we avoid that?
7. What are some things you find you have in common with other students that you didn't know about before?

Remind students that these posters are very special and not to be written on by anyone in the future.

COMPLETION Give credit for the project to everyone in a group if each group member has a poster on which there are contributions and signatures of everyone else in the group.

SUBJECT—S, SS, C,
A, R
FORMAT—CLASS
PROJECT

Something Special about Me _____

OBJECTIVES To provide a time when each student can be the center of the whole class's attention
To encourage appreciation of each other in ways not based on class status or life opportunities
To encourage a group to create a cooperative gift for one person

MATERIALS Paper or oaktag, markers, pencils

IMPLEMENTATION This is an alternative to the standard "Show and Tell." The standard format subtly reinforces the idea that if your family has money you have more to share that your classmates will value. Also, when many students share in a single session, the listeners tend to think about their own turns. They miss what is being shared! This version solves these problems.

If you are in a self-contained class, pick one day of the week when you can set aside a half hour for this activity. Assign a different student to each week. Each week at the given time (for example, Friday after lunch) a student may share with the class for fifteen minutes. If you rotate classes and have a shorter class period, cut the time down.

A student may bring in:
    something he made
    something someone made for him
    something he found
    something obtained from an accessible public place

He can share by:
    reading a favorite story to the class
    teaching something from his cultural background
    teaching a song
    telling about some place he's been that didn't cost money

The class focuses full attention on the one sharing and asks him questions.

Examples

Read aloud a story or poem.
Show old family photos from country of ancestors.
Tell a story that your parent has told you.
Teach a song.

Afterwards, the class works together to make an affirmation poster for the focus student. Use a flashlight to cast the student's shadow on a piece of paper taped on the board. Trace his face in profile. Or make a large outline of the letters of his name connected together. Students write affirmations on the posters. The focus student takes his affirmation poster home.

DISCUSSION

1. How did you feel when you were the focus? In what ways was that fun? Was it at all frightening? If so, why?
2. What have you learned about your classmates in this activity? What did you learn about their knowledge and skills?
3. What did you learn about yourself as you read what your classmates wrote about you?
4. How did you feel when you read your affirmation poster? How do you feel when you look at it in your room?

SUBJECT—A, LA
FORMAT—CLASS
PROJECT

Classroom Yellow Pages _____

OBJECTIVES

To encourage students to feel good about stating and sharing their own skills
To have students appreciate the wide variety of skills within their classrooms
To help students realize you don't have to be the "best" at something to enjoy it or teach it

MATERIALS   Colored paper, markers or crayons, yarn

IMPLEMENTATION   Tell students that within the class there are many skills that are known and acknowledged and others which perhaps have not yet been shown. They will make Yellow Pages to share this information so that students can take advantage of each other's skills.

Start out with each student suggesting one skill she can teach the others. Stress that students need not be expert at something; they simply have to know how to do it well enough to teach someone who knows it less well. If students have trouble coming up with a first idea, encourage the class to prompt them if you think ideas will come quickly. Otherwise prompt them yourself. Don't overlook some common, but still appreciated, skills.

Examples of Common—But Still Appreciated—Skills

arranging flowers, tying knots in blown up balloons, teaching ultimate frisbee, doing headstands, naming bugs, baking ethnic specialties, teaching popular dances

---

Write each skill separately on a piece of construction paper—one skill per page. Draw about ten boxes on each page. First have each student draw herself doing the skill she suggested on the appropriate page. Then have students circulate those, drawing themselves on any other pages which fit. Circulate more sheets of blank construction paper. As students think of skills not yet listed, they can create new pages. If enough pages are moving around the room, and if some students spend more time on drawing than others, it will not be obvious how many times each student is including himself.

After students have had time, collect all the pages. A few students—especially those who need the practice—can alphabetize them. Have other students make a cover and bind the book.

Place your Classroom Yellow Pages in an accessible place. Use it when you need skills taught and encourage student-use when they want to learn something.

DISCUSSION   1.   In what ways was it easy, and in what ways difficult, to think of skills? Were there some skills you thought of but didn't list? Why not?
2.   Which skills did you think of because your classmates suggested them, although you hadn't thought of them as skills yourself?
3.   In looking through the entire collection of yellow pages, what did you discover that you want to learn?
4.   Did you discover some surprising skills that your classmates have? What are they? Why do you think these were surprises to you?
5.   Were there some things you didn't think you were "good enough" at, and then during the activity you realized you could include? If so, why do we tend to think we have to be experts at skills in order to teach them? Why is this not so?
6.   What are some things you discovered that you have in common with others in the class?

COMPLETION   Class members get credit for this project if everyone in the class has made a contribution to the Classroom Yellow Pages.

Feelings In Common _____

OBJECTIVES

To learn to identify and share feelings and understand feelings of others
To enable students to find feelings they have in common with others in the class
To discover that no matter how different people appear, we often are very alike in our
    feelings

MATERIALS

"Feeling Scavenger Hunt" worksheet (see end of chapter, page 73) and pencils

IMPLEMENTATION

Divide students into heterogeneous groups of 5 or 6. Explain to the children that we
all have feelings and, that in order to work together well as a class and in groups, it's
important to be able to name our feelings and understand what causes us to feel the
way we do. This exercise will help practice this skill. Also explain that many times we
are so focused on our own immediate feelings that we think we're the only people to
have the kinds of feelings we do. Usually many people have the feelings we do. In fact,
people who seem very different from us may have feelings very much like our own.

Give each student a "Feeling Scavenger Hunt" worksheet. As a class, discuss the
feelings listed. Have students interview each other in their own group and complete
their form. Remind them that they are to work slowly. There is no rush. They are to
interview every other person in the group at least once. Tell students they should share
only those things they want to share. Some things we prefer to keep private. Ask students
not to tell the same situation to more than one person in their group.

Perfect Writing?

Help students determine when spelling and English mechanics should be perfect
and when an emphasis on perfection is a poor use of time and energy. You might
want to create two categories of work: (1) work which will be read by others, (e.g.,
bulletin boards, letters, booklets, stories for other classes); and (2) work which will
be read only by the group involved and the teacher (e.g., worksheets, rough drafts,
notes). The first category should contain the most accurate work students can do.
Work in the second category should be readable but energy need not go into correcting
spelling at the expense of focusing on content. This lesson would fall in
category 2.

When completed, have students share scavenger hunt findings with others in their
group. They take one feeling at a time.

Each person tells others who had the feeling and what experience caused it. When
finished, collect "Feeling Scavenger Hunt" worksheets. Come together for discussion.

1. Was it hard or easy to talk about feelings? In what ways was it hard? In what ways was it easy?
2. Which feelings did you find that others also felt? Were the situations that caused the feelings similar to each other?
3. What feelings did you find in common with students who are very different from you in other ways?
4. How can we learn more about the feelings of people different from ourselves?
5. How well did you listen to others? How much did you feel listened to?
6. How could listening be improved in your group?

COMPLETION   Students get credit for "Feelings in Common" if each group member turns in a worksheet on which there is at least one contribution of everyone in the group.

Talking with Parents

Be well-prepared when you talk with parents about cooperative learning, especially at conference time. Since for many it is a new concept, provide the necessary rationale and background. Review Chapter 2 and summaries of research mentioned there and in the other suggested readings. Most will be strong supporters of cooperative learning when provided background information.

Parents of a fifth-grader came to a local teacher to tell him they didn't like cooperative groups and wanted their daughter taken out of them. The teacher made a strong case for the value of cooperative learning and responded to parental concerns. He did not agree to remove the student from cooperative activities.

The teacher talked with the student the next day. The student said that her parents didn't want her to be in an interracial group. The student told the teacher she liked cooperative groups and wanted to stay in them. Cooperative groups can allow children's sensitivity and good will to hold sway!

B. GETTING RID OF THOSE PUT-DOWNS

SUBJECT—C, LA
FORMAT—PARTNERS

Change That Vulture _____

OBJECTIVES   To help students understand the ways they put themselves down
To enable students to pinpoint ways to build, rather than tear down, their self-images

MATERIALS   Worksheet—"Changing Those Vultures," page 74, paper cut in shapes of feathers, crayons or markers

IMPLEMENTATION STEP 1   The students define, or you define, a put-down. Students think about put-downs they've said or thought about themselves in the past few days. For example, "I'm so dumb, I messed up my math homework last night." Ask for examples from the class.

Tell students that they'll be thinking more about these self put-downs and finding ways to get rid of them. Tell them you will begin with a story and ask them to think about how they're similar to the main character in the story.

STEP 2   Tell the "Vulture Allegory" and discuss with the class.

DISCUSSION
1. In what ways are you like Paul? In what ways different?
2. What have you done to keep vultures away from you?
3. What can we all do to change those vultures in this classroom?

STEP 3   Discuss with the class "Vulture Feather Coloring—Four Easy Steps." Divide students into partners. Each student fills out the worksheet, "Changing Those Vultures." Students color in vulture feathers as appropriate. They discuss their worksheets with their partners and make a contract to help each other color vulture feathers. Collect worksheets. Be sure to return them the next day. Come together for discussion.

DISCUSSION
1. What is one put-down you often give yourself? What is one way you will change that vulture?
2. Partners, what are you going to do to help your partner color vulture feathers?

Tell students you will have them work together about once a week to see how well they are helping each other color those vultures.

COMPLETION   Students receive credit for "Change That Vulture" if they hand in a worksheet signed by themselves and their partner.

Reminder

Remember, students are evaluated as a group for cooperative projects and only if everyone has participated in the task as assigned does any member of the group receive credit.

For example:
1. A student would be given credit for People Posters if she has a poster on which there are contributions and signatures of everyone else in her group.
2. A student would receive credit for ''Change That Vulture'' if he handed in a worksheet signed by both himself and his partner.

At the beginning of each lesson, be sure to tell students the criteria for getting credit.

Review the Evaluation Section in Chapter 2 and see the Resources section for a more detailed discussion of evaluation formats. Use these evaluation formats to evaluate more carefully **each** student's learning.

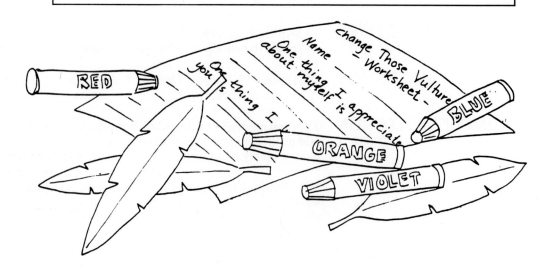

THE VULTURE ALLEGORY

This is a shortened and revised version of "Vulture: A Modern Allegory on the Art of Putting Oneself Down," by Dr. Sidney Simon, Argus Books, 1977.

Vultures are big, nasty-looking birds with sharp talons and cruel sword-shaped beaks. They are usually seen circling high in the sky—waiting, watching—or perched on jagged rocks or bare tree limbs, close to something dying.

But this story is not about real-life vultures. The vultures we're going to talk about are vultures we create in our heads, the ones that do damage to people.

What the invisible vultures are after . . . is you. Not your body, it's true, but a very real part of you called your self-image. Self-image is the way you see yourself, your own opinion of yourself, your private self-rating system. You may be perfectly healthy-looking to everyone else—walking, eating, and talking as you always do. But if you are putting yourself down, even part of the time, your self-image is wounded. A wounded self-image is bound to attract the attention of the vultures.

PAUL AND THE VULTURES

Here is a story about Paul, a young man who attracts many vultures.

To look at him you wouldn't think Paul Putdown has much to worry about. He has no big troubles—with school, his parents, or life in general. But Paul has one big problem with a capital "P"—himself, Paul. And Paul is scared. He is being threatened every day by the whole flock of vultures that circle overhead every waking moment.

In the morning Paul opens his eyes, looks at the clock and says, "Oh, what a nerd I am! Why did I sleep late again? Can't I do anything right?" Paul heads off toward the bathroom and slips on the hall rug. "Clumsy, stupid klutz! You'll trip on the way up to the stage at graduation! That's providing you ever manage to pass enough courses to graduate." The boldest of the vultures makes a quick dive and nips off the tiniest part of Paul's self-image.

In the bathroom, Paul takes a sleepy-eyed look at his face in the mirror. "Look at that, will you! If you've got a strong stomach. A face that only a plastic surgeon could love." Three vultures dive like fighter planes and score direct hits on Paul's self-image.

When Paul gets to school, he passes one of his teachers, Ms. Vega, in the hall. "Why Paul, it's good to see you. I'm certainly looking forward to seeing you in the school play next week."

This makes Paul feel suddenly very good about himself . . . for a second or two. In fact, two vultures who were about to dive at him nearly have a head-on collision in mid-air. They get completely dizzy when faced with such positive thoughts.

Paul sees his best friend Grace. But Grace is walking and laughing with another guy, a new student.

"I can already tell. Grace likes that new guy better than she ever liked me. But who could blame her?"

With more room to work, the vultures dive from higher altitude and use the extra speed to rip off really bite-sized pieces of his self-image.

"Hi Paul!" Grace says cheerily, "I'd like you to meet Bill. Bill, this is Paul, my very best friend in the whole world and a super person!"

This is, of course, too much for Paul to handle. He blushes a nice shade of red, and replies, "Oh, come on Grace, boring old me. Cut it out."

In gym, where he usually relaxes and has fun, Paul hits the volleyball into the net on his own team's first serve. He yells to himself all the nasty things that no one on his team has even thought.

Music class—Paul forgets the word to one of the new songs they've been rehearsing, and feeds four vultures at once—one for each space on the treble clef.

And so Paul's day continues.

 **VULTURE FEATHER COLORING**

Four Easy Steps

We can change vultures from plain, nasty birds to festive birds that don't bother us. We do this by coloring in their feathers.

1. **You color a feather every time you feel good about yourself.**

   If you were to sit down right now and appreciate just a few things about yourself, you would see many colored feathers. . . .

   Like the way you made yourself go down and try out for the school newspaper reporting job in spite of being scared to—and how much you enjoyed seeing your name in print.

   Like how you managed to stop that stupid argument between your two best friends by reminding them how much you liked them both—and how much they liked each other.

   Such positive lists confuse vultures, make them dizzy so you can color feathers. Vultures live on self put-downs, remember, and when you start thinking "yes" instead of "no" it is usually more than they can handle.

2. **You color a feather every time you say something true and good about another person.**

   Be sure that what you say is more than just a breezy compliment. Feathers change color only when what you say is genuine and really adds to other people's opinions of themselves.

3. **You color a feather every time you block a self put-down and start thinking positively.**

   Every time you recognize that you are feeling sorry for yourself, worrying about your appearance or abilities, put it into perspective. It's not the end of the world. You build up your positive habit by turning off that nasty voice that tries to get you to brood about things that are only your opinion in the first place.

4. **You color a feather when you turn your head around and use the energy of the old, negative way of thinking about yourself to run over self put-downs and make positive points.**

   Say "I used to believe people didn't like me, but now I feel sure that people who take the time to know me actually like me and want to be with me. After all, I do have friends. If I work at getting to know the new girl, I'll have more."

   So, join the change-the-vulture club! The price of membership is cheap. Color a feather on the first vulture that makes a dive at you.

Put-Downs Don't Really Make It Better ____

OBJECTIVES To have students increase their awareness of why put-downs happen: why we use them and why others use them
To find realistic alternatives to that behavior
To work cooperatively to create a product which can be shared with others

MATERIALS One situation card for each group, "Alternatives" worksheet for each group, see pages 75–76

IMPLEMENTATION PART A 1. Read one of the situation cards to the whole class. Then divide the blackboard into three columns: "Turning my bad feelings in on myself" "Turning my bad feelings out on others" "Changing the situation to get rid of my bad feelings." Have students brainstorm on possible ways to deal with the situation you just read. List those ideas in the correct columns. If a column is blank, solicit suggestions for it.

2. After you have a few ideas in each column, discuss the pros and cons for each idea, for each of the students involved in the situation.

DISCUSSION
1. What is a put-down?
2. What do put-downs do for the person making the put-down? What does the person making the put-down want it to do for her?
3. What do put-downs do for the person being put down?
4. Why do people put other people down?
5. Instead of putting someone else down, what happens if you put yourself down? If you do that inside your head? If you say it aloud?
6. What makes some people put themselves down when they feel bad while other people put others down?
7. When you are in a situation where you are tempted to put yourself down, or put someone else down, what are some alternatives?
8. What do you have to do in a situation in order to end up feeling good? What can you do so other people end up feeling good?
9. How can you change a situation so no one is put down? Why is that hard?

How I Feel

When you're angry or upset about something someone has done, try communicating those feelings, directly to the person, in terms of how **you feel,** *not* in terms of what **they are doing.** For example, "I feel hurt when you make fun of my drawing" rather than "You're mean to make fun of my drawing."

PART B 1. Divide the class into heterogeneous groups of 4–5 students. Give each group a situation card. Give students ten minutes to plan skits which show their situations being dealt with by each of the three methods listed on the board. Use three columns.

2. Each group presents its skit, with all three versions, to the class.

3. Then each group discusses and answers the "Alternatives" worksheet for another group's skit. Assign these so each skit is covered.

4. Discuss responses to the "Alternatives" worksheet for each skit. The group that filled in the worksheet on that particular skit shares its observations first.

COMPLETION   A student gets credit for this activity if each person in her group participates in planning and presenting a skit based on the information cards and if each person contributes to a signed "Alternatives" worksheet, which is handed in.

Example: Working Through a Situation Card—#2

Column 1—turning bad feelings in on myself

Jason sits and sulks saying to himself, "I'm so uncoordinated, I can't do anything right. Why did I have to be born so clumsy?"

Jason starts playing ball but says, "Even my ball game is lousy. I drop the ball more than I catch it."

Jason lies down on the ground, staring at the sky and lists all of the things he can't do. "I can't walk on the fence. I can't even get on it. I never get a math page all right. My handwriting is messy. Adam was mad at me yesterday. Jamal can do everything."

Column 2—turning bad feelings out on others

Jason goes over and shakes the fence, knocking Jamal off and saying, "See, you're not so good. You fell!"

Jason goes over and taunts Jamal, "You think you're a big shot because you can walk on the fence. Well, I can print neater than you can. That's more important than walking on a stupid fence."

Jason goes back to Joey and Danny and says, "You're such lousy ball players. Learn to catch, why don't you?"

Jason goes over to Matt and Rick and says, "How come you two are talking? Bet you can't even get up on the fence."

Column 3—changing the situation to get rid of bad feelings

Jason goes over to Jamal and says, "Could you help me get up on the fence and walk along with me so I can learn how to do that? I think it's neat that you're so good at that."

Jason goes back to playing ball with Danny and Joey, saying, "I'm not as good at balancing as Jamal. That's something he's better at. But I can do lots of things well and I really enjoy ball. I'm glad Joey and Danny like playing with me."

Jason goes up to Rick and says, "I want to learn how to walk on the fence, but I know that's too hard for me now. Will you help me get up on the balance beam so I can practice balancing and get good enough to walk on the fence?"

SUBJECT—A, LA
FORMAT—CLASS
PROJECT

Unbirthday Treats _____

OBJECTIVES   To provide an alternative to putting others down, and to set a positive tone in the classroom
To allow students to share compliments in an unthreatening way

MATERIALS   Assorted materials, possibly none

IMPLEMENTATION

Tell students that there are much better ways to deal with people than by using put-downs. Explain to students that they are each going to pick, out of a hat, the name of another student. They should tell no one. For a week the "treater" will do nice things for her "treatee." "Treaters" may not spend any money. They may make things out of readily available classroom supplies, write compliments, or do favors. At the end of that week, the "treatee" will discover his "treater."

Write each student's name on the same size slip of paper and put it in a hat. Students pick without looking. Then they check that they do not have their own name. Make a list of each student and the name each pulled. This is important so that if someone is not receiving anything you can help the treater to begin. If a student hasn't followed directions and writes something negative, speak with that student.

At the end of the week have a treater call out the name of her treatee. Then that student calls out his treatee and so forth around the room.

Examples of Unbirthday Treats

1. Make a fancy name sign for your treatee to use on her desk.
2. Bring in wildflowers you've picked for your treatee.
3. Write a poem.
4. Write a compliment letter to your treatee.
5. String a beaded bracelet.
6. Make a friendship pin.
7. Make an origami peace crane.

DISCUSSION

1. How did you feel when you received notes and surprises? How is this different from getting a put-down?
2. How did you feel while you prepared notes and gifts for your treatee?
3. How did you feel when you got to see your treatee receive his surprises? How is this different from giving a put-down?
4. What was different about the tone in our classroom this week? In what ways could we keep this in the future?
5. Without making treats we can tell other people positive things about themselves all during the year. What are examples of compliments we could give each other every day?

Tell the students you will help them avoid put-downs. Encourage them to give each other compliments every day.

I Am Lovable and Capable

Sidney Simon has written a story called "IALAC"—the need of everyone to know that "I Am Lovable and Capable." Read that story to your class. (See bibliography for source.) Or, create your own, based on your school building and routines. After you tell it, create a bulletin board called "IALAC" with an envelope of cards. Every time something is done which is good for another person's IALAC, the recipient writes an anonymous description of it on a card and attaches it to the bulletin board. Watch positive feelings in your class increase!

Rebecca's Always Crying _____

OBJECTIVES To have students distinguish between constructive and destructive ways to try to change another student's behavior
To help students learn constructive, cooperative ways to help each other change

MATERIALS Worksheet "Rebecca's Always Crying," pages 77–78, paper, pencils

IMPLEMENTATION Divide students into pairs. Students read worksheet to each other or, if one student can't read well enough, his partner may read to him. Students then work in pairs to complete questions.

Combine pairs into groups of four to share their answers. Collect worksheets. Then gather as a class for general discussion.

DISCUSSION
1. Discuss answers to questions on worksheet.
2. When we don't like something someone does, why do we often cope with that by making fun of it? Why is that not helpful? How can it actually make that behavior happen more, rather than less, often?
3. How can a group of people help someone change more easily than one person might be able to? In this story why would a method used by Rebecca and the whole class work better than something that Rebecca and one other child would try?
4. Are there problems in our class that we could work together to solve? If so, what are the problems and what could we do?

Build in Success

Using the format of "partners" is one of the most effective ways to build successful cooperative learning experiences early in the year.

Therefore, many of the lessons in Chapters 3 and 4 use partners. More complex formats follow in later chapters and can be introduced to students as the year progresses.

COMPLETION Students receive credit for this lesson if they turn in a signed worksheet on which they have taken turns writing the answers.

Compliment Sheets

A way to make change easier is to give compliments. In my classroom we have an envelope labeled "compliment sheets." Sometimes, we will take five minutes and everyone will fill out a compliment sheet for someone in the building. Sometimes, we just take one as we wish, fill it out, and deliver it. I divided a regular-size paper into quarters, created a form, and made many copies.

It reads:

Dear _____ ,

I think you're good at _____ .

or
I liked it when you _____ .

Ellen

Help!

OBJECTIVES
To have students see helping others as an alternative to put-downs
To enable students to recognize their feelings regarding helping and being helped
To encourage students to ask for help when they need it and give help when it is requested

MATERIALS
"To Help and Be Helped" worksheet, pages 79–81*

IMPLEMENTATION
Tell students that an important expectation in their class will be to ask for help when they need it and give help when it is requested.

Remind students that instead of putting others down when they don't know something, we could help them learn it. For example, instead of telling Renee that she's spastic because she can't hit the softball with the bat, Pedro could teach her. Remember, too, that when we teach someone, they don't always learn. This isn't because they're "stupid" or you're a poor teacher. Not everyone is good at everything. People can have fun playing baseball together even if some hit further than others.

Tell them that sometimes we're afraid to ask for help when we really want to. Because we don't ask, we don't learn, and then we feel stupid, unhappy or worried. Often, then, we take out these bad feelings about ourselves on others, and put them down. For example, John doesn't understand how to do the math problem his group is working on. He's afraid to ask for help because he thinks he'll look stupid. He fools around and doesn't do the problem. Then John makes fun of Lydia and calls her dumb when she gets an answer wrong.

Tell students that in this class you want everyone to give help rather than put people down. Encourage students to ask for help whenever they need it. No one should be embarrassed. It's by asking for help that we learn.

Go over the following guidelines. Then post them.

HELPING
1. Help a person learn how to do his work. It's **not** helpful to do another's work for him.

2. **When you think a person needs help:**
Ask her if she wants your help. Never give help without another's permission. If the person wants a few more minutes to figure something out, respect that. If a person then needs help, give it.

3. **When you need help:**
Ask for it! Try to say exactly the kind of help you need. Don't ask a person to do something for you.

4. **When a person asks you for help:**
Give it.
Find someone who can help her if you can't.
Never put her down for asking for help.

Divide students into pairs. They each fill out the "Help and Be Helped" worksheet. They share their worksheets with each other and discuss the situations. They each make sure the other has written an answer to each question. They check grammar and punctuation and turn in the pages. Come together for discussion.

*Worksheet adapted from *The Interdependence Journal,* Philadelphia Affective Education Project.

1. Ask for responses to question 1 on the worksheet. What feelings do we have in common when someone asks us for help? What are the best ways we can respond to a person who asks for help?
2. Ask for responses to worksheet question 2. What feelings do we have in common when we ask someone else for help? What can people do to make it easier to ask for help?
3. Have students share responses to question 3.
4. Ask for responses to worksheet question 4. What did you like about your decision? What would you do differently next time?
5. Refer to question 5 on the worksheet. What do you do when you realize you need help? How satisfied are you with that? What would you like to do differently?
6. Discuss questions 6 and 7 on the worksheet.

COMPLETION   Each person gets credit for the activity if their partnership hands in two completed worksheets signed by each partner.

C. RESPECTING AND LEARNING FROM DIFFERENCES

SUBJECT—C, LA

More of the Same _____

OBJECTIVES   To enable students to increase their valuing of diversity by providing an exaggerated experience of sameness
To increase students' listening skills

MATERIALS   Worksheet—"Please Listen to Me," page 82

IMPLEMENTATION   Tell students that the class will participate in an experiment. Pick a day. Tell students
DAY ONE   that on "Sameness Day" you want them all to wear a white top and dark pants or skirt to school. Tell them to bring a peanut butter and jelly sandwich for lunch.

DAY TWO   On "Sameness Day" do everything possible to make life the same for everyone. Have all students do the same thing every minute of the day. Lead the class in reading passages in unison and make sure everyone keeps together. Use your creativity in providing experiences that they all do the same. The "bottom line" is not to allow for diversity!

Toward the end of the day or during the next class period, divide students into groups of three. Students will interview each other about their reaction to "Sameness Day." Tell students to listen very carefully to each other because at the end of the interviews they will evaluate their listening skills.

Students take turns asking questions of the third. Brainstorm questions as a class or you suggest some. Possible questions might be:
1. Today was a day of sameness. How did you feel today?
2. What did you like about today? What did you not like about today?
3. How were your experiences today different from other days?

When students finish the interviews, pass out the "Please Listen to Me" worksheet. After each student has completed his own, have students share results. Then come together for discussion.

DISCUSSION The students will first discuss their reactions to Sameness Day. Then they'll talk about the process of their group—how effectively they listened to each other.

Content
1. How did you feel during Sameness Day?
2. What did you like, or not like, about the day?
3. Everything was the same and we had very few differences. What are some of the things we missed by not having differences?
4. What do differences among people bring to our lives?
5. From now on, how can we learn to appreciate differences?

Process—Listening
1. Discuss worksheet questions 1 and 2.
2. What differences were there, if any, in how much you felt you were listened to? What were others' feelings about how well they listened? How do you account for this?
3. What differences were there, if any, in how well you thought you listened to others and how much they felt listened to? How do you account for this?
4. What can we do to become better listeners?

Summarize the listening aspect of the lesson by making a classroom chart, "Behaviors that Encourage Listening." Refer to it in the future. It might look something like the list below.

Tell students that they will use the "Please Listen to Me" worksheet during the year to help them examine and improve their listening skills.

Behaviors that Encourage Listening

1. Look at the speaker.
2. Think about what the speaker is saying rather than the ideas in my own head.
3. Let the speaker finish before I talk.
4. Comment on what the speaker said to show I understand.
5. Ask questions if I don't understand something the speaker said.

Responding to the Previous Speaker

Older students can increase their listening skills by practicing responding to the previous speaker.

Pick an issue to discuss as a class. Before a student states her opinion, she must look at the previous speaker and comment on—not paraphrase—what he said. Then she makes her point. Continue in this manner.

SUBJECT—LA, R, A
FORMAT—GROUP
PROJECT

A Change of Heart _____

OBJECTIVES To encourage students to appreciate others who initially seem different
To help students understand what makes their feelings change about other people or peoples
To give students an opportunity to work cooperatively on a project

MATERIALS   One copy of *The Stranger* by Kjell Ringi (New York: Random House, 1968), lined paper, pencils, markers, drawing paper, yarn, staples, "Evaluating Contributions" worksheet, page 83

Interlibrary Loan

Don't be daunted if you don't have copies of books needed for lessons in *Cooperative Learning, Cooperative Lives*. Your local library can get almost any book through the interlibrary loan system. Use it!

IMPLEMENTATION PART 1   Read aloud *The Stranger* to the entire class. In this book, the people are scared by a stranger who is a giant, but they come to feel differently when they can communicate on the same level and learn about each other's feelings.

DISCUSSION

1. Why were people in the book initially suspicious? How did they react because of that suspicion?
2. What caused them to change their feelings? How did this improve life for them and the stranger?
3. Why are people often scared of those who look different? What are some physical differences that particularly scare people?
4. Why are people often scared or uncomfortable around those who act differently? What are some of those differences that are especially frightening?
5. What are some things that make you less scared of someone who is different?
6. If someone is scared of you because you are different, what are some things you can do to make them less scared?

PART 2   Divide students into heterogeneous groups of 2–4. Ask each group to think of a real or fictitious example of when they have benefited from people who initially seemed different. For example, a girl and boy were playing jacks on their porch. A purple child with green hair walked up to their porch and stood watching. The children got scared and went inside. They watched through the windows and saw that the purple child was just standing there. They felt safer and went outside to continue. The purple child wandered over and looked at them and the jacks. They gave their jacks to the child who then showed them some totally new moves. Soon they were all playing together, everyone enjoying the new ways to play with jacks.

After each group develops a draft idea, gather the class. After someone from each group reads aloud their group's ideas, discuss them as a class. After making any changes, groups get back together and draft stories.

Choose one or two members to be writers, one illustrator, and a binder. Groups then make a bound book. (See bibliography for books on bookbinding.) These can be shared with other classes.

Pass out "Evaluating Contributions" worksheets and have students fill them out. Ask them to discuss their results with their group and decide what they'd do differently next time.

DISCUSSION

1. In what ways was it hard to think of a story on this theme? In what ways was it easy?
2. What were some of the things you had people appreciate about the people they met?
3. What were the advantages of writing a story with other people? What were the problems? How did your group overcome them?
4. What did you learn from your evaluation worksheet? What would group members do differently next time?

COMPLETION Group members receive credit for this project if they comp̶___ ___ __ ____ ___ _ _____
showing what can be gained from people who appear differ___. All group members
must contribute to the book if credit is to be given.

Evaluation Worksheet

Use the "Evaluating Contributions" worksheet with other lessons throughout the
year. It is an excellent way for students and you to assess the extent to which all
group members are contributing to the group task.

Dividends of Difference _____

OBJECTIVES To help students think about what they can learn from people different from themselves
To train students to listen more closely and precisely to what others are saying
To have students feel affirmed by being truly listened to

MATERIALS A clock with a second hand or a timer

IMPLEMENTATION Tell students that they will be thinking about things they've learned from people different from themselves and they will also be practicing their listening skill. If you think it will be difficult, do a trial run of this exercise with the whole class in a circle.

Divide students into pairs. Write one of the following topics (or comparable ones you develop) on the board. Read them aloud.

• Some things I learned or could learn from people who are different from me are. . . .

• Some things I like or respect, or could like or respect, about someone who is different from me are. . . .

• Some people different from myself whom I would like to meet (real or imaginary) are. . . .

Give students the following rules: (1) When the speaker is speaking, the listener may not give any verbal responses at all. (2) If the speaker runs out of ideas on the given topic, the pair may sit quietly and the speaker may resume at any time he has a new idea. (3) The speaker may not speak about anything but the given topic. Give one topic to the partners. When you say, "Begin," one person in each pair will talk to the other person about her answer to the given topic. Allow one or two minutes, depending on your group, then call time.

When time is called the listener must then repeat to the speaker, in the listener's own words, as much as she can remember about what the speaker said. After the listener has recalled all she can, the pair may discuss the listener's recall and the speaker may add anything the listener forgot. Then switch and allow the original listener a chance to be speaker. Give a new topic. Again allow one or two minutes. Then the second listener should repeat back to the speaker. Complete this set in the same way.

Gather as a class for discussion.

DISCUSSION   First let's talk about what you learned.

1. What are some examples of things you learned from people who are different from yourself?
2. What are examples of things you like or respect about people different from you?
3. In this class or school, do we usually focus on how we are different from others who aren't in our group of friends, or do we focus on what we can learn from them? In what ways do we do this?
4. How can we practice focusing on what we like or respect about others rather than on differences?

Now let's talk about listening.

5. What was hardest about this activity when you were the speaker? How about when you were the listener?
6. What did you learn from this about the way you listen? What changes would you like to make in your own listening?
7. How is this different from the way we usually speak and listen?
8. What are some advantages of this method? Some disadvantages?

COMPLETION   Students receive credit for this activity if both partners can write something their partner learned from, or liked about, people different from themselves.

GOING FURTHER   If there is an unsolved controversial issue in your school, you might use that as a topic— "We could cut down on name-calling in this school by. . . ."

You can use topics from a curriculum area, "If we were living 200 years in the past, I think my life would be different because. . . ." If the quality of listening in your class declines periodically, re-do this activity.

SUBJECT—LA
FORMAT—PARTNERS

Different Skills, Wonderful Skills _____

OBJECTIVES   To increase respect for people who seem to be "different"
To increase awareness of the advantages of diversity
To get students to look at each other more openly

MATERIALS   Copies of "Not What We First Thought" worksheets for each pair, pages 84–85, pencils, extra paper

IMPLEMENTATION   Divide students into pairs. Give half the pairs "Not What We First Thought—Sleepover Party" and the other half "Not What We First Thought—Camping Trip." Instruct students to read the worksheet to themselves or aloud to each other. Then each pair cooperatively writes an ending to their worksheet.

Students read their endings aloud to the whole class. They also make neat copies to post on a bulletin board. Follow by discussion.

DISCUSSION
1. Share some of your feelings about the story endings students have written.
2. Why do we sometimes think other people are "weird"? What is it that makes someone else seem strange to us?
3. In what ways is "differentness" frightening? Why?
4. Why are we sometimes uncomfortable with people we think are different?
5. How is it helpful for people to be different from each other? What problems would we have if we all had the same skills?

70

6. In the stories, why were the other kids reluctant to have Lizzie or Jimmy with them? In what ways do their feelings make sense to you? In what ways are those feelings hard for you to understand?
7. How did their feelings change? How did they learn to appreciate Lizzie/Jimmy?
8. What are some other ways they could have appreciated her/him?
9. a. In the story about the sleep-over, Samantha asks Jimica if she thinks Lizzie is gay? Why are many students uncomfortable with people they think might be gay? How does our society encourage this discomfort? What could you do to handle this discomfort for yourself? For others?
   b. In the camping trip story the boys were especially uncomfortable with the fact that Jimmy didn't have traditionally male skills. They may well have thought he was gay. Why might this be a problem to them? How could they deal with that in a way that would be constructive for Jimmy and for them? How could they work through their feelings?
10. Think of someone you know whom you consider to be different. Do not say the person's name.
    a. Why do you see that person as different?
    b. In what ways do you dislike that difference?
    c. Sometimes the difference the other person shows makes us afraid. What might make you afraid of something in the person you see as different?
    d. What are some characteristics of the person you could appreciate?
    e. What are some things you have in common with that person?
    f. What can you do to act on what you appreciate and what you have in common?

FOLLOW-UP Start a bulletin board with students on appreciating differences. Post relevant newspaper articles, cartoons, life stories, where people with different skills turn out to be helpful and important group members.

COMPLETION A student receives credit for the activity if she and her partner have completed an ending to the "Not What We First Thought" worksheet, have both signed it, and have posted it on the bulletin board.

71

About Me

A. **What I say about myself**—These questions are for YOU to answer.

1. Something I do well . . .

2. Something that made me proud of myself . . .

3. Something special I did for someone else . . .

4. Something special about me . . .

B. **What others say about me**—These questions are for OTHERS to answer. Before you start, fill your name in the blanks.

1. A parent:
   Something I like about _____ is . . .

2. A sister, brother, or friend:
   Something special about _____ is . . .

3. An older person (grandparent, teacher, neighbor):
   _____ is an important person to me because . . .

4. Someone in this class:
   I like _____ because . . .

Feeling Scavenger Hunt

Find someone in your group who recently had the feeling listed on the left. Ask her to explain what made her feel the way she did. On the right, include a few words to remind you of her reason. **Do not use any person more than two times.** You may include yourself.

Find someone who felt . . .	person	reason
1. happy		
2. angry		
3. proud		
4. disappointed		
5. sad		
6. helpful		
7. strong		
8. left out		
9. competent		
10. put down		

CHANGE THAT VULTURE WORKSHEET

Changing Those Vultures

Step 1—You color vulture feathers every time you feel good about yourself.

One thing I appreciate about myself is _____

_____

Step 2—You color a vulture feather every time you say something true and good about another person.

One thing I like about you, _____ , is _____

_____

(Tell this to the person before the end of the day.)

Step 3—You color a vulture feather every time you block a self put-down and think positively.

Next time I start giving myself this put-down _____

_____
(Fill in put-down.)
I will think to myself "STOP, VULTURE, you can't get me today!"

Step 4—You color a vulture feather every time you reverse a put-down to a positive point about yourself.

I used to believe _____

But now I feel sure _____

Signed _____

Partner Contract

One way I will help my partner change those vultures is _____

_____

_____

Signed _____
(partner)

PUT-DOWNS DON'T REALLY MAKE IT BETTER WORKSHEET
Situation Cards

---

1. Evan is finishing his history report. He looks over at Benji's and sees that it is longer than his. He also thinks that it looks better. He then looks at Adam's and sees it has lots of spelling mistakes and is very messy.

---

2. Jason is playing ball with Joey and Danny. He looks up and sees Jamal walking along the top of the playing field fence. Jamal never even wavers. Jason goes to try and can't even boost himself up onto the fence.

---

3. Jeffrey works for two hours on a cover for the class calendar. He erases a lot and smudges his picture. The teacher says he would like to use the picture if Jeffrey will copy it over. Jeff refuses, and in fifteen minutes, Belle draws one which is used.

---

4. Arjuna comes in with a new coathook which he can't put up himself. He goes over to Dexter, who is finishing his math homework, and asks if he'll put it up. Dexter says, "No." Then he goes to Elaine who is talking with a new student. She says, "No." Then he goes over to Rebecca who is drawing.

---

5. Rachel is typing a story into the computer. Every time she tries to load her disk, the computer says, "Atari: Memo Pad." After the fourteenth try she knocks the disk drive onto the floor. Next to her the whole time are three students playing PacMan on another computer.

PUT-DOWNS DON'T REALLY MAKE IT BETTER WORKSHEET

Alternatives

1. List the characters in the situation.

2. Which character was feeling bad about himself or herself? Why?

3. In the version where that character turned those feelings inward, what did he or she do?

4. How did that character feel afterwards?

5. How did the others react?

6. How did they feel?

7. In the version where the character turned those bad feelings out on others, what did he or she do?

8. How did that person feel afterwards?

9. How did the others react?

10. How did they feel?

11. In the version where the character tried to change the situation, what did she or he do?

12. How did that person feel?

13. How did the others react?

Rebecca's Always Crying

"I didn't do anything to her and there she is, crying again," Benji complained.

"Yeah. It's ridiculous. All I did was stretch and yawn and maybe my arm touched her and she starts crying," added Evan.

Jason joined in the conversation, "I don't see why we always have to be so careful of her. You can't even get near her."

"What do you usually do when Rebecca starts crying?" Anne, their teacher, asked.

"Tell her to stop, obviously," Benji answered.

"And tell her it's stupid and there's no reason she should be crying," said Clorae as she came into the room.

"And does that help?" asked Anne.

"No, then she starts crying because she says we're being mean to her," said Jason.

Milo put in another point, "And then we have to all wait to get to do something until she stops crying. You won't explain stuff to us or let us go anywhere while she's crying. She makes us late all the time."

"Could you do something else that would work better?" questioned Anne.

Rebecca's Always Crying—continued

Discuss these questions together. Take turns writing the answers.

1. Why do some children cry more easily than others?

2. In what ways are Rebecca's classmates making her cry even when they don't mean to?

3. What could Rebecca's classmates do to help her cry less often?

4. If they do something that causes Rebecca to cry, what could they do to help her stop?

5. What are some behaviors besides crying that we might want others to stop?

6. What could we do to help change those behaviors?

signed _____

_____

HELP! WORKSHEET

To Help and Be Helped

1. When someone from our class asks me to help them I usually feel _____

and I think to myself _____

_____

and then I _____

_____

(Your behavior)

An example of this was when _____

_____

_____

(Describe the situation.)

An example of a time I did not act, think, or feel in that way was when _____

_____

_____

_____

_____

_____

(Describe the situation. Include your thoughts, your feelings, and what you did.)

_____

_____

2. When I ask someone from our class to help me I usually feel _____

and I think to myself _____

_____

and then I _____

_____

(Describe your behavior.)

An example of this was when _____

_____

_____

_____

To Help and Be Helped—continued

An example of a time I did not act, think, or feel in that way was when _____

_____

_____

_____

_____

3. Was there a time when members of the class were helpful to you and you didn't thank them? Here's your chance.

_____ , I appreciated it when you _____

_____

_____

4. One time that I needed help recently was _____

_____

_____
(Describe situation.)

What I did about it was _____

_____

_____
(Describe your behavior.)

I was _____
(Describe your feeling . . . happy? sad? other?)

about my decision because _____

_____

_____

To Help and Be Helped—continued

5. When I realize I need help I usually. . . .
   (Circle one or more answers that are typical of you.)

   a. ask for help from anyone who is around.

   b. ask for help from one or two good friends.

   c. try to figure something out before I ask for help.

   d. tell the situation to others and hope someone offers to help out.

   e. look sad and hope someone asks what's wrong.

   f. don't ask for help and feel sad or angry.

   g. don't ask for help and feel bad about myself, and put others down instead.

   h. other

6. One way my partner and I are alike regarding helping is _____
_____

One way my partner and I are different regarding helping is _____
_____
_____

7a. Next time I need help, I will _____
_____
_____

   b. Next time someone asks for help, I will _____
_____
_____

   c. My partner will help me do these things by _____
_____
_____

signed _____

_____

Please Listen to Me

1. How well did I listen to others in my group?

1	2	3	4	5	6	7

I wasn't
listening
at all.

Sometimes
I listened.

I listened
very carefully
to others.

I let others know I was listening by . . .

I could have been a better listener by . . .

2. How well was I listened to by others in my group?

1	2	3	4	5	6	7

I wasn't
listened
to at all.

Sometimes
I was
listened to.

My ideas were
carefully
listened to.

Someone made me feel listened to by . . .

Someone made me feel I wasn't listened to because they . . .

3. Next time I listen to others I will . . .

A CHANGE OF HEART WORKSHEET

Evaluating Contributions

Name _____

Other group members a. _____

b. _____

c. _____

1. I feel I contributed to this project by:

2. I feel _____ contributed to this project by:
   (your name)

signed _____
(group member a)

3. Without _____ 's contribution to this project . . .
   (your name)

signed _____
(group member b)

4. The extent to which _____ did his or her fair share of the
   (your name)
work was:

1	2	3	4	5
did nothing		did some work, but not a fair share		did fair share

signed _____
(group member c)

Not What We First Thought—Sleep-over Party

Samantha is having a sleep-over for her twelfth birthday. She and her best friend, Jimica, are going through their class list, picking names for the party. They decide upon Aviva, Lisa, Juanita, and Maggie. When they get to Lizzie's name, Samantha says, "I don't think we should have her. She's weird. We're gonna be talking about boys all evening and she doesn't even **like** boys. Do you think she's gay?" Jimica agreed, "I don't think I'd want her around and she'd be bored anyway."

That evening Samantha went over the list with her mother. Her mother was surprised that Lizzie wasn't included. "You used to be such good friends." "Yeah, but things changed. She's not interested in what we're interested in. She hasn't grown up yet. Maybe she never will. It'd be dumb to have her." Samantha's mother pointed out to Samantha how old the friendship was and how important it had been. Finally, reluctantly, Samantha agreed that Lizzie wouldn't ruin the party, and invited her.

The girls all arrived for dinner. They made five kinds of pizza so everyone would be satisfied. They had ice cream sundaes for dessert. During all the talk about boys Lizzie was very quiet. At midnight they decided to make a snack. Lizzie knew how to make crepes. They filled them with leftover ice cream and covered them with hot strawberry sauce. Then they decided to play charades. When they were little, Lizzie had been very good at acting. During the last year the other girls hadn't gone to any of her shows because they thought they'd all be boring. They were amazed to see how funny and convincing Lizzie was. She started to teach them techniques she'd learned in her Friday night drama workshops. They acted out scenes until 3 A.M.

Not What We First Thought—Camping Trip

Matt, Josh, Carlos and Ethan were going on a hike. Josh said that he thought he'd have to take his cousin Jimmy along since Jimmy was staying at his house that month. The others said,

"But he's such a sissy."

"It'd be awful to have him on a hike!"

"All he'll do is cry and complain."

"He'll never make it up the hills."

"I bet he won't even be willing to fish; he probably thinks it's mean to kill fish."

Finally though they agreed to take Jimmy, figuring that if they made fun of him enough he'd stop his silly behavior.

The first day Jimmy dragged behind all the others all day. He couldn't get the fire started. The boys were thinking that they had been right not to want him.

The next day they went fishing early in the morning. Carlos slipped on a rock and fell into the lake. Josh and Ethan dragged him out and thought he was okay even though he was crying very hard. When they got him seated, they realized that his ankle was swelling up very fast. They kept telling him he was all right, but he wouldn't stop crying. They were getting really scared. Jimmy came over from the tent where he'd been reading instead of fishing, just as they'd expected. He started slowly patting and rubbing Carlos with a towel to dry him off. He kept saying in a quiet voice, "It's okay to be crying. It must hurt a lot." Then he held Carlos gently. The other boys were relieved to have someone take over who wasn't scared or uncomfortable in the situation.

4 JOINING TOGETHER AT SCHOOL

"Joining Together at School" contains lessons that enable students to examine their immediate environment to discover patterns of competition and cooperation. It provides opportunities for increased student interdependence and cooperative endeavors.

Through lessons in Section A, "Competition Can Hurt," students evaluate the benefits and prices of competitive and cooperative behavior in themselves and others. They learn to recognize how a competitive or cooperative perspective affects perceptions of, and actions taken in, daily events. By examining their own behavior, students determine the extent to which the socialization to compete in our society has affected them. They explore ways in which stereotypes and discrimination can encourage competition and hinder cooperation. Common negative effects of peer pressure are contrasted with ways peers can provide mutual support to each other. Finally students learn the importance of getting into others' shoes and seeing their points of view.

Often diversity among students creates competition rather than cooperation. Lessons in Section B, "Valuing Group Diversity and Resolving Conflict," help students understand how they can use diversity in helpful ways rather than allowing it to trigger competitive individualism and feelings of superiority over others. The strengths and creative potential of diverse groups of people are explored. Students learn a variety of conflict resolution skills and strategies that allow them to work creatively through the controversies and problems that differences may generate.

"Together for a Creative and Cooperative School" is comprised of cooperative activities that students can carry out in their school. Students participate in cooperative sports, art projects, and computer activities. They practice peer tutoring, cross-age teaching, and reaching consensus. These lessons help make student interdependence a reality.

In addition to a content focus on cooperation, lessons in this chapter concurrently teach skills that enable students to work effectively together. These skills for improving group process, building cooperation, role play, conflict resolution, peer and cross-age teaching can be used again and again throughout the school year in activities in any subject area.

New cooperative learning formats are also included in this chapter. In addition to partners and group projects, the jigsaw format, peer teaching, and cross-age projects are introduced. Students thereby gain experience in a broader range of ways to learn cooperatively.

A. COMPETITION CAN HURT

Competition and Cooperation: What's to Gain? What's to Lose? _____

OBJECTIVES   To have students define competition and cooperation
To enable students to evaluate the benefits and prices of competitive and cooperative behavior as it affects themselves and others

MATERIALS   Worksheets—"Competition and Cooperation: What's to Gain? What's to Lose? A. Jigsaw stories, B. Questions, pages 127–130

IMPLEMENTATION   Tell students that they will define two important words—competition and cooperation—and examine what people gain and lose from each.

STEP 1   In a large group discussion, ask students to define competition and cooperation. Write key ideas on oaktag or newsprint. The final definition might look something like the box here.

Definitions

Competition: People learn and work as individuals against each other in order to succeed or win over others.

Cooperation: People learn and work together toward common goals so that everyone succeeds and wins.

Competition	Cooperation
I think of myself before others. What I want comes first.	I think of myself and others at the same time. What we both want is important.
I feel good about myself when I win over others.	I feel good when we all succeed together.
I keep my ideas, information, and possessions to myself.	I share my ideas, information, and possessions with others.

Now ask students to share examples of competitive and then cooperative behavior in different settings: family, friendships, school. Help students make explicit why each example shows competition or cooperation. Examples might look like those listed on the next page.

Examples	
Competition	**Cooperation**
Family	
I fight with my sister over our favorite game. Because I'm older and bigger, I take the game when I want it.	I take care of my younger brother and sister on Saturday morning so my mother can get her schoolwork done. Then we can all go to the park in the afternoon.
Friends	
I felt great when I won over Diane for the pitching position on the softball team.	Our group of friends helps each other improve our soccer skills.
School	
I'm happy when someone raises his hand and gets the answer wrong because then I have a chance to be called on and get it right.	Our whole class worked on a mural that was displayed in the public library. All our names were on it. We had our picture in the newspaper too.

Encourage students to watch for examples of competition and cooperation in their daily lives.

STEP 2   Remind students that in many situations we have a **choice** to behave competitively or cooperatively. Point out that many messages we get from parents, friends, and society encourage competition. Explain that while we can gain individually by acting competitively, often we pay prices—that is, we lose out on or give up things by doing so. Often alternative cooperative behaviors bring benefits we don't think about.

Tell students that in order to better understand the benefits and prices of competition and cooperation they will examine examples of typical school situations.

For practice read the following account to the class. Then help them identify the gains and losses by asking the questions listed below and discussing their responses. Examples of typical responses are in parentheses.

Where Can We Find the Information?

Mr. Fleet assigned a social studies report on the Wampanoag Nation of Native Americans (American Indians).

Nora was excited about the project because she had a book and magazine article that described the culture of the Wampanoags. Her mother had given them to her. Her mother was an expert on Native American cultures. Nora had so much information that she knew she'd get an A on the report.

Most of the other students in the class couldn't find much material on the Wampanoags. All of the books had been checked out of the library. Some asked Nora, "Do you have much information yet?" Nora thought about sharing her books with them. She decided not to because then everyone might get good grades. Her report wouldn't be the best.

"Oh, I don't have that much information. Anyway I have to keep my materials at home." Her friends looked disappointed. Where would they get their information?

Questions

Self

1. What did Nora gain by what she did?
   (She gained the chance to get an A on the report.)
2. What price did she pay? What did she lose out on?
   (She wasn't fully honest with her classmates. She lost out on being able to help others. She lost out on discussing the material with others and gaining insights she would have gotten from hearing their interpretations.)

Others

3. How will what Nora did help others?
   (It won't help others.)
4. How will it hurt others?
   (It will keep them from learning as much as possible about the Wampanoags.)

Alternatives

5. What could Nora have done that could have been cooperative?
   (She could have: a. brought in her materials for others to use; b. shared the information she had orally; c. invited her mother to come to class to speak to everyone on the Wampanoags.)
6. How would that benefit her?
   (She would feel good about helping others learn. Other people would like her more for being willing to share. She would feel proud when her mother came to talk to the class. She would have the benefit of others' interpretations, choice c.)
7. How would it benefit others?
   (Others would learn more. It would make everyone in the class feel supported in their work. The class as a whole would learn as much as possible about Wampanoags.)

STEP 3

Divide students into heterogeneous groups of five. Explain that they will work together using the jigsaw method of cooperative learning. Everyone will have information necessary to the successful completion of the task. Give each student one part of Story A. Each reads her paragraph aloud to the group. Then students work together to put the paragraphs in sequential order. All students must agree on the order. Spot check to see that everyone in the group is able to read the story and explain why the cards are in the order they are. Once they do, they go on to discuss and answer the questions on the worksheet according to the directions. They turn in their group response. Encourage students to try to reach agreement. If, after discussion, there are divergent opinions, record them. Repeat for Story B.

Finally come together as a class for discussion. If there were differences of opinion among group members on questions, encourage the students to bring these out in discussion.

Hints to Make Group Worksheets Work!!

Some students do very well with group worksheets. For other students, the process is difficult because non-writers must wait while the scribe writes an answer.

Suggestions
1. Instruct scribes to write clearly but quickly. Neatness and spelling will not be criteria for success here.
2. Have several scribes and alternate with each question.
3. Limit the number of words or sentences in the answer.
4. a. You or students copy the 8 ½ by 11 worksheet onto a larger paper so all group members can gather around while one person is writing.
   b. When possible, post this large worksheet on a wall so students can easily see what is being written.
5. Give each student a worksheet. While the scribe writes the answer on the group worksheet, each student writes on her individual worksheet. She keeps that worksheet in her own notebook. Credit is given if the group worksheet—the only worksheet usually handed in—is correct and if all group members have a completed worksheet in their notebooks. Content need not be corrected on individual worksheets. If it is, correct to provide individual student feedback. The content of individual worksheets must not be connected to receiving credit or to a grade.

DISCUSSION

1. For each story discuss worksheet questions 1–7.
2. What are examples of competitive behaviors in our class?
   What do we gain? What do we lose out on?
3. What are cooperative alternatives to these competitive behaviors? What would we gain from these alternatives?

Ask students to point out competitive and cooperative behaviors when they see them in the classroom. Keep a class logbook or poster on positive cooperative behaviors. Place in an available location so anyone can easily add to it. Remind them that only when they recognize these behaviors can they make a **choice** about which will be most beneficial to themselves and others.

Everybody Can Gain through Cooperation

Sometimes it's hardest to think of the **benefits** of cooperation.

In "The Field Trip," if she had been Hector's buddy, Susan could have gained new insights and understanding about what it means to be disabled. By taking time to get to know Hector for a day, she might have gained a new friend. She might have enhanced her creative ablity and that of the class by posing Hector's dilemma to the whole class, and brainstorming ways of doing things on the trip so Hector could be a part. The whole class could gain a sense of greater community.

In "The Art Contest," Aaron might have gained leadership and interpersonal skills if he had accepted the idea for the mural and shared his skill in working on a large collective work. The class could have created a complex, diverse product that no one of them could have done alone. The class would have gained a sense of group accomplishment through community recognition. They would have gained the opportunity to educate and inspire many community members about Martin Luther King Day.

There can be gains for all through cooperation!

COMPLETION　A student receives credit if each member of his group has participated in answering the worksheet as indicated by signatures.

In discussion of worksheets, a student receives credit if all group members called on by the teacher are able to provide the group's answer for the questions asked.

Dealing with Time Constraints

This lesson, as some others in *Cooperative Learning, Cooperative Lives,* may take longer to complete than you imagined from reading it. This, and others, can easily be broken into sections, begun one day, and continued the next. Clearly there are time constraints in our classrooms. At the same time, important ideas and concepts take time to digest. Why not, therefore, divide up such lessons rather than move through them too quickly. Learning takes time!

SUBJECT—C, LA
FORMAT—GROUP
PROJECT

Switch Those Glasses—From Me to We! ___

OBJECTIVES　To use "seeing eyeglasses" to help students see the difference between a competitive and cooperative perspective
To help students see opportunities for cooperative perspectives and action

MATERIALS　Pairs of glasses—one for every three students
Worksheets—"From Me to We Situations" (one for every three students), "Observing Me-First and We-First Behaviors and Words" (one for every three students), pages 131–132

IMPLEMENTATION　Tell students that they will get to wear some very special glasses—"seeing eyeglasses." The glasses will enable them to see the world in different ways. Use actual sunglasses or old eyeglass frames.

Explain that today we will use two types of seeing eyeglasses—"Me-first glasses" and "We-first glasses." When you wear "Me-first glasses" you are thinking of what's best for yourself. When you wear "We-first glasses" you are thinking of what's best for you and other people. Your friend's needs or wishes are as important as your own.

Role-model the difference in the glasses by putting them on and speaking briefly, wearing each.

Divide students into heterogeneous groups of three. Hand out both worksheets. Tell students they will role play some typical daily situations. For the first role play one person will be "A," one "B," and another "C." "A" wears the seeing eyeglasses, "B" role plays with that person, and "C" is the observer. In situations 2 and 3 the roles shift. The person wearing the glasses begins the role play by wearing me-first glasses. Tell students after about one minute you will call "switch glasses." Continue the role play. The goal is to come up with a solution to the situation. On the worksheet, the observer records the key phrases and behaviors of the role player who wears the me-first and then the we-first glasses.

Ask willing students to volunteer to do a sample situation for the class. You can use any situation relevant to your class or school.

During this trial run, all students practice observing. After the trial run, discuss the differences in behaviors, using observers' notes.

Now have students do role plays. Move from group to group helping any trio having trouble. Allow about three minutes for a role play and a couple of minutes for the observer to finish recording observations. Groups continue with next role play until all three situations are finished. The three group members make sure they agree with each other's observations. Then they each write the response to one situation on the worksheet. While one is writing, others start making a permanent list of "me-first" and "we-first" behaviors. They discuss and answer the last two questions and sign the worksheet to indicate agreement. Then, join together for discussion.

DISCUSSION

1. How did you feel wearing the me-first seeing eyeglasses? How did those people who were partners feel?
2. How did you feel wearing the we-first glasses? How did your partners feel?
3. What are some examples of me-first and we-first behaviors and statements that you recognized?
4. How are these behaviors and sayings like what happens in our class or in our school?
5. What can we do to help each other see the world with our we-first glasses? What can we say to someone when they are wearing their me-first glasses?
6. What can you do to help yourself remember to wear your we-first glasses?

COMPLETION

Students get credit for this lesson if each member has answered one situation on the worksheet and all indicate agreement with signatures.

GOING FURTHER

Tell your family about the me-first and we-first glasses. When your family faces a problem ask if they'd like to wear we-first glasses when trying to solve it.

Evaluation: Group Project Format

Student achievement is most significant in cooperative groups where students are actively engaged with each other and where each group member is accountable for his learning.

A group project format doesn't necessarily guarantee, by its structure, such accountability. We all have observed groups where one person does all the work. Therefore, it's important that you monitor students' group work to make sure all are engaged and that you intervene to solve problems that block that. Group-member signatures on worksheets help build in individual accountability, but they don't assure it.

To further insure learning by **all** students:

1. After completing a lesson in *Cooperative Learning, Cooperative Lives,* evaluate content-learning of individuals by using content-evaluation formats in Category III in the Resources section of this book.
   a. Quizzes, short answers, and so forth (completed individually and evaluated as a group) tie individual success to success of others in the group.
   b. Direct discussion questions to individual group members. The group is evaluated according to the response of its individual members. For example, in discussion of worksheets, a student receives credit if all persons in her group called on by the teacher are able to provide the **group's** answer for the questions asked. If there were several points of view at the end of the discussion, she must present each.
2. Increasing equal group participation helps insure learning. Once students have improved their group process skills, tie them into the group evaluation. Use Process Evaluation Formats in the Resources section of *Cooperative Learning, Cooperative Lives.*

Roles to Make or Break a Group _____

OBJECTIVES
To increase student understanding of the different roles people play in groups

To increase student understanding of how each role helps and hinders a group from accomplishing its task

To increase student understanding of how each role makes others in the group feel good or bad

To give students an opportunity to have a structured group discussion

MATERIALS
Twelve copies of "Observer" worksheet, page 133, four per group; enough copies of "Participant" worksheet for each student, page 134; three copies of each chair sign; single chairs for each student placed in three circles of seven to nine chairs each

Chair Signs	
Helpful Roles	**Not Helpful Roles**
Idea-giver	Distractor
Peace-keeper	Silent one
Encourager	Teaser
Clarifier	Dominator

IMPLEMENTATION STEP 1
Explain to students that during any group discussion we each may play one or many different roles during the course of the discussion. Go through the chair sign cards one by one, being sure students understand the terms and the implications.

STEP 2
Divide class into groups of seven or nine students. Alternate helpful and not helpful roles. One chair is the observer. Pass out Participant Worksheet to each student. Review it. Give each observer an Observer Worksheet. Review it with all. Have students cross out any role not being used. Each observer will get a new worksheet.

STEP 3   During this activity, the three groups of students will concurrently have a discussion. (See box below.) Whoever is sitting in a chair will play that role in terms of her contributions to the discussion and style of participating. Every three minutes you call out "clockwise" and each student moves one chair over, and takes on a new role. Include observer role in rotation. During these discussions, observers for each group fill out an "Observer Worksheet." Each observer gets a new worksheet.

STEP 4   After four rotations stop and have the group talk about the activity. Each small group discusses the Participant and Observer worksheets. This should be done as follows: First the group discusses the "Idea-Giver" role. Each student who had this role talks about how she felt and what she likes and didn't like. Then the observers each share their observations of those who were idea givers. The group proceeds role by role until all have been discussed.

STEP 5   Gather as a whole class and go through discussion questions.

Discussion Ideas

1. How we can cooperate to welcome and work with the new non-English speaking Cambodian student in our class?
2. How we can work together to make life easier and more satisfying for the secretaries in our school?
3. What we can do about all the garbage that keeps being thrown in the public park near the school?

DISCUSSION

1. Which roles did you like playing? Why?
2. Which roles did you not like playing? Why not?
3. What role is typical for you? How helpful, not helpful, is that role to you? To others?
4. Were there any roles that surprised you in terms of how helpful or harmful they were to the group decision making? To people's feelings? Explain.
5. Which roles does this class need more of in order to do cooperative discussion and tasks successfully? How could we get people to play those more often?
6. Which roles does this class need less of? How could we work together to get rid of some of those roles?

COMPLETION   Students get credit for this activity if every member in their group completes and hands in a Participant worksheet and Observer worksheet (if relevant).

WORD SEARCH

Cooperation—Where Everyone Wins

EASY WORDS	HARDER WORDS
PLAY	TOGETHER
WITH	NOT AGAINST
ALL	RESPECT
FUN	COOPERATE
FRIEND	NO ONE LOSES
CARE	RECEIVES
GIVE	WINNERS
ENJOY	MUTUAL
HAPPY	INCLUSIVE
SHARE	EQUAL
	EVERYONE WINS

```
P L A Y T O G E T H E R
L R E S P E C T N P C N
A B M U T U A L O U O O
Y F R I E N D G O H O T
W U E B Q S W I N A P A
I N C L U S I V E P E G
T P E N A D N E L P R A
H H I D L E N J O Y A I
A E V C A R E Y S B T N
L L E S H A R E E A E S
L P S L P Y S N S P O T
E V E R Y O N E W I N S
```

Jacqueline Haessley, "Peacemaking Activities for Children," Book 1.
Milwaukee Peace Education Resource Center,
2437 N. Grant Blvd., Milwaukee, WI 53210. Copyright 1984.

Resisting Peer Pressure

OBJECTIVES   To give students the opportunity to learn role-playing skills
To demonstrate how easy it is to give in to negative pressure
To show students some positive alternatives for dealing with negative peer pressure

MATERIALS   None

IMPLEMENTATION PART 1   Go over *Guidelines to Role Playing* (see box on page 98). Be sure students understand that actors will be playing a role, not playing themselves, and that audience responses need to be to the *roles,* not the actors.

Acknowledge that, for students and adults, it is often easier to give in to peer pressure and go along with a group even if you do not like what they are doing. At times we all do that when we don't really want to, and when we know that the group is doing something wrong. It takes practice to resist a group's decision but, if we can do so, we feel much better about ourselves and our friends, and they feel better about us and about themselves.

Present situation 1. Ask for volunteers for roles. Pin name signs on volunteers. Give instructions to the audience. (See box.) Have them act out Scene 1, then have them leave the stage area and act out Scene 2. Do this again for situation 2.

SITUATION 1   Cam, Rachel, Scott, and Jeff go into a comic book store. Rachel, Scott, and Jeff are making fun of Cam because she doesn't want to steal comic books the way they do.
Scene 1: She goes ahead and steals one herself.
Scene 2: She convinces them they should pool the money they have and buy two comic books for the four of them to share.

SITUATION 2   Josh, Matt, Rick, and Toure are studying for a math test for the next day. It is 3 P.M., right after classes have ended.
Scene 1: Josh suggests that they copy from Matt since he does most of the problems correctly. Then, instead of spending time studying, they can all go to the Y.
Scene 2: Josh suggests that they go through the topics and help each other. As soon as they finish, they can all go to the Y.

DISCUSSION

1. How did Cam feel in the first scene? What satisfied her about her behavior? What bothered her? How did she feel about herself? Her friends?
2. How did Cam feel in the second scene? What satisfied her about her behavior? What bothered her? How did she feel about herself? Her friends?
3. In each scene how did Rachel, Scott, and Jeff feel about Cam? About themselves? About each other?
4. What were the advantages for each of the four in the first scene? How did their choices help them? What were the disadvantages? How did their choices hurt them?
5. What other alternatives did Cam have?
6. How did Josh feel in the first scene? What satisfied him about his behavior? What bothered him? How did he feel about himself? His friends?
7. How did Josh feel in the second scene? What satisfied him about his behavior? What bothered him? How did he feel about himself? His friends?
8. In each scene how did Matt, Rick, and Toure feel about Josh? About themselves? About each other?
9. What were the advantages for each of the four in the first scene? How did their choices help them? What were the disadvantages? How did their choices hurt them?
10. What other alternatives did Josh have?
11. Describe a situation where you had to make a choice about your own behavior when it was different from what your friends wanted. What did you do? Why? How did you feel about yourself? About your friends?
12. How can you help a friend who is trying to make a choice which is different from the group choice? How can your friends help you to make a choice that is different from the group's?
13. What are the prices that we sometimes pay when we do not go along with our friends? What do we gain? In what ways is it worth it?

PART 2

Divide class into heterogeneous groups of three. Each group creates a situation with two scenes. In the first scene the focal character goes along with peer pressure even though she doesn't like the decision. In the second scene she convinces the group to make a different decision. Groups write situations on cards. All group members sign to indicate agreement.

Gather as a class. Skim cards and choose two or three to use with the class or have students pick by lot. Follow the role-play directions in Part 1. Have other groups volunteer to do the role plays. Use discussion questions, with appropriate name changes. Save remaining cards and use during the year when appropriate, especially when resisting peer pressure becomes a classroom issue.

COMPLETION   A student gets credit for this activity if each person in his group participated in developing a situation in Part 2, and so indicated by signing the card.

SUBJECT—SS, LA, C
FORMAT—GROUP
PROJECT

United We Stand: Divided We Fall _____

OBJECTIVES   To have students define and recognize prejudice, stereotypes and the "isms"
To help students understand how these forms of inequality hinder cooperation among people
To teach students a process for observing and changing their behavior in groups

MATERIALS   One copy of "Spotting Inequality" (Part One) for each student, one copy of "Spotting Inequality" (Part Two) per group, "The Playing Field Conflict" and "Group Process Observer Checklist" (one per group) pages 135–140

IMPLEMENTATION STEP 1   Gather students together as a class. Explain that prejudice, stereotyping, and the "isms" hinder cooperation among people. Note that some people use stereotypes to keep people from cooperating and others do it without understanding. Hand out worksheets "Spotting Inequality." Read and discuss the definitions together. Divide students into small groups of about four. One group member reads the first situation and tells what "ism" it is. She asks if others agree. She then writes the answer and passes the worksheet to the person on the right who continues the process. All sign to indicate agreement. Collect worksheets.

DISCUSSION   1.   Go over the worksheets with students.
2.   What are examples of prejudice, stereotypes or "isms" that we see in our class, school, community, or society?

Open Minds to Equality

For more detailed background and a myriad of activities on stereotypes and the "isms" see *Open Minds to Equality: Learning Activities to Promote Race, Sex, Class, and Age Equity* by Nancy Schniedewind and Ellen Davidson (Englewood Cliffs, NJ: Prentice-Hall, 1983).

STEP 2   Divide students into small groups of about four if they are not divided so already. Tell them that when they work together in groups there are two areas on which to concentrate. One is the **task**—getting the job done. The other is the **process**—how well they work together. In this activity they will practice concentrating on both.

Tell students that stereotypes and the "isms" block cooperation and that people sometimes try to keep others from cooperating by encouraging these. Pass out "The Playing Field Conflict" worksheet to all students. One group member reads a paragraph aloud, the student on her left reads the second, and so forth to the end. Tell students that the **task** for this activity is to find examples of how stereotypes and the "isms" block cooperation and to find alternatives to that.

Tell students that you also want them to focus on watching the **process** of the group—**how** they work together. In order to help this happen, one person in each group will be a **process observer.** A process observer doesn't participate in the task. He sits outside the group and observes how people work together.

Pass out the worksheets, "Group Process Observer Checklist" and go over it with all students. Choose one process observer for each group. Explain that the process observer will put a check under each person's name when he does one of the behaviors listed that either helps or hinders their group. Encourage students to try very hard to use helpful behaviors and not harmful ones.

DISCUSSION

First let's talk about the **task** of your group.
1. Discuss questions one and two on the "Playing Field Conflict" worksheet.
2. What examples do you see in your lives or in the world where stereotypes and "isms" hinder cooperation? What would alternatives be?
3. Students read their stories. Discuss ways the stories get rid of stereotypes and "isms" and encourage cooperation.

Stereotypes and "Isms" Thwart Cooperation

- Using racist and sexist arguments, employers sometimes pit white workers against black workers and men against women in order to hinder attempts at unionization which could bring higher salaries and better conditions for all.

- Affirmative action efforts often prompt racist or sexist responses by white males. Blaming minorities and women for also wanting an opportunity for a job keeps everyone from collectively asking more basic questions. Why isn't our economy structured to provide decent jobs for *all?* Who does the present hierarchical and competitive economic system serve? How do racism, sexism, and classism keep all workers from asking those questions and cooperating to change the system?

Now let's talk about the **process** of your group. First give process observers time to share their checklist with their group. Ask the group to discuss the checklist and decide how they could improve as individuals and as a group next time they work together.
4. Process observer, in what ways was it hard or easy to see the helpful and not-so-helpful behaviors of group members?
5. What did you learn by observing?
6. Group members, what did you learn from the checklist your process observer shared with you?
7. Did anything surprise you? If so, what?
8. What would you do differently next time to work more effectively as a group? Pick one specific behavior you will work on.

Use the "Group Process Observer Checklist" with other small group activities so students become more aware of their behaviors and can then work to change them. Later in the year, use this form as part of the evaluation or grading process.

COMPLETION

Students receive credit for this lesson if their group hands in: (a) a completed "Spotting Inequalities" worksheet signed by all group members, (b) "The Playing Field Conflict" worksheet signed by all group members, (c) an alternative end to "The Playing Field Conflict" with a list of the important contribution of each group member, (d) "Group Process Observer Checklist."

Cooperation at the Phoenix School

The children at The Phoenix School wanted to give one of their teachers a baby shower. Some children at the Phoenix School come from families with minimal incomes and buying presents can be economically stressful. Also, for young children, using parental money to buy a present is not very empowering. Instead, the children each gave the new baby something used that they had owned and loved themselves. These presents included well-loved books, stuffed animals, toys, overalls, and blankets. The teacher and his wife were delighted to receive such already-loved presents for their baby.

At the Phoenix School children are often responsible for helping each other, rather than turning to adults for all help. When a child is hurt, another child may well go for an ice pack or wash off a paper cut and put a band-aid on it. The students do a great deal of the office work, such as putting together school mailings, collating assignments, and preparing materials for games. Children work together to clean the school, dump the trash and put it out for the garbage collectors, wash off the sinks, etc. Thus they feel the environment is more theirs and feel more of a responsibility toward it.

SUBJECT—M, C

Score as Much as Possible* _____

OBJECTIVES

To provide students an experience that offers them the choice of competing or cooperating with others
To enable students to see the extent to which they are typically socialized to compete
To examine the results of such competition

MATERIALS

Worksheet—"Score as Much as Possible" (one worksheet for every two students), page 141

IMPLEMENTATION

Tell students they will participate in an activity, "Score as Much as Possible," that will give them practice with logical thinking and decision making. Divide students into heterogeneous groups of eight, and within the group of eight form four sets of partners. Students sit on the floor or around a big table so they can be next to their partners and across from another set of partners. The whole group will form a square as indicated in the drawing here.

Give each pair a worksheet: "Score as Much as Possible." If, by working together, your students can figure out the directions, give them time to do that. If the rules are too complicated, explain the rules to the class.

If a student asks directly, "Who are we working for, the partnership or the group?," never directly answer that question. Just remind students that the name of the activity is "Score as Much as Possible." The point of the activity is for students to make that decision—whether to work for themselves or the group. The greatest amount of learning comes if they make that decision for themselves.

Make sure all students understand the rules. If there is a great deal of confusion, you might do one trial run. Once you've begun, keep up the pace. Partners keep their own scores and, at the end of round ten, tally their total score. Then bring students together for discussion.

*From *Teaching Human Beings* by Jeffrey Schrank. Copyright © 1972 by Jeffrey Schrank. Reprinted by permission of Beacon Press.

This can be a powerful experiential activity. Sometimes students get very angry at each other, feel deceived, or feel guilty if players break agreements. Allow plenty of time to talk about these feelings. Help students see how a competitive structure encourages such tricking, so students can avoid overpersonalizing blame. Allow plenty of time for processing the activity.

DISCUSSION

1. What were some feelings you had during that activity? What made you feel the way you did?
2. Did any group make an agreement that was then broken by a partnership? If so, how did that affect the group after that?
3. How did partners who broke an agreement of the group justify it? What arguments did they use?
4. Let's tally the scores. Add all the points of your group of eight and I'll write the group scores on the board. Now let's get the score for the class. (Also write this on the board.) How do you feel about the group score and the class score?
5. Were you more competitive or cooperative? What caused you to be that way?
6. What assumption did you make about who you were working for—yourself or the group? Why did you make that assumption?
7. What could we have done differently if we wanted to "score as much as possible" for our class? What did we lose by competing?
8. As we grow up, what encourages many of us to think competitively? What would need to be changed so we grow up seeing cooperation as an equally visible alternative?
9. People can choose to work against each other or to cooperate with each other. Why do we or groups of people often choose to compete? What would be the results of cooperation?

B. VALUING GROUP DIVERSITY AND RESOLVING CONFLICT

SUBJECT—R
FORMAT—PARTNERS

Head Starts: For Some or All? _____

OBJECTIVES

To enable students to recognize competitive individualism and find alternatives to it
To help students learn that diversity can provide a chance to share skills rather than trigger competitive individualism and feelings of superiority

MATERIALS

Worksheet: "The Solar Design Project," one per partnership, pages 142–144

IMPLEMENTATION

As a review, ask students to define competition and cooperation. Tell them that now you want them to learn about competitive individualism, another block to cooperation.

Write these definitions on the board or oaktag and talk about them with students.

> **Competitive Individualism**
>
> **Individualism:** A belief that people should look out for themselves first before thinking of other people.
>
> **Competition:** People work against each other to get something for themselves. There is a winner who is rewarded.
>
> Add individualism and competition and stir:
>
> **Competitive Individualism:** A belief that competition is fair and that each person has an equal chance at succeeding or winning in a situation. The individual may feel:
> - If I win, it's because of how good I am.
> - I must compete with others and win in order to feel successful.
> - I must feel better than others in order to feel good about myself.
>
> The individualist forgets that people usually don't have an equal chance to succeed because some people have a head start, in that they have more advantages **to start with!**

Divide students into partners and give one worksheet to each partnership. They take notes, read the dialogue aloud to each other, and complete the worksheet together.

DISCUSSION

1. Discuss questions one and two of the worksheet. (Examples of possible responses are in the boxes below.)
2. Can you think of any other examples of competitive individualism in our school or community? How can people with head starts share their advantages with others in cooperative ways?
3. How can we use diversity in helpful ways rather than let it trigger competitive individualism and feelings of superiority over others?

COMPLETION

A student receives credit for this lesson if he and his partner have read and discussed "The Solar Design Project" and participated in answering the worksheet, as indicated by signatures.

> **Examples of Competitive Individualism
> in The Solar Design Project**
>
> 1. Boys said everyone had an equal chance.
>   **In reality,** boys had lots more practice wtih carpentry.
> 2. Boys said they're better carpenters because boys are **naturally** better.
>   **In reality,** most girls hadn't been encouraged to get practice in carpentry. If they had, they could develop a well-constructed project.
> 3. Boys feel good about themselves, because they know how to build a model. They put the girls down.
>   **In reality,** their feeling of success is not deserved. They had a head start. They put the girls down to make themselves feel good.

> **Examples of Alternatives
> for The Solar Design Project**
>
> - Boys would understand that girls have less practice in carpentry. They would choose mixed groups of boys and girls. The boys would teach the girls some carpentry skills. The girls might have ideas about space, color, and design. They have had practice in those areas. The quality of the solar buildings would improve, the design would show more creativity, and all would learn new skills.
> - The students could write letters to their parents asking them to teach carpentry skills to girls. Students could explain their reasons.
> - Students could invite a woman carpenter to class. This would be encouragement to girls and would teach both boys and girls special skills.
> - Boys could teach girls a few basic skills. Then mixed groups of boys and girls could teach them to kindergartners and help younger children have an *equal* start.

Controversy Is Constructive! _____

OBJECTIVES

To define and discuss controversy
To learn the positive value of controversy
To work creatively with controversy in a group

IMPLEMENTATION

Take ten minutes to define and talk about controversy with the whole class. Explain that controversy is a **conflict of ideas.** In group work, controversy is inevitable and **positive!** When people have different ideas, it's important to listen carefully to each other's ideas. You may criticize other students' **ideas** without criticizing them as people. For example, you might strongly disagree with some of your friends about how to spend the group's limited money letting people know more about pollution in the local community. Even though you might disagree regarding the use of the money, you still like the people in your group.

Ask students to think about this situation. As a class, brainstorm all the ways of solving this problem.

Ask students to write down what they think is the best way to solve this conflict.

Divide students into heterogeneous groups of five. Tell them that, as a group, they are to decide which two ways of solving the problem **the group** feels would be most effective. First, each student is to state his #1 choice, with the reason why. After all people in the group have had a chance to talk, the group then tries to reach a decision as to which are the two best solutions. Allow about ten minutes.

Return to the whole class and report decisions.

DISCUSSION TASK

1. What solutions did each group choose, and why?
2. What are some strengths and weaknesses of the different solutions?
3. How can we use some of these ideas when we have conflicts in our class?

PROCESS

1. How many different solutions did your group have? Was there controversy—a conflict of ideas?
2. Did you listen carefully to each person and her reason before you began debating? If not, why not?
3. How convincing were other people's reasons for their choices? Did these reasons convince you to change your mind?
4. How did the group finally resolve the conflict of ideas?
5. Are you pleased with the result? If so, why? If not, why not?

Conclude by reminding the class that they will often have differences of opinion with others. They will often disagree on ideas. Write on the board or on oaktag:

Controversy Is Positive and Healthy

_____ , even though I disagree with you about
(name)

_____ , I accept you as a person.
(idea)

Conclude by having each student say this to anyone in his group with whom he disagreed.

Problems? Try Something New! _____

OBJECTIVES

To teach students a process for resolving a conflict or solving a problem

To encourage students to see problems as something which, to be solved successfully, must meet everyone's needs

To free students to think more creatively about solving problems and resolving conflict

MATERIALS

Large sheets of paper, markers

IMPLEMENTATION

Do this lesson with the entire class. Teach brainstorming. (See box on page 106.) Have students brainstorm the types of problems you have in the classroom. You may insist names not be used initially if that would cause too much open conflict. Create a list on the board. Students decide on one problem which they think applies to many people, or which they think happens often. Write that problem at the top of a large sheet of paper and post it in front of the class.

Next, students brainstorm possible solutions. They say anything they want, even if an idea is clearly advantageous to only one person or group of people and is harmful to others. Write these solutions under the problem. Continue this list until you have at least ten ideas. Take no more than five minutes.

Then have students note the possible solutions for person or groups one and two. A + for person or group one means that person would be satisfied with the solution, a − means he wouldn't be. Use the same system for person two. Write the +s and −s next to each solution. Now students look at all the solutions which have a + for both people or both sides. Those are win-win solutions. Take two or three of those and work out the practical measures to implement them. (See example at end of lesson.)

> **Brainstorming**
> 1. Students call out ideas as they think of them.
> 2. Accept all ideas.
> 3. Allow no discussion on any ideas, no reactions to anyone else's ideas.
> 4. Encourage ideas which are follow-ups of previously suggested ones.
> 5. Have more than one scribe if necessary in order to take notes at the pace at which ideas are suggested.
> 6. Write down ideas in a way everyone can see and read.

DISCUSSION

1. Why is it important to try to come up with win-win solutions for problems? Why do win-lose solutions often mean that, really, the "winner" doesn't get what she wants after all?
2. Why, at first, do we find it hard to think of solutions which meet both our needs and the other person's?
3. How can a group sometimes think of ideas which are more helpful than any one of us would come up with on our own?

Tell students that this process for resolving conflict is one they will use throughout the year. Ask each person to practice it during the next week when they have, or see, a conflict or problem that needs to be solved.

COMPLETION

Students receive credit for this activity if they participate in the class brainstorming sessions.

Example

Problem

Adam distracts the class with jokes and anecdotes which prevent the students from discussing the class material. Scott really wants to learn all the content in the class and gets very angry at Adam's comments which use up time and get discussions off course.

Possible Solutions

- Throw Adam out of class every time he talks.
- Throw Adam out of class every time he makes an irrelevant comment.
- Throw Adam out of class when his irrelevant comments aren't funny.
- Switch Scott to a different section.
- Give Adam three minutes at the beginning or end of every class to tell jokes and stories.
- For a week, count the number of times Adam interrupts the class. The next week allow him three fewer interruptions, and the next week three fewer, and so on. Throw him out if he goes over that.
- Require that Adam do a favor for Scott each time he, Adam, interrupts the class.
- Make Scott responsible for giving Adam a handmotion each time Adam begins to interrupt.
- Put Adam and Scott in a locked room to talk about the problem until they come up with a solution they both like.
- Have all the students take turns motioning to Adam to stop.
- Have Adam and Scott try to explain to the class why they feel the way they do.

Adam	Scott	Idea
−	−	Throw Adam . . . talks
−	+	Throw Adam . . . irrelevant
−	−	Throw Adam . . . not funny
−	−	Switch Scott
−	−	Give Adam three minutes
+	+	Count the number of times
−	−	Adam do favor
+	+	Scott responsible for handmotion
−	−	locked room
+	+	students take turns motioning
+	+	Adam and Scott explain

Note: Your coding ideas may differ from that of the class. Go with the group's opinion, since all will need to agree that a solution is a win-win in order to try it.

Practicalities

Students take turns motioning.

- Step 1: Students brainstorm on what sorts of comments are disruptive. They list those and give Adam a copy.
- Step 2: All students, including Adam, agree on a signal which will tell Adam he should stop doing what he's doing. The signal should not, in any way, disrupt the class.
- Step 3: Class role plays Adam doing something disruptive and someone signaling him to stop.
- Step 4: Class and Adam try out this method.
- Step 5: Entire class evaluates and modifies this method.

Work Through That Conflict* _____

OBJECTIVES   To teach students a process for conflict resolution
To give them practice using that mediation process

MATERIALS   Worksheets: "Guidelines for Mediator," "Contract," pages 145–146

IMPLEMENTATION STEP 1   Tell students that you will teach them a process of resolving conflicts. It can be used throughout the year. The process is called mediation. The person who helps others resolve a conflict is called a mediator. Explain that as the teacher, you will be the mediator today and will work with small groups of students over the next few weeks to mediate conflicts that arise in the classroom.

Brainstorm hypothetical conflicts in the classroom or school. Pick one to use as an example. Save the whole list for later use.

Pass out both parts of "Work Through That Conflict" worksheet and go over it with students, step by step. You may want to teach "I-messages" for use in Step 2. See "We Have to Do It Differently" in Chapter 5. Explain that the mediator asks the questions aloud to the persons in the conflict. The mediator asks herself the questions for the mediator in her mind.

Ask for two volunteers to role play the conflict the class picked. You mediate. Stop at each step and point out the role of the mediator.

Over the next several weeks take students aside when a conflict arises and use this process to mediate the conflict. When such a conflict is resolved successfully, and if students are willing, share the process with the class. This rewards students for effective efforts at conflict resolution.

STEP 2   About one month later, or when students are used to the mediation process, tell students they will now have a chance to learn some skills for mediation.
Option 1—Choose another conflict from the list brainstormed above. Divide students in trios. Ask students who have been through the mediation process with you to be the mediators. Each of the others take one side of the conflict. Encourage each student to represent this assigned side of the conflict, even if in reality they might not take that position.
Option 2—This option is more complex and involves more risk, but potentially can have a greater long-term effect on your class. Ask students who have already gone through the mediation process with you to be mediators. Limit the numbers to a third of the class. Ask other students to think of conflicts they have with others in the class and to choose as a partner one of those persons. If it is hard for students to think of conflicts specific to each partnership, they may choose simple and general conflicts, such as interrupting. Some juggling may be necessary to get everyone ready.

Pass out both worksheets to each group. Review the mediation process. Remind mediators to go step by step. As students talk in their groups, move around the groups and assist any student having difficulty. Students fill out contracts at the end.

When all groups have finished, ask for a group that followed the process carefully and came up with a workable solution to redo their mediation process in front of the class. Interrupt to point to each step in the process or ask students to watch for them. In a large group, discuss both the example and other experiences from their trios. Praise students for their efforts and remind them that learning mediation is difficult at first.

*Based on a process developed by Allen Main and Albert Roark, reported in the *Personnel and Guidance Journal,* June 1975.

The Mediation Process: A Short Example

Introduction

Teacher: I am here to help you find an agreeable solution to this conflict. You may each need to change a little in order for this to happen.

Step One

Teacher: Jenny, how do you see this conflict?
Jenny: I'm so mad at Jamilla. She's always moving her desk close to mine and trying to copy my language arts assignments. Sometimes she'll even ask to see my work.
Teacher: Jamilla, how do you see the conflict?
Jamilla: Jenny shows her papers to her friends. All the white kids share information with each other. They won't share it with us. Last year that happened in Mr. Murphy's class too.
Teacher: Jamilla, let's focus on the conflict now, not last year.

Step Two

Teacher: OK, we do have a conflict! Jenny, how does the conflict make you feel?
Jenny: I work hard and I don't like people taking my information.
Teacher: Can you find feeling words to describe this?
Jenny: I feel mad and I feel cheated.
Teacher: Jamilla, how does the conflict make you feel?
Jamilla: I feel left out. I also feel upset when I don't understand the lesson.

Step Three

Teacher: What would be the best outcome to the conflict?
Jenny: I would like to do my work without being interrupted.
Teacher: Jamilla?
Jamilla: I would like someone who understands the material to help me so I can get the lesson done.
Teacher: Is there an outcome you can agree on?
Jenny: After you give an assignment, I could work with Jamilla to make sure she knows how to do it. Then she could work on her own.
Jamilla: But sometimes I have a question in the middle of a project and you won't explain things to me.
Teacher: What other alternatives are there?
Jamilla: When Jenny shares with other people she could share it with me.
Jenny: OK, just as long as you work really hard on it first. Also, you should ask other people sometimes.
Teacher: What does Jamilla do well that you'd like her to help you with?
Jenny: Jamilla is great on math problems on the computer. I get confused at that sometimes.

Step Four

Teacher: What changes are you willing to make to make this happen?
Jenny: When we have individual written assignments, I'll check with Jamilla to make sure she's off to a good start. If I share my information with my friends, I'll share it with her too.
Jamilla: I won't interrupt Jenny after the beginning of her work. When I have a question, I'll also ask the teacher or other students, not always Jenny. I'll help Jenny on math computer problems when she wants help.
Teacher: As a mediator, I'm going to check with each of you every day next week and ask about your contract.

The above situation is not atypical, especially in desegregated schools. Because white students often have had more educational advantages than many minority students, they can have higher skill levels. White students can perceive minority students as not trying hard, "copying," or always wanting information. Minority students can perceive whites as hard working, cliquish, and unwilling to help. What is a difference in skills—usually resulting from a disparity in educational opportunity—sets up a dynamic that reinforces racial stereotyping.

The teacher could have helped alleviate both the individual conflict described above and the general problem by setting up interracial cooperatively-structured groups for assignments and projects. He would be sure to place a value on things minority students in his class do well, and in some lessons structure those into the assignments. Fewer individual resentments would develop, learning would be enhanced and racial stereotyping decrease.

> For more detail, see Janet Schofield, "Cooperation as Social Exchange: Resource Gap and Reciprocity in Academic Work" in *Cooperation in Education.*

DISCUSSION

Students in conflict
1. How do you feel about the mediation process?
2. What did you learn by doing it?
3. What did you agree to change?

Mediators
4. In what ways was being the mediator hard? In what ways was it easy?
5. What did you do that helped the others work through the conflict?
6. Did you come to a resolution? Why or why not?

Everyone
7. What examples are there of solutions to the conflict that all agree on? What did people agree to change?
8. What would you do differently next time you use mediation?

Tell students to save their worksheet, or collect them and save them yourself, since they'll be using mediation as conflicts arise throughout the year.

COMPLETION

A student receives credit for this activity if each member of her group has participated in the mediation process, as indicated by signatures on "Work Through That Conflict: Contract."

Youth Mediators Have Success

"Sometimes kids understand what makes other kids do things better than grownups do" was a fourth grader's explanation of the Student Advisory Council. SAC is part of the student government of P.S. 75, an elementary school in Manhattan.

Students were trained by the Children's Creative Response to Conflict Program to help each other resolve conflicts. They learned listening skills, affirmation skills, and how to help others solve their problems. They then met with kids whose behavior caused problems in the school and helped develop solutions.

The sessions were successful because the council members understood that they weren't there to punish, but to listen and give tools. They learned again and again that affirmation and attention produce an atmosphere where the problem becomes comprehensible, where working together can solve it.

"Sharing Space," *Bulletin of Children's Creative Response to Conflict Program,* (April 1983).

110

It Depends on How You Look at Things —

OBJECTIVES

To enhance student appreciation of validity of different points of view

To encourage students to see a problem through another's eyes

To encourage students to see solutions to problems as being ones which meet the needs of all people involved

MATERIALS

One copy of worksheet "It's All Her Fault; No, It's All His Fault" (page 147) for each student and extras for each group, paper, pencils

IMPLEMENTATION STEP 1

Give each student a copy of the worksheet. Direct students to work independently to devise a solution which would meet both students' needs.

STEP 2

Divide students into groups of three or four. Give each group a copy of the same worksheet. Groups work together to devise a group solution which would meet both students' needs.

STEP 3

Instruct each group to think of a classroom problem involving two people or two groups. Each group describes the problem in writing from the two different points of view. They should use fictitious names. For each point of view, students must show understanding and sympathy with regard to the people involved. Then students write a solution which seems to them to be satisfactory for all the people involved in the conflict.

STEP 4

Groups share their problems and solutions aloud with the entire class. If appropriate, post these on the bulletin board to be read.

DISCUSSION

1. In what ways was it hard or easy to think of a problem which had two genuine points of view? Do you think all classroom problems can be seen from more than one point of view? Why or why not?
2. Was one point of view easier for you than the other? Was one point of view easier for your group? If so, what did you do to try to understand the other point of view?
3. How did you pool your ideas to create your characters? Your solutions?
4. How was it different working to devise a solution by yourself and working with a group? What were the advantages and disadvantages of each?
5. Did you have more diversity of ideas in the group? Why or why not?
6. Were you able to build on each other's ideas when working in a group? Did other people's ideas help you think of more ideas of your own? How?

COMPLETION

A student receives credit for this lesson if he and all other group members have written a solution to both the worksheet and classroom problem—a solution that shows an understanding of the people involved, as indicated by signatures on the written solutions.

C. TOGETHER FOR A CREATIVE AND COOPERATIVE SCHOOL

SUBJECT—A, SS
FORMAT—GROUP
PROJECT
(CLASS PROJECT)

Blessed Are the Quilters, for They Are the Piecemakers _____

OBJECTIVES

To learn about the history of quilting

To demonstrate that a cooperative group project can be larger and more beautiful than those created by individual students

To create an artistic object which can be appreciated by the entire class and school

To encourage appreciation of each other's ideas and skills

MATERIALS

One large piece of printed fabric at least 6 ft. by 6 ft., print or solid fabric 4 ft. by 6 ft., one square of muslin for each student 9 in. on a side, needles, regular thread, quilting thread, either scrap fabric or crayons, iron

IMPLEMENTATION

Introduce students to the history of quilting in this country. Colonial women made quilts out of scrap fabrics, using traditional patchwork designs. Designs were passed down in families from generation to generation. White women most often made geometric pieced quilts in blocks. Black women more often created applique quilts, frequently with religious themes.

A particular type of quilt was the friendship quilt. These were typically created as leave-taking presents for pastors moving on to new churches, and for weddings. Today, they are also made for births and retirements. Usually each quilter created her own square, and signed her name in the center of the square. Often all quilters used the same pattern. Then, at a quilting bee, the squares were sewn together and the quilt was filled and bound. The quilting was done as a group with many women sitting around the quilting frame together.

Have interested students do further research on women quilters and present that to the class.

> Background Reading on Women and Quilting
> • *The Quilters: Women and Domestic Art*—Patricia Cooper and Norma Buford
>
> Curriculum
> • *Quilting as a Traditional Women's Art Form: A Kit*—Mary Ruthsdotter
>
> Practical Books—Making a Quilt (Adults)
> • *The Sampler Quilt*—Diana Leone
>
> Practical Books—Making a Quilt (Students)
> • *A Patchwork Applique and Quilting Primer*—Joellen and Elyse Sommer
> • *The Beginner's Guide to Sampler Quilts*—Caren Caraway

MAKING A QUILT STEP 1

For this project, the class will create a quilt around a specific theme. Each student gets one square of fabric. Either assign the theme or have the class use consensus to pick a theme. Here are two suggestions:

Working and Living Together Peacefully: Each student creates a square showing people of mixed cultures working or playing cooperatively.

People with Differences: The quilt as a whole shows people of different races, genders, ages, cultures, classes, and some people with handicaps. All should be involved in a variety of activities. Brainstorm ideas for pieces.

STEP 2 Each student works individually to make her square. (See the next box for specific directions.)

STEP 3 After all the squares are made, students take turns sewing them together on a sewing machine.

STEP 4 Have a quilting bee in your classroom. At a quilting bee, the top of the quilt with the designs and the filling and the backing are sewn together. The quilt is stretched out. Students sit around it and work. At any one time, you can have six to eight students quilting.

STEP 5 Hang the finished quilt in your classroom, in the school lobby, in the public library, town hall, or an historical building.

Notes on Quiltmaking

For Inexperienced Sewers
Consult books on quilting listed above.

For Experienced Sewers
Here are a few general ideas to provide background.

The easiest type of quilt to make is a crayon quilt. Each student first colors a design on scrap paper. When students are satisfied with their designs, they tape muslin over their squares. They trace over them and color them in with regular crayons. Then they put clean scrap paper over these and press with a hot iron to set the color.

Another possibility is for students to design squares on paper and then cut each piece out of scrap fabric. They can then sew these onto the muslin, folding under rough edges.

After the squares are made, the quilt top needs to be sewn together. A sewing machine works well for this. See illustration. Place the backing fabric wrong side up, put quilt batting on top, cover with pieced top. Fold edges of backing fabric over top, miter corners, fold under rough edges. Baste. Quilt.

DISCUSSION
1. In what ways did quilting historically give women a sense of community?
2. Why were quilts more commonly used in the past than today?
3. Recently, there has been a revived interest in quilting. What reasons can you think of for this?
4. How did our combining of squares produce a quilt that is stronger and more interesting than any one class member could have made on his own?
5. Why do you think quilting bees originated? What were some of the good things that happened at our quilting bee?
6. What does each square in our quilt tell us about ways people live together? What do all the squares together tell us? In what ways is that a fuller message?

COMPLETION A student gets credit for this activity if each student in the class makes a piece for the quilt and participates in the sewing in the quilting bee.

SUBJECT—M, LA, S
FORMAT—GROUP
PROJECT

Creating Cooperative Curriculum _____

OBJECTIVES

To enhance student appreciation of their own and each other's creative ideas
To encourage student realization of positive effects of synergy of their ideas
To reinforce the concept that students can capably create learning materials for their peers
To enable students to create classroom academic content that is cooperative

MATERIALS

Scrap paper, pencils, good paper, stapler, yarn, markers

IMPLEMENTATION

Explain to students that they are going to create learning materials for each other. They will use regular subject matter being taught, and the materials they create will emphasize cooperation. Following are examples in different subjects.

MATH

If your class is divided into math groups, have each group make a word-problem book for another group. If the class is not divided into math groups, form such groups. Each group makes a problem book for others. Give examples based on the content you are studying. For example:

Clorae and Jason's class has decided to have a communal pencil and pen supply bought by money the class earned collectively so that all children can have equal access to these. Pencils were on sale at the drugstore. Clorae buys 15 packages of pencils which used to cost $14 for a dozen packages. The sale price is 15% off. What does she pay for the pencils? Jason buys pens at the sale price of 5 packages for the price of 4. They used to cost 29 cents a package. He buys 10 packages. What does he pay?

Each group makes up about fifteen problems. They exchange them with another group to check for spelling and practicality. They also make sure each problem emphasizes cooperation. The problems are then returned to the original group for any revisions which may be needed. Then each group creates a booklet and neatly copies over problems. Use these in future math classes or assignments.

SPELLING OR VOCABULARY

If everyone in your class studies the same spelling or vocabulary words, divide your class into heterogeneous groups of three to five. If you have spelling groups by level, give each group a set of words appropriate for spelling practice for a different group. Each group makes a set of sentences with blanks, using the spelling words. These should stress cooperation and be antiracist and antisexist.

For example:

    because, could, where

1. Do you know _____ we could get glitter for the sign we're making for our nursing home party?
2. We did the marketing for Aunt Tillie _____ she was busy fixing her furnace.
3. _____ you please help me carry in this crate of apples for the Halloween party?

SCIENCE

Divide class into heterogeneous groups of three to five to make ecology booklets. Each group works on making a list of community ecology ideas. Students brainstorm in small groups on possible ideas. For example: (a) making posters for store windows and telephone poles encouraging people not to throw trash on the street; (b) making signs for trash cans encouraging their use; (c) setting up pick-up places for newspapers, bottles and cans for recycle. Groups trade ideas and check for spelling, grammar, practicality, and scientific accuracy (for example, what type of metal cans can be recycled and which can't). As a class, work together to eliminate overlap. Then each group writes up its ideas, with illustrations, for a booklet. Make copies and bind into booklets. Distribute to community places such as stores, laundromats, day-care centers. Students also carry out one of the ideas as a project.

LANGUAGE ARTS

Divide class into heterogeneous groups. Each makes up a set of sentences practicing whatever punctuation or capitalization skills are being taught. The sentences must reflect cooperation. They write these so other students will put in the needed corrections.

For example:
1. When we finish buying compost, let's go in and make some popcorn, Rose suggested
2. Jordy yelled loudly can someone grab the other end of this shelf these books are about to fall on my head

Original groups correct others' work.

DISCUSSION

1. In what ways was making up sentences and problems with a group easy? Difficult? Satisfying? Frustrating?
2. How was it different to make up examples where people were cooperating? How, if at all, did you have to change your thinking?
3. How did it help to have a group making up the examples rather than doing it yourself?
4. Were there any ways that the group made it harder? If so, what could you do about that the next time?

Avoiding Stereotypes

Be sure students create examples which avoid stereotypes based on age, sex, race, handicap, sexual orientation or class. Get them going by giving your own nonstereotypic examples. Help them to modify their ideas if the first drafts come out reinforcing stereotypes.

COMPLETION   Students get credit for this activity if their group completes the project with a final product and each individual group member writes a paragraph explaining her contributions to the product. Those paragraphs must be signed by each of the other group members.

The Peaceful Classroom

Each morning after opening, I present my ESR "TEACH PEACE" button to a student who has demonstrated courtesy, good listening and cooperative behavior during that time period.

The student is instructed to pass the button to a classmate s/he observes practicing peaceful, cooperative behaviors, such as those for which s/he received the button. That classmate then watches for another student behaving peacefully and passes the button to him/her. This goes on all day. In the final ten minutes of school, all students who received the button are called to the front of the class by the student who awarded him/her the button. The awarder tells why the button was passed—what specific behaviors were noticed that prompted the passage of the button. As the year progresses, students are required to be aware of their own behaviors which earned them the button, thus further reinforcing a positive self-image.

This activity has many purposes. It provides for student-controlled behavior management; it helps students learn to see good behaviors in their classmates; it makes students aware of a range of cooperative, positive behaviors; it provides an opportunity for brief oral speaking; and it helps the less popular students get recognition from their peers by requiring them to recognize and publicly proclaim appropriate behavior.

Positive reinforcement and peer reinforcement are strong tools for maintaining a healthy classroom climate/learning environment and for teaching active concepts of peace.

Tony Catalano, sixth grade teacher, Paradise, CA,
in *Forum,* Educators for Social Responsibility (Summer 1984).

Peer Teaching: What Makes It Work? _____

OBJECTIVES   To have students think about values and skills necessary in successfully helping each other
To have students create something which is visually appealing and amusing and that has lasting power
To emphasize that there are many different constructive ways to help each other

MATERIALS   Worksheet: "Words to the Blurb"—several for each group (page 148), pencils, markers, poster board

IMPLEMENTATION STEP 1   Divide students into pairs. Give each pair two copies of the worksheet "Words to the Blurb." On the first worksheet they draw in facial expressions and write conversation which shows one student teaching another in a supportive, helpful way. On the second worksheet they do facial expressions and conversation with one student teaching another student in a way which is either useless or destructive.

STEP 2   Gather as a whole class for discussion questions:
1.   How did you portray positive ways of helping? How negative ways?
2.   Did you and your partner agree on what would be helpful and supportive and what would be useless or destructive? If not, in what ways did you disagree?
3.   If you disagreed, how did you resolve the disagreement?
4.   How did you decide on wording of conversation and on facial expressions? How did you split the tasks?
5.   In what ways did you come up with funnier or more interesting ideas by working together than either of you might have if you had done it on your own?

STEP 3   Title a space on the blackboard **The Do's and Don'ts of Peer Teaching.** As a class, decide on and make a list of five or six very important positive things we can do when we are helping another person learn something. Make a list of five or six destructive things we can do in that situation.

STEP 4   Combine pairs into groups of four or six. Give each group *large* poster board divided in half. Assign, or let groups choose, one of the positive behaviors and one negative. Label one half of each board **DO** and the other half **DON'T**. Each group creates a cartoon for each side showing one student teaching another: On the "DO" side this should be illustrating the helpful supportive method and on the "DON'T" side a destructive one. Color if desired. All group members sign. Post finished worksheets on bulletin board titled **Do's and Don'ts of Peer Teaching.** Put posters on top of blackboards or bulletin boards around the room.

STEP 5   Discussion
1.   Each group shares its poster and explains it. What do others especially like about each poster? Why?
2.   Do these remind you of real situations that happen in school? If so, in what ways?
3.   How did your group decide what to have the characters on the poster say? How did you decide on their facial expressions? If there was disagreement, how was that resolved?
4.   In what ways did your group come up with funnier or more interesting ideas than any students would have individually?
5.   What skills did group members pool to come up with good cartoons? (e.g., drawing, printing, sense of humor, use of words)
6.   How can we use these cartoons and comic strips to improve peer teaching in this classroom?

COMPLETION   A student receives credit for this activity if each student in the partnership completes and signs the "Words to the Blurb" worksheet and each student in her larger group contributes to the group poster and indicates this by signing.

Help with Homework

Fifth grade teacher Marny Panuska found that some students in her new class had great difficulty taking responsibility for their homework assignments. Marny used cooperative groups to help deal with the problem. She assigned those students to a group whose members had responsibility for checking each other's assignments before handing in, and who were encouraged to call each other after school if they were ever unsure of what they were to do for homework.

By the fourth week, these students were handing in their assignments on time!

Adventuring in Cooperative Computer Programming

OBJECTIVES

To give students opportunity to learn a new skill and teach it to peers

To give students an opportunity to create a learning material for other students

To teach students to analyze commercially-produced material for its ideas and values and to improve on these in the creation of their own materials

MATERIALS

A commercially-designed computer adventure game connected with your social studies curriculum; computers, blank disks, worksheet "The Values in the Game," page 149

A Board Game Alternative

If you do not have computers in your school, or do not have the help of a skilled programmer, this lesson can be modified to be used with any commercial games. For example, students could first play *Monopoly*, then work out a theme for a board game which focusses on your social studies theme. Then one group could create the board, other groups create each set of cards, another group create the necessary pieces, and another group work on the specifics of the rules. Use the same methods for revisions and trials as in the computer description.

IMPLEMENTATION STEP 1

Choose a computer game with an adventure format which fits in with your social studies curriculum and can be played in small groups. Teach five students to play the game. Then divide remaining students into five groups. Have each student who has been taught the game teach the other members of her group.

STEP 2

As students play the game in small groups, meet with each group to discuss the game. Focus on what they enjoy and do not enjoy about the game and what they are learning from it. Focus on the way they can play the game together.

STEP 3

Have students analyze the game for its values. Distribute worksheet, "The Values in the Game." They complete it together. Go over their responses to the questions, emphasizing the hidden messages we learn about men and women, whites and people of color, violence and nonviolence, and competition and cooperation—through games. Discuss the fact that the class will be creating its own computer game. Go over the "Challenge" at the bottom of the worksheet. Evaluate accordingly the game you create.

STEP 4

Discuss with the whole class a computer game that they could design as a group and which would be connected with your social studies curriculum. As a class, you must create a theme for the game and a basic outline. Then create a list of tasks involved in making the game. These can include: designing each piece of graphics, designing necessary maps, designing the plot line and possible opportunities at each step, programming into the computer situations and possible responses.

STEP 5

Each group picks an element of the game design and works on it cooperatively. Periodically, groups need to show others their progress so that a coordinated effort is made. Have groups look at and critique each other's elements. Groups then go back and revise their pieces.

STEP 6 Put all the pieces together and have each group try out the game and make notes for revisions. When the game is in a format where it can be played by students other than the creators, lend it to another class—same age, younger, or older. Again request critique. When the game is in a finished stage, make copies and have it become a permanent part of the school software library.

DISCUSSION
1. In what way was the commercial computer game you played designed to be played as a small group? Designed to be cooperative? Designed to be competitive? How?
2. How did playing as a small group differ from what it would have been like had you played individually?
3. What behaviors hurt your playing as a group? How? What things did group members do or say that helped you play cooperatively?
4. Compare the experiences between groups. How were they similar? Different?
5. What was it like to be taught how to play the game by another student? What worked well for that? What could be done differently?
6. How did the game you designed differ from the commercial game? How was it similar?
7. In what ways was working as a class easy? In what ways was it hard? What would you do differently next time?
8. What made your small group work well in designing your piece? What could you have done to make it better?
9. How did suggestions from other groups help in your revisions?
10. In what ways does your class game work to help you learn more about what you're studying in social studies? What did you learn while designing the game? What will others learn while playing it?
11. Did your class meet the "Challenge" to promote fair, nonviolent and cooperative values? Was this hard or easy? How?

COMPLETION A student gets credit if: (a) the peer teacher successfully teaches the game to other students in her group, (b) her group completes "The Values in the Game" worksheet, and (c) each group completes its section of the class game, and it works!

The Lessons of Arcade Video Games

What do (the majority of these arcade video) games teach their avid players? First they teach automatic responses . . . The player has no time to think, only to respond. You develop eye-hand reflexes that are amazingly quick. This is useful in warfare, doubtless. So is automatic obedience.

Second they make killing, smashing or winning the goal . . . To win, you must obliterate every enemy or obstacle in sight . . . Third they are mindless. . . .

Games reflect society. If games teach us to shoot on sight, to regard everything that appears as an enemy, to feel without thinking and to indulge hateful feelings, to strive to be ''men,'' they are perpetuating values that exist in society.

Adeline Naiman, ''Video Games, Mindless, Macho, Materialistic''
in *CIBC Bulletin*, vol. 13, nos. 6, 7.

Crossing That Age Line _____

OBJECTIVES
To give students practice working with younger children
To teach students guidelines for effective cross-age cooperative projects

MATERIALS
Worksheet: "Guidelines for Cross-Age Projects," pages 150–151, strips of paper about 36″ long and 8″ high, crayons or markers

**IMPLEMENTATION
STEP 1**
Tell students that one form of cooperation is the sharing of information and skills with younger students. They'll be doing such cross-age projects during the year. Today they'll develop guidelines that will make such cross-age projects effective.

Gather the whole class together. Students think of an older student, sibling, or friend who taught them something. As they recall what the person did that helped or hindered learning, list these "do's and don'ts" on newsprint. The list may look something like that on the "Guidelines for Cross-Age Projects" worksheet.

STEP 2
Tell students they will teach younger students how to make accordian books, books that are cooperatively written.* First they'll make these books themselves.

Accordian books open and close like an accordian. Take a long strip of paper about 36″ long and 8″ high and fold it back and forth six or eight times. Students work in pairs to write and draw a story. One student does the first section, the other the next and so on. Students write a story with a cooperative theme. It's also fun to write in a dialogue format. For example, "The Story of the Goat and the Can" might begin with the can talking to the goat in the first segment. The goat would talk back in the next section and so on, and in some way they would cooperate before the story's end.

When completed, students share books with each other.

DISCUSSION
1. What did you like about working with your partner on the accordian book?
2. What problems did you have? How did you solve them?
3. What problems do you foresee younger children having in making accordian books? How could the problems be solved?

STEP 3
Arrange for students to go to younger classes. In advance, you and the cooperating teachers assign one older student to two younger students.

Distribute the "Guidelines for Cross-Age Projects" worksheet, adding the criteria your class developed in Step 1, or develop a worksheet of your own based on your students' ideas. Encourage students to follow the "do's" and avoid the "don'ts" during the accordian book project. Tell them that when they return, they will evaluate their effectiveness by using the worksheet.

The teacher reads the accordian books to the class. Then, each older student teaches his or her two younger ones how to make accordian books. They provide a cooperative theme, for example, "Doing something together I couldn't do alone." When finished, students organize a reading of accordian books by the teacher to the whole class.

*Idea from Rosemarie Tanner, Columbus School, Poughkeepsie, NY.

Upon return to their class, each student evaluates her cross-age interaction using the worksheet, "Guidelines for Cross-Age Projects." Join together for discussion.

DISCUSSION
1. How did you feel participating in this cross-age project?
2. What things did you do that helped the project go well?
3. What problems did you encounter? How did you solve/try to solve them?
4. Look at your worksheets. Where are your strengths and weaknesses? What weaknesses could you eliminate next time? How?
5. From what you've learned, what advice would you give to another student doing a cross-age project?

COMPLETION
Since this is the first cross-age project, credit is given for handing in a signed worksheet.

GOING FURTHER
On future cross-age projects, students might work in partners. One observes the other working with the younger child and using the guidelines. In some cases, feedback could also be given by the child being taught.

Cross-Grade Learning

Mary Pezzo, science teacher at the Poughkeepsie Middle School, New York, assigns science reports to cooperative groups. When completed, these are posted on the bulletin boards in her science class. Students in one class must read and learn from the reports of the other classes as well as from their own. Some of this material will be included on their quiz. Pezzo also has groups in her classes make cooperative science card games that are used in other classes in the same grade. Such procedures build cooperative learning across tracked classes in her school's science program.

SUBJECT—C
FORMAT—CLASS
PROJECT

Coming to Consensus _____

OBJECTIVES
To teach students the skill of coming to a consensus
To give students an opportunity to make a real life decision as a group by consensus

MATERIALS
Copies of "Consensus Guidelines" worksheet, page 152, chart paper, markers, paper and envelopes, stamps, use of telephone, phone books

IMPLEMENTATION
Explain to students the field trip policy of your school district. This may include a specific number of trips per year, cost of trips, use of transportation, and so forth. Tell them that they, instead of you, will decide on the trip or trips. List district-mandated conditions on chart paper and post in front of the room. Add any nonnegotiable conditions.

Review brainstorming. Then brainstorm on guidelines that should be used for the group to decide on field trips. Be sure to include reasons for field trips, money, distance conditions, and so forth. After class brainstorms, correct any factual errors.

Then, the class brainstorms on possible places for field trips for this year. After you have a reasonably long list, open it up for discussion. Students should give pros and cons of all the ideas. They ask each other questions regarding the suggestions which some know more about than others.

Pass out "Consensus Guidelines" worksheet. Read with the class. Explain any confusing points. Explain that, in this case, there is no reason to reach an immediate decision. Consensus is often a slow process, not good for emergencies, but useful when it is important for everyone to be satisfied.

The class continues discussion on field trip possibilities with the idea of reaching a consensus. At this stage, they should come up with a list of all possibilities which might be realistic—all ideas that some people strongly like and that no one strongly hates. It is appropriate to have between three and seven ideas.

Divide class into as many groups as there are possible trip ideas. Avoid large groups. Have two groups work on one place, if necessary. Each group researches a different possibility. This research can include making phone calls to places, writing letters, getting written materials, inquiring on costs and transportation, figuring out relevance to curriculum, speaking with classes who have been to the places before, and so forth.

After the groups have had enough time to complete their research (probably several weeks later), hold another class discussion. Each group presents its information, not pushing its idea, but providing all the necessary facts. Then open discussion to the whole class on all the possibilities. Review consensus guidelines. Make a chart for each possible place, listing pros and cons of each idea. Work toward a consensus.

DISCUSSION

1. Were you able to reach consensus? What helped or hurt your reaching consensus? In what ways did you like using consensus, rather than a vote, to try to reach this decision? In what ways did you dislike it?
2. In what ways will a field trip be more successful if the decision is reached by consensus? In what ways might it be less successful?
3. What satisfied you about working towards consensus rather than voting? What frustrated you?
4. How attached to (or turned off to) the idea that you researched did you get? Why? How strong were your feelings about that idea compared to your feelings about the other ones?
5. The larger a group, the harder it often is to reach consensus. What small groups are you in at school, or outside school, in which consensus might be used to reach a decision?

Example: Field Trip Guidelines

1. Must be related to something we're studying
2. Can't be more than one hour away
3. Can't cost more than $2 each for admission and transportation
4. Can't have furry animals since Tony and Belle are allergic

---

SUBJECT—P.E.
FORMAT—PEER
TEACHING, CROSS-
AGE PROJECT

A Fair Game

OBJECTIVES

To give students the opportunity of creating athletic games in which everyone has a fair chance

To give students experience playing cooperative games

To provide opportunities for students to share athletic skills and/or experience

MATERIALS

Athletic equipment, depending on the games chosen

IMPLEMENTATION

Explain to students that while most sports and games are competitive, there are many ways to make them more fair and more cooperative—and just as much fun!

The first two versions below create conditions for appropriate competition—that is conditions that give everyone a fair chance of winning. The third version is of a totally cooperative game.

A: REVISING THE RULES

When people have unequal skills or experience in a sport or game, the negative results of competition are exacerbated. Changing rules or equalizing skills creates a more fair game.

Have students choose an athletic game that can be played in your gym or school yard. Have students rank themselves from one to ten on their perception of their ability level in that sport or game. Encourage honesty.

Divide students into heterogeneous groups of four or five with mixed ability levels. Each group works together in suggesting handicaps or changed rules so everybody has an equal chance of succeeding. For example, in basketball the players with the most developed skills might be allowed to use only one hand and would have to run backwards. Players with moderately developed skills might not be allowed to talk or yell to other teammates. Encourage students to create a game that would be fun and fair. All group members participate in a trial run of the game and revise it accordingly.

Groups then join together as a class and share their plans. Discuss the strengths and weaknesses of various versions and allow groups to make minor changes. Go outside, or use the gym, to teach the games to others. After play, join together for discussion. Also have students write down their group's revised rules, all sign, and hand in.

DISCUSSION

1. How did the people with fewer skills in this sport feel playing the new games? Why do you think you felt the way you did?
2. How did people with more developed skills feel? Why did you feel this way?
3. What do highly-skilled people gain in a game where all have an equal chance?
4. Which game variations were more fun? Which most fair? Which both?
5. When is it particularly important to you to win and when is it important to you to know that others are having fun? How does this affect your feelings during a game?

COMPLETION

A student receives credit if she and her group have cooperatively revised a sport or game, taught it to others, and recorded the rules on a sheet signed by all.

The Winning Player

We must come up with a new definition of a "winning player"—a definition which every coach must strive to instill in each player. In *What Do You Say After You Say Hello?*, Dr. Eric Berne writes that a winner is defined as a "person who fulfills his or her contract with the world and oneself. That is, he sets out to do something, says that he is committed to doing it, and in the long run does it." In applying this to sports it suggests that each time a player sets to play she should determine what she wishes to get out of the participation. The goal is what's important.

B: SHARING SKILLS

Another way to make games—or life situations—more fair is for those with well-developed skills to teach them to others. In this case, students with many skills increase their ability to be effective teachers and those with fewer skills become better in the sport.

Divide students into heterogeneous groups of about five each. Have students pick a sport, design a drill, practice activity, or simple game in which more experienced students teach other students a key skill of that sport. Remind students to use what they've learned about peer teaching in designing and teaching the activity.

Arrange for students to go to the gym or playground. First, experienced students within the small groups teach the others, using the activity. Next, each group teaches the other groups.

DISCUSSION

1. How effective were the activities you made up in the teaching of skills? How effective would they be over time?
2. Which activities were more effective than others? Why?
3. What were some things the "teacher(s)" did that helped you learn the skills? What kind of things did they do that hindered your learning?
4. As teachers, what did you learn about teaching? What will you do differently next time?
5. What did skilled persons gain from teaching others?
6. What are other skills or information that we can share with others in our lives in order to give more people an equal chance?

C: COOPERATIVE GAMES

Tell students that you will teach them a few cooperative games that they in turn can teach to others.

In the box below are several examples exerpted from *The Cooperative Sports and Games Book,* by Terry Orlick. Copyright © 1978 by Terry Orlick. Reprinted by permission of Pantheon Books, a Division of Random House, Inc. The idea of two or more individuals or groups working together toward mutually beneficial ends is central to cooperative games theory.

Cooperative Games

Bump and Scoot

Materials: beach ball and volleyball net

Begin with two teams of about 6–8 students on each side of the net. When a player hits the ball over the net, he scoots under the net to the other side. The collective goal of the game is for teams to completely change sides with as few drops of the ball as possible.

This is a particularly good game for classes where boys tend to monopolize play. In Bump and Scoot, if you start with boys on one side and girls on the other (although not a good practice in general), boys must pass to girls in order to succeed at the game.

Bump and Team Scoot

Materials: beach ball and volleyball net

This variation of Bump and Scoot provides more action and enables more students to play. Form four teams of about 6 students. Teams A and B start on one side of the net and C and D on the other. Each team names itself. When a player on one team hits the ball over the net, she yells her team's name and the whole team scoots to the other side of the net. The collective goal is to score as many points as possible before the ball hits the ground.

Try another version where only those who have touched or assisted to set the ball up scoot under the net. This encourages even more cooperation.

Collective Score Blanketball

Materials: beach ball, two blankets—one for each team

Divide students into two teams and position on each side of the net. All team members hold onto a blanket. A point is scored each time the ball is tossed over the net from one blanket and caught successfully by the other team in its blanket. The common objective is to score as many points in succession as possible.

DISCUSSION   Be sure to encourage equal discussion from those who usually do well in sports and those who don't.

1. How did you like these cooperative games? What did you like about them? What didn't you like about them?
2. What were some feelings you had while playing? How are these feelings different from those you experience when you play more competitively?
3. What is the difference, if any, in your feelings about cooperative and competitive games—if you're a skilled player or a less skilled player?
4. Is it important to you to have fun and to include everyone? Why? In what ways is winning important to you? Why?
5. How do you think our society would be different if people grew up playing more cooperative sports?

Arrange to have students teach these cooperative games to younger students. Review with students what they learned about cross-age projects (see pages 120–121) and remind them to use what they learned.

GOING FURTHER   Ask students to teach their new games to their brothers, sisters, and neighborhood friends. Have them teach other skills they have. Have students report the results.

Parent Barter: Cooperation with Parents

At our school we send parents a form at the beginning of the year asking if they would like to help in our classroom or school during the year. Our suggestions for areas where we can use help include: office work, driving, chaperoning on subway trips, cooking, supervision at play time, writing, teaching a lesson about one's heritage, maintenance, cleaning, and so forth. The list affirms many kinds of skills. We also try to balance times when the help can be used so that parents with jobs during the school day still have an opportunity to contribute if they want to. On parent workdays, we get high school students to provide child care for young children.

Ellen

COMPETITION AND COOPERATION WORKSHEET

Part A: Jigsaw Stories

Story A—The Field Trip

Ms. Lum's class is going on a field trip to Seneca Falls, New York. The first women's rights convention was held there in 1848. The class will see historic sites and do a great deal of walking around the town.

Ms. Lum asks everyone to choose a partner to be her "buddy" for the field trip. Buddies will stay together for the whole day.

Susan plans to ask her best friend, Latisha, to be her buddy. Before she can do this, Hector turns to her and asks if she'll be his buddy. Hector is not very popular at school. He has a limp and has to wear a brace.

Susan thinks to herself: If I have to be Hector's partner, I'll be slowed down all day. We won't be able to keep up with everyone else or do all the walking everyone else does. I want to see everything.

Susan tells Hector she won't be his buddy. She walks over toward Latisha, leaving Hector standing there alone.

Part A: Jigsaw Stories—continued

Story B—The Art Contest

For the past few years Humiston School has held an art contest. Students draw posters to illustrate one of the school holidays. The first place winner gets a prize and has her picture in the newspaper. This year the art work will illustrate Martin Luther King Day—January 15.

Aaron is excited about the contest. Last year he came in second and this year he thinks he can win. He has read a book about Martin Luther King and already has an idea for the poster.

Ms. Hernandez, the school principal, calls Aaron into her office. "Aaron, since you're such a good artist I want you to help me make a decision. What would you think if we don't have a contest this year? Instead, each class could work together to draw a mural about Martin Luther King. Each class would put their mural in a different building in town—for example, in the bank or library. Everyone would sign the mural and **everyone** would get praise for their work."

Aaron thought to himself. If we don't have a contest how can I win? How can everyone see what a good artist I am? I won't even get my name in the paper!

"Ms. Hernandez, I like the idea of a contest better. Then everyone will work harder at their art work and we'll get better drawings. **Please** have the contest!"

COMPETITION AND COOPERATION WORKSHEET

Part B: Questions

Directions: One student reads the first question. He gets the opinion of every group member. Group members then decide on an answer. The reader writes the answer or answers on the worksheet. Pass the worksheet to the student on the right. Repeat the process. Check the spelling and grammar of the person before you. If you find an error, ask him to change it. Check over the whole worksheet for content, grammar, and punctuation before handing it in. Sign your name to show agreement.

Story A—The Field Trip

Self

1. How did Susan gain by what she did?

2. What price did she pay? What did she lose out on?

Others

3. How did Susan help others?

4. How did she hurt others?

Alternatives

5. What could Susan have done that would have been cooperative?

6. How would this benefit her?

7. How would it benefit others?

8. How would it hurt her?

signatures _____

_____

_____

_____

_____

COMPETITION AND COOPERATION WORKSHEET

Part B: Questions—continued

Directions: One student reads the first question. She gets the opinion of every group member. Group members then decide on an answer. The reader writes the answer or answers on the worksheet. Pass the worksheet to the student on the right. Repeat the process. Check the spelling and grammar of the person before you. If you find an error, ask her to change it. Check over the whole worksheet for content, grammar, and punctuation before handing it in. Sign your name to show agreement.

Story B—The Art Contest

Self

1. How did Aaron gain by what he did?

2. What price did he pay? What did he lose out on?

Others

3. How did Aaron help others?

4. How did he hurt others?

Alternatives

5. What could Aaron have done that would have been cooperative?

6. How would it benefit him?

7. How would it benefit others?

8. How would it hurt him?

signatures _____

_____

_____

_____

_____

From Me to We Situations

Situation 1

A is one of the best basketball players in your class. It is near the end of the game and the score is tied. Time out is called. **B** is a good player but hasn't played much. She's sitting on the bench. **B** asks **A** if she can take **A**'s place.

Situation 2

A has been working to get a social studies assignment done. **A** just finished and can go work on a computer game that he really likes. **A** notices **B** is having trouble with his social studies assignment.

Situation 3

Your class is going on a field trip to the zoo. The teacher asked everyone to bring in a dollar to help pay for the bus and for refreshments. **A** has already decided what treats she wants to buy at the zoo. On the day of the trip her teacher says that several children haven't been able to bring in a dollar. She suggests everyone pool their money so the children with none can have refreshment money. She asks all of you to talk that idea over with your neighbor for a couple of minutes. Then the class will decide. **A**'s neighbor, **B,** is one person who couldn't afford to bring in $1.

Observing Me-First and We-First Behaviors and Words

Me-first behaviors and words	**We-first behaviors and words**
Situation 1	
Situation 2	
Situation 3	

Something we learned about me-first behavior and words is

_____

Something we learned about we-first behavior and words is

_____

Signed _____

_____

_____

ROLES TO MAKE OR BREAK A GROUP WORKSHEET

Observer

Role	Classmate in Role	Description
Idea-Giver		
Peacekeeper		
Encourager		
Clarifier		
Distractor		
Silent One		
Teaser		
Dominator		

ROLES TC MAKE OR BREAK A GROUP WORKSHEET

Participant

————— ————————————————————————————————

When I played the ——————————— role, I said or did ———————————
——

————— ————

I felt ——————————————————————————————— about

myself and ——————————— about other group members.

****

When I played the ——————————— role, I said or did ———————————
——

I felt ——————————————————————————————— about

myself and ——————————————— about other group members.

****

When I played the ——————————— role, I said or did ———————————
——

I felt ——————————————————————————————— about

myself and ——————————— about other group members.

****

When I played the ——————————— role, I said or did ———————————
——

I felt ——————————————————————————————— about

myself and ——————————— about other group members.

****

Usually in a group I play the ——————————— role. I feel ———————————
——————————————————— about that. Another role I would like to play

is ——————— because ———————————
——————————————— . A role I don't want to play is ———————————

because ———————————
——
——

UNITED WE STAND: DIVIDED WE FALL WORKSHEET
Spotting Inequality (Part One)

1. **Prejudice:** An unfavorable opinion about a person or group of people formed without knowledge.

   For example:

   > Marie says, "Jews are stingy."
   >
   > Marie has never met a Jew. She is prejudiced against Jewish people.

   An example of prejudice we have observed is:

2. **Stereotype:** A general viewpoint about a group of people based on a misinterpretation of fact or limited understanding of the facts.

   For example:

   > Stereotype: Disabled people are helpless.
   >
   > Fact: Many disabled people are able to do a variety of things for themselves. Many live independent lives.

   An example of a stereotype we have observed is:

3. **Isms**

   _____ People are seen and treated differently because of (1) _____ .

   A, B, C, (2) _____ is/are viewed as better or more important than others

   D, E, F, and people in that group have more power in society. In our society those

   or G people are (3) _____ . Values and practices of institutions (schools, families, churches, media, etc.) support these inequalities.

Key Words (Fill in according to "ism" being discussed.)

A: **Racism** (1) skin color; (2) one race; (3) whites.

B: **Sexism** (1) being male or female; (2) one gender; (3) males.

C: **Classism** (1) their socioeconomic background; (2) people from certain classes; (3) upper and upper-middle class.

D: **Ageism** (1) age; (2) certain ages; (3) adults (not elderly).

E: **Anti-Semitism** (1) religion; (2) one religion; (3) Christian.

F: **Ableism** (1) physical ability; (2) certain abilities; (3) disabled people.

G: **Heterosexism** (1) sexual orientation; (2) one sexual orientation; (3) heterosexuals.

Spotting Inequality (Part Two)

Match the correct "ism" with the examples below:

• Jonah examines his school calendar. Only one of the holidays honors minority people or minority culture. Jonah concludes that his school system enforces _____ .

• Pauline did a survey of the books in her school library and fewer than 1 percent of the main characters were people with physical handicaps. The publishing industry reinforces _____ .

• Louise is interested in computers and wants to take a special course after school. Her parents won't allow it because they feel girls don't need to know about computers. Louise's family encourages _____ .

• Bette did a social studies report on the city budget. She learned that the city council cut out money for the minibus and cut back money for mass transit. Bette knows most older people depend on the bus system to travel. Bette's city council enforces _____ .

• Ralph learned that the club his uncle belongs to does not allow Jews to be members. The club enforces _____ .

• Hector did a study of TV shows and finds that 90 percent of people shown are middle or upper class. When low income or poor people are portrayed, many are shown as lazy or troublemakers. Hector concludes the television industry promotes _____ .

• Josh's mother is a lesbian and lives with another woman. Josh is doing a project on families and can find only one book in both the school library and public library that positively describes homosexual families. The publishing industry reinforces _____ .

An example of an "ism" we have observed is:

signatures _____

_____

_____

_____

The Playing Field Conflict

Students at the Benjamin Banneker Middle School have a special opportunity. A vacant field near the school will be given to the city. The City Athletic Board asked all interested groups to put in a request for the field. The Board will decide which group will use the field.

Some students at Benjamin Banneker belong to the Youth Soccer Program. Other boys play baseball with teams on the Community Center League. The girls just formed a new Girls' Sports Club and have started to play field hockey. Everybody wants to get the new field for their group.

Sarah is a captain of one of the teams in the Youth Soccer Program. She asked her sixteen-year-old brother, Paul, about an idea. "What if all the middle-school sports groups could get together to make a request for the field together! Then we'd be sure to get it."

"Oh, don't do that," said Paul. "You wouldn't want to share the field with those dudes who play on the Community Center League, some of them are black and Puerto Rican. Watch, they won't do their share of keeping up the grounds."

John, a member of the Jets, plays for the Community Center League. He was trying to figure out the best way to get the field. He asked for ideas from his neighbor, Roland, a high school football player.

Roland warned, "Whatever you do, don't join forces with the Girls' Sports Club. Would you want to use the same field as a bunch of girls who think they can play sports?! You guys would look like sissies."

Liana, an organizer of the Girls' Sports Club, tried to convince all the middle-school students to work together with the Club to put in a bid together. "We'd have such a good chance to get the field because we'd represent so many students if we work together," Liana argued.

Sarah thought about the words of her brother. She said, "We're going at it alone. We'll get the field on our own. It's too complicated to work together."

John remembered what Roland said. John replied, "We don't need any help to get the field, especially from girls!"

The next week the City Athletic Board met. Students from four different groups made requests for the field.

    Youth Soccer Program—45 students—represented by Sarah.

    Community Center League—70 students—represented by John.

The Playing Field Conflict—continued

Girls' Sports Club—50 students—represented by Liana.

High School Athletic Association—100 students—represented by Roland and Paul.

The City Athletic Board studied the requests. Then the chairperson spoke. "All of your groups have fine requests. We have decided to assign the field to the High School Athletic Association. They represent more of the young people and will use the field for several different sports. Thank you all for your effort."

Roland looked at Paul. They smiled at each other.

Sarah, John and Liana left the room mad at each other. Each promised themselves that their team would get the field next year.

John was heard muttering, "Those girls, always spoiling things for us."

Sarah told her friend, "Those Community Center kids always want everything we have. It makes me so mad."

Roland and Paul went out to celebrate.

The Playing Field Conflict—continued

Work together as a group to answer these questions. Turn in one worksheet and story from your group.

1. At the end of the story, the middle-school students went away mad at each other.
   a. Given what the middle-school students know and feel, why is it understandable that they are mad?

   b. As the reader of the story you have more information than they did. Who would you be mad at? Why?

2. How did Roland and Paul use cooperation between themselves, along with competition with others, to hurt other groups? How did they use stereotyping and the "isms" to do that?

   signed _____

   _____

   _____

3. Work together as a group, and on a separate piece of paper write an alternative ending to this story. Use cooperation in a helpful way to benefit ALL those involved. Write an ending that overcomes stereotyping and "isms" rather than one that uses those to benefit some people and hurt others. Include dialogue among characters, and be creative. Indicate at the bottom of the story one important idea each person gave that helped make the story a good one.

UNITED WE STAND: DIVIDED WE FALL WORKSHEET

Group Process Observer Checklist

Make a check each time a person shows one of these behaviors.

Students' names

Positive Behaviors					
1. Gives ideas					
2. Asks others for their ideas					
3. Gives praise to others					
4. Shares					
Not Helpful Behaviors					
1. Interrupts					
2. Puts someone down					
3. Disrupts the task					
4. Bosses					

Process Observer's Signature _____

Score as Much as Possible*

Directions

In ten rounds, you and your partner will choose either an X or a Y. The points scored in each round are dependent on the pattern of choice made by everyone in the group. Scoring will be as follows:

4Xs	Lose 1 point each
3 Xs 1 Y	Win 1 point each Lose 3 points
2Xs 2Ys	Win 2 points each Lose 2 points each
1X 3Ys	Win 3 points Lose 1 point each
4Ys	Win 1 point each

Strategy: You can confer with your partner once each round and make a joint decision. Before rounds 5, 8, and 10 you can confer with other members of the group.

Score Sheet

Round	Time	Confer With	Choice	Points Won	Points Lost	
1	1 min.	Partner				
2	30 sec.	Partner				
3	30 sec.	Partner				
4	30 sec.	Partner				
5	2 min. 30 sec.	Group Partner				Bonus Round Double Score
6	30 sec.	Partner				
7	30 sec.	Partner				
8	3 min. 30 sec.	Group Partner				Bonus Round Triple Score
9	30 sec.	Partner				
10	3 min. 30 sec.	Group Partner				Bonus Round Multiply Score by 5
						Total

*From *Teaching Human Beings* by Jeffrey Schrank. Copyright © 1972 by Jeffrey Schrank. Reprinted by permission of Beacon Press.

The Solar Design Project

Vanessa: Hi Mom. You're late getting home from work.

Ms. Jackson: Yes, I missed my bus and had to wait twenty minutes for the next one. I'm tired!

Vanessa: Cheer up, Mom. I have the supper all ready. It's spaghetti.

Ms. Jackson: Terrific! That makes me feel better already. How was school?

Vanessa: So, so. There were two good things. One was that our sixth grade had a play in assembly about Sojourner Truth, who was an abolitionist and women's rights activist. The second thing was that Mr. Smaldone told me I had improved a whole lot on the saxaphone.

Ms. Jackson: Congratulations! I can't wait to hear you in the spring concert.

Vanessa: Two lousy things happened. First, I lost one of my gloves . . . but I'll look for it again tomorrow. The other thing was that we had a project in science and all the boys are making fun of the girls. I was so mad.

Ms. Jackson: Oh dear! Tell me more about that.

Vanessa: We've been studying solar energy in science. Ms. Ryan gave us a project to work on in groups. We have to design and build a model of a solar-heated building. She said the best models would be displayed in the local library. I was so excited because it could be a neat project. Ms. Ryan told us to divide into groups of four. All the boys picked to be with boys and the girls with girls.

Ms. Jackson: Why did it work out that way?

Vanessa: The boys said they wouldn't work with girls because girls were spastic model builders. Then, when we started planning our buildings, the group of boys next to us kept saying things like, "Girls are lousy carpenters." "Girls are all thumbs." "Boys are better model builders than girls." "Our model will be the best and will be displayed and yours won't."

Ms. Jackson: How did you feel about all that?

Vanessa: I felt hurt. I was mad too. I wanted to say something back, but I didn't have much practice with carpentry and I wondered if our model would turn out right anyway. Then the boys said, "You girls have an equal chance to build the best model. If you don't, it will prove that boys are better carpenters than girls." I wondered if they were right.

The Solar Design Project—continued

Ms. Jackson: Did Ms. Ryan see what was going on?

Vanessa: Not at first, but then she heard it and interrupted the class. She asked the boys if they really thought that, because they were boys, they were better carpenters than girls. They all said yes.

Ms. Jackson: Then what?

Vanessa: Then she asked the boys what practice they had in carpentry. They said things like, "I helped my father fix the front steps." "I got a carpentry set for my birthday and built a doghouse." "I work with my older brother in the shop." "My uncle's a carpenter and he took me to work with him." Most of the boys said things like this.

Ms. Jackson: What about the girls?

Vanessa: Only two girls in the whole class had an example like that. Most of us had never been given practice with carpentry.

Ms. Jackson: Then what?

Vanessa: Ms. Ryan reminded us that we had been learning about competitive individualism. She said this sounded like a good example. She asked us to think about why.

The Solar Design Project—continued

Work together with your partner. Write down ways the solar building project became an example of competitive individualism.

1.

2.

How could this situation be changed, to show an alternative to competitive individualism?

Signatures _____

_____

WORK THROUGH THAT CONFLICT WORKSHEET

Guidelines for Mediators

Introduction

Tell the two persons that you will not decide who is right or wrong. You will help them find a solution they both can live with. Tell the persons that in order to find a solution each will need to make some changes.

Step 1—Ask each person in conflict:
Describe the conflict from your point of view.

Mediator check: Did the persons describe the situation now and not examples from the past? If no, ask them to focus on the present.

Step 2

How does the conflict make you feel?

Mediator check: Did the persons use feeling words? If no, ask them to use feeling words.

Step 3

What would be a good outcome to this conflict, from your point of view?

Mediator check: Did the persons agree on a good outcome? If not, help them find one outcome they could live with.

Step 4

What changes are you willing to make in order to bring about the outcome that's best for both?

Mediator check

a. Has each person agreed to a change? If not, help them do that.

b. Have they thought of all possible alternatives? If not, suggest others.

WORK THROUGH THAT CONFLICT WORKSHEET

Contract

Person 1: _____

I agree that I will:

1.

2.

3.

Person 2: _____

I agree that I will:

1.

2.

3.

Mediator: _____

In order to help _____ and _____ keep their agreement I will:

1.

2.

signed _____

_____

_____

IT DEPENDS ON HOW YOU LOOK AT THINGS WORKSHEET

"It's All Her Fault"
"No, It's All His Fault"

Wendy's view

He's always making fun of my work. Whenever we do a project together, he always writes or draws on my paper and tries to change my work. I don't see why he always thinks his stuff is better; I have good ideas too. It's no wonder I hit him; he doesn't understand anything else.

Sidney's view

She never listens when I try to tell her something about work we're doing together. I think she has lots of good ideas; it's just that sometimes she makes a mistake or doesn't draw something perfectly. I'm just trying to help so the work we do together can come out good. I think it's stupid, unfair and mean that she hit me when I was just trying to get our projects to be right.

Solution Possibilities

Words to the Blurb

ADVENTURING IN COOPERATIVE COMPUTER PROGRAMMING
WORKSHEET

The Values in the Game

1. **Sexism**

    a. Number of male characters, number of female characters, number of androgynous characters and their roles _____

    b. Is the main character male or female or androgynous? _____

2. **Racism**

    Does the game portray different racial groups, e.g., Native Americans? Does it do so in stereotypical ways? _____

3. **Violence**

    Is violence used in the game? In what ways? Does violence help you "win"? _____
    _____

4. **Competition/Cooperation**

    In order to succeed in the game, in what ways do you compete with other characters? In what ways do you cooperate?

    _____
    _____
    _____

    _____

The **challenge** to your group is to create a game that is:

a. **Not sexist**

Shows females and males equally

b. **Not racist**

Has no racial group stereotyped

c. **Nonviolent**

People win through creativity, intelligence or skill—not violence!

d. **Cooperative**

Characters succeed in the game by working together, rather than against each other.

Guidelines for Cross-Age Projects

Do's		Don'ts	

Do's

1. Be friendly. Learn the younger student's name and ask her questions about herself.   —

   "Hi, I'm Tony. What's your name? What kinds of things do you like to do?"

2. Tell him about yourself.   —

   "You're probably wondering about me. I'm in 6th grade and am on the gymnastics team."

3. Talk to her using words she can understand. Check with her to see if the words are too hard, and be careful not to patronize her by defining easy words.   —

   "Today we're going to work on a maze. Do you know what a maze is? Have you ever done one before?"

4. Give clear directions. Ask him to repeat back to you what the task is so you know he understands.   —

   "Now, before we start, can you tell me what we're going to do?"

Don'ts

1. Make fun of him because of his age.   —

   "How big are you anyway, pee wee, 30 pounds?"

2. Criticize her for not knowing something or doing something right.   —

   "You mean you don't know how to do multiplication?"

3. Talk to your classmates about her in front of her.   —

   "Hey Bob, this kid is really something—look at the funny way she writes."

4. Do things for her.   —

   "Josh, give me that paper (grabbing it). Hold it like this."

Guidelines for Cross-Age Projects—continued

5. Go at her pace, taking one step at a time.   ___

   "Now that you've finished that, let's go on to the next step."

6. Give praise.   ___

   "Terrific, you draw such colorful pictures."

7. At the end tell him what you liked about working with him.   ___

   "Gene, I like working with you because you have very creative ideas."

8.

9.

5. Be impatient.   ___

   "Hurry up Penny, you should have finished that page long ago."

6.

7.

8.

9.

Signature _____

Consensus Guidelines

Consensus is a way of working together as a group to reach a decision with which everyone is comfortable. It is informal discussion involving talking things through, understanding what other people are saying and feeling, and trying to work out decisions which are acceptable to everyone. Everyone must be part of the decision and satisfied with it. When a decision is reached, the group shapes it and puts it into words which everyone understands.

Here are some helpful attitudes in consensus:

Unity—trying to come up with things the whole group can accept.

Cooperation—understanding that the needs, feelings, and ideas of everyone are important.

Openness—checking our own beliefs and changing them if new ideas make us feel differently.

Diversity—bringing out disagreements and seeing value and truth in what everyone says.

Creativity—coming up with new ideas.

Patience—working until we find something acceptable to everyone.

Respect—recognizing that everyone has rights, whether they agree with us or not.

5 PULLING TOGETHER IN FAMILIES, COMMUNITIES, AND WORKPLACES

In Chapters 3 and 4, students have focussed on the competitive aspects and co-operative potential of their own behavior and of their relationships with their peers in school. Now they are ready to explore their local surroundings.

Section A, "Does Competition Pay?" is comprised of lessons that enable students to compare the positive and negative effects of competition in families, workplaces, and communities. Ways in which those same settings can be the foci of collaboration are set forth in lessons in Section B, "Cooperative Alternatives All Around Us."

Competitive ways of relating and competitive patterns in institutions can hurt people. Even so, because competition is ingrained in our society, it is far from easy to direct energy toward cooperation. Section C, "Getting from Here to There," offers some of the many ways this can happen. For example, students examine such efforts as developing nonviolent conflict-resolution strategies in the family and reversing competition among workers through union activity. Finally, through the lessons in Section D, students themselves develop cooperative projects that will benefit their families, communities, and workplaces.

New cooperative learning formats are included in this chapter too. Learning center, cooperative board game, cooperative card game and research project formats provide additional ways for students to learn through a cooperative goal structure.

A. DOES COMPETITION PAY?

SUBJECT—SS
FORMAT—JIGSAW

All in the Family

OBJECTIVE | To have students examine the ways competition can hurt families

MATERIALS | Worksheets—I—"Competition Can Hurt Families—Jigsaw Sections," and II—"Competition Can Hurt Families," pages 185–187

IMPLEMENTATION STEP 1 | Divide students into heterogeneous groups of three and give each student one of the three jigsaw sections from worksheet I—"Competition Can Hurt Families." Section A is the simplest to understand and C the most difficult. Distribute accordingly.

Students read the material to themselves. Each then teaches the other two group members one way competition can hurt families. Then, as a group, they discuss an example **they** have observed in which competition hurts families. Students fill out that section of worksheet II.

STEP 2 Put slips of paper into a hat. Include an equal number of the three topics—"brothers and sisters fighting," "competition between families," and "sexism sparks competition." Have each group draw a slip.

Each group plans a two-minute skit demonstrating how that kind of competition can hurt families. They also plan a one-minute skit that shows a cooperative alternative to the same situation. Move around to help as needed. Once groups have planned and practiced the skits, each group that is willing presents the first part of its skit. The class identifies what kind of competition it shows. Then the group presents the cooperative alternative.

DISCUSSION
TASK
1. How hard or easy was it to think of ways you've seen competition hurt families? Why?
2. What are examples of positive, or appropriate, competition in families?
3. What can we do to reduce hurtful competition in families?

PROCESS
1. What helped your group work together on your skit?
2. What hindered cooperation?
3. What would you do differently next time?

COMPLETION For an individual to receive credit for this activity the group must:
1. turn in a worksheet that each member has discussed, written one part of, and agreed with as evidenced by signatures
2. develop a skit that involves each person in their group.

SUBJECT—A, SS

One, Two, Seven, Nine: Get It Off the Assembly Line

OBJECTIVES To provide students an experience of a competitively structured work situation
To enable students to examine the consequences of competitively structured work
To enable students to participate in a cooperatively structured work situation

MATERIALS Materials to make bookmarks, such as oaktag, markers

IMPLEMENTATION This activity is a simulation that enables students to experience a competitive, routine work situation. It is purposely not cooperative. Tell students they will do a simulation of a workplace.

PART 1 Divide students into groups of five. Arrange each group, except for one, with desks side to side and facing in the same direction. Students in each team number off from one to five.

Tell students that the school board has honored them by asking them to make bookmarks that the board can sell for a dollar apiece at their meeting. The profit will pay for a special dinner for board members and community leaders. Explain that they want as many bookmarks as possible so they can make a lot of money. Explain, therefore, that each person on a team will make one part of the bookmark. Make a bookmark pattern with five parts and draw it on the board. Number each section. The bookmark starts with the first student in the line and each succeeding person adds her part.

Tell students that the board will pay each of them $.25 for a half hour's work. The team that makes the most bookmarks will be rewarded with special stickers for each team member. The person who is the best worker, as judged by the teacher, will get two special gifts. (Decide yourself what these gifts will be.)

Explain that the one group *not* set up in a line will observe. Tell students that if you see a slow worker you will ask that person to sit in the corner and replace him with one of these students who is standing by. The dismissed student will not get a quarter. Ask students not to complain since the job is so important. If anyone complains about the job or talks to their neighbor, he will be dismissed to the corner. Further, remind students that the quality of the work must be excellent. Distribute materials.

During the simulation, you play the role of boss. Be firm. Don't allow students to get out of their seats. As students work, admonish them to work hard. Urge them to hurry. Dismiss several students who are "slow workers," who are talking or who are complaining. You can do this fairly or arbitrarily. Dim lights to make it difficult to see. Keep students working for about thirty minutes, or until you judge they have experienced enough for a fruitful discussion. Distribute stickers and gifts.

DISCUSSION

1. First, ask everyone to write a brief description of how they felt during the activity. How did you feel as you were working? What made you feel that way? (Be sure to get all feelings out, since this activity can generate feelings of stress, anger, incompetence and so forth.)
2. Workers who were dismissed, how did you feel? Are there any feelings or experiences you have in common?
3. Those of you who got a special sticker or a gift, how did you feel? Other workers, how do you feel about that?
4. How did you feel about people on your team? Other teams?
5. What are your opinions and feelings about the bookmarks? Are you proud of them? Why or why not?
6. How do you feel about the money you received?
7. The profit from the sale of the bookmarks will go to the school board for a dinner. What are your opinions and feelings about the use of that money?

Remind students that since this was a simulation, you were taking on the role of boss. The way you acted was not **you.** Explain that you designed the activity so they could feel what many work situations are like.

8. In the way the work situation was structured, what stimulated competition?
9. In the way the work situation was designed, what brought out negative feelings about others? about yourself? about the product itself?
10. Explain to students that the way this work was structured is similar to the way much work is structured in our society. Ask them for examples. Discuss with them the points in the next box.
11. What would be an alternative to the work situation you have just experienced?

Competitively Structured Work

- Work is structured so that there are limited rewards—in our society, money, power, and status—and people must compete with each other for these rewards. These rewards are distributed unequally.

- To "get ahead," workers must prove that they're better than someone else.

- Workers are accountable to a boss who has the power to make decisions about the work situation, including hiring and firing and working conditions.

- People who do the work make a small amount compared to those who manage or own the business or institution where people work.

- In the competition-for-rewards, making money or keeping power can be more important to owners and managers than people's needs, feelings, or working conditions.

While not all work situations in our society fit this description, many do, because the economic system itself is so structured.

PART 2   Now provide students an opportunity to experience an alternative work structure—a cooperative one.

Returning to their original groups of five, they put their desks in a circle. They are to work cooperatively—either to create a bookmark they all like or to produce any product they want. They can make one large item together, or make a small group product and plan more of the same, or each make his own. They will sell their products at the PTA meeting and then decide what to do with the money. For example, they could divide the money equally among themselves. Or, the class as a whole could spend it on something for the class or for a trip. Remind them that the more effectively they work together, the greater chance of making creative, marketable items. Also remind them to be conscious of the feelings and needs of others.

DISCUSSION   1. How did you feel while you were working? What made you feel that way?
2. How did you feel about the people in your group? In other groups?
3. How did you feel about your products? Are you proud of them? Why or why not?
4. How do you feel about the plan for money?
5. How did you feel about working on this item, compared to the last one?
6. How did the structuring of the work stimulate cooperation?
7. How did the structure help bring out feelings about others? What were they? About yourself? What were they? About the product itself? What were they?
8. Explain to students that some workplaces are structured cooperatively, and that they will learn more about these. Ask them for examples. Discuss with them the points in the box below.

Cooperatively Structured Work

- Work is structured in such a way that rewards are shared.

- People work together and support each other. All are rewarded for a successful product.

- Workers make decisions about their work and working conditions.

- Profits are shared among the workers.

- The feelings and needs of the workers are very important.

SUBJECT—M, SS
FORMAT—BOARD
GAME

Community Challenge Game _____

OBJECTIVES

To have students consider the effects of living in a community in which families, neighborhoods, and institutions are based on competition

To have students consider the effects of living in a community in which families, neighborhoods, and institutions are based on cooperation

To compare feelings and experiences of families living in both types of community situations

MATERIALS

For each student: Family-Needs Checklist, page 190; pencil; blank paper titled "Income"

For each group playing the game: Directions, page 188 or page 189; Community Challenge Cards—cut up and color coded (one color for the cooperative version of the game and one for the competitive one), pages 191–204; dice; game board

To make a game board, take a board from an old game and cover it with plain paper. You or the students should then draw a game path with about forty-five spaces. Label one-third of them "Family and Neighborhood," one-third "Workplace," and one-third "Public Institutions" (example below). Around the game path, add drawings or pictures of communities, families, and workplaces. If the students play as individuals, make one game for every five students. If they play as partners, make one game for every eight students (leave out one family). Have the students help make the game boards, cut up cards, and so forth.

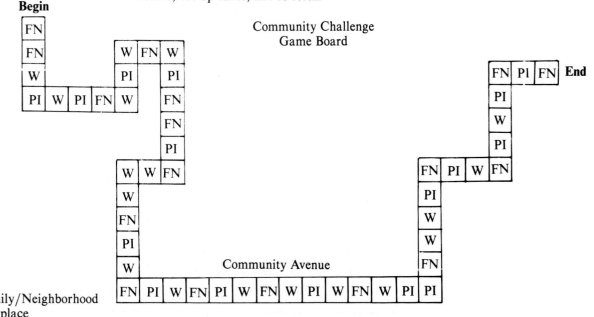

Community Challenge
Game Board

FN—Family/Neighborhood
W—Workplace
PI—Public Institutions

IMPLEMENTATION

Tell students they will be examining the effects on families of living in a community that is based on competition as compared to living in a community that is based on cooperation. To do that, they will play two versions of a board game, the Community Challenge Game. Tell them they will discuss each version after playing it and then compare the two versions at the end.

Divide students into groups of five. Give each a game board and cards for the competitive version and a set of directions. Students read the directions. Answer questions. They begin. As students play, move around the room providing help as needed.

DISCUSSION QUESTIONS COMPETITIVE VERSION

1. How do members of each family feel now that the game is over? What makes you feel that way?
2. Who were the winners in each group? What helped you to win?
3. Who were the losers? What caused you to lose?
4. In what ways were families and neighborhoods competitive? How did that help or hurt different families?
5. In what ways were institutions, businesses, and schools competitive? How did that help or hurt different families?
6. In what ways would you like to change this game? Why?

On a subsequent day, distribute directions, questions, and cards for the cooperative version of the Community Challenge Game. Again, move around the room to help as needed.

DISCUSSION QUESTIONS COOPERATIVE VERSION

1. How do members of each family feel now that the game is over? What makes you feel that way?
2. Did the group reach its goal? What helped or hindered that from happening?
3. In what ways were families and neighborhoods cooperative? How did that help or hurt different families?
4. In what ways were institutions, businesses, or schools cooperative? How did that help or hurt different families?
5. How would you compare your feelings about yourselves as families in the cooperative version compared to the competitive one?
6. In what ways was the competitive version of the game like real life?
7. In what ways was the cooperative version of the game like real life?
8. How can we make some aspects of the second game happen in our communities?

CONCLUSION

Students return to groups. Each student responds to the following "I Learned Statements" in writing:
Something I learned about how competition in communities affects people is. . . .
Something I learned about how cooperation in communities affects people is. . . .
Students proofread each other's papers for grammar and spelling. They make sure others' ideas are clear. Sign and hand in.

COMPLETION

A student receives credit for this activity if his group completes the Community Challenge Game (credit is given whether they win or lose!) and completes and submits five "I Learned Statements," one from each group member.

A Cooperative Community—Unrealistic?

The community represented in the cooperative version of this game may seem unrealistic to many students. In that case, it is important to explain that the individual examples of cooperation in the communities described in the game do exist in reality, although most may not exist in their community and rarely do we find a single community with all these examples of cooperation. It is important for students to have an alternative version of what **can** be, because only then do they truly know their options and only then can they decide what kinds of communities they want to help create.

Check Out Those Books _____

OBJECTIVES
To learn to read more analytically, looking for overt and covert examples of cooperation and competition in different settings
To practice compiling analyses from different sources
To communicate information and to interpret information in a way which is useful to others

MATERIALS
"Book Analysis" worksheets (average 6 per student or pair), page 205, poster board, markers, books

IMPLEMENTATION
Divide students into heterogeneous groups of six. Within these groups, students can work individually on the first part of this lesson or they can work in partnerships with a strong reader working with a poorer one.

Explain to students that they will be analyzing their reading books, or books written for younger students, for examples of cooperation and competition. They can choose books from the school or public library, or work with ones you provide (see Bibliography for ideas). This lesson is appropriate for contract grading (see the Resources section of this book). If you choose contract grading, each student contracts for a grade before beginning the project. After reading each story students work individually to complete the worksheet, "Book Analysis." If working in pairs, they take turns reading the story aloud to each other, with the stronger reader helping the weaker one. Then they work together on the worksheet.

After all the members of a group have completed their worksheets, the group works cooperatively to complete a project which will communicate this information to others. An example of this is a handout for the library which gives a short summary of each book and a rating for cooperation and competition. Another possibility is a chart of all the books which summarizes the information on the worksheets. Another project would be the making of posters about the books which are most cooperative, stressing the ways those books work.

DISCUSSION
1. What kinds of cooperation were most common in these books? Least common?
2. What kinds of competition were most common? Least common?
3. Was cooperation most common within families, with friends? In a community? Between communities? In school or workplaces? Why is this so?
4. In which places was competition most common? Why?
5. How integral to the story was the competition or cooperation?
6. If you were to rewrite this story to make it more cooperative, what else would have to change? Explain why.

COMPLETION
A student gets credit for this project if each student in her group completes the number of worksheets agreed upon and if her group completes a group project with contributions from all members' worksheets.

B. COOPERATIVE ALTERNATIVES ALL AROUND US

Ingrid and Jeffery's Cooperative Households

OBJECTIVES To learn about the experience of a young person who lived in a cooperative household
To think about the benefits and the prices of living in individual families and the benefits and problems of living cooperatively

MATERIALS Worksheets—"An Interview with Ingrid" (one per student), "An Interview with Jeffery" (one per student), "Thinking about Households" (one per partnership), pages 206–209

IMPLEMENTATION Tell students there are people and families who apply the idea of cooperation to their living arrangements. They form cooperative households.

Often several families and individuals rent or buy a large house together. People have their own bedrooms, but they share kitchen and living areas. In this way, everyone can have both privacy and company.

Tell students they will learn more about cooperative households by reading two interviews: one with Ingrid Lakey, a twelve-year-old girl who lived in a cooperative household in Philadelphia, Pennsylvania, and one with Jeffery Pardo, fifteen, from Cambridge, Massachusetts.

Divide students into partners. Distribute interview worksheets.

One student takes the role of Ingrid and the other is the interviewer. They read the interview aloud. Then they switch roles and do the same for Jeffery. Distribute "Thinking about Households" worksheet. Students respond to questions. When partners are finished, come together for discussion.

DISCUSSION
1. What are some benefits of living in an individual household? Some costs?
2. What are some advantages of living in a cooperative household? Some costs?
3. Some families live in cooperative households for many years and then choose to move. What might be some reasons they would make that decision?
4. A cooperative household could work out perfectly for some family members and not be working well for others. What might be some reasons for that?
5. What family problems might a cooperative household help to solve? What problems might a cooperative household have?
6. Do any of you live in extended families where other relatives are in the household? What are benefits and costs to this?
7. Do you think you might want to live in a cooperative household someday? Why or why not?
8. What do you think are some characteristics of people who do particularly well in cooperative households? What might be some characteristics of people who do particularly well in individual households?

COMPLETION A student gets credit for this lesson if she and her partner each contribute to answering the questions on the "Thinking about Households" worksheet and hand in a signed copy with clear, thoughtful answers.

FOLLOW-UP Invite people who live cooperatively in your community to talk to your class. Help students prepare thoughtful questions in advance.

New Ways to Work _____

OBJECTIVE To examine a way of organizing work that is cooperative and meets the needs of workers regardless of sex and class background

MATERIALS One copy of "A Women's Factory" worksheet* for each student, one copy of "A Women's Factory: Questions" worksheet for each group, pages 210–212

IMPLEMENTATION Tell students they will be learning about an example of a cooperatively-structured workplace in Georgia.

Tell students that McCaysville Industries is a "workers' self-managed" factory. Explain that in both the United States and in other countries, there are factories run by the workers themselves. Workers make decisions about their workplace and share the profits from their work. Production is often greater than in traditionally-structured factories and workers are usually more satisfied with their work.

Divide students into groups of four, with some good readers in each group. Go over difficult vocabulary words as a class before groups begin. Each student takes roles for an interview, with one person the interviewer and the other three the workers. They will read the dialogue aloud to their small group.

After they finish reading the interview, they work together as a group to fill out the questions on the worksheet, making sure each person has written an answer to one part of the worksheet. They hand that in. Join together as a class for discussion.

DISCUSSION
1. First discuss responses to worksheet questions. Then discuss the following questions:
2. How does the way the work is organized at McCaysville Industries avoid the sexism that is found in some jobs?
3. How does the way McCaysville Industries is organized deal with the unhealthy competition that is found in some jobs?
4. How does the way McCaysville Industries is organized avoid the class discrimination of some jobs?

COMPLETION In order for a student to get credit for this lesson, her group must hand in "A Women's Factory" worksheet, with one section completed by each group member and signed by all group members. Each person's signature means she agrees with the content of the answers and that spelling and grammar are correct.

FOLLOW-UP If possible, order the film "When Women Get to Hurting," a thirty-minute documentary about McCaysville Industries. Students can then see the women whose roles they played and can also see McCaysville Industries in action.

An article on McCaysville Industries can be found in "Women Taking Charge: New Ways to Economic Power," by Sharon Grant, *et. al.*

---

*"A Women's Factory" Worksheet was written by the authors. The material is taken from "McCaysville Industries: A Women's Factory," by Cynthia Burton and Sharon Grant in *Women Taking Charge: New Ways to Economic Power.*

Freedom Farm Cooperative _____

OBJECTIVE To provide students an example of a cooperative model of community organization and responsibility

MATERIALS Worksheets—(mount on cards) "Freedom Farm Cooperative—Jigsaw Sections,"* "Question Cards," pages 213–215

IMPLEMENTATION Divide students into groups of four. Tell them they will learn an alternative form of a working community. If this lesson is overly simplistic for your class, transform it into a cross-age project. Tell students that after they complete it, they will be sharing it with students in a lower grade.

Distribute jigsaw sections of the "Freedom Farm Cooperative" worksheet. Students read their sections silently. When all are finished, they report their information to others in the group, reading sequentially from A to D.

Then students choose a question card with a different letter from their jigsaw section. (Mark the letter on the back of the card.) Each answers his question in writing without conferring with others. Then they exchange papers with one other person in the group. They check each other's work for content, grammar, punctuation, and spelling. A student may add to or revise an answer if convinced to do so. No one may change another student's paper. Together students then answer the group question. All papers are clipped together, without individual names, and handed in. The group's papers are evaluated for correct content and for spelling and mechanics.

DISCUSSION
1. The Freedom Farm Cooperative is an example of a community of people working cooperatively for what they need. They share the work with everyone. Imagine your neighborhood, community, town, or city organized so everyone worked for what was needed, with income and resources shared by all. How would it be different from the way it is now? How do you feel about that?
2. What examples are there of people cooperating with each other in our community today? How could cooperative work be expanded?
3. In our community today, what examples are there of people sharing with each other and making things needed by all? How could this be expanded?

COMPLETION A student gets credit for this activity if his group hands in a set of papers, each written by a different group member, answering the questions on The Freedom Farm Cooperative. The group's papers are evaluated for correct content, spelling, and mechanics.

*Adapted from *Fannie Lou Hamer* by June Jordan (New York: Thomas Crowell, 1972).

Community Child Care _____

OBJECTIVES

To give students an example of community cooperation in the providing of services needed by that community

To encourage students to think about the cooperation implicit in child care

To train students to turn to local community people for information, particularly community members who are not often in that role

To provide students the opportunity of working together to create a cooperative game

MATERIALS

Six sheets of large poster board, 200 or so file cards for game cards, spinners, dice, markers, crayons, rulers, "My Contributions to the Game" worksheet (one for each student), page 216

IMPLEMENTATION STEP 1

Explain that students are going to be creating games on the theme of how day-care centers involve the cooperation of many community members. Games must give correct information on day care and stimulate players to think about the cooperation that is a natural part of day-care centers.

Ask which children were in day care before they started school. Ask them to describe their centers—structure, buildings, teachers, programs. Record the information the children have from their own experiences.

Now discuss people from community day-care centers and the skills each needs. You and your students will modify this list:

- director—certification, training and/or experience in early childhood education, skills in relating to young children, staff, and parents
- child care workers
- custodian, repair person—understanding of equipment to be found in day-care centers, simple carpentry, cleaning skills
- health care person—skills, probably certification in advanced first aid and/or nursing
- parents—willingness, as volunteers, to work with individuals or small groups on special projects, to help on field trips, and to share special skills or information from their own backgrounds
- community resource people—willingness of skilled people (in music, art, dramatics, cooperative games, and so forth) to lead special events and projects at the center
- fundraisers: willingness of people to help raise money for the center by organizing concerts, book sales, and so forth
- optional: food personnel—understanding of nutrition, finances, cooking ability
    van driver (if transportation is offered)—driver's license, good driving skill while driving children

Talk about how this wide array of community people must work together for a community-based day-care center to function well.

STEP 2

Explain that the games to be created should be cooperative games where the whole group either wins or loses. They should be games that children will want to play. They must also give accurate and thought-provoking information which emphasizes the community cooperation necessary for a day-care center to run well.

Brainstorm with the class on what makes a board game or card game satisfying. Then have students analyze their list for ways in which they could create cooperative games which meet these needs. For example, if suspense (not knowing who will win) is important, can they come up with ways to make a cooperative game suspenseful by trying to beat the clock or beat another power that is controlled by dice or cards? Copy lists in a way that they will be available as guidelines to groups once they start working.

STEP 3 As a class, brainstorm on resources for more-detailed information about day-care centers. Examples: parents who work in day care, day-care staff from centers children previously attended, or staff from centers their siblings currently attend. Make a list.

STEP 4 Divide children into heterogeneous groups of four. Each group begins planning a game which would teach other students about the community cooperation necessary for day care. Each group needs to plan both strategy ideas and content for their game. As groups begin planning, they list questions they have and information they need. Groups then divide the task so some students contact the people resources listed in "Step 3" above, while others work on game boards, game cards, or gather information from books or magazines.

STEP 5 a. After each group has a preliminary game plan they try it out and make adjustments.
b. Groups exchange games, still in preliminary form, and try out games for other groups. They give feedback to designing groups.
c. As a class, discuss all the games. Are some groups having trouble developing cooperative strategies? Other class members can give ideas. Do some groups need more information that other groups may have? Each group shares problems and requests help.

STEP 6 a. Each group makes one good-quality copy of its game and the directions.
b. Share with other classes. Make available in school library. Lend copies to the day-care centers where staff or parents served as resources.

DISCUSSION
1. In what ways are day-care centers examples of community cooperation?
2. Why can't a day-care center be a one-person operation?
3. How do day-care centers affirm a variety of skills, training and backgrounds?
4. What did you learn about day-care? What insights did you have about their cooperative nature?
5. Contrast the information of students who had been in day care themselves with those who had not. How much cooperation did you notice when you were in a day-care center?
6. How did day-care teachers and parents feel about being resources for information? Had they had that opportunity before? Why or why not?
7. How did students who had been in day-care feel about being resources? Had they had that opportunity before?
8. How did your group decide on what information to include in your game? Why was what you chose important? Interesting? Thought-provoking?
9. What is it like to devise cooperative game strategy? What is hard about that? Easy? How does it compare to the more common competitive game strategy?
10. How did it help to have a whole group work on the game instead of doing it alone? Would there have been any advantage to doing it alone? Explain.

COMPLETION A student receives credit for this activity if each member of her group hands in a signed worksheet "My Contributions to the Game" and her group completes a cooperative game about community child care.

Facts About Day Care

- In March, 1986, 62.8% of all women with children under eighteen years old worked outside the home. The highest increase in the rate of labor force participation was in women with children under three years old.

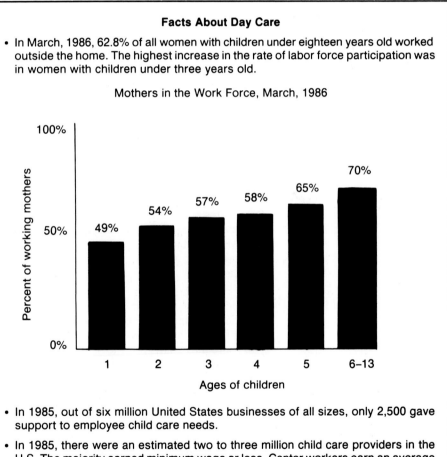

Mothers in the Work Force, March, 1986

- In 1985, out of six million United States businesses of all sizes, only 2,500 gave support to employee child care needs.

- In 1985, there were an estimated two to three million child care providers in the U.S. The majority earned minimum wage or less. Center workers earn an average of $9200 per year, with the middle 50 percent of workers making between $6800 and $12,500. Family day-care workers averaged about $1.00 per child. The National Day-Care Home Study (1981) estimated that 87 percent of family day-care workers earn less than minimum wage. In 1985, 97 percent of all child care providers were women.

National Commission on Working Women,
2000 P St. N.W., Suite 508, Washington, DC 20036.
Copyright 1986.

C. GETTING FROM HERE TO THERE

SUBJECT—M, LA, A
FORMAT—LEARNING
CENTER

We Have to Do It Differently _____

OBJECTIVES

To encourage students to look at a wide variety of family problems in an open-ended way, looking for many creative cooperative alternatives

To have students understand that some of their family problems are common to other families and see possible cooperative ways of handling those

To have students understand problems which don't or couldn't happen in their families, develop empathy for members of those families, and find cooperative ways of working with them

To reinforce the concept that a group of people can often generate more solutions to problems than any single individual can generate

MATERIALS

All stations need enough paper and writing implements for all the children in a group. In addition each station needs the following (pages 217–223):

Station I: Sign should read **PROBLEM CARDS.** Worksheet—"Problem Cards" (cut up). Make one copy of each card, covering with clear contact paper or laminating. Make one copy of the directions.

Station II: Sign saying **JOURNALS.** Worksheet—"Journal Entries" (cut up). One copy of each journal entry covered with clear contact paper or laminated. One copy of the directions.

Station III: Sign saying **DEAR ABBY.** Enough copies of "Dear Abby Sample" letter for each group member. One copy of the directions.

Station IV: Sign saying **SKITS WITH I MESSAGES.** Worksheet—"Skits with I Messages" (cut up). Make three copies of each scenario and one copy of the directions.

Station V: Sign saying **FAMILY REMINDER POSTERS.** One copy of the directions. Poster board, markers, ruler, scrap paper.

Station VI: Sign should read **FAMILY MATH PROBLEMS.** Worksheet—"Family Math Problems" (cut up). Copy each problem on a task card, cover with clear contact paper or laminate. Make one copy of the directions and one copy of the answer card.

IMPLEMENTATION

Divide students into six groups. Each group will have a turn at each of the six learning stations. Assign the order. Explain to students that all stations have to do with problems that families have. Some might relate only to certain types of families and some might be more universal. At some stations they will be looking at violent and/or competitive ways families deal with these problems. In all cases they will be looking for nonviolent cooperative ways to handle them.

In one station students practice "I-Messages." Teach them about these now. Tell students that an I-message is a way to share with another person how a behavior of theirs makes you feel. It is a way that helps people resolve problems cooperatively. It must follow the following format.

When you _____
                    (behavior)

I feel _____
                    (feeling)

Because _____
                    (consequence)

For example: When you take my pencil and don't return it
I feel angry
Because I don't know where to find it and can't do my homework as I planned.

An "I-message" doesn't blame another person or tell her what to do. It tells that person how their behavior makes you feel.

Have students give a few examples and try one themselves to make sure they have the right idea. Leave the "I-message" format on a chart in the room so students can refer to it during the lesson and use for interpersonal communication during the rest of the school year.

Have each group begin at its first station. Directions should be posted at each center.

After all students have completed all learning centers, gather as a whole class. Share samples of work. Put some on bulletin boards. Use the discussion questions.

DISCUSSION   1. How do you feel about the cooperative solutions to family problems that different groups suggested? Do you think they would be effective? Why or why not?
2. How hard, or easy, was it to come up with cooperative solutions to family problems? Why was that so?
3. Why do different families have different ways of dealing with family problems?
4. Why is it hard for many families to try new ways? How can that be made easier?
5. What strategies can you try with your family?
6. What would be good ways to suggest those alternatives or begin using them?

Have students develop additional problems themselves. Integrate them into the centers as well.

COMPLETION   A student gets credit for this lesson if each member in her group hands in
Station I: A written response to the Problem Card, proofread and signed by writer and partner.
Station II: A series of journal entries, proofread and signed by writer and partner.
Station III: A letter to, or response from, Abby, proofread and signed by writer and partner.
Station IV: "I learned" statements (from the group).
Station V: One or more "family reminder posters" (group or individual) with her signature.
Station VI: Responses to family math cards (from partners) and either member can explain how they got the answer.

HENRY.. THIS IS NOT THE PATH TO PEACE!

Bread and Roses

OBJECTIVES

Students will learn about one form of social cooperation—a strike
Students will examine an example of a strike—the Great Strike in Lawrence, Massachusetts, in 1912

MATERIALS

Make titles for centers. Cut and mount materials from worksheets as needed.
Worksheets for each learning center: A: "Letters from Angelina," B: "Bread and Roses," C: "The Prices of Profit," D: "The News Tonight," and E: "Solidarity Forever," pages 224–231
A cassette tape recorder. Tapes (D) and materials to make posters (B). A record player and record of labor songs including "Solidarity Forever" (E) (Many albums of labor songs include "Solidarity Forever." Check your nearest record library.)

IMPLEMENTATION

Set up your room in learning centers with appropriate materials at each center. Have groups of four students cooperatively complete tasks at each center. It is advisable for them to start with task A—"Letters from Angelina." Have background material available for further reading.

Background for Students

Among the materials available we recommend:

Reading
Lawrence 1912: The Bread and Roses Strike, William Cohn.
Bread and Roses: The Struggle of American Labor 1865–1915, Milton Meltzer.

Slide Show
"Bread and Roses: The Lawrence Strike of 1912."

Before beginning, tell students that they will work cooperatively on tasks at various learning centers. Explain that all the tasks are about a very important strike in American history—The "Great Strike" in Lawrence, Massachusetts in 1912. (1) Ask students if they know what a strike is. (2) Explain that a strike is an example of co-operation among many people. Solicit current examples. Ask if anyone has seen a strike, felt the effect of a strike, or know someone who has been on strike. Tell them that, after completing the different tasks, they will make a display or bulletin board about the Lawrence Strike and will use the products and work they complete at the centers.

Have students work on center projects over a period of several days. Give assistance as needed.

When students have completed the centers, help them organize a display or bulletin board. Post a sampling of: Angelina's letters and answers to questions, math problems and answers, and picket signs. Play the tape of the radio show. Choose only some items to display, but make sure every student's work is included in some form.

DISCUSSION Come together for discussion of the whole activity.

1. What is the most important thing that you've learned in working on the tasks about the "Great Strike"?
2. In what ways was cooperation important to the Lawrence Strike?
3. How did workers overcome barriers to cooperation?
4. What examples of strikes today can you think of? What are people striking for in these cases? How are they organizing? Bring in relevant clippings to discuss.
5. Why is management not giving in to strikers' demands, in the case of the current strike? How is it organizing itself?
6. Why, when people join together, do they have a better chance of improving their lives than they would on their own?
7. How can others support people who are on strike?

COMPLETION A student receives credit for this lesson when her group has completed the number of tasks assigned, with evidence of all group members' participation. This would include: (1) "Letters from Angelina" worksheet with written work and signatures of all group members, and (2) one or more of the following: a slogan and picket sign with signatures of each group member, correct answers to "Prices of Profit" math problems, a tape recording from "The News Tonight," and an original verse to "Solidarity Forever" said, or sung, in unison by the group.

If you wish to evaluate content-learning or grade this lesson, contract-grading formats are appropriate. In this case, all students would not necessarily complete all activities. (See the Resources section of this book.)

A General Strike

A very powerful mass cooperative effort is a general strike in which **all** workers in a locale protest a situation by striking together. In this way a whole city, state or nation can be immobilized.

In February, 1919, workers shut down the city of Seattle for five days. Workers called a general strike in support of shipyard workers who were striking for better wages. In order not to penalize citizens, the strike committee made several exceptions to the general strike. For example, firefighters stayed on the job. Drugstores were closed except for prescription counters. Laundry workers only cleaned hospital laundry.

A labor-war veterans guard was formed to preserve law and order without the use of force. They carried no weapons, using persuasion instead.

The general strike was totally nonviolent. It was ended after five days because of the threat of bloodshed when the national guard was called in.

For more information on strikes in American history,
see Jeremy Brecher, *Strike* (Boston: South End Press, 1977).

Ties to Your Curriculum

This lesson can easily be integrated into the standard U.S. History curriculum when studying the Industrial Revolution.

Food Co-ops: The Choice Is Up to You ___

OBJECTIVES
To give students information on three different methods of organizing food co-ops
To have students compare different organizations and see advantages and disadvantages of each as they would apply to different situations and groups of people
To encourage students to look at their own group and that of their families and analyze what methods would work for them

MATERIALS
Food Co-op Information Sheets—"Mariposa Co-op," "North Country Co-op," and "West Bank Co-op Grocery" (information from "Dandelion," Movement for a New Society); worksheet, "Co-op Comparison Chart" (see Step 1, Implementation for numbers & distribution), worksheet, "A Food Co-op for Our Class" (one per group), pages 232–236

IMPLEMENTATION STEP 1
Divide students into four groups. Give one group "Mariposa Co-op" information sheet, another group "North Country Co-op" information sheet, the third group "West Bank Co-op Grocery," and the fourth group the entire set of information sheets. The first three groups are each to prepare a scenario which shows the history of the co-op and how it functions in the community. Particular stress should be given to the type of people the co-op serves and the organization of the co-op in terms of management and rights of workers and members. The fourth group completes the "Co-op Comparison Sheet" and prepares a panel which presents this information in a factual format.

STEP 2
Gather the class together. The first three groups each present their scenarios, then the fourth group presents its panel.

STEP 3
Discussion Questions A
1. What have you learned about co-ops that you didn't know before?
2. Why are there different ways to organize co-ops? What factors are crucial to insure that the structure is effective in the situation?
3. Why do co-ops have different policies about what they carry? Do you think that is good or bad? Explain why.
4. What are the advantages of hiring members as staff? The disadvantages?
5. What are the advantages of hiring staff with different cultural, social and economic backgrounds? The disadvantages?
6. What appealed to you about each of the different co-ops? Why? What did you not like about each? Why?
7. Describe a composite of the co-ops that would seem to you especially effective.

STEP 4
The class brainstorms on the class's characteristics and the type of food co-op which would work for class members and their families. Post a large list where students can readily see it.

STEP 5 Divide students into heterogeneous groups of four students per group. Each group takes the brainstorm list and creates a description of the organization and policies of a food co-op which would work for the class and its families. Each group fills in "A Food Co-op for Our Class" worksheet. Groups then gather together to present and compare their descriptions. Then go on to Discussion Questions B.

Discussion Questions B
1. What factors about your class and families were important to you in designing a co-op?
2. What factors were not so important? Why?
3. Which of the three co-ops is your vision most similar to? Why?
4. What would be the best benefits of a co-op to your class community? Why?
5. What would be the biggest problems? Why?
6. Why would some families choose to shop at the co-op and some at supermarkets?

COMPLETION To get credit each student in her group must participate in her group's scenario or panel, and sign as a participant in her group's description of the class's food co-op.

D. STUDENTS MAKING A DIFFERENCE

Whose Job Is It Today? _____

OBJECTIVES To practice taking a representative family problem and trying a cooperative solution
To show that there is often no "right" answer to a problem and that testing various options cooperatively will often yield the "best" solution for a particular group
To enable students to use other students' experiences to help them

MATERIALS Cardboard, poster board, markers, brass fasteners, rulers, pencils, small bags, worksheet "Here's How It's Working" for each student, page 237

IMPLEMENTATION
1. Discuss with students the issues which develop around family chores. Encourage discussion about who does which chores in different families and how people feel about it. Discuss what works and what doesn't work. Discuss why people feel angry and exploited. Then students brainstorm a list of possible cooperative ways to divide chores fairly. Here are five possibilities (your students might think of others):
   a. Job wheel
   b. Job Spinner
   c. Job in a bag
   d. Week by week chart
   e. Permanent job chart (see samples below)

2. Divide students into design groups. Each group picks, or is assigned, one of the methods. Make sure each group has a different method. Each student makes a sample relevant to her household jobs.

3. Students go home and discuss with families—are they willing to try out this method for a week? They explain that they will have choices of other methods later. (If a family is not willing to try a chart, pair that student with a student whose family will try a chart. Maintain the pairing for the remainder of the lesson.)

These examples are all for the O'Connell-Gillespie Family. This household consists of:

Kathleen O'Connell
Kathleen's son, Ryan, age 10
Kathleen's friend, Maria Gillespie
Maria's mother, Lucia
Maria's daughter, Karen, age 12
Maria's son, Joe, age 8

Job Chart by Weeks

Job	10/7–10/13	10/14–10/20	10/21–10/27	10/28–11/3
Dust	Kathleen	Joe	Karen	Lucia
Cook Dinner	Ryan	Kathleen	Joe	Karen
Do Dishes	Maria	Ryan	Kathleen	Joe
Clean Bathroom	Lucia	Maria	Ryan	Kathleen
Vacuum	Karen	Lucia	Maria	Ryan
Free	Joe	Karen	Lucia	Maria

Job Wheel

Turn one space clockwise each day.

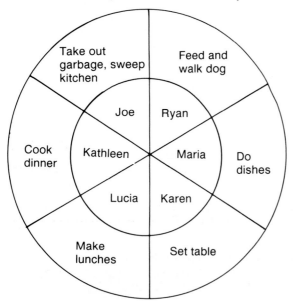

Job Spinner

Each day it gets spun and wherever it lands shows the jobs for the day.
Same wheel as Job Wheel. Spin inner circle.

Permanent Job Chart

Job	Person
Dust	Joe
Vacuum	Lucia
Dishes	Maria
Cook Dinner	Ryan
Bathroom	Kathleen
Clean Kitchen	Karen

Job in a Bag

Job cards in the bag, each household member closes eyes and picks out a job.

bathroom
dust
cook
sweep
dog
vacuum

4. Divide students into new groups such that each group now has students trying different methods. These groups should meet every few days. Students should discuss with each other how their particular method/s are working. They should try modifications suggested by other students. They fill in worksheets, "Here's How It's Working."

5. Students return to their original design groups to implement the suggestions from the trial experiences and the worksheets. Students report revisions to the class, noting reasons for the revisions.

6. Each student (either alone or with her family) makes a decision about which method her family would like to continue trying. To use with her family, each student makes a final, visually-appealing, job wheel, spinner, bag or chart using art materials. Students whose families aren't participating can make a hypothetical model to be posted on a bulletin board.

DISCUSSION
1. How hard (or easy) was it to explore with your family the issue of cooperative division of household chores? Why do you think that was so?
2. What did you learn by completing and sharing the "Here's How It's Working" worksheet?
3. What are some of the benefits to different family members of the cooperative job-sharing method you tried? What are some of the problems? What is the effect on your family as a whole?

COMPLETION
A student receives credit for this activity if each member of her mixed-method group completes the "Here's How It's Working" worksheet (if family is participating) and if each member of her design group completes a visually-appealing cooperative job-sharing chart, bag, wheel, or spinner.

SUBJECT—M, SS,
LA, A
FORMAT—CLASS
PROJECT

A Cooperative Enterprise

OBJECTIVES
To have students set up a school-based cooperative enterprise
To provide a product or service that will help others or be enjoyed by them
To use math in a practical way with relevant life applications

MATERIALS
Materials for the project the students select—this will vary.

IMPLEMENTATION
Review with students the difference between work that is structured competitively and that which is structured cooperatively—see "Competition and Cooperation" (page 88). It is recommended that this review be completed first. Tell students they will have a chance to set up an enterprise that is structured cooperatively.

Brainstorm with the class regarding all the possible things they could make or provide and then sell. The criteria for the items must be that they help others and/or are good for people.

Idea Starters—Cooperative Enterprises

1. Long term, challenging

Pizza—Class buys or makes pizza to sell at lunch each week. Negotiate with cafeteria staff to avoid any potential conflict.

Community Guide—Students create a booklet about the community, giving times and prices for skating rinks, bowling alleys, and so forth. Include phone numbers of all the movie theaters, hours for storytelling at the public library, and so forth.

Newspaper—Students write, print, and develop an ongoing newspaper with news about students and events in your school—as well as other news. Sell to students and community members.

Birthday Parties—Students form a collective to organize birthday parties for preschool and primary school children. They learn how to play and teach party games, make favors, and bake birthday cakes.

Plants from Seeds—Students grow plants from seeds and sell them to other students, parents, teachers, and community members throughout the year.

2. Short term, cooperative

Food—Students make and sell special food items. Make sure they're **healthy** foods that are good for people!

Jobs—Students list jobs each person is willing to do, with the cost, for example: Sue, rake leaves at $.75 a bag; Jose, wash windows at $.50 a window. Sell the job cards to students, parents, or other people in the community.

Clothes—No need to buy new clothes from the store!—create a clothes exchange. Bring in clothes you or your siblings have outgrown. Sell them to other students at inexpensive prices.

Postcards—Students do black line-drawings the size of regular postcards. Four fit on standard page. Make copies and cut.

Calendars—Some students draw pictures for each month, others make the grids. Have copies made and bound.

Cookbooks—Gather ethnic or other special recipes from each student's family. Make cookbook and sell to parents and other community members.

Decide on a cooperative class enterprise from the list of suggested projects. As a class, discuss the decisions that would need to be made to organize the enterprise. Discuss them together or break up into work groups for discussion. Students research the cost for each project, the amount of work, and the amount of money that can be earned. This provides the students with good practice in using fairly complex math in ways which are useful (and helps answer the question of why we have to do word problems). Students return with ideas and information for the class decision. For example, if the class decided to turn their room into a restaurant for noon hours the last Thursday and Friday of the month, decisions might be:

1. What jobs are needed for the enterprise to operate?
2. a. What shall we serve on the menu?
   b. How much should we charge?
3. a. Who shall we invite to the restaurant?
   b. How shall we contact them?
4. What will be done with the profits?
5. How much will it cost us to buy the supplies? Subtract that from the amount we will charge to see how much profit we can make.

Next, students make a management plan—who will do what, when. Students assign different group tasks. For example, in the restaurant idea, there may be shoppers, cooks, public relations people, decorators, servers, and entertainers. Remind students that jobs could rotate the next month. After planning, groups come together to coordinate aspects of the workers' self-managed restaurant. Remind them that a student will receive credit for the project only if all other students have completed their assigned tasks.

Discuss in advance ongoing use of the profits. Remind students that, in a cooperative enterprise, profits are shared equally among workers and/or are put back into the enterprise. For example, in the workers' self-managed restaurant, students might decide to use the profits to buy ingredients for next month's restaurant, to invite ten senior citizens who need and would appreciate a free lunch, and to provide free lunches to the class members themselves.

DISCUSSION

After the first experience with the enterprise, take an extended time for discussion.
1. So far, what are the most successful things about our cooperative enterprise?
2. What are our problems? How can they be solved?
3. Did all the different groups responsible for the enterprise do their parts? Why is this important?
4. What makes our enterprise cooperative as compared to competitive?
5. Compare this project to "Work Design," a competitive experience. What are the differences?
6. How do other people feel about our enterprise? How does it serve them or bring them happiness?
7. The profits from our enterprise are put back into the enterprise and also shared among the workers. To what extent do you believe this is fair? Unfair? Why?
8. What would be the advantages or disadvantages of having more cooperative enterprises in our society? Who would gain? Who would lose?

COMPLETION

Assess accountability periodically, especially for a long-term project.

A student receives credit for the cooperative enterprise if all students have completed their assigned tasks satisfactorily.

**Business Simulations in American Schools . . .
Are They Realistic?**

Many classroom business simulations used in American schools today are based on myths about American business.

For example an article in "Learning Magazine" describes Florence Bailey's third and fourth grade class. She wanted her students to learn about economics so she decided to set them up in the cookie business. Students baked and sold cookies. All students talked together to make decisions about the business. At the end of the year the profit was divided equally and each student earned $20.

In reality most Americans don't have the capital to open a business for themselves. In most American businesses the owners are not also the managers and workers. Workers seldom make binding decisions about how the business will be run. Most importantly, workers very seldom get to share all the profits; rather, they go to owners and stockholders.

Actually, Ms. Bailey's class ran a workers' self-managed business, but it was not described as such. Workers' self-management is seldom even discussed as an economic alternative.

Through such simulations students learn an unrealistic and idealized view of American business. What else do they learn? The article ends with Arthur's feelings—"I love money."

Nancy Tieken-Weber,
"The Cookie Concession: Economics for Fun and Profit,"
Learning Magazine (October 1981).

SUBJECT—M
FORMAT—
COOPERATIVE GAME,
CROSS-AGE

Earning Power

OBJECTIVES

To have students practice basic math skills using problems involving cooperation
To enable students to work together to make and play a cooperative math board game
To provide students an opportunity to teach others a cooperative game about work

MATERIALS

A recycled board game or a large piece of poster board and markers to make a board game
Worksheets—Directions, Question and Luck Cards (cut up), pages 238–243

IMPLEMENTATION

This project is applicable to the whole class or to a small group. If you have the whole class work on it, divide students into groups of four to five and have enough materials for each group to make a game board.

If you have students for whom some of the problems would be too hard, make a color coded game. Choose the appropriate cards to cover the range in your classroom and color code those in several categories according to your students.

After students are divided into heterogeneous groups, tell each student which color or colors he should move on. Thus, you can have heterogeneous groups of students doing math at their own levels, working toward a common goal.

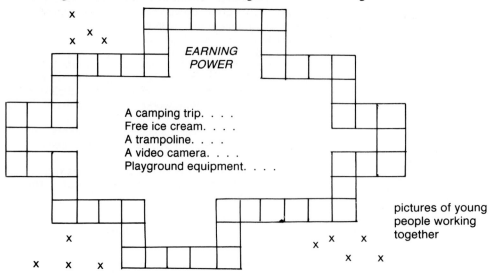

EARNING POWER

A camping trip. . . .
Free ice cream. . . .
A trampoline. . . .
A video camera. . . .
Playground equipment. . . .

pictures of young people working together

PART 1
MAKING THE GAME

Tell students they will help make a cooperative math game, play it, and then teach it to others. Have students:

1. Make a path on the game board with squares the size of the problems on the worksheet cards. Leave twenty-six spaces for the question problems and additional spaces for cards students make up. Leave about six spaces marked "Luck." Explain that the problems they make up must be examples of people cooperating to earn money. Students look over problems, color code them, and paste them on spaces on the game board. Then they develop problems of their own. They check to make sure the problems reflect cooperation. Paste on other spaces. Check difficulty and color code.

2. Intersperse word problems with luck squares.

3. Write the following on a large space in the middle of the game board.

   > A camping trip for your class—$110
   > Free ice cream at lunch for the whole school each Friday for the year—$135
   > A trampoline for the school—$175
   > A video camera and tapes for your class to make movies—$230
   > Playground equipment designed for kids with disabilities—$265

   Add other choices or alternatives if you like. Remind students these are fictitious goals, used for the game only.

4. To fill in free areas of the game board either:
   a. Cut out pictures of young people working together, or
   b. Draw such pictures

PART 2
PLAYING THE GAME

Tell students they will now play the cooperative board game, "Earning Power." In a cooperative game they win or lose as a group. They work together as a team.

Reiterate that the game has word problems that describe young people working together to earn money. It will be used to buy something for all.

Students follow the directions and play "Earning Power."

DISCUSSION

1. How did you feel playing "Earning Power"? What made you feel that way?
2. Did your group win? What helped or hindered that?
3. If you play "Earning Power" again, what will you do differently?
4. "Earning Power" is a cooperative game. What made it cooperative? How is that different from most other games?

PART 3
TEACHING THE GAME

Prepare students to teach the "Earning Power" game to students in another class by having them review the rationale for a cooperative game and by having them develop useful questions for after-play.

Students teach the "Earning Power" game to students in another class. They describe their part in making it. They explain the rationale for a cooperative game, assist as needed during play, and lead a follow-up discussion.

COMPLETION   A student receives credit for this activity if her group completes "Earning Power." (They receive credit whether they win or lose.)

SUBJECT—A, SS
FORMAT—
RESEARCH
PROJECT, CLASS
PROJECT

People's Art

OBJECTIVES   To give students an opportunity to cooperate in the creation of change in their community

To provide the community with a mural representing the contributions of many diverse groups of people who helped their community

MATERIALS   Butcher paper or newsprint for mural design plans, paint, brushes, rags, and other materials for painting a large outdoor mural (Request donations from local paint and hardware stores.)

IMPLEMENTATION   Check with students to see if they know that art doesn't have to be the product of one person alone, but can be created cooperatively. Elicit or explain that art doesn't have to hang in a private home or museum, but can be displayed in open public places, for the enjoyment and inspiration of the community. Tell students they will create art for everyone in the community to enjoy.

Ask students if they have seen community murals. Elicit or offer background information. Explain that, in towns and cities across the country, people have designed and painted large murals on the sides of buildings, walls, and so forth. These depict the history and/or peoples of their community. If there are such murals in your city or town, visit them. Tell students that they will create a community mural depicting the ways different groups of people, often forgotten in history, contributed to the development of their communities.

PART 1 RESEARCH

Work with students to list those groups who are often left out of history. Be sure to include: Native American women and men, minority women and men (Blacks, Chicanos, Asians, Puerto Ricans) and white women. Add ethnic groups representative of your community.

Divide students into research groups of four to five. Assign each group to research one of the groups listed. Students should check to see if members of that group have been present in their community. With students, make a list of sources of historical information. To make this most effective, you will have had to seek out some of these sources before you begin. Be sure it includes: historical associations, older people in the community, minority associations, professors, women's groups, librarians. Students in each group divide contacts and tasks, so each student has a specific responsibility. Each person brings a written account of his findings back to the group.

The history of different groups of people in a community is not always easy to find. Yet, with some creative research, information can usually be uncovered. For example, even if yours is a predominantly white community, there is surely a history of Native American peoples in the area and most likely of other minority peoples though perhaps this history is not commonly known or appreciated. Give students assistance and encouragement. Explain how important their research is since most recorded history is limited and distorted, being written almost solely by and about white males. In fact, **many** diverse people have made history.

After learning of each member's findings, each research group is to identify and decide what to depict—what is most significant. The selections should be ones which could be depicted on an outdoor wall-mural. Encourage students to focus on *people's* history—the experiences, accomplishments, and cooperative efforts of "ordinary" people, not "leaders."

When all research groups are finished, they share their findings with each other and together determine an event or accomplishment that will be included in the community mural.

DISCUSSION
1. What resources did your group use to find the information it needed?
2. How hard or easy was it to find the information on Native American men and women, minority men and women, and white women, who contributed to the building of the community? What made it hard or easy?
3. What were some of the most interesting things that you learned about the group you were researching?

COMPLETION: PART 1
A student gets credit for this section of the project if her group hands in a series of research findings with at least one page from each member, and a statement of reasons why the event or accomplishment was decided on for the mural.

PART 2 PLANNING PAINTING THE MURAL
In the meantime, seek out sides of buildings or walls in your community that would be appropriate for a mural. Discuss the project with the owner. Continue looking until you secure permission from an owner. Provide sample sketches on plywood for owner-consideration.

Request assistance from the local council on the arts, other groups committed to the arts, parents, and the art teacher.

With students, plan the mural in such a way that each group can design and paint one separate section. In this way everyone can work at once if you have a very cooperative class. Otherwise, they can work in shifts. Students stay in research groups to design their section of the mural. Have each group get feedback from other groups to ensure that the whole mural will be acceptable to all.

For one-half day, assign one artistically-skilled student from each group to work with a professional artist. The outline of each section of the mural must be drawn at the chosen site. The next day bring students to the site to paint, again utilizing assistance from professional artists and from parents.

Upon completion, invite community members and reporters from local papers to see the mural and hear student-accounts of its making. Be sure to give special invitations to the diverse groups depicted on the mural. Student artists sign their names on the mural.

DISCUSSION
1. How do you feel about the community mural you created?
2. How did people in the community feel? What did they most appreciate?
3. What did your group members do that helped the successful completion of the mural?
4. What did your group members do that hindered the project?
5. If students in another school were starting a community mural, what advice would you give them?

SUBJECT—S, LA, SS
FORMAT—SMALL
GROUP, CLASS
PROJECT

Keep Your Community Clean

OBJECTIVES

To teach students to analyze a problem in their own community
To give students practice in working together to deal with a community problem
To give students the opportunity to work with others in the community
To teach students how to plan a multi-step project
To validate the skills and contributions of different class members

MATERIALS

Poster board, markers, bags, tape

IMPLEMENTATION STEP 1

Suggest a community problem to your students. Pick one that you think is obvious and important in your community. The example we use here is a community which is not as clean as many residents would like. Have the students brainstorm on reasons for the particular problem. In this example some reasons could be: not enough garbage cans in well-traveled areas, garbage cans not emptied often enough so overflow onto sidewalks, not enough pretty areas which are tempting to keep clean, not regular litter clean-up so that areas get messy and thus look unappealing, no returns on bottles, or not enough convenient recycling places or services.

STEP 2

Students divide into small groups, each group picking one of the reasons that the community isn't as clean as it should be. Groups brainstorm ways the class can deal with that. These ways can include: tasks group members or entire class members can do, tasks which would need parent help, tasks which could be done by the whole school, tasks which would include cooperation from local merchants or people living in the neighborhood.

STEP 3

Groups share their ideas with the entire class. Students pick tasks which interest them and divide into new groups according to these interests.

STEP 4

Students go out and begin tasks. After a few days, class time should be spent updating each other on progress, describing problems and getting suggestions for modifications, getting more help in areas where it is needed, and so forth. This should be done every few days. If a group comes up with an idea for a task which none of the group members feel they can do as well as another class member could, this would be the time to ask for that help.

STEP 5

Discuss and evaluate the project and decide on continuation.

STEP 6 This is a second part to this project. The class brainstorms on other community problems. Then the class uses consensus to pick one problem on which to work. (See lesson on consensus, p. 121) Then proceed as in the first project beginning with Step 2 and following the same steps.

DISCUSSION
1. Why is garbage in the streets a frequent problem in many communities?
2. Why is that a problem which is often not "solved" by existing groups?
3. How did it feel to work with members of the community on this problem? With others in your school?
4. What reactions did you get from those outside your class—to you, as young people, working on a community problem?
5. What kinds of cooperation did you get?
6. What other kinds of cooperation would have helped? What could you do to get more cooperation?
7. What kinds of publicity did you get? How did that help? What other publicity could you have gotten? What could be done to get that publicity?
8. How was your class able to work as a group to deal with a problem?
9. What kinds of skills were valuable in working on this problem? In what ways did working as a group prove more efficient than working as individuals?
10. How easy or hard was it to pick another problem to work on? Why? If you had an easy consensus, what does that tell you about your class? About the problems in your community? If consensus was hard to reach, what does that tell you?
11. What were the similarities and differences in working on an assigned problem and working on one chosen by you as a class?

COMPLETION A student gets credit for this lesson after detailing, in writing, the ways she contributed to this project.

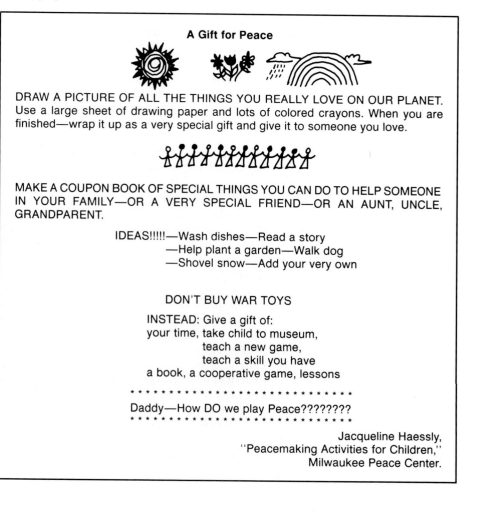

A Gift for Peace

DRAW A PICTURE OF ALL THE THINGS YOU REALLY LOVE ON OUR PLANET. Use a large sheet of drawing paper and lots of colored crayons. When you are finished—wrap it up as a very special gift and give it to someone you love.

MAKE A COUPON BOOK OF SPECIAL THINGS YOU CAN DO TO HELP SOMEONE IN YOUR FAMILY—OR A VERY SPECIAL FRIEND—OR AN AUNT, UNCLE, GRANDPARENT.

IDEAS!!!!!—Wash dishes—Read a story
—Help plant a garden—Walk dog
—Shovel snow—Add your very own

DON'T BUY WAR TOYS

INSTEAD: Give a gift of:
your time, take child to museum,
teach a new game,
teach a skill you have
a book, a cooperative game, lessons

* *
Daddy—How DO we play Peace????????
* *

Jacqueline Haessly,
"Peacemaking Activities for Children,"
Milwaukee Peace Center.

Educating Ourselves, Our Friends, and Our Neighbors

OBJECTIVES

To provide a model of students developing a cooperative research project, with findings to be shared with families and community

To have students learn to challenge the stereotypes they have, in this case particularly about Native Americans

To have students learn how to gather correct information and to share it in a useful way

MATERIALS

Worksheet—"Stereotypes of Native Americans," page 244, fiction on Native Americans from your local library, reference books on Native Americans, pencils, use of copying machine, an agreeable librarian, "Unlearning Indian Stereotypes" filmstrip and activity book

IMPLEMENTATION

Tell students one way to make a difference in their communities is to gather accurate information on a topic and share it with others. Explain that they will do such a cooperative research project about Native Americans (American Indians).

**PART A
STEP 1**

Students share what they know about Native Americans. Where did they get this information? Do they think it is correct? Is any of it contradictory? How do they check whether it is true? Have students list stereotypes about Native Americans. For each stereotype analyze what might be true, what might not be true, and why. Put in list form in an accessible place in the classroom.

DISCUSSION

1. What are some beliefs we have about Native Americans?
2. Where did you get the information that led to those beliefs? What comes from reading? comic books? television? movies? advertisements? toys? toy boxes? What other sources give you your image?
3. Do you question some of these beliefs? Why?
4. Are there some that you are sure are true? Why?

STEP 2

From your public library and your school library, take out all the books you can on Native Americans. Make sure these books are either at or below your students' reading levels. Students should work in pairs (or threesomes), each group reading the same two or three books.

STEP 3

Students work together to complete the worksheets on all the books each pair (or threesome) reads.

STEP 4

Gather as an entire class. Each pair (or threesome) should share information from its worksheets. Include areas where no useful information was found. Other students can help either with information, or with ideas on how to do the research. Other students can also challenge information on worksheets about what the stereotypes are or what the "correct" information is.

DISCUSSION

1. What were some stereotypes that were easy to find? Why were they easy?
2. Was there some information in the books that you weren't sure about?
3. Were there some stereotypes that were easy to correct?
   For example, your book about Massachusetts Indians might have said they lived in tipis. You could check and find out that tipis were used on the plains, not on the coast.

4. Was there information you couldn't get? What? Why was it unavailable?
5. How could you find out if the information in your reference books was correct? Why is so much information in encyclopedias and history books also incorrect?
6. Why do we know more about certain Native American nations than others? Which are the ones we tend to see as "American Indians"? Why?
7. What sources of information do you think are most reliable? Why?

STEP 5 Show and discuss the filmstrip "Unlearning Indian Stereotypes." As needed, do additional activities provided in the Activity Booklet. Then students make modifications in their worksheets and do more research if needed.

STEP 6 Each pair records its final information in a one-page summary report about each book read. They divide writing equitably and then check each other's work.

PART B Tell students that once they've gathered accurate information on a topic, it is important to share it with others. This is how their collective efforts can make a difference in many people's lives.

Students go back to their partnership or group and discuss some of the ways they can share the research they did with their school, family, or community. Here are some examples:
1. Give the school librarian multiple copies of the one-page summary report about each book. Ask the librarian to hand these out when the books are borrowed.
2. Do the same for the town library.
3. Bring reports home to families and share information with adults and siblings.
4. Find out when the school or local library is having a book fair. Talk with the organizers and show them your reports. Encourage them to select stereotype-free books for the book fairs.
5. Work with your teacher, librarian, or interested parents in compiling a list of stereotype-free books about Native Americans. Use when ordering new books.

Have each student take one action step and complete it. They report back to the partnership on how it went. As a partnership or group, write a brief statement of what they learned from their action step. How can what they learned help educate others about Native American stereotypes? Come together as a class for discussion.

DISCUSSION
1. What kinds of action steps did different partnerships take?
2. How effective were they, or will they be?
3. How did other people respond to you and the research you had done?
4. What did you learn from this project?

COMPLETION **Part A:** A student gets credit for Part A of this activity when both partners have written, had checked by their partner, and handed in, the page summary of a book their partnership researched.

Part B: A student gets credit for Part B after each student has taken an action step and cooperated with his partner to write and hand in a summary statement of what they learned by doing this project.

GOING FURTHER This process can be used for any ethnic group, socioeconomic class, disability, and so forth.

ALL IN THE FAMILY WORKSHEET

I: Competition Can Hurt Families—Jigsaw Sections

A. Brothers and Sisters Fighting

Explanation: Brothers and sisters often compete in families for possessions, for having "their way," and for attention from adults.

Example: Rebecca wants to use Jack's bike. He doesn't let her because it's **his.** They fight!

Costs of Competition

• Rebecca and Jack lose time and energy for doing other things they enjoy.
• They lose good feelings about each other.
• They lose a chance to share and they lose the warm feelings that come from sharing.
• Jack might lose a chance to use something of Rebecca's the next time he wants to.

B. Competition Between Families

Explanation: Sometimes a family, or people in a family, compete with other families to be the "best." The best can be defined in many ways—having the best possessions like clothes and cars, having the most money, being the toughest, being the most athletic, and so forth.

Example: The Jackson's TV works well. It's an eight-year-old black and white set. The Jacksons are very satisfied with black and white. The other families on the block, however, have color TVs. The Jacksons don't want to be outdone by their neighbors. They decide to buy a color TV.

Costs of Competition

• The Jacksons lose the money that they could have used for other things like family outings, books and games, and so forth.
• They lose their independence—doing things because they **want** to and not because other people do them.
• They think "new" is best, and lose out on an appreciation of the value of the old.

I. Competition Can Hurt Families—Jigsaw Sections—continued

C. Sexism Sparks Competition in Families

Explanation: Sometimes sexism exists in families. Boys learn to do only certain things (like carpentry or outdoor work) and to act in particular ways (like being strong and unemotional). Girls learn to do certain things (like housework and taking care of children) and to act in particular ways (like being emotional and caring for others). Family members come to feel they are better than others in some areas but are "losers" in others.

Example: The Holiday family is planning to go to a movie at the library tonight. Mrs. Holiday calls Mr. Holiday at work just before he is to leave to take the bus home at the end of the day. She tells him that the family car won't start, but she thinks she can fix it by working under the hood. Mr. Holiday tells her not to play with it and to leave it for him to fix when he gets home. She reminds him she just completed an auto mechanics course. He still says no, even if it means missing the movie.

Costs of Competition
- The Holidays will probably miss a trip to the movies.
- They miss a chance to cooperate in getting something done.
- Mrs. Holiday misses the chance to use her new skills and build up her confidence in auto mechanics.

ALL IN THE FAMILY WORKSHEET

II: Competition Can Hurt Families

Discuss the answers together. Try to come to an agreement. Each person writes the group answer to one of the three sections below—A, B, C. If there is strong disagreement, note that as well. Then read the worksheet. Sign if you agree with the answers and if spelling, punctuation, and grammar are correct.

A. An example we have observed of brothers and sisters fighting is . . .

The costs of that competition are . . .

An alternative is . . .

B. An example we have observed of competition between families is . . .

The costs of that competition are . . .

An alternative is . . .

C. An example we have observed of sexism sparking competition in families is . . .

The costs of that competition are . . .

An alternative is . . .

Signed _____

_____

_____

COMMUNITY CHALLENGE GAME WORKSHEET

Directions: Competitive Version

Object

To meet all your family needs and arrive at the end of Community Avenue.
The winner is:

1. The first family to meet its needs and also arrive at the end of Community Avenue, or

2. The family with the most needs met when time runs out

Materials

Pencil; "Family-Needs Checklist;" blank sheet of paper titled "Income;" movers (use coins, paper clips, rings, etc.); dice; three sets of cards—"Family/Neighborhood," "Workplace" and "Public Institutions" for the **competitive** version of "Community Challenge" (cards are marked FN, W, PI).

Steps

1. Place movers at beginning of game board.

2. Choose to play with **either** Set One or Set Two of the Family Cards. Draw a Family Card. You are that family for the game. Write down your income on the blank sheet of paper.

3. Throw a die. Highest goes first. Others will continue counterclockwise.

4. Move according to the number shown on either of the die.

5. You will land on a "Family/Neighborhood," "Workplace," or "Public Institutions" space. Pick a card from the corresponding pile. If there are no more cards for the space you landed on, wait until your next turn and roll again.

6. If you can use the card, keep it. If it meets one of your needs, check it off on your "Family-Needs Checklist." If you can't use the card, place it at the bottom of the pile.

7. You must keep all Luck Cards. Luck Cards may affect your income. If so, revise your income. Keep the family's current income in sight, on the income sheet.

8. Special moves
   - *Landing on the same square as someone else:* You lose a turn.
   - *Doubles:* Take an extra turn.

9. Please note:
   a. Workplace cards affect all wage earners in the family, except when noted otherwise.

   b. A family's child-care needs are met when all children are accounted for. Some families will have no needs, some will need one card, and others two. This will depend on the ages of children in the family.

COMMUNITY CHALLENGE GAME WORKSHEET

Directions: Cooperative Version

Object

The group wins if all families meet all their needs and arrive at the end of Community Ave. The group wins if:

1. Everyone gets to the end of Community Avenue and all families have met all their needs, or

2. Time runs out and all families have met their needs

Materials: Pencil; "Family-Needs Checklist;" blank sheet of paper titled "Income;" (use coins, paper clips, rings, etc.); dice; three sets of cards—"Family/Neighborhood," "Workplace," and "Public Institutions" for the **cooperative** version of Community Challenge (cards are marked FN, W, PI).

Steps

1. Place movers at beginning of game board.

2. Choose to play with **either** Set One or Set Two of the Family Cards. Draw a Family Card. You are that family for the game. Write your income on the blank sheet of paper titled "Income."

3. Throw a die. Lowest goes first. Others will continue counterclockwise.

4. Move the number shown on either die.

5. You will land on either a "Family/Neighborhood," "Workplace," or "Public Institutions" space. Pick a card from the corresponding pile. If there are no more cards for the space you landed on, wait until your next turn and roll again.

6. If you can use the card, keep it. If it meets one of your needs, check it off on your "Family-Needs Checklist." If you can't use the card, give it to someone who can.

7. You must keep Luck Cards. Luck Cards may affect your income. If so, determine your revised income. Keep the family's current income in sight, on the income sheet.

8. Special Moves
   - *Landing on the same square as someone else*—Move the other family ahead to where it wants to go.
   - *Doubles*—Give the family you land on an extra turn on its next turn.

9. Please note:
   a. Workplace cards affect all wage earners in the family, except when noted otherwise.
   b. A family's child-care needs are met when all children are accounted for. Some families will have no needs, some will need one card, and others two. This will depend on the ages of children in the family.

COMMUNITY CHALLENGE GAME WORKSHEET
Family–Needs Checklist

Community Challenge Game
Family-Needs Checklist

1. Housing   ____

2. Transportation   ____

3. Medical Care   ____

4. Child Care   ____

5. Recreation and Entertainment   ____

6. Education   ____

7. Food and Clothing   ____

Community Challenge Game
Family-Needs Checklist

1. Housing   ____

2. Transportation   ____

3. Medical Care   ____

4. Child Care   ____

5. Recreation and Entertainment   ____

6. Education   ____

7. Food and Clothing   ____

Community Challenge Game
Family-Needs Checklist

1. Housing   ____

2. Transportation   ____

3. Medical Care   ____

4. Child Care   ____

5. Recreation and Entertainment   ____

6. Education   ____

7. Food and Clothing   ____

Community Challenge Game
Family-Needs Checklist

1. Housing   ____

2. Transportation   ____

3. Medical Care   ____

4. Child Care   ____

5. Recreation and Entertainment   ____

6. Education   ____

7. Food and Clothing   ____

COMMUNITY CHALLENGE GAME WORKSHEET
Family Cards

Set One   Set Two

A You are a single mother with two children ages two and six. You recently moved to the mainland from Puerto Rico. You are being trained to be an electrician and will then earn $15,000 a year.	**A** You are a white, single father with two children ages three and five. You sell cars and make $50,000 a year.
B Your family is composed of a mother, grandmother, and five children ages fourteen, ten, nine, six, and three. The mother is a check-out clerk at a local store. The grandmother babysits at home. Your income is $8,000 a year.	**B** Your family is composed of a father, aunt, and four children ages four, six, seven, and nine. The father is unemployed and the aunt is disabled. The aunt's disability income is $7,000 a year. All are white.
C Your family is composed of a mother who is a lawyer, a father who is a photographer, and an infant. You are white. Each year Mom makes $50,000 and Dad makes $30,000.	**C** Your family is composed of a mother, father, and two children ages three and six. You are black. The mother is a teacher and father a social worker. Each makes $20,000 a year.
D Your family is made up of a mother, her female friend, and two children, four and seven, all white. The mother is a computer programmer and makes $20,000. Her friend is a nurse practitioner earning $15,000.	**D** Your family is composed of a father, his woman friend, and one child, age seven. You are all Asian. The father is a bus driver and makes $18,000 a year. The woman friend is a student.
E You are a black, elderly single woman who is disabled. You live off your disability income—$4,000 a year.	**E** You are a white, elderly, single, able-bodied woman. You earn an annual income of $10,000 from Social Security and a pension.

COMMUNITY CHALLENGE GAME WORKSHEET

Cards—Competitive Version

W	FN
Your neighborhood grocery store charges high prices. The big supermarket across town is much cheaper. You can shop there and meet your food and clothing needs—if you have transportation.	This is a small apartment with two bedrooms. If your income is $12,000 or more, you may keep this card to fill your need for housing.
W	**FN**
You shop for clothes at a department store. Since family members worry about style, they often buy more than they can afford. You meet your food and clothing needs, but lose 1 percent of your salary.	This single-family, three-bedroom house is yours if your income is $40,000 or more. It fills your need for housing.
FN	**FN**
You find a single-family, four-bedroom house. If your income is over $40,000, keep this card to fill your housing need.	If your income is $25,000 or more you may keep this single-family, two-bedroom house to fill your need for housing.
FN	**FN**
This is a single-family house with two bedrooms. If your income is $25,000 or over, you can keep this card to fill your need for housing.	This is a small one-bedroom apartment. If your income is $8,000 or more and if you are a small family, you may take this card to fill your housing need.

Cards—Competitive Version—continued

W	**PI**
Your workplace has health insurance. It covers 70 percent of your health costs. This meets your medical care needs.	Someone in your family has a fall and might have a broken arm. If you earn $8,000 a year or more, go at once to your private doctor. If you make less, wait 2 hours in the emergency room. Miss two turns. Meet your need for medical care.
W	**PI**
Your workplace has health insurance. It covers 70 percent of your health costs. You are in a car accident. Doctor and hospital bills are $50,000. Your medical needs are met if you make over $45,000 so you can pay the owed $15,000.	Your community government helps support an excellent theater company. The actors are paid well for their work. If your salary is over $20,000, you can afford to buy a season ticket. In that case, meet your recreation and entertainment needs.
W	**W**
You can afford to buy a health insurance policy if you make $20,000 a year or more. You are healthy all year. This meets your need for medical care.	In your community is a club with a pool, tennis courts, and golf course. If you make over $25,000 you can afford to join. In that case, meet your recreation and entertainment needs.
W	**PI**
You can buy health insurance if you make $20,000 or more. This meets your medical care needs. You have a heart attack and need doctor and hospital care. The bill is $30,000. All but $4,000 is covered. Take that off your salary or lose four turns until you pay it off.	Your community has a public park on the other side of town. If you have met your need for transportation, you are able to get there and meet your recreation and entertainment needs.

Cards—Competitive Version—continued

FN	W
There is no free pool in your community. People who want to swim build their own pools. You can afford to do this if you make $50,000 or more. In that case, meet your recreation and entertainment needs.	You see a car for $10,000. If your income is between $16,000 and $30,000, you need a loan. If you make more, you can buy it outright. This fills your need for transportation.
W	**W**
Your family loves movies. If you make $15,000 or more, you can afford to go to the movies once a month. In that case you meet your recreation and entertainment needs.	You want to buy a car for $9,000. You can afford it if your income is $28,000 or more. You need a bank loan if between $15,000 and $28,000. This fills your transportation need. If you earn less than $15,000, forget it!
FN	**PI**
The children in your family want a new toy. Each has saved some money, but not enough. Since each wants to buy the toy for himself, no one gets it. Do not meet your recreation and entertainment needs.	You have access to public transportation, ten blocks away. It fills your transportation need unless your family has more than one child under five or anyone sick or disabled. Otherwise, it is too far away.
W	**W**
You go the car dealership and find a car you like for $10,000. If your family income is more than $30,000 you can afford to buy it. This fills your need for transportation.	You buy a used car for $2,000. You suddenly find it needs many repairs. Only if you have a family income of $10,000 or more to fix it does it fill your transportation need.

Cards—Competitive Version—continued

W There is one good nursery school in your community. If you earn $20,000 or more you can afford to send your child there. In that case, you meet your need for child care.	**FN** A child in your family has a serious learning difficulty. If you earn over $20,000, you can pay for a private tutor to work with the child every day. If you can afford this, your educational need is met.
FN In your community, there is no child-care center with any space for your child. You have to hire a sitter. If you earn $25,000 or more you can afford this. In that case, you meet your need for child care.	**W** Your family wants your child to go to the best college. If you make $50,000 or more you send the child to computer camps and summer language and art programs. If you can afford this, your educational need is met.
FN The elementary school gets out at 3:00. You don't get home from work until 6:00, so you hire a sitter. If you make over $20,000 a year, you can afford this. In that case, you meet your need for child care.	**PI** In the early grades, the children in your family were tested for their ability and are tracked. Because they were put in lower tracks, they feel dumb and do poorly. Your educational needs are not met.
PI The children in the family work very hard in school and do good work. Because they don't get A's and aren't the best in the class, they feel badly about themselves. Your educational needs are met, but for a price.	**W** You go food shopping in the local grocery store. If you make $10,000 or more you can afford to buy nutritious food for your family. In that case, you meet your food and clothing needs.

Cards—Competitive Version—continued

Luck **W**	Luck **W**
Someone in your workplace is bored with his job and wants your job. He criticizes you and your work and works day and night to get ahead of you. He gets your job. You are demoted. You lose 15 percent of your salary.	You work fast at your workplace in order to keep up with all the work and with the other workers. You get praise and power—and ulcers and have to go to the hospital for three weeks. Lose two turns and take $1,000 off your salary for medical bills.
Luck **W**	Luck **W**
This card applies to anyone making $30,000 or less. You and others have complaints about your job. You try to organize a union at your workplace to deal with them. The management doesn't like it. You are fired supposedly for different reasons and lose your salary.	Your workplace experiences economic difficulty. You are put on half time. Cut your salary in half.
Luck **W**	Luck **W**
This card applies to anyone making $15,000 or more. You work fifty hours a week, six days a week to get ahead. You receive a bonus from the workplace. Add 20 percent to your salary.	Your child is sick for three weeks and you have to stay home. Lose 5 percent of your salary. If there are two wage earners in your family, decide which one will be affected.
Luck **W**	Luck **W**
You work as hard as a co-worker. You spend more time with the boss and work hard to become her friend. She gives you a $1,000 raise to add to your salary. Your co-worker doesn't get it. You like the raise, but lose the friendship.	You work very hard in order to get ahead. You get a bonus of $1,000 to add to your salary. Yet you have hardly any free time to spend with your family and friends.

Cards—Competitive Version—continued

Luck **W**	Luck **FN**
Your workplace had serious economic problems. You were laid off and have to go on unemployment. Cut your salary by one-half.	Your family needs a new sofa. There is a sale that you can take advantage of if you can get a truck to move the sofa. If you make $18,000 or more, you can rent a truck. In that case, take an extra turn. Otherwise lose a turn.
Luck **PI**	Luck **FN**
Your community does not have a recycling center. Each family must pay for garbage pick-up. The community is full of litter and broken bottles. You step on a piece of broken glass. Lose a turn.	Your family doesn't want to do the household chores. If you make $25,000 or more, you hire someone to clean and do repairs. You lose out on learning many skills. If you make less, your house is dirty and you lose a turn.
Luck **PI**	Luck **FN**
Someone in your family needs help with problems. If you make over $25,000 you can afford a counselor. Move ahead two spaces. If you make less, community mental health can see you for five visits. After that, hang in there!—go back five spaces.	Your lawnmower breaks. You have to use money you've saved to buy a new one. Lose a turn.
Luck **PI**	Luck **FN**
You need a loan to buy a car. You go to the bank. If you earn $15,000 or more, you get the loan. Otherwise, please strengthen your legs and walk. Take an extra turn.	You need a ladder to do some painting. If you make over $20,000 you already own one. If you make less, go out and buy one. Go back two spaces.

COMMUNITY CHALLENGE GAME WORKSHEET

Cards—Cooperative Version

PI	**FN**
Your community runs a nursery school. Fees are paid on a sliding scale. Pay 5 percent of your salary to have your child-care needs met.	Families in your neighborhood organize a tutoring program. Adults help high school students. Older students tutor younger ones. You can share this card with two other families. All your educational needs are met.
FN	**PI**
The families in your neighborhood get together to start a child-care center. You hire a teacher. Adults in each family work four hours a week. If two other families join, and pay 5 percent of their income, your child-care needs are met.	Your community offers summer programs in dance, music, computers, math, drama, and languages. If you make $15,000 or under it's free. Over $15,000 pay 1 percent of salary. Your educational needs are met.
PI	**PI**
The elementary school gets out at 3:00. After school your child goes to a community-run afterschool program. Everyone in your community pays 1 percent of their salary for this service. Your child-care needs are met.	The school your children go to doesn't track students by ability. Everyone is helped to work hard and do his or her best. Teachers expect good work from all. Your educational needs are met.
PI	**W**
The children go to a school where students work together to help each other learn. Everyone does her best and helps others do their best. Your educational needs are met.	You belong to the community food cooperative. If you work four hours a week, you get a 10 percent discount on all food. Meet your food and clothing needs. Share this card with two other families.

Cards—Cooperative Version–continued

PI Your community has set aside land for gardens. If you get one other family to work with you, you can plant a garden. This allows you to cut down your grocery bill and meet your food and clothing needs.	**PI** You find a community subsidized apartment with three bedrooms. If your income is under $15,000 you may move in. Fill your housing need.
FN Your community opens a clothing exchange. You sell clothes you've outgrown and use the money to buy clothes other families have sold. Every family that wants to use it gets their food and clothing needs met.	**FN** You discover a cooperative house with space for two families. If your income is $6,000 or more you and any other family with that income may move in. Both fill their housing needs.
FN You find a two-family, four-bedroom house. If your income is $15,000 or more and you find another family with that income to share with you, both have met your housing need.	**W** Your workplace provides full medical coverage to all workers. It covers all your health costs. This meets your medical care needs.
FN You find a cooperative house where several families live together. If your income is $7,000 or more and you have no more than two children, you can move in. Fill your housing need.	**W** Your workplace provides full medical coverage to all workers. It covers all your health costs. You are in a bad car accident. Your doctor and hospital bills are $50,000. Your medical needs are met.

Cards—Cooperative Version—continued

PI You belong to a community medical plan. Membership is 2 percent of your salary. It covers all your health costs. You are healthy all year. You meet your medical care needs. At any point during the game you may share this card with one other family.	**PI** Your community has a public park with a pool, tennis court, and playing fields. Admission is free. If you have transportation, this meets your recreation and entertainment needs.
PI You belong to a community health plan. Membership is 2 percent of your salary. It covers all your health costs. You have a heart attack and need hospital and doctor care. The bill is $30,000. Your medical needs are met.	**W** The owner of a vacant field will let community residents use it. Families will rotate jobs: grass-cutting, clean-up, and scheduling events. People make a baseball diamond and set up a volleyball net. Everyone who is willing to work gets recreation and entertainment needs met.
PI Someone in your family has an accident and might have a broken ankle. Go to the community hospital. There are enough doctors to examine the ankle right away. Meet your medical care need.	**FN** There is no swimming pool in your neighborhood. If all the families decide they want one, contribute 1 percent of your annual income to build one. This will meet your recreation and entertainment needs.
PI Your community organizes a program of music and plays in the park. People in the orchestra and plays are local residents of all ages. Admission is free. Meet your recreation and entertainment needs.	**PI** Your family loves movies. Your library shows free movies every Saturday. This meets your recreation and entertainment needs.

Cards—Cooperative Version—continued

FN The children in your family want a new toy. Each has saved some money, but not enough for the toy. You pool your money and get the toy. You get your recreation and entertainment needs met.	**PI** Your community has an excellent system of public transportation. If you are not disabled, it meets your transportation need.
W You see a car you want to buy for $10,000. If your family makes $30,000 or more, buy it. If you make between $10,000 and $30,000 you can go to the credit union for a loan. Fill your transportation need.	**PI** Your community has developed an excellent system of public transportation, with provisions for the disabled. It meets your transportation need.
FN Your transportation is a car pool. You need a car, and one other family who wants to participate needs a car. You each save $1,000 a year by car-pooling. Add that to your income. Both fill your transportation need.	**FN** This is for someone who doesn't own a car. Find one family with children and a car. You take care of the children three hours a day for use of the car one hour a day. This meets your transportation need.

Cards—Cooperative Version—continued

Luck **W** Workers at your workplace have been working 45 hours a week to keep up. Together you decide you don't have enough time for family or friends. You agree to hire another person and cut your hours to 40. You cut your salary 3 percent but are not so rushed. You have more fun with family and friends.	**Luck** **FN** You and your friends chipped in to buy shares in a small truck years ago. It cost each family $100. Now you see a sale on a sofa. You can afford it because you can use your truck to move it from the store to your home. Take an extra turn.
Luck **PI** Your community government operates a recycling center for bottles, cans, and newspapers. They are sold and reused. In this way the community earns some money for other projects. Give another family an extra turn.	**Luck** **FN** Your family cooperates to do all the household chores. You don't have to pay anyone to do work for you. Go ahead either one, two, or three spaces.
Luck **PI** Your community government starts a switchboard. Whenever anyone has a problem, they call the switchboard and are referred to a community agency. No one has to face life's problems alone. Move another family which wants to go ahead two spaces.	**Luck** **FN** You convince two other families to share a lawnmower with you so it costs less to each. Go to any free space ahead.
Luck **PI** You need a loan to buy a car. Go to the Consumer Credit Union. Many citizens invest money in the Credit Union so that when any family needs a loan it is there. Because everyone is helping each other, you get your loan. Give the other families a handshake.	**Luck** **FN** You need a ladder to do some painting. Your block already bought a ladder for any family to use when they need it. Go borrow it from the person storing it. Move ahead either one, two, or three spaces.

Cards—Cooperative Version—continued

Luck **W**	Luck **W**
You are getting bored with your job and want a change. You switch jobs with another person in your workplace and learn new skills. You make the same amount of money as before, but are happier.	You work hard, but feel your health is being negatively affected. You arrange to work five fewer hours a week and someone else picks up the time. You lose 5 percent of your salary. You save your health and big doctor bills later.
Luck **W**	Luck **W**
You have complaints about your job. You get together with other workers and decide to make needed changes. All are happier.	You work in a cooperatively-run workplace. It is experiencing economic difficulty. You and all the other workers each lose 5 percent of your salary.
Luck **W**	Luck **W**
You work in a cooperatively-run workplace. Everyone is working hard and business is excellent. All receive a bonus. Add 10 percent to your annual salary.	You work in a cooperatively-run workplace. Your child is sick for three weeks and you have to miss work. You make up the time over the course of the year. Lose no salary.
Luck **W**	Luck **W**
You work as hard as a co-worker with the same job as you. You often share ideas and help each other with projects. Your teamwork helps all and improves the workplace. Everyone gets a 1 percent bonus.	Your workplace is a cooperative. The workers are owners and managers. Your workplace experiences serious economic problems. Everyone cuts 10 percent from their salary. No one is laid off.

Cards—Cooperative Version—continued

Luck	**PI**	Luck	**FN**
Southern Cooperative Development Fund— The S.C.D.F. is a bank that lends money to cooperative organizations in the South. Any group that borrows money becomes an owner in the corporation. You might try to start a similar fund in your community. Take an extra turn.		In the Shared Living household in Boston fifteen people of low and moderate incomes live in a cooperative house. The house is 70 percent older people and 30 percent younger. Older people have both privacy and companionship. You like this idea and may try something similar. Take an extra turn.	

Luck	**PI**	Luck	**PI**
Many communities have People's Yellow Pages. These directories list cooperative services in those communities. Services include legal aid, free clinics, food co-ops, recycling centers and day care. With the People's Yellow Pages citizens can know where to go to get their needs met. You decide to start a People's Yellow Pages in your community. Move ahead three spaces.		The Beach Area Community Clinic provides low cost medical and social services. It has a general clinic, a seniors' clinic, community workshops and counseling. Fees are on a sliding scale. No one is refused services. This gives you ideas for your community. Move ahead one space.	

Luck	**PI**	Luck	**FN**
In Minneapolis, there are many cooperatively-run businesses and services that people can use. These are: a food co-op, clothes stores, a press, a day-care center, a builder's co-op, a book-store, a tenants' union, a theater group and a bakery. The All-Cooperating Assembly is the federation that links these co-ops together. This example inspires your community. Move ahead four spaces.		In the Detroit area, about 1,500 senior Americans live in seven buildings developed and managed by Cooperative Services. The residents run their buildings cooperatively. The cooperatives do not try to make a profit. Therefore people can live there cheaply. You might try to develop cooperative housing like this in your community. Move ahead three spaces.	

Book Analysis

Book Title _____ Author _____

Number of pages _____ Reading level of book _____

Setting (time and place) _____

Characters (names, ages, roles) _____

_____

_____

Families

Examples of cooperation:

Examples of competition:

Friends

Examples of cooperation:

Examples of competition:

Community

Examples of cooperation:

Examples of competition:

Between Communities

Examples of cooperation:

Examples of competition:

School and/or Workplace

Examples of cooperation:

Examples of competition:

General statement of this book in terms of cooperation and competition:

INGRID AND JEFFERY'S COOPERATIVE HOUSEHOLDS WORKSHEET

An Interview with Ingrid

Interviewer: You lived in a cooperative household that is part of a bigger group of people called Movement for a New Society. What is MNS?

Ingrid: Movement for a New Society is a network of people working to make the world a safer place in which to live.

Interviewer: How long did you live in a cooperative household?

Ingrid: I lived in a cooperative household from the time I was a baby until two years ago.

Interviewer: What were your feelings about life in a cooperative household?

Ingrid: I liked living with other people because they were nice. I could talk to them about things. They were understanding people and it was fun!

Interviewer: How was the household organized?

Ingrid: The grown-ups would meet in weekly meetings and discuss what needed to be done. They discussed who would cook what day, who would do child care what day, and talked about questions that had to be dealt with.

Interviewer: How were jobs taken care of?

Ingrid: All the adults shared chores and cooking. We had a sign-up sheet and people would sign up.

Interviewer: What were the positive things about living cooperatively?

Ingrid: There was always someone home for the four children. There were people to pay attention to us. We all shared experiences. When my father had cancer, there were people always by my side, and they helped me get through it all. It seemed less frightening.

Interviewer: What were the problems of living collectively?

Ingrid: I was not aware of any problems.

Interviewer: What were the effects of living cooperatively on you?

Ingrid: Cooperative living is hard to explain, but it helped me grow up to be a good person. I am now twelve years old and I am very glad that I lived communally for nine years.

INGRID AND JEFFERY'S COOPERATIVE HOUSEHOLDS WORKSHEET

An Interview with Jeffery

Interviewer: How long have you lived in a cooperative household in Cambridge?

Jeffery: My father moved into the house about three years ago. At first, I lived with him there only on weekends. Then, for almost two years, I lived in the house during the week and on some weekends. Now I spend most of my time at the house. Before my father and I moved into this house, we lived in another cooperative house but with fewer people.

Interviewer: How many people live in this cooperative household? How are they related?

Jeffery: My father is the oldest member of our household, I'm the youngest. Everyone else is between twenty and forty. Some of the people have typical outside jobs like working for computer companies. Others do full-time political work like organizing against local companies that produce parts of nuclear reactors. Right now, there are seven people living here.

Interviewer: What are your feelings about living in a cooperative household?

Jeffery: I like parts of it and I don't like other parts. I'm the only one here who isn't an adult. We work on issues about ageism but I still sometimes feel that I get excluded from conversations or that people in the house don't seek me out as much because I'm younger than they are. Also a couple of the people in this house like to argue. There can be loud and drawn out fights. I find that hard if they happen often. Everyone here has definite opinions about who I should be and what I should do. That gets really tiring.

Interviewer: In what ways is your father clearly the one who parents you and in what ways do the other adults take that role?

Jeffery: My father is responsible for seeing that I get out to school. He's the one the school calls for conferences. He pays my expenses. Otherwise, I talk with whomever I'm comfortable with; it doesn't matter about the person's role. I'm responsible for myself and have a full adult role in chores and meetings. If people in the house have strong opinions on something, they'll try to convince me in the same way they try to convince each other, not in a way that is patronizing.

An Interview with Jeffery—continued

Interviewer: How are chores worked out?

Jeffery: Each of us has a night to cook. We share all the cleaning chores. We have very long house meetings once a week to work out problems.

Interviewer: What are the positive parts of living cooperatively?

Jeffery: I like having so many interesting people with different points of view in the house. I like having people to talk with really late at night or having great discussions at the dinner table. We all save money!

Interviewer: What are the problems?

Jeffery: One problem is the amount of arguing that goes on sometimes and the tensions between some people. Also I don't like the pressures that get put on me. Sometimes chores don't get done. Also I'd like not to be the only one who isn't an adult.

Interviewer: What are the effects on you of living cooperatively?

Jeffery: I think it's been very good for me. It's been a way my father could afford to have me live with him. I've been exposed to more adults with more diverse opinions. I've learned tremendous amounts about politics through the discussions we always have. I've learned to cope with tensions. I've taken adult responsibility in cooking and cleaning.

Thinking about Households

Think about the way most people live now in individual families. Below list three benefits (things people gain, advantages) and three prices (things people lose out on, disadvantages) of living in individual families.

Think about the possibility of your living in a cooperative household. List three benefits and three prices.

Benefits	Prices
Individual household	Individual household
1.	1.
2.	2.
3.	3.
Cooperative household	Cooperative household
1.	1.
2.	2.
3.	3.

Signatures _____

_____

A Women's Factory

Below is an interview with women of McCaysville Industries, a factory that sews women's clothing. Each student should take a role and read the interview aloud.

Interviewer: What makes McCaysville Industries so different from other factories?

Eva Chancey: McCaysville Industries is located in the hills of northern Georgia. As far as we know, it's the only completely woman-owned and operated factory in the country.

Interviewer: Why is that so special?

Bernice Ratcliffe: The garment industry is a man's world. Women do most of the work, but women supervisors are rare. Except for McCaysville, there are no women owners.

Interviewer: How did McCaysville get started?

Lorraine Miller: The factory grew out of a strike against Levi-Strauss, the nearby blue-jean factory. Conditions were bad there. The strike was a long one. We needed jobs, so we decided to start our own factory.

Interviewer: How is McCaysville different from Levi-Strauss or other factories?

Eva: Oh, it's different in so many ways! One is that here everybody works together. The four women who are owners and managers are also workers. They work right along with us.

Bernice: All jobs are pretty much equal. For example, we have no janitor. The workers and owners clean up their work areas at the end of the day.

Lorraine: There was always so much pressure at Levi-Strauss. They kept pushing us so hard for more work. Here we don't have the same pressure. One example is production.

Interviewer: Please explain what production is, and how that's different.

Lorraine: Sure. At a typical factory, production is the number of items a worker has to make each week. Production numbers at Levi-Strauss were set by the fastest worker. You got more money if you made more than the production number. If you met production for four days, but not the fifth, you lost it for the week. This puts too much pressure on people. Slower people could never catch up and were soon fired. It was a very competitive system.

A Women's Factory—continued

Bernice: To me that form of production isn't fair, because the workers who don't make production work just as hard as the ones who do. We want to set a production system based on the group, not the individual.

Eva: Yes, in this way a factory sets a quota each day—for example, 100 dozen blouses. If the workers as a group reach or go over the quota they receive a bonus. This reduces pressure and creates cooperation. It's a chance to feel like, "We earned this together."

Interviewer: That sounds like a very interesting alternative! What else is different about McCaysville?

Eva: McCaysville is a very safe and happy factory. Since the owners work in the factory and experience the environment like everyone else, they make sure it's safe for all.

Interviewer: I noticed one woman leave before the end of the day. Why is that?

Bernice: She got a call from school that her child was sick, so she went to take her home.

Interviewer: Can she just walk out and leave?

Bernice: Many women working here are mothers. We understand family emergencies. I'll fill in for her. She can make up the time later this week. Most factories don't understand that parents do need special consideration. We try to understand women's needs.

Interviewer: In many factories or businesses, the profit that is made goes for higher salaries for owners and top managers. Some goes to stockholders—people who own part of the business, but don't work there. Where does McCaysville Industries profit go?

Eva: At McCaysville, all the money we make goes to pay the workers or goes back into the factory. The owners and managers here *are* the workers. They get only a little more than everyone else. We all work very hard because we know the profits will come back to us as wages and better working conditions. This is very different from most factories.

Interviewer: Do you have any final comments?

Lorraine: Yes, I do. Here at McCaysville women are respected. We are given dignity, asked for our opinions, and treated as human beings. This is very different from most factories. I hope I can continue working here for a long time.

A Women's Factory: Questions

Directions: Discuss one question at a time. Take turns writing the answer in the space provided. When the worksheet is finished, check to make sure everyone agrees with the answers and that spelling and mechanics are correct. When there are major differences of opinion, summarize all ideas.

1. How do the women of McCaysville Industries feel about their workplace?

2. What would you like or dislike if you worked at McCaysville?

3. McCaysville Industries is different from many other workplaces. It is structured more cooperatively. List four examples of this. Explain why the women of McCaysville Industries like those differences.

Example of Cooperation	**Reason Women Like That**
a.	a.
b.	b.
c.	c.
d.	d.

Signed _____

_____

_____

_____

FREEDOM FARM COOPERATIVE WORKSHEET

Jigsaw Sections

A.   Fannie Lou Hamer was born on October 6, 1917, in the state of Mississippi. Her parents were Jim and Ella Townsend. They worked very hard to support their family. Life was hard.

Fannie Lou's parents worked picking cotton on land owned by a rich white man. They picked tons of cotton for the owner, but they stayed poor. The owner paid them very little for their work.

Fannie Lou, her family, and the other people who worked the land were black. The children who lived on this plantation were hungry all the time. They could only imagine how good it would be to have three meals a day. That was only a wish, never something real.

B.   When Fannie Lou was six years old, the boss of the workers saw her playing. He asked her to come pick cotton in the field. If she did, he promised to bring her to his store and give her anything she wanted.

Fannie Lou was hungry. She didn't have good clothes. She decided to go with him. She tried to work as hard as she could so she could get things from the store. She strained and struggled in the field. She picked thirty pounds of cotton!

The boss took Fannie Lou to the store, and she picked out special treats. She was happy for a day. Yet she was sad for many days to come. The boss had tricked her. He found out that she could pick so much cotton even though she was a little girl.

From then on, Fannie Lou had to work in the fields. The sun was hot, her back ached, and her fingers hurt. Still, she had to pick cotton.

Fannie Lou got to go to school for a few years. She loved to learn! But her family was so poor that they needed each and every child to work in the field. After sixth grade, Fannie Lou had to drop out of school. This made her very sad. If her family was to eat, she would have to work.

Jigsaw Sections—continued

C.   During the 1960s, Fannie Lou Hamer became a leader in the Civil Rights Movement. She was brutally beaten for trying to get black people registered as voters. Nevertheless, she continued to fight for equal rights for black people year after year.

Even when she was older, she never forgot how hungry she and her brothers and sisters were as children. She knew that, even in the 1960s, poor children were still hungry.

Fannie Lou had a dream that she worked to have come true. Her dream was that poor black and white people could work together to buy a big piece of land and farm it together. They would plant and reap their food. They would share everything so they would never be hungry again.

She would call this the Freedom Farm Cooperative. People would work together to grow what they needed. They wouldn't have to work for a boss. They would be paid with the food they harvested. All members of the cooperative would share with each other.

D.   Fannie Lou Hamer asked for help from citizens all over the United States to start the Freedom Farm Cooperative. She got the help she needed.

For example, in 1971, 176,000 white high school students in Chicago walked in a March Against Hunger. Each student found a storeowner who would give a certain amount of money for each mile the student walked. The students walked miles and miles. They made a large donation to Ms. Hamer.

Fannie Lou Hamer bought a large piece of land near her home in Ruleville, Mississippi. She bought it, not for herself, but for the Freedom Farm Cooperative. All who worked on the farm were the owners.

Over 5,000 people came to the Freedom Farm Cooperative to plant and harvest food. In this way, many people who were once hungry worked together to create a better life for all.

FREEDOM FARM COOPERATIVE WORKSHEET

Question Cards

A. Fannie Lou Hamer's early life

Describe Fannie Lou's life as a child.

B. The boss's trick

How did the boss trick Fannie Lou?

C. Ms. Hamer's idea for Freedom Farm

Explain Ms. Hamer's plan for the Freedom Farm.

D. Beginning Freedom Farm

Describe ways people cooperated to start Freedom Farm.

COMMUNITY CHILD CARE WORKSHEET

My Contributions to the Game

1. Background Research

I researched:

2. Production of Game

I made:

3. Ideas and Feedback

Ideas I contributed:

Feedback I gave:

signed _____

_____

_____

_____

Group Members

WE HAVE TO DO IT DIFFERENTLY WORKSHEET

Directions

Station I—Each of you picks one problem card. Read your card silently and think of possible ways to handle the problem. Think of steps that different people in the situation could take. Make sure your ideas are cooperative and nonviolent. When all the students in your group are ready, one of you reads your card aloud to the group. Then give your ideas of how to handle the problem. Other group members can then give you more ideas. Take notes on these. Then the next group member reads his card aloud and follows the same process. Continue until all group members have had a turn. Then work independently to write up the ideas for your own card. Exchange with another group member for proofreading and signature.

Station II—Pick one journal entry. Read it and then write two more journal entries for the same child. These two entries should be ones where the child uses competition and/or violence to cope with the problem. Then write three additional entries where the child uses cooperative nonviolent means for dealing with the same problem. After each student in your group has written five entries, gather as a group to read your work aloud, receiving suggestions from other group members. You can then modify your entries if you wish to. Exchange with another group member for proofreading and signature.

Station III—Read the sample "Dear Abby" letter. Discuss family problem letters an advice columnist might receive. Talk about responses the advice columnist might give. If you are in the first, third, or fifth group to come to this station, you should discuss possible family problems. Work independently on a letter to Abby. When everyone is finished, read the letters to the group. Receive suggestions and make revisions. If you are in the second, fourth, or sixth group to come to this station, take the set of letters written by the previous group. Each of you should pick one letter and write a response to it. Then read these aloud to your group, receiving suggestions and making revisions. Exchange with another group member for proofreading and signature.

WE HAVE TO DO IT DIFFERENTLY WORKSHEET

Directions—continued

Station IV—Pick one scenario and the correct number of group members to act it out. Each of those students picks a role and reads the scenario to himself. Then the actors portray the scene, as it is written, for the other group members. Discuss how each family member felt, what each family member wanted, and whether those needs were met. Then the same group of students should act out the same scenario using "I-Messages." By sharing feelings in this way, people can often work out nonviolent solutions to problems. Each character tells how a behavior of another person makes her feel. Remember to use the format learned in class. Here's a reminder: "Burt, when you won't help with chores, I feel angry and taken advantage of. When that happens, I don't have time to do other things that are important to me." That type of I-phrasing is used instead of: "You are bad. It's mean of you not to do your chores. You're being inconsiderate. You don't care if I don't have free time." Again, discuss how each family member felt and wanted, and whether those needs were met. Your group should do more than one scenario, being sure everyone gets at least one turn to be an actor.

As a group, write some "I learned statements"—what you learned by resolving family problems cooperatively.

Station V—Work together as a group listing helpful, nonviolent, cooperative ways in which you and your family can solve problems and help things go smoothly. For example: Using "I-Messages" rather than "You-Messages," offering to help with chores, listening to someone else in the family when he has a problem, being more tolerant of someone else if she is having a hard day. Students in your group can then work individually or together to create posters which remind people of these types of behaviors and why they are important. Posters can have words and drawings on them. You may also want to make smaller single-color copies of your posters which can then be copied and distributed to all class members to color and take home to post. Each group member signs the poster she drew or contributed to.

Station VI—Work in partners. Each pair starts with one math task card. If you finish it, go on. You can solve the problems by talking about them or drawing or acting them out. If you get stuck, ask other group members for help. Check your answers with other group members. Your teacher will call on one member of your partnership to explain how you got your answer.

WE HAVE TO DO IT DIFFERENTLY WORKSHEET
Station I: Problem Cards

Adam Greenberg works on the assembly line in a car factory, five days a week from 7 A.M. to 3 P.M. Three evenings a week he works as a night watchman from 6 P.M. to 1 A.M. Leah Greenberg works as a nurse's aide from 9 A.M. to 5 P.M. Saturday through Wednesday. Rachel, who is ten, is expected to cook dinner on the evenings her mother works. Sometimes seven-year-old Rebecca helps her. Josh, eleven, and Daniel, thirteen, are never expected to help with dinner. They are responsible for shoveling snow, mowing the lawn, and taking out garbage. Both parents feel very strongly that this is the right way to do it.

Corinne Gray is a bank loan officer. Her husband, Samuel, is a lawyer. Sometimes Samuel drinks too much. When he does so, he often hits his wife Corinne or his oldest son, Nathan. He never hits the younger children, Gloria or Sarah. When he doesn't drink, Samuel is loving and involved with his family.

Paul's birth mother was Asian-American and his father was white. They died when he was an infant. He was adopted by the Johnsons, a white family. Now Paul is twelve. While he loves his parents, he is unhappy that they live in a white neighborhood and have all white friends.

Janet, fourteen, babysits every afternoon for her younger siblings: Joan, who is seven, Julian, four, and Jessie and Jeremy, both two years old. Her father is a single parent who works at his house painter job until 7 P.M. Janet tries to do her homework and cook dinner while watching the four younger children. Often she gets frustrated with them and locks them in their rooms to keep them from hurting each other or getting in trouble.

Billy lives with his father, Mike, and Mike's friend Sam. Billy likes Sam a lot but is upset that some children tease him about his father living with another man. Billy makes up stories about women his father dates so the children won't tease him about Sam.

WE HAVE TO DO IT DIFFERENTLY WORKSHEET
Station II: Journal Entries

Dear Diary,

Today has been a crummy day. All day I kept having to go into places that had steps. All day people have been annoyed with me. I do my best with my crutches but I'm still much slower than kids who don't need crutches. I want to be able to go places and do stuff and I want people to understand that usually I won't be as fast as they are.

Dear Diary,

I'm furious! I can't believe it! Evan came over to play today and I was really excited. I've wanted to be his friend all year. Then my neighbor, Mrs. Penn, came over and told my mother she didn't want Evan playing on our street because he's black.

Dear Diary,

Sometimes I don't know what to do. The kids at my new school are nice enough in their ways. Pamela and Duke really seem to be trying to include me in their activities. This makes me feel pretty good, but it seems that everything they do costs money. Today, I could have gone roller-skating with them and on to the video arcade and out for ice cream. I would love to play with them, but they spend in a day what I can spend in a month. Today, I lied to Pamela and told her that I had to go home and help my mother. I'm afraid that if I say no to them too often, they will stop asking me out.

Dear Diary,

Maybe I should just give up! My sister says I need a psychiatrist just because I like to cook. She says boys should be outside playing and it's "unnatural" for me to like cooking.

Dear Diary,

Jimmy has been here overnight three times this month. We love playing with our transformers and have a good time together. Today, he invited me to stay overnight at his house. He has a super set of Legos and he's fun and I want to go. Dad doesn't want me to go because Jimmy's mom has another woman living with her. I don't see how that matters at all.

WE HAVE TO DO IT DIFFERENTLY WORKSHEET

Station III: Dear Abby Sample

Dear Abby,

I'm ten years old and a boy. My parents have always taught me to express my feelings. They've taught me that it's okay to cry when I'm sad. My father and mother both cry when they're feeling bad. Lately, friends have started teasing me and saying I'm not a "real boy." What should I do?

Sincerely,
I want to be me

Station IV: Skits with I Messages

Characters: Mother, Father, Douglas—age eleven

Douglas is upset because his father yelled at him for spilling molasses on the floor his father had just scrubbed. Douglas didn't mean to spill it; he was just making himself a molasses sundae. Father called him a "stupid, inconsiderate idiot."

Characters: Grandpa, Luis—ten, Carmen—seven

Luis and Carmen are fighting over who will feed the cats. Grandpa is exhausted, having had a fight with a co-worker, gotten stuck for an hour on the subway coming home from work, and dropped the groceries, including a dozen eggs, on the front steps. He sends them both to their bedrooms and feeds the cats himself.

Characters: Father, Jeffrey—age twelve

Jeffrey won't get up in time for school. He gets in trouble for being late. The school nurse calls his father and tells him he's an irresponsible parent for not getting his child up on time. When Father wakes Jeff and he refuses to get up, Father tells him he's getting Father in trouble and he's a mean, useless, pain-in-the-neck kid.

WE HAVE TO DO IT DIFFERENTLY WORKSHEET
Station VI: Family Math Problems

---

1. Your mother has been complaining that she has to do all the cooking. She has a full-time job and is tired when she gets home. She doesn't think it's fair. So you all decide that each family member will cook dinner one night a week. That works out well because you live with your grandfather, both your parents, and your three siblings. You have a wonderful eggplant recipe from camp. The problem is it serves forty-two people! You realize that's too much. You decide to make one-sixth of the recipe. Here's the original. Rewrite this recipe so it makes the correct amount for your family.

15 lbs. eggplant

3 quarts ricotta cheese

2 tablespoons salt

12 cloves garlic

½ cup parmesan cheese

1 teaspoon pepper

9 lbs. tomato sauce

1⅓ cups salad oil

4⅔ cups chopped mushrooms

¾ cup parsley

6 eggs

---

2. Your father has been frustrated by your youngest sister's tangled hair. She returned from two weeks at camp with a head full of tangles. You decide to comb it out. You sit her down while your older sister reads her a story. You get out thirty-three knots. Your older sister starts to get laryngitis from reading. You need a new distraction. You start singing to your little sister. You get out twice as many knots as you did during the reading. Then you ask her to tell you stories and you get out two-thirds as many knots as during the singing. While your sister plays with the dog, you get out eight more knots than you had gotten during her storytelling. If your sister now has seventy-eight knots left in her hair, how many knots did she have when you started?

Station VI: Family Math Problems—continued

3. You and your two brothers decide to earn money to buy your father a large ceramic bread bowl for his birthday. He loves to cook and feels sad that your family can't afford special cooking implements. You know that a good bread bowl will be a real treat for him. Your brothers are old enough to babysit. George can earn $1.15 an hour and Dennis earns $.90 an hour. George babysat for seven hours and Dennis babysat for nine hours. You earned $.60 an hour for twelve hours of work delivering groceries. The bread bowl costs $24.90. How much more do the three of you need to earn?

4. Even with your glasses you are legally blind. Some things are much harder for you than they are for other children. One of the things that you have learned to do very well is to make baskets. The pieces are big and you can do a lot of it by feel. You invite three students in your class over to make baskets for the school winter fair. You help them figure out how many yards of basket-reed they need. Gigi is making a square basket with nine strips going each way. Each strip is 18 in. long. Irene is making a rectangular basket with eight strips one way and twelve the other. The eight strips are each 20 in. long. The twelve strips are each 16 in. long. Kendall is making a small square basket with six strips each way, each strip 15 in. long. You are making a heart-shaped basket which would start off with a square base of twelve strips each way, 16 in. long. How many feet of basket-reed do you need to get altogether?

5. Your family is hosting a block party for a new family in the neighborhood. They are the first Hispanic family to move there and they've received a few rude phone calls. You hope that gathering friendly neighbors will help them feel at home in the neighborhood. You decide to arrange flowers. You make three arrangements that each have four daffodils and twice as many tulips. You make two arrangements with seven lilies in each. You make four arrangements that each have four jonquils and eight daisies. How many flowers do you need?

Learning Center A: Letters from Angelina

Directions: Each person in your group chooses a letter to read. The person with the earliest-dated letter reads it aloud. As a group, discuss the question. Continue in the same way for each letter. Each reader writes the group's answer on a separate paper. Hand in answers after all four letters are finished and all sign names to indicate agreement.

Letter 1

Lawrence, Massachusetts
January 11, 1912

Dear Anna,

I have two very exciting things to tell you. Today is my 11th birthday! Mother gave me a peppermint stick. She cried because she didn't have more money to get me other presents. I said I didn't care. I'm excited just to be eleven!

You know how sad I was last year when I had to stop school to work in the woolen mills. Well, the second exciting thing is that I didn't have to go to work today. There is a strike! Maybe if the strike lasts a long time, I can go back to school.

Anyway, a strike means that everyone stops working in protest. Yesterday the American Wool Company cut all the workers' pay. You know, don't you, that Mother, my brother Anthony and I work fifty-six hours a week and each make $8.50 for a six-day week! That's hardly enough to buy food for us all. I don't tell Mother, but I'm always hungry. When I saw our pay this week which was even less than before, I wanted to join the strikers. I called out slogans with the other workers as we left the factory—"Better to Starve Fighting than Starve Working." I'm proud to be a striker.

Your cousin,
Angelina

As a group, decide on three words or phrases that describe Angelina's life.

Signed _____

Learning Center A: Letters from Angelina—continued

Letter 2

Lawrence, Massachusetts
January 24, 1912

Dear Anna,

The strike at Lawrence is very hard, but it's also very exciting! All the mills are closed down and no cloth is being made. Hopefully this will make the owners pay us a fair wage.

We march in the streets with signs explaining why we are on strike. This brings attention to our strike because reporters from many newspapers are here. This is the first time in the United States that so many people have picketed at once. Oh, to picket means to march with signs outside the workplace during a strike. I hope it helps alert other Americans to our terrible working conditions and the low pay we get working in the mills. The picket lines have thousands of people in them. Sixty percent of the whole city of Lawrence is out on strike. The soldiers and policemen patrol the city and guard the factories. Our leaders help keep our spirits high. One leader, Elizabeth Gurley Flynn, called out to our crowd, "Can they weave the cloth with soldiers' bayonets or policemen's clubs?" We all responded, "No!" We know the mill owners cannot run the mills without us.

The union that is organizing the workers is the IWW—the International Workers of the World. This is a union that tries to get all the workers together. Other unions wouldn't allow my mother to join because she was Italian, couldn't speak English, and was a woman! The IWW is different! They believe that only by getting everybody together—men and women, people of different races, immigrants and native-born—can we be strong enough to win better conditions for *all*.

In Lawrence, there are twenty-five nationalities who speak forty-five languages! This is because many people have just come to the United States. The strike committee—the people directing the strike—is made up of one person from each nationality group. In this way, every group gets their ideas listened to and their representative brings back plans to the group.

Over half of the workers are women. My mother and the other women march on the picket lines and help organize the strike. Sometimes my mother and brother and I march together. My mother holds a sign—"Bread and Roses." We are fighting for enough money so we can eat and also for a chance to enjoy the beauties of life. Maybe if we win the strike this will happen.

The IWW holds meetings for us children. Some of my friends still go to school and don't have to work in the mills. They were told by some of their teachers that strikers were lazy and should go back to work or else go back where they came from. These friends were ashamed of their parents for having plain clothes and going out on strike. Elizabeth Gurley Flynn and other union leaders explained to all of us children how going out on strike meant fighting for a better life. It was something to be proud of and not ashamed of. They asked us if we thought it was fair that mill workers who made the finest wool fabrics in the country didn't have enough money for decent clothes? We said, "No!" Now that they stopped to think about it my friends see the courage and strength their parents have and are proud!

It's getting dark and we have no more lamp oil. Goodbye for now.

Your cousin,
Angelina

---

1. Why was it difficult to organize the workers in Lawrence and to go on strike?

2. What did the IWW and its leaders do to overcome those difficulties?

3. If you were a child in Lawrence, would you agree or disagree with your parents if they went on strike? Why?

Learning Center A: Letters from Angelina—continued

Letter 3

Philadelphia, Pennsylvania
March 3, 1912

Dear Anna,

The past week has been the most frightening and most exciting of my life! Let me tell you the story.

Anthony and I were getting very sick and hungry because the strike lasted so long. Remember we had no pay for weeks! There was very little food to eat and I lost ten pounds. We have run out of fuel so we have caught colds easily. This is true for other children too.

People living in New York City and Philadelphia who support our strike got worried. They agreed to take us children into their homes while the strike lasted. That way we could be cared for. We were going to go to Philadelphia.

My mother took my brother Anthony and me to the train. There were about forty children and their parents. The mayor had said that no children should leave Lawrence. The police tried to stop our mothers from putting us on the train. The policemen pushed us and beat us. My mother was choked by a policeman and I was hit with a club. I will never forget how terrible it was!

Thank goodness some reporters were there. They wrote newspaper articles about what happened. This helped other people in America see what we were fighting against. Some people wrote letters to important people about what happened to us. These letters will help us win the strike!

Yesterday we were able to get on the train and go to Philadelphia. I am happy to be safe and have enough food to eat, but I miss my mother and my friends!

With love,
Angelina

What would you write back to your cousin after receiving this letter? Write that short letter.

Learning Center A: Letters from Angelina—continued

Letter 4

Lawrence, Massachusetts
March 23, 1912

Dear Anna,

I arrived home in Lawrence yesterday. I cannot tell you how happy I am! We won the strike! The American Woolen Company has agreed to give workers pay raises and more pay for working overtime. Maybe now our family will have enough to eat. Maybe now we can enjoy life more and be happier.

This strike taught me a lesson. It showed me what people of many different backgrounds can do if they stick together. Because **everyone** struck, the mills couldn't run. We all created one big union—"all for one and one for all." Now I hope **everyone** will have a better life!

Your cousin,
Angelina

1. In what ways did people cooperate in Lawrence? How did that help win the strike?
2. What might have happened that would have caused the strike to fail?

Learning Center B: Bread and Roses

Directions: Take turns reading parts of the background section aloud. Then work together to complete the task.

Background

When the workers at Lawrence were on strike, they made up slogans and sometimes wrote them on picket signs. The slogans would tell others why they were striking and what they wanted.

Some slogans were:

- "We Want Bread and Roses, Too"—Strikers wanted enough pay to feed their families. That was "bread." They also wanted working conditions that allowed them to enjoy the beauties of life. That was "roses." Young girls and women especially carried these signs.
- "Better to Starve Fighting than to Starve Working"—Workers were working fifty-six hours a week and making so little money that families were very hungry. They would be hungry during a strike, too, but they'd be fighting for a better life.
- "With One Big Union We Will Win"—This slogan told outsiders that **all** workers were united and everyone would work together for changes. It was the slogan of the IWW—the International Workers of the World. It was the only union at the time that tried to unite **all** workers.

Task

As a group, make up a slogan that the young people at the Lawrence Strike might want to say to others. Then decide on a design for a picket sign that would have both words and art work. Create that picket sign as a group. Divide work so **each** person has a task. Sign your names on the picket sign.

Learning Center C: The Prices of Profit

Directions: Work as partners on these problems. When you and your partner are finished, check the answers with the other set of partners. Work together until you all agree on the answers and each person can explain how she got the answers. Call the teacher when you are ready. The teacher will check your answers and ask one of you to explain how you got an answer.

1. The highest paid workers in Lawrence made $10.50 a week. They worked fifty-six hours a week. How much did they make an hour?

2. Most workers in Lawrence earned about $8.75 a week. They worked a six-day week. How much did they earn a day?

3. Strikers in Lawrence formed picket lines composed of 20,000 people. If each person, with arms stretched holding on to the next person, took up five feet, how many miles long were the picket lines?

4. In 1905 mill owners in Lawrence made profits of $212,690,048. They took 20% of the amount to pay the workers. How much profit did they have left?

5. Since the workers were on strike, they did not have money to buy food. People from across the United States contributed money for food. Five soup kitchens fed a total of 2,300 people each day. If workers had a bowl of soup for breakfast and one for dinner, how many bowls of soup did each soup kitchen serve in a week?

Learning Center D: The News Tonight: February 20, 1912

Roles

Margaret Adams, reporter
Jacques Renard, age 12, mill worker and striker
Laura Panuska, mother, mill worker and striker
William Wood, owner of the American Woolen Company

Directions

1. Draw Roles

Each person draws a role.

2. Develop Questions

As a group, decide on three important questions that the reporter should ask each person in order to get both information and feelings about the Lawrence strike.

For example: 1. Please tell us about your life before the strike.

2. Why are you on strike?

3. How have you been involved in the strike?

4. Why do you pay the workers so little?

Reporter—write these questions down.

3. Trial Run

Reporter: Conduct a practice interview with each person, one at a time. As one person is being interviewed, others observe.

Observers: At the end of the interview, give praise for what the reporter and person interviewed did well. Give suggestions for improvement.

Reporter and interviewees: Consider making the changes the observers suggested in the final radio broadcast.

4. Taping "The News Tonight"

Using a tape recorder, work as a group to make a radio broadcast from Lawrence in February, 1912. In addition to the interview with each person, you can include an introduction, commercials, and closing comments.

BREAD AND ROSES WORKSHEET

Learning Center E: Solidarity Forever

Background

Music played a very important part in the Lawrence Strike. Thousands of workers sang songs together and marched to the music of bands and drum corps. The music and the songs gave people courage to struggle even though the strike was hard.

One of the favorite songs of the strike was "Solidarity Forever." Below are two verses of the song followed by the refrain. Number off 1, 2, 3, 4, and each read a line of each verse. Say the refrain together. Discuss what these words mean.

"Solidarity Forever"

They have taken untold millions that they never toiled to earn,
But without our brain and muscle not a single wheel can turn.
We can break their haughty power; gain our freedom when we learn
That the Union makes us strong.

Solidarity forever!
Solidarity forever!
Solidarity forever!
For the Union makes us strong.

In our hands is placed a power greater than their hoarded gold;
Greater than the might of armies, magnified a thousand-fold.
We can bring to birth a new world from the ashes of the old.
For the Union makes us strong.

Solidarity forever!
Solidarity forever!
Solidarity forever!
For the Union makes us strong.

Listen to the record or tape of "Solidarity Forever" and practice singing with it.

Imagine you are children your age during the Lawrence strike. Work together to write another verse to "Solidarity Forever." In the verse, express your feelings about your life, your work, and the strike. Practice saying or singing your new verse in unison.

When every group has finished this learning center, you will say or sing all your verses together as a class.

Information Sheet: Mariposa Co-op*

Mariposa means "butterfly." A small food co-op in Philadelphia is similar to a butterfly. Two days a week 250 people, from 100 different households, come to pack, pick up, and buy food. They have pre-ordered it by leaving orders at the store the week before. On the other days the store looks like a cocoon but on those days it looks like a colorful butterfly. Food is bought in bulk quantity from the pre-orders so it all gets sold. The lack of waste keeps prices down.

Mariposa has three part-time paid staff people—a treasurer, a personnel manager, and a store manager. The members all meet every three months to make all the important decisions. All the members, unless they are disabled, must work two hours every month. Some co-ops will allow members to pay more and not work. Mariposa will not. Thus everyone who participates in decision making also knows what it is like to work at the co-op. They all understand the situation. Also, they can all gain skills in working together, in running a small business, and in cooperative problem solving.

Much of the work in this co-op is done at home by members. People drive to different places to pick up the food. They work together to pack and store it. Most of the members live within walking distance of the co-op. They use the bulletin board for all sorts of different information. They talk together and become friends. They exchange information on plumbers, babysitters, carpenters, and dentists.

On all items, the co-op charges 20 percent more than it pays. That money is used for rent, electricity, supplies, and the salaries of the part-time staff.

Mariposa has decided to stay small. They believe it's the only way all members can know each other and be part of all decisions. If many more people want to join, Mariposa will help them start a small new neighborhood co-op.

*Information from "Dandelion," Movement for a New Society.

Information Sheet: North Country Co-op*

North Country Food Co-op is not just a food store. They also serve as a community center and a nutrition-information center. Their sales hit a million dollars last year.

North Country is run by eleven paid staff members who work as a collective. When the store was started in 1971, it was on one family's back porch. Now they have a storefront on a busy street. When they first started, people were simply expected to put their money into a coffee can when they bought food. Now they have electronic cash registers and weigh all items carefully. Instead of the store closing when the staff wanted to go on vacation, it is now open twelve hours a day every day of the week. They sell a wide variety of foods, including those traditionally found at health food stores and those traditionally found at supermarkets.

In spite of all these changes, the philosophy of the food co-op has stayed the same. Members are committed to educating people about food, giving people control over getting food, and building a community.

There is flexibility in the scheduling of work hours as well as an expectation that everyone will help in a crisis. All the workers regularly write evaluations of each person's work. There is also a coffee can labeled "appreciations" where people can write compliments to each other. These are read at the staff meetings.

North Country does not want to get too big. They would rather share their expertise to help another small group start an additional food co-op nearby.

*Information from "Dandelion," Movement for a New Society.

Information Sheet: West Bank Co-op Grocery*

West Bank is a consumer-owned co-op designed to serve its whole neighborhood. They stock a whole variety of food including items not usually found in food co-ops, like Pepsi and Twinkies. West Bank members and shoppers are a cross-section of the community: older people, students, folks of many nations, races and cultures, poor and middle income. The food available ranges from brown rice and seaweed to TV dinners.

The difference at West Bank is not so much in what food they sell but in how they're run. The members, most of whom are neighborhood people, elect a board of directors. That board directs the managers. The managers tell the workers what to do. The workers are all members and have a seat on the board.

When there are worker-openings at West Bank, the co-op advertises for workers in varied cultural settings: the state unemployment office, the Indian Center, the Afro-American Center. They often hire new workers who have no experience with co-ops or with worker self-management. Often this is a problem since, at first, workers don't understand the concept fully enough to be committed to it. However, West Bank believes in open hiring and is willing to make some changes so it will work. They have moved to a system with a hierarchy and with consequences for workers who show up late or don't work well.

West Bank would like to grow larger. They believe more community people would then be exposed to the idea of co-ops. Even in a larger co-op they see members as having much more control than at the supermarket. Recently, they bought the drugstore down the street and it is now being run by the same board of directors.

*Information from "Dandelion," Movement for a New Society.

FOOD CO-OPS WORKSHEET

Co-op Comparison Sheet

Name of Co-op	Mariposa	West Bank	North Country
Pre-order or Storefront			
Organization			
Members (geographic location, socioeconomic class, age)			
Paid Staff			
Members' Work Responsibility			
Decision Making			
Hiring/Firing			
What's Sold			
Role in Community			

Signed _____   _____   _____

A Food Co-op for Our Class

Pre-order or Storefront—Explain why:

Organization

Requirements for Members

Hiring and Managing of Paid Workers

Type of Items Carried

Method for Making Policy Decisions

Signatures of Group Members Participating in This:

_____   _____   _____

WHOSE JOB IS IT TODAY? WORKSHEET

Here's How It's Working

1. Which cooperative job-sharing method are you trying with your family?

2. Complete the following chart:

Name of Person	Chore(s) Done	Likes about This Method	Dislikes about This Method

3. Does your family have ideas for how this method could be improved? List them.

4. Does your family have other job division methods which the class isn't yet trying? List them.

EARNING POWER WORKSHEET

Directions

Needed

One piece of paper, entitled "Our Group's Earning Power"

Pencils with erasers

Scratch paper for each person

One token for each person

Dice

Getting Ready to Play

1. Look at the items in the middle of the game board. As a group, decide which item you want to work for. Take into consideration the amount of time you have to play. Make sure everyone in your group is included in the decision. Place Luck Cards in a pile on the side of the board.

2. Put your token on any space. Throw the dice. Lowest goes first.

3. Move the number of spaces shown on the dice. Your teacher may assign each student a color or colors. If your teacher does this, only count and move on the squares of that color or colors. Read what it says on the square you land on. If it says Luck, draw a Luck Card from the pile. Do what it says. Then return it to the bottom of the pile. If it is a word problem, read it aloud. Everyone works out the problem on paper. Wait until everyone is finished. Then tell the answer. If others agree—fine! If anyone in the group disagrees, work together to find errors. Once everyone agrees, the reader writes the number of the problem and adds the money amount to a paper titled "Our Group's Earning Power." Pass the paper to the next person, and continue in turn. Add the amount earned from your problem to the total amount earned by the group. This will make a column of addition that represents the earnings of the whole group. As you go, check the addition of the person before you.

To Win

When you have earned what you need to buy the item you selected, ask your teacher to check your calculating. Your group wins when you've earned enough to buy what you decided on, and have no math errors. You lose if you have not earned what you needed or if an error is found.

Good luck!

EARNING POWER WORKSHEET

Cards

Question Laura went grocery shopping for Mr. Blum, who had arthritis. She earned $1.50 a week for five weeks. Mr. Blum gave her a $1 bonus at the end of the five weeks. How much did she earn?	Question George, Bette, and their grandmother baked 4 dozen cookies to sell. They each ate 4 cookies. The dog got 6 cookies. How much did they earn if they sold the cookies for $.15 each?
Question Lin-Su and Jessica share a paper route. They deliver 40 papers a week. They made $.01 on weekday papers and $.03 for each Sunday paper. How much did they make in four weeks?	Question Juanita and Rebecca made homemade Christmas and Hanukkah cards. They sold 32 cards for $.15 each. How much did they earn?
Question Mr. Lum's class collected newspapers to be recycled. They were paid $.75 a tied stack. Fifteen students collected 4 stacks each, 12 students collected 5 stacks each, and 6 students collected 7 stacks each. How much did they earn?	Question Jose, Maria, and Peter participated in a walkathon. They got neighbors to pledge $.50 a mile. Jose walked 12 miles, Maria walked 13 miles, and Peter 11 miles. How much did they earn if each had pledges from 4 neighbors?
Question While fishing, Mary and her dad caught 20 fish. They kept the 12 largest and threw the smaller ones back. They ate 2 fish and sold the others for $1.25 each. How much did they earn?	Question Rodney and Angelina made homemade pumpkin pies at Halloween. The ingredients cost $6.13. They sold 7 pies at $2.75 each. How much did they earn?

Cards—continued

Question	Question
Polly and Paul tutor younger children. Each has two students for an hour each Monday, Wednesday and Thursday. How much do they earn a week?	Sally and Ruth shoveled Mr. Kesselman's sidewalk. They earn $4 for a snowfall of 5 in. or less and $6 for a snowfall of more than 5 in. The snowfalls this winter were 2 in., 4 in., 7 in., and 14 in. How much did they earn?
Question	Question
Mr. Gonzalez is confined to bed. Liana reads stories to him each Saturday afternoon. She earns $2 each Saturday. How much did she earn in 14 weeks?	Mr. Smith's class wanted to help clean the neighborhood and earn money. They collected 10 large bottles, 35 small bottles and 52 aluminum cans. They get $.05 for a large bottle, $.02 for a small bottle and $.01 for a can. How much did they earn?
Question	Question
Clayton's class wanted to raise money cooperatively. There are 23 children in the class. Each student will sell a raffle ticket worth $1.50. The prize will cost $7. After paying for the prize, how much will the class earn?	Latisha mows lawns and made $21.45 this week. Her brother Roderick babysat and made $10.90. They pool their resources. How much do they have?
Question	Question
John and Julie ran a Saturday play school. They took care of five children. Each parent paid $4 per child. John and Julie spend $3.73 for refreshments. How much did they earn?	Becky and Paul raised $17 selling books. They gave $5 to the Cancer Society. How much do they have left?

Cards—continued

Question Rosa and a neighbor planted a garden. Each tomato plant cost $.30 and each cucumber plant $.20. They bought a dozen of each. At the end of the summer they had sold $25 worth of vegetables. How much did they earn after paying for the plants?	Question Jake, Sue, and Mei-ling washed 8 cars at $2.20 each. How much did they earn?
Question Tyrone and Beth made a wishing well. Each student paid $.10 a wish. Tyrone and Beth put prizes at the end of the strings. They paid $2.10 for prizes. Twenty students took 1 turn each and 13 students took 2 each. How much did they earn?	Question Maura and her mother raised daffodils. The fourth grade sold them in the spring. They bought all the flowers for $15. They sold them for $.75 a bunch. Mr. Smith's class sold 15 bunches, Ms. Steinberg's class sold 16, and Ms. Lee's class sold 17. How much did they earn?
Question Loretta, Carlos, and Jamila wrote a play and presented it to neighbor children. They spent $4.40 for costume material. They charged $.25 per child. Fifteen children came to the first show and 35 to the second. After paying for costumes, how much did they earn?	Question Luke cleaned the whole house the Saturday his father was sick in bed. His dad thanked him. When he was better, he paid him $2.
Question Larry and Abe made granola bars and sold them at the senior citizens center. They spent $4.45 for ingredients and $1.50 for bus fare. They sold 41 bars for $.30 each. How much did they earn?	Question Paul reads stories into a tape recorder to send to blind people who can't read. Paul earns $1.50 a tape. If he did three tapes each Saturday how much did he earn in a five week period?

Cards—continued

Question Roy and Rebecca take care of pets. They charge $3 a day for cats and $3.50 a day for dogs. This weekend they cared for three dogs and one cat. How much did they earn?	**Luck** You and Laura add your own homemade cookies to Mr. Blum's grocery order just as a present. Go ahead 3.
Luck You and Amber are on your way to get ice-cream sundaes. You see a dog lying in a car with the windows up. The dog is panting. After you eat, you come back out. The dog looks worse. You go from store to store and find the dog's owner. She's very grateful. Take another turn.	**Luck** Your friend Kim is sick. You do her paper route for her and share the earnings. Take an extra turn.
Luck You are helping Marny make tomato sauce. She's never done it before and she's worried. You give good suggestions and encouragement and you chop lots of onions. Go ahead 5.	**Luck** After collecting newspapers for recycling, you can't be bothered taking them in. You stuff them all in your basement. Lose a turn.
Luck You and Ed are baking bread for the hot-lunch program. He's telling lots of funny jokes. Unfortunately, you forget to put in the yeast. The bread doesn't rise right, but you have a good time baking and the kids are pleased to have hot bread, even if it's flat. Take another turn.	**Luck** You get mad at your friend José while fishing with him. You push him in the lake and row away. Go back 10.

Cards—continued

Luck After you and Susie baked cookies for your school fair, you left them all on the counter while you went out to play. The dog ate all but two of them and he licked those. Lose a turn.	**Luck** Your neighbor, Mr. Lin, is upset because a skunk just sprayed his pet wolf-hound. He stands there holding his nose shut. You and Tamitha go to the store for tomato juice and give the dog a bath in it. Go ahead 5.
Luck During the walkathon you are very good at encouraging Tameka who is having trouble walking. Go ahead 4.	**Luck** You, Anthony, Arlene, and Adam just finished building a clubhouse. You each took responsibility for building one wall. You're really pleased until you realize that no one left an opening for a door. Go back 5.
Luck Your friend Matthew is in a grumpy mood. You invite him to go apple picking and tell him how much you like him as a friend. Go ahead 3.	**Luck** Justin offered to help you shovel your driveway. Then you can both go shovel other driveways. You are pleased, but you get mad at him because he's not as fast as you. You dump a shovelful of snow down his back. Lose a turn.
Luck You and Charisse are raking leaves to earn money. You get a huge pile and Amina comes out and scatters them. You convince her to help you repile them. Take another turn.	**Luck** Lizzie hadn't combed her hair for a week. She'd been swimming twice a day. Her grandparents are coming to visit and don't like tangled hair. You spend 6 hours helping her unknot it. Go ahead 4.

EDUCATING OURSELVES, OUR FRIENDS, AND OUR NEIGHBORS
WORSHEET

Stereotypes of Native Americans

Name of book _____

Author _____

Is the author a Native American? _____

Setting of story _____

Time period of story _____ Native American group _____

List three words which describe how you feel about the book.

_____

Write a sentence or two which summarizes the plot. _____

_____

_____

What can you tell about the author's attitude toward Native Americans? Is the author Native American? _____

_____

_____

What attitudes or views does this book show about Native Americans? Give specific examples and page numbers. _____

_____

_____

From the information you have, do you think those are stereotypes? If so, explain why. Do you think those stereotypes are true? Why or why not? What information are you using? Where did you get it? How will you know if it is accurate? _____

_____

_____

_____

What more information do you need to check if these stereotypes are true? How can you get it? How will you know if it's accurate? _____

_____

_____

Signed _____

_____

244

6 MAKING EVERYONE WINNERS ACROSS THE LAND

What would be the potential for our nation if cooperative ideas and programs were implemented? Lessons in this chapter ask students to consider this question and examine ways to make everyone winners.

First students investigate the effects of excessive competition on our nation, and its people as a whole. While some lessons in section A, "Societal Repercussions of Competition" highlight individuals and families, students are asked to think about the broader implications of these situations for millions of people across the country. Lessons provide ways to explore the U.S.-wide effect of competitive individualism and blaming-the-victim. Students examine how competitive policies and practices of particular institutions, and of our economic system in general, can foster conflict between diverse groups of people, rather than unity and common purpose.

"Collaborating Nationwide," section B, contains lessons that give students examples of the ways diverse groups from all over America have cooperated to change the effects of a competitive system. From the Underground Railroad to the United Farmworkers' boycott, lessons provide models of those things which people have accomplished interdependently. These models present a vision of what is possible.

Roadblocks to a more cooperative nation are many. Lessons in section C, "Overcoming Barriers to a Cooperative Society," help students examine some of them. Lessons offer examples of ways in which society has attempted to overcome competitive individualism. Students consider the ramifications of seeing problems as national ones rather than individual ones. They explore how antagonistic groups have overcome their differences in order to work for common goals. Students learn to investigate the needs of *all* people, in order to structure institutions and systems to work for everyone. Through activities, students are able to examine their connectedness to other people across the nation, especially people they don't know. Students then determine how their choices and actions can have positive (or negative) effects across the entire country.

The final section, "Students Networking for Change," suggests ideas and activities for cooperating with other people nationwide. From becoming active in a national student group to stop nuclear war, to writing articles on peoples' cooperative community endeavors for national magazines, to jointly developing a book, slide tape, or video that will be valuable to other young people across the country, students learn that they can act with and for others they don't know to help make everyone winners!

This chapter introduces a new cooperative learning format, the treasure hunt. It offers additional lessons with cooperative card game, learning center, cross-age and research formats in addition to the more basic ones.

Lessons in this chapter are based on the assumption that excessive competitive practices and institutions in our nation can be counterproductive to many citizens' well-being. This is not a commonly examined idea, and some teachers and students may find it unpalatable. For any lesson, a teacher can have some students present the prevailing notion of the benefits of competition and others do further research and give support to ideas implicit here. In this way, critical thinking and stimulating discussion can be generated.

Because of the increased complexity of the learning formats, some lessons may appear quite involved or confusing at first. At this point in the year, students should be used to the more basic formats and need more challenge to stay stimulated. Some lessons appear long, but this is only because most of the hard work is done for you. For example, game cards are made, treasure hunt slips designed and so forth. This saves you work and makes the lessons easier to use. Once prepared, you can use them year after year. So don't let the initial complexity of some lessons deter you. Jump in!

A. SOCIETAL REPERCUSSIONS OF COMPETITION

SUBJECT—SS, M
FORMAT—GROUP
PROJECT

With the Odds Against Them _____

OBJECTIVES   To define and understand the effects of competitive individualism on a national level
To examine how competitive individualism can cause a "blaming-the-victim" mentality
To explore the price the whole society pays for competitive individualism

MATERIALS   A deck of playing cards for each group (four to five students per group)
Worksheets—"Life Hurdle Cards" (to be cut up), "Information Sheet," pages 294–298

IMPLEMENTATION   Tell students that they will play a card game called Life Chances. The game will test their skill in hand-eye coordination, math number matching, and group cooperation. If they work quickly and efficiently, they can do well. You will reward the most skilled group.

In preparation for this lesson, arrange decks of cards to reflect the resources and opportunities of different groups in our society.

GROUP A   Upper-class white men: Full deck of cards minus aces, twos, threes, no hurdle cards

GROUP B   Upper-class women or upper-class minority males: Full deck of cards minus aces, twos, threes, group B hurdle cards

GROUP C   Middle-class white men: Full deck of cards minus kings, queens, jacks

GROUP D   Middle-class women or middle-class minority males: Full deck of cards minus kings, queens, jacks, hurdle cards for groups B and D

GROUP E   Poor white men: Aces through tens, with only three of each type

GROUP F   Poor women or poor minority males: Aces through tens, with only three of each type, hurdle cards for groups D and F

Divide students into heterogeneous groups of about five. If groups are to be uneven, put extra students first in group A, then B, and so on. Call the groups by their letter name and distribute decks accordingly.

Explain these rules. Each group gets a pack of cards. There will be three rounds of four minutes each. Choose a dealer and scorekeeper for each round. Dealer shuffles and deals cards. At your signal, "go," students begin to play. Each person turns his top card over. If there are any matches, they make the match and call out the combined value of the cards. The scorekeeper writes the score down. Score cards according to their value with Aces—1, Jacks—11, Queens—12, Kings—13. The matched cards are put to the side. Unmatched cards go under each person's deck and play continues. Groups may reshuffle the cards once during each round. Tell students there may be a few chance cards in the deck. If they turn one up, read it, and follow the directions. Then place it aside.

Call time at four minutes. Ask groups to double check their points and mark them on the board. Praise the high-scoring group for their excellent hand-eye coordination, math matching skills, and group cooperation. Blame low groups for their lack of skill and hard work. Tell them to work harder. If any group complains about the hurdle cards, say something like, "If you work hard, you can succeed," and quickly move on. Many classes will realize they have been set up. Nevertheless, continue the activity.

Proceed in the same way for two more rounds. Supervise groups C–F to make sure hurdle cards are shuffled into the deck. Make note of pertinent student comments when scores are posted or at other appropriate points during the game. These comments can be discussed later.

DISCUSSION

It's important to leave plenty of time for discussion of this activity. Be sure to begin by discussing feelings. Encourage all students to share their feelings.
1. What were some of the feelings you had during this activity? Why did you feel that way? (Ask people in different groups separately.)
2. The group that won, how do you feel about how well you did? Why do you think you got so many points?
3. Groups that did poorly, how do you feel about how you did? How do you account for not doing as well?
4. Did you think that all groups had an equal chance to win? Why or why not?
5. Was it a fair game? Why or why not?

After student responses, if it hasn't come out in discussion by now, tell students that groups did not begin equally. Explain the distribution of cards and the existence of hurdle cards, or have students share the composition of their decks with each other.

6. How do you feel knowing this?
7. Now do you feel it was a fair game? Why or why not?
8. Did the losers lose because they didn't work hard? Did they deserve to lose?
9. Did the winners deserve to win? Why or why not? Was it really because they were more skilled that they won?

Tell students the groups represented various groups in our society. Distribution of cards was in proportion to the amount of money groups have. The hurdle cards point out the actual roadblocks and the discrimination different groups face. Have students read the hurdle cards aloud to the whole class.

Explain to students that you were playing a role in the activity. You blamed slow groups for not doing well and told them to work harder. This wasn't the way you **really** felt! You told other groups how wonderful they were. You knew that no matter how hard people worked, they couldn't catch up because of how they started out and the hurdles they faced. You knew it wasn't because of hard work or skill, but because of their high cards and lack of hurdles that the top groups did well. You said what you did because that's what people say. And that's what institutional practices reflect in our society. The idea behind this is competitive individualism.

Remind students that they learned in the lesson on the Solar Design Project ("Headstarts: For Some or All?", Chapter 4) how competitive individualism affects individuals. Ask someone to remind the class what they learned in that lesson.

Competitive Individualism

Discuss the following with students: Competitive individualism is based on the belief that competition is fair and that each individual has an equal chance to succeed or win in a situation. An individualist feels that each person succeeds on his or her own merit. The individualist doesn't take into account the advantages his group has to begin with and the disadvantages others have.

Explain that competitive individualism also affects whole groups of people in our society. In society, as in the game, groups of people begin life with unequal opportunities. Some groups have more money than others. Some face discrimination because of their race or sex. This is shown by the life hurdle cards.

When groups with less money or more hurdles are not as successful in society, groups with advantages often blame *them* for their problems, rather than blaming the unequal opportunities. This is called "blaming-the-victim." For example, when poor minority people are without jobs, some people blame them for being lazy. In fact, the lack of money, the discrimination faced in education, and the job market itself present hurdles to getting jobs. Furthermore, there are not enough jobs for all of the population . . . though there could be. Equal education and employment opportunities and more equal financial resources for everybody would best create fair chances for all. Blaming-the-victim doesn't make sense. It makes things worse—because it hides the truth. And it hurts people who're already hurting. It is a way of avoiding change . . . change we all need . . . to be healthy and happy and free.

10. In what ways does our nation lose out because of competitive individualism and blaming-the-victim?

Pass out the information worksheets. Students work in small groups to complete worksheets. After all groups are finished, discuss these final questions:

11. Based on the information items, what are your feelings and ideas about competitive individualism?
12. Who benefits from it? How? Who does it hurt? How?
13. What could be done to change the negative effects of competitive individualism?

COMPLETION   A student receives credit for this activity if she participated in the Life Chances game and contributed to completing the worksheets, as indicated by her signature.

The Slide, Scream, and Splash Water Slide Company

OBJECTIVES

To understand how competition among workers for jobs in the U.S. affects the perceptions and feelings of workers

To examine ways in which competition between different groups of workers affects options for improved job opportunities for all

To understand how an economic system based on competition fosters divisiveness among groups of workers

To consider alternatives that diverse groups of Americans have in dealing with a competitive economic system

MATERIALS

Worksheet—"Group Information Sheets" (cut up), "Individual Information Sheets" (cut up), pages 299–302, small tokens students will appreciate—e.g., peanuts, novelty pencils, wrapped candy, and so forth.

Video This Lesson!

If you have access to a video camera in your school, this is one of a number of lessons that would be good to videotape. The camera is technically simple to use even for novices. Though it seems you and the students would be self-conscious about the camera, experience shows that this eases quickly. A major advantage of videotaping is that students can look back at their interactions and analyze what was going on. This is much more effective than trying to remember correctly, especially if the activity was complex and was a simulation where students were actively, emotionally involved.

IMPLEMENTATION

Tell students they will participate in a simulated experience—an experience in class that is like a situation in real life. Some of them will be owners of a company and others will be members of different groups of people who want jobs. The situation they will role play is very much like what happens to groups of workers across our country every day!

Divide students into five groups. Announce the five groups: owners of the Slide, Scream, and Splash Water Slide Company, white male workers, white female workers, minority male workers, and minority female workers. Give each group "General Information: Slide, Scream, and Splash Water Slide Company" for background and discussion.

Provide small tokens (see Materials above). At the beginning of the simulation each owner is given ten tokens and each person who gets a job will be given one token.

Explain to students how the simulation will proceed. The Board of Directors of Slide, Scream, and Splash have decided to open up ten new jobs and the Board will decide who will get the jobs. Each group will have one minute to present reasons why members of their group should be hired. Then each person will have ten seconds to say why she as an individual should be hired. Owners of SSS may make any kinds of decisions they want to during the simulation.

Give the groups fifteen minutes for planning. Give each group its information sheet to read and discuss. Give each student an individual Information Card. Groups wanting jobs plan what they will say in their argument to the owners. Members of the Board of Directors can discuss how they will decide who will get jobs. After ten minutes, potential workers have five minutes to interact with the Board of Directors. They can ask the members questions, make requests, or do anything they feel is needed. Then they have five minutes left for planning in small groups.

Don't announce initially that groups can talk among themselves; however, if they ask, indicate that they can. During the planning, subtly remind students the Board of Directors can make any decisions. For example, if workers ask if they can "make up things" to help them get the jobs, tell them they can. If members ask if they can increase or decrease the number of jobs, tell them they can. The simulation may go on in any way the students want to take it. As a teacher, you will need to use your judgment about when to intervene, if at all, and when to end the role play.

At the end of the planning period, the Board of Directors hear each group's argument. Members listen next to individual arguments. Encourage members to be strict in limiting groups and individuals to the prescribed time. The Board of Directors has ten minutes to make its decisions. Then it announces the decisions to the whole class and gives each new employee a token.

During the ten-minute period, if other groups, singly or collectively, try to influence the Board of Directors, allow that to continue. If groups just sit and do nothing, have each student write responses to the following open-ended questions:

- Feelings I have now about myself in my role are . . .
- Feelings I have now about the other groups are . . .
- Feelings I have about other individual workers are . . .
- Feelings I have about the owners are . . .

Rainbow Coalition

In Boston, when organizing his mayoral campaign, Mel King named his group *The Rainbow Coalition*. His support crossed all color and ethnic lines. Betsy Rose, a local folk singer, wrote a song entitled: *We All Came over on Different Ships But We're in the Same Boat Now* about the various origins of current "Americans" and our common current needs.

DISCUSSION   Leave plenty of time for discussion of this activity since strong feelings may be generated.
1. How do you feel now, and why? (Go around the room and give each student the chance to respond, if she wishes to.)
2. How do members of the job-seeking groups feel toward people in other job-seeking groups? Why do you feel that way?
3. How do you feel about the other individual workers? Why do you feel that way?
4. How do members of the different groups wanting jobs feel about the Board of Directors? About their decisions?
5. Was this situation competitive or cooperative? Why? How did this affect your feelings toward other people?
6. Was this situation fair? Why or why not? If not, what could have been done to make it more fair?

7. Did the Board of Directors have other choices? Like what? Why didn't they think of these or act upon them? (For example, the owners had the choice of expanding the number of jobs.)
8. What other choices did the workers have that they didn't act upon? Why didn't they think of them or act upon them? (For example, the worker-groups had the choice of getting together to convince or to pressure the owners to increase the number of jobs so there would be enough jobs for all.)

If students don't raise these options themselves, discuss other choices with them.

Tell students that what happened in the simulation today is what happens across our country all the time. Many people are forced to compete for few jobs. It is understandable that people in this situation would develop competitive and angry feelings toward other people who need those same jobs!

Have You Heard . . .?

- "Women are taking away men's jobs. Men need jobs to support their families."
  Reply—What about women who have families to support? Most women work because of economic necessity.

- "Minorities and women aren't qualified."
  Reply—This isn't true. It is used as an excuse to keep minorities and women out of jobs. Besides, what are critics doing to see that job-training and education programs are set up so *all* people have a fair chance to become qualified?

- "Minorities fought for affirmative action and now women are taking the jobs," or "Women fought for affirmative action and now minorities are taking the jobs."
  Reply—Both groups fought for affirmative action. The problem is there just aren't enough jobs to go around.

In all these cases, women and minorities are pitted against each other. The real problem is that there aren't enough jobs to go around. To change this situation, business and government could create enough jobs for all—if they wanted to.

---

9. Being part of a system that makes workers compete against each other for jobs often encourages each group of workers to see themselves as "we" and other groups as "they." What is another way to look at this situation?
10. What could workers do to try to create a more fair situation for all?

Working Together for Jobs for All

- Minority and white workers have organized unions that fight for more jobs and better working conditions for all.

- Women and minorities have fought together for affirmative-action policies in order to give both women and minorities an equal chance for jobs.

- Minorities and whites, men and women, are working together for "jobs with peace." "Jobs with peace" is a plan that would cut down on military spending in order to create more jobs that will meet the human needs of all people. (See lesson "Jobs with Peace," Chapter 7.)

- Women and men, people of color, and whites can get together and insist that some of the high profits corporations make (that usually go to shareholders and top management) be shared more with workers and be used to create more jobs for more workers.

11. What could owners do?
12. To what extent do you believe that everyone in our society should have the right to a job so they can support themselves and their family? What, if anything, should businesses and the government do about that?

Explain to students that many companies in the United States make high profits which go to owners and stockholders. At the same time, there are many people competing for the few jobs that there are. Many of the jobs that there are have terrible working conditions. Such competition keeps workers from getting together to demand more jobs for all. Also our nation is losing out on the talent, skill, and hard work of many many of its citizens.

Companies could create more jobs and reduce their profits. Few people take the time to stop and ask this question: "Is it fair that some people are making huge profits while other people are without work?"

The goal of a cooperative economic system would be to insure jobs for all. People would not have to compete against each other to be assured a job—a job that means their survival and sometimes that of their family. Tell students they will learn more about those alternatives soon.

Profit for Whom?

In 1982 General Motors made a profit of .963 billion dollars. In that same year, G.M. workers signed a contract that included concessions. In 1983 the profits of G.M. rose to 3.730 billion dollars.

In 1983 G.M. gave bonuses of 181.7 million dollars to its top 5,805 managers. They received an average of $31,284 each. The average worker received a profit sharing "bonus" of $640.

G.M.'s top officers gave themselves over 1 million dollars each in bonuses.
For example: Chairman of the Board of G.M. $1,490,000.00
              President of G.M. $1,329,970.00

Corporate profits in the U.S. in 1982 were 69 billion dollars. In the same year, the unemployment rate was 9.4%—close to 20,000,000 people. This figure does not include discouraged workers who had lost their jobs and stopped looking or underemployed people, people who have part-time jobs because they can't find full-time jobs.

At the same time, the corporate tax rate has been declining steadily since 1953 while the tax on individuals has been increasing. In the early 1950s corporations paid over $.70 in federal taxes for every one dollar individuals paid. In 1981 corporations paid $.21 for every dollar an individual paid.

Institute for Labor Education and Research

254

SUBJECT—M, LA, SS
FORMAT—JIGSAW

Moving

OBJECTIVES

To explore how groups of people in our country can work against each other to the detriment of all groups, rather than cooperating for the good of all

To explore how policies and practices of institutions can cause groups to work against each other

To examine a specific case (housing) of lack of cooperation and to discover the prices paid for that by individuals, groups, and our nation as a whole

MATERIALS

Worksheets—"Dialogues" (cut up), "Questions," pages 303–308

IMPLEMENTATION

Explain to students that they will examine an example of the prices groups of people pay—that is, what they lose out on—by working against each other, rather than cooperating.

Divide students into groups of four and into partners within them. Make sure each student with reading problems is paired with a good reader. Assign pairs of Hector and his mother, Ms. Morales, to one set of partners and Theresa and her father, Mr. Riley, to the other.

Distribute a set of dialogue sections to each group. Students place them in chronological order and divide them among the Morales and Rileys. Students read their parts aloud, in sequence. Encourage spirited reading. If students are confused at any point, they stop and discuss that dialogue section as a group.

When students are finished reading, pass out one copy of the worksheet, "Questions," which students discuss and answer as a group. Then come together as a whole class for discussion.

DISCUSSION

1. Discuss each of the questions on worksheet "Questions." Questions 4 and 5 can be difficult. If students have trouble, use information from the box below in discussion.
2. What happened in Greenwood happens in other cities across the U.S. today. What are the prices people pay for this? What prices does our nation pay?
3. Sometimes one group of people sees itself as "wes" and sees another as "theys," when in fact both groups have things in common. In this case, whites and Puerto Ricans had in common the wish for affordable housing in a friendly neighborhood. If whites and Puerto Ricans had cooperated, who would have been the "wes," who the "theys"? How could we all be "wes"?
4. What examples can you think of in your life or in society where groups see each other as "we" and "they"? What are the prices of this competition to the nation? How could they work together for gains for all?

You might want to tell students that blockbusting is illegal and most realtors and banks don't engage in such practices. Nevertheless it has been, and still is, one form of institutional discrimination practiced to maintain racially segregated areas.

COMPLETION

A student gets credit for this activity if each person in his group participates in the dialogue and contributes to completing the "Questions" worksheet, as indicated by their individual written contributions and signatures.

FOLLOW-UP

1. **Expository Writing**
   a. Write a statement as the real estate agent who tries to convince Ms. Morales not to consider buying a house in the Lakeview or Parkside areas of the city. Then write a response from Ms. Morales.
   b. Write a statement that might be written by a neighborhood group opposing Puerto Ricans moving into the neighborhood. Then write a response from Theresa.

2. **Math**
   Sample word problems for "Moving"
   a. Mr. Riley said his house should sell for at least $35,000. If he gets only $30,000, how much money does he "lose"? What fraction of the total worth of the house does he lose? If he had a $105,000 house and he lost at the same rate, how much would he be selling that house for?

   b. If Ms. Morales pays $50,000 for a house instead of the $45,000 she could afford, how much more money is she paying? What fraction of the $50,000 is that?

   c. The Morales can afford the mortgage on $50,000 if Aunt Carmen lives with them. Suppose the monthly mortgage and interest payments are $510 and Aunt Carmen pays one third. How much does Ms. Morales pay each month? How much does she pay in a year?

   d. The Rileys were paid $30,000 for their old house and bought a new one for $48,000. How much more did they pay for the new house?

   e. If their old mortgage and interest payments were $370 a month and their new one is $440 a month, how much more are they paying each month? How much more in a year?

f. Ms. Morales has a take-home pay of $460 a check, and receives two checks a month. If she is paying the mortgage/interest you calculated in problem c, how much does that leave her a month for other expenses? If her food costs for the family are $250 a month and utilities average $110 a month and medical insurance is $90 a month, how much does she have left for other expenses?

What's to Lose? What's to Gain?

Policies and practices of institutions often keep people of different backgrounds or races from seeing what they have in common, and working together. Minorities and whites lose out when banking and real estate institutions use blockbusting, steering, and redlining, as depicted in the account, "Moving."

Loses
Theresa: Loses friends
Mr. Riley: Loses $5,000
Hector: Loses a chance to live in Parkside
Ms. Morales: Loses $5,000

Whites and Puerto Ricans could have
1. Worked together to make Greenwood an integrated neighborhood. Whites would stay and Puerto Ricans be welcomed.
   and/or
2. Worked together to oppose and then change bank and real estate practices—steering, redlining, and blockbusting—so people could choose where they want to live.

Gains of such cooperation
Theresa: New Puerto Rican friends, Hector as a neighbor
Mr. Riley: A better relationship with his daughter, since he wouldn't force her to move. He might gain her respect. Not having to move
Hector: If he moved to Parkside: living near his friend Tanya and the city pool
       If he moved to Greenwood: living in an integrated neighborhood
Ms. Morales: If she moved to Parkside: a house she could afford
           If she moved to Greenwood: an integrated neighborhood

---

Janice Bernstein describes the results of redlining in Boston, Massachusetts. "The banks didn't lose anything. The only ones who lost out were the people. The blacks were bilked and so were the whites. It was a deliberate scheme to make a lot of money."

Nancy Seifer, *Nobody Speaks for Me,
Self Portraits of Working Class Women.*

Team Players? _____

OBJECTIVES   To understand the effects, in terms of daily life, of a competitively-structured economic system

To explore the benefits and losses of "winning" in such a system

To examine the effects of unemployment on the people that a competitive economic system sets up to be losers

To understand the connection between those who gain privileges from, and those who suffer from, such a system

To explore the prices and the benefits (to all people and to the nation) of a more co-operatively-structured economic system

MATERIALS   Worksheets—"Dialogue" and "Questions," pages 309–313

IMPLEMENTATION   Divide students into heterogeneous groups of four. Either assign the following roles to group members or have students choose roles: two readers, one questioner, and one writer.

Distribute the "Dialogue" worksheet to all students. Tell students that the two readers are to read "Team Players?" out loud while the other two group members follow along silently. Then distribute the "Questions" worksheet to the questioner and writer. The job of the questioner is to read the question and ask each person in the group for opinions. She helps the group decide on an answer. On questions of opinion, if there is no consensus, she helps people clarify the different points of view. The writer writes the group answer on the worksheet. If there are two opinions, he summarizes each point of view.

Encourage group members to listen to each other carefully because in the group discussion you will call on anyone to present the group answer to any question. (Of course, remind students that they also listen because it's polite and they learn more that way!) If there are two points of view, the person answering must state the two opinions.

When groups are finished, come together for discussion.

The Hidden Costs of Unemployment

The cost of unemployment is not only the waste of potential income—the wages, taxes, and output that are lost to society when people aren't producing.

In 1981 one in four Americans went through the experience of losing a job. The experience of being out of work imposes heavy personal and social costs, few of which can be measured in money.

- Headaches, upset stomach, ulcers, insomnia and hypertension often follow job loss.
- Because for pregnant women and their babies unemployment means poor nutrition, a 1% rise in unemployment is quickly followed by a sharp rise in the mortality rate of newborn babies.
- Family instability often surfaces in the forms of depression, alcoholism, juvenile delinquency, child neglect and abuse.
- Each time the unemployment rate goes up 1%, 320 more suicides occur that can be directly traced to job loss.

Dollars and Sense (December 1982)

DISCUSSION

1. Discussion questions 1–13 from the worksheet.
2. Explain to students that the situation of Rodney's father and Stacey's father is similar to that of thousands of Americans. Millions of people are unemployed and millions of others are overworking and some of those are stepping on others in the effort to become winners. What effects does this have on our country as a whole?
3. Tell students that the economic system **does not have to be** organized competitively. If it were organized more cooperatively, many more people could have jobs. Status, power, and money could be distributed more equitably. What would the benefits to individuals and society be in this situation? The losses? How could the losses be lessened?

COMPLETION

A student receives credit for this activity if, in discussion, all group members called on answered the questions satisfactorily.

Connections: Winners and Losers

In a competitive capitalist economic system the gains of "winners" are often directly connected to others' losses. For example:

- Because of the size and amount of money available to them, big companies can bid highest and buy out parts necessary to make a product and put smaller companies out of business.
- Baseball teams with the most money to spend can buy the best players and poorer teams more often end up in the cellar.
- Companies with the most resources can undercut others in price wars until others go out of business. Then the "winner," having eliminated the competition, can set prices as high as it wants.

GOING FURTHER

1. Interview someone who has been unemployed. Find out: how he felt, how unemployment has affected his family, what he believes should be done to deal with unemployment.
2. Find out what percentage of the U.S. population is unemployed. How does this affect our country?

The Voice of Martin Luther King

In our society it is murder, psychologically, to deprive a (hu)man of a job or an income. You are in substance saying to that (hu)man that s/he has no right to exist. You are in a real way depriving him (or her) of life, liberty, and the pursuit of happiness, denying in his (or her) case the very creed of . . . society. Now, millions of people are being strangled that way. The problem is international in scope. And it is getting worse, as the gap between the poor and the "affluent society" increases.

WIN, November, 1967 (reprinted in August 1983).

B. COLLABORATING NATIONWIDE

SUBJECT—SS, M,
LA, MUSIC
FORMAT—LEARNING
CENTER, CROSS
GRADE

Underground Railroad—The 1800s _____

OBJECTIVES

To learn about a historical example of citizens across the United States cooperating to run an underground railroad

To learn about the growth and development of a cooperative movement and the impact it had on a wide variety of people in a variety of roles

To learn about how a large group of people can accomplish a task which would have been impossible for any one person or even for a small group of people

MATERIALS

Copies of records: Pete Seeger, *I Can See a New Day* and *Bright Morning Star, Arisin* or *Holly Near, Lifeline,* (records are often available at the public library) record player, large newsprint, markers, thin cardboard, crayons, tongue depressors, file cards

Dictionary, recent fifth grade American history textbooks with information on the Underground Railroad and several of the following books: *Freedom Crossing* by Margaret Clark; *Harriet Tubman: Conductor on the Underground Railroad,* Ann Petry; *Runaway to Freedom,* Barbara Smucker

One copy of each worksheet, pages 314–317

IMPLEMENTATION

Review with students an overview of the Underground Railroad. Be sure all students know that it existed from 1790, in Ohio, until the Civil War. It was most active in the 1840s and 1850s. Be sure students understand that it was an illegal method to help slaves escape, first to the north, then later to Canada. Read aloud from some of the books listed above or from current American history textbooks.

Divide students into six heterogeneous groups. Explain that the first task is for all members to complete the project at their assigned station and present it to others in the class. They are then to modify the activity in order to present the information to a younger class with whom they'll be working. (You need to select the class ahead of time and work out an arrangement with the teacher.)

DISCUSSION

1. What did you learn about the Underground Railroad? Did people cooperate on the Underground Railroad? How?
2. In what ways was cooperation essential for the Underground Railroad? What would have happened otherwise?

3. What did you learn because of the way information was presented to your group (in song, through math, through reading . . .)? How did that method help you to learn?
4. What was it like to modify the activity for younger children? In what ways was that hard? Easy?
5. How did the younger children do when working cooperatively?
6. How did the younger children do when learning about the Underground Railroad?

COMPLETION A student gets credit for this lesson if each member of her group:

Language Arts: Writes a story with a partner, corrected by others.

Math: Completes a math problem correctly, checked by others.

Puppets: Makes a puppet and contributes to the puppet show.

Vocabulary: Makes four vocabulary cards and indicates how she contributed to making the cooperative game.

Music: Learns a song and teaches it to others.

And when each group member has documented her contribution to the teaching of the material to younger students.

**American History: A Rich Source of
People-to-People Cooperation across America**

Another period filled with many examples of people working together, often in defiance of the law, is the American Revolution. Have students examine their texts (and/or supplementary books) for examples of boycotts or acts of noncompliance that united people in cooperative action across state lines.

For your information, see Howard Zinn's *A Peoples' History of the United States.* It provides numerous examples of ordinary citizens working cooperatively in peoples' movements for change.

Whose Birthday Is It?

Many classrooms celebrate the birthdays of George Washington and Abraham Lincoln. In recent times many celebrate Martin Luther King's birthday. Here are some suggestions for celebrating the birthdays of other important people who worked cooperatively for a more just world.

Some possible birthdays are:
      Martin Luther King, January 15
      Lucretia Mott, January 31
      Frederick Douglass, February 12
      Susan B. Anthony, February 15
      Mother Jones, May 15
      Mohandas Gandhi, October 2

1. Read aloud a short biography, or sections of a biography. Have students look especially for examples where the person helped other people, was helped by other people, accomplished something by working cooperatively that she couldn't have accomplished alone.
2. Have students develop a time line for the person. The time line should include events and efforts which show the person working with others toward a common goal.
3. Have students develop a commemorative stamp designed to show how this person worked with others for a specific goal—for example, not a picture of Susan B. Anthony's profile, but one showing her at a meeting with a group of women planning a demonstration.
4. Do role plays with the person and others with whom he worked. Show scenes where the person worked with others to accomplish a goal that he couldn't accomplish alone.

Follow the Drinking Gourd

Many slaves escaped bondage along the Underground Railroad, a system of secret, safe places to hide and people to give food and shelter on the way to the free states of the North and Canada. This song provided a map and time-table: Follow the Big Dipper, it points the way to the North and freedom!

Go Down, Moses

When Israel was in Egypt land —
    let my people go
Oppressed so hard they could not stand —
    let my people go
Go down, Moses, way down in Egypt land
Tell ol' Pharoah let my people go!

    Em B⁷ Em–(2x) Em B⁷EmC/Em B⁷Em–
    Em–Am–EmAmEmAm/Em–Bm–Em B⁷ Em–

Thus speaks the Lord, bold Moses said —
    let my people go
If not I'll strike your first born dead —
    let my people go! . . .

No more in bondage shall they toil . . .
They're comin' out with Egypt's spoil . . .

Your foes shall not forever stand . . .
You shall possess your own good land . . .

O let us all from bondage flee . . .
And soon may all the earth be free . . .

"Moses" in slavery era songs usually refers to Harriet Tubman as well as the earlier emancipator (Tubman led thousands of slaves to freedom on the underground RR). In SONGS OF WORK & PROTEST, SONGS OF THE SPIRIT, PEOPLES SONGBOOK, & POCKETFUL OF SONGS.

Harriet Tubman

Walter Robinson

One night I dreamed I was in slavery,
'bout eighteen fifty was the time.
Sorrow was the only sign;
nothing around to ease my mind.
Out of the night appeared a lady
leading a distant pilgrim band.
"First mate," she yelled, pointing her hand,
"make room aboard for this young woman," saying

    Em—/C–CD Em/G—B/C–CD Em://

Chorus
"Come on up," uh uh huh, "I've got a lifeline,
Come on up to this train of mine."
"Come on up," uh uh huh, "I've got a lifeline,
Come on up to this train of mine."
She said her name was Harriet Tubman,
and she drove for the Underground Railroad.

    Em—/C–D Em Em:// D–C–/G–D—Em—

Hundreds of miles we traveled onward,
gathering slaves from town to town,
Seeking ev'ry lost and found,
setting those free that once were bound.
Somehow my heart was growing weaker,
fell by the wayside's sinking sand.
Firmly did this lady stand,
lifted me up and took my hand, saying (Chorus)

Love Canal Treasure Hunt _____

OBJECTIVES   To learn how people in a community can cooperate to create change both for themselves and other people across the country

To learn about a national problem—dumping toxic waste—and to understand how it
affects people and what can be done about it

MATERIALS   Worksheets—"Message Cards: Scavenger Hunt" (cut up and color coded), "The Class
Treasure" (cut up), "Treasure Hunt Key," "Examples of Clues" (optional), pages
318–328

A treasure. Choose something you know students will like and that all will be allowed
to have. Consider asking a parent or local business for a contribution.

IMPLEMENTATION   This activity is a treasure hunt. Most of the work has been done for you. The clues are
written and the treasure hunt key organized. Yet time is needed to set up the treasure
hunt. It is advisable to set it up after school on the day before the hunt and conduct
the hunt as early as possible in the morning.

Follow the "Treasure Hunt Key" for set up. Be sure to color-code the message
cards so groups take the correct ones. Use the "Treasure Hunt Key" to make sure you
have the right clues at the right hiding places. The clues provided may be used if not
too simplistic for your class, otherwise make up your own. Enlist cooperation of school
personnel who will participate in the treasure hunt, and alert others that it will be
taking place.

Tell students that they will be learning about a national problem that people
cooperated to solve. Explain that the way they will get information is to go on a treasure
hunt. Have students who know the process of a treasure hunt explain it to others.

Explain that this treasure hunt is a little different from others. They will find
information in addition to getting a series of clues. Divide students into five groups,
each of which will be a family. Explain the sequence of the treasure hunt, as outlined
below.

**SEQUENCE OF
TREASURE
HUNT**

1. Teacher gives first clue to each family.
2. Families find their message card, read it aloud to each other, and return to class.
3. Families receive more information from other families by sharing their information in the whole class.
4. The teacher asks discussion questions for the round.
5. Teacher gives next clue to each family.

Remind students that there will be more than one message at each hiding place.
Explain the color-coding and urge students to be sure to take their clue, and not one
belonging to another family. Tell students not to tell others where the hiding places
are, otherwise, it spoils the fun for other groups.

Continue accordingly through four rounds. Be sure that students share information from each message card before you ask your discussion questions and give the
next clue card.

Some student groups may return with their clues before others do. If this will present a problem for your group, have some vocabulary words from the lesson for them to review or a short crossword puzzle containing these words to work on until all groups return.

When students are clear about the process, begin the treasure hunt.

DISCUSSION ROUND ONE

What do the five families represented here have in common?

ROUND TWO

1. What more do you know now that you have in common with other families in Love Canal?
2. What health problem does each family have?
3. How do you feel now that you've heard about the problems of others as well?
4. Those who are concerned by what you know, why don't you move from Love Canal?

ROUND THREE

1. What new information about Love Canal have you found out from your neighbors?
2. What are some of the effects of the chemicals buried at Love Canal?
3. What did other members of the Love Canal Homeowners Association do to push for a change?
4. What are your feelings now? Why do you feel that way?
5. How do you feel about taking action together with your neighbors? Is this different from how you used to feel about taking action?

ROUND FOUR

1. What did you and other residents of Love Canal do together to bring change to thousands of other Americans?
2. How do you feel about the statement, "Ordinary people can't make changes."?

When students have found the treasure, give them time to enjoy it. Then come together for a final class discussion.

DISCUSSION AT COMPLETION OF TREASURE HUNT

1. In Love Canal a crisis brought people together. Do people need an emergency to learn to cooperate? How can people come together and fight for their rights without needing a crisis to motivate them?
2. Love Canal residents worked very hard to get help from people who didn't live in Love Canal. Do you think it's important to cooperate with others and support them even if we don't think their problem is ours? Why or why not?
3. How have other people in different parts of America worked together for a change that affects many others?
4. What is an important issue that you feel people all over America could cooperate to solve?

Now have each student write three "I Learned" statements based on information in the Love Canal Treasure Hunt. Return to groups to proof each other's work for punctuation, grammar, and clarity of ideas. Hand in as a group.

COMPLETION

A student receives credit for this activity if each member of her group (1) participates in, and completes, the Treasure Hunt; and (2) hands in three signed "I Learned" statements.

FOLLOW-UP

Love Canal is only one of many communities that faced the problem of toxic waste. Assign student groups to do research on what other communities are currently doing to deal with this problem. You or students can write to:
The Citizens' Clearinghouse for Hazardous Wastes
P.O. Box 926
Arlington, VA 22216

SUBJECT—SS, LA, M
FORMAT—LEARNING
CENTER

The United Farmworkers' Boycott _____

OBJECTIVES

To gain knowledge about the use of a boycott by the United Farmworkers' Association

To understand how the boycott of the U.F.W.A. used the cooperation of different groups of people all across the country

To learn how people all over America can cooperate toward a common goal, even if they don't know each other

MATERIALS

For all centers: Name of center in large letters on sign posted at center; Directions—mounted on cardboard at center

A—Rita's Learning Center: Worksheet "Rita's Diary" (sections mounted on cards), paper and pencils

B—The Mothers' Learning Center: Worksheet "Family Role Cards" (cut in sections and mounted), tape recorder and blank tapes

C—The Priest's Learning Center: Worksheet "Meet the Truck" (cut up on cards), two maps of the United States with time zones indicated

D—The Young Girl's Learning Center

E—The Union Members' Learning Center: Worksheet "Worker Cards" (cut up)

F—The Students' Learning Center

Worksheets are on pages 329–340.

Cooperate to Create Centers

Learning centers are time-consuming for one teacher to make. Why not get together with other teachers in your grade and choose a common theme. Each teacher can make one center and then pool your creations!

IMPLEMENTATION

Tell students that they will be completing a series of activities about the United Farmworkers of America and their use of a boycott of grapes to gain better working conditions and lives. Check to see if students know the term, boycott. If not, boycott means that many people refuse to buy or use a certain thing until those selling the product or running the service make certain changes. Ask if students can think of any examples where boycotts were used. If no one suggests the Montgomery bus boycott, remind them that Rosa Parks' refusal to go to the back of the bus catalyzed that very successful boycott. Explain that many different people from all over the United States cooperated to make the United Farmworkers' Association grape boycott a success.

Give students background on the situation of Chicano farmworkers and the early years of Cesar Chavez. Borrow *Mighty Hard Road, The Story of Cesar Chavez,* by Terzian and Cromer through interlibrary loan. If you are unable to get that book, get one of the other resource books listed below and summarize relevant background information to the class.

Resourcebooks on the Farmworkers, Chavez, and the U.F.W.A.

For students
Mighty Hard Road: The Story of Cesar Chavez, James Terzian and Kathryn Cromer, Doubleday (upper elem., M.S.).
For easy reading use *Cesar Chavez,* Ruth Franchere, Crowell Publishers (elem.).

For teachers
Cesar Chavez: Autobiography of La Causa, Jacques Levy, W. W. Norton.
Chavez and the Farm Workers, Ronald Taylor, Beacon Press.
Sal Si Puedes: Cesar Chavez and the New American Revolution, Peter Matthiessen, Random House.

Either assign all centers, or only some. Or use contract grading and let student groups choose the number of centers to complete. (See the Resources section.)

Stagger beginnings so all groups can do Rita's Diary Center first. As students continue, move from center to center to make sure they are doing the work correctly. For example, make sure they know how to calculate time changes at the Priest's Center. After all groups have finished, hold a final discussion.

People from labor, the churches, and the universities were so well "organized" by abusive cops and store officials that they remained to convince a substantial segment of the American people first to boycott grapes, then head lettuce and Gallo wine. In giving these up, the people gave up some of themselves to the farmworkers, and eventually increased ten-thousand-fold the field of organization of La Causa.

Jacques Levy, *Cesar Chavez:
Autobiography of La Causa*
(New York: Norton, 1975).

DISCUSSION Before the discussion, post student work on the United Farmworkers Bulletin Board and have student groups read each other's work.

1. At Rita's Center you learned about the conditions the farmworkers had to work under. Describe those.
2. What are some important things people should know about the United Farmworkers' Association?
3. If you were Rita, would you have gone to New York City to help with the boycott? Why or why not?

Play tapes produced from the Mothers' Center. Have students listen for the reasons mothers gave for joining the boycott.

4. What were the most convincing reasons mothers on the tape gave for joining the boycott? Do you agree with them? Why or why not?
5. At the Young Girl's Center you wrote a story about the young girl who was blocking the trucks and facing the police. You read each other's stories too. How do the stories show an understanding of why a young girl might be involved in the boycott?
6. Workers who didn't know the farmworkers helped the boycott. Why? In what ways did they do this?
7. How did it help the boycott for people to picket trucks arriving with grapes in major cities?
8. Describe what boycotts exist in the United States today.

Boycott Information

An excellent resource for information on current boycotts is "The Grapevine: A Boycott Information Newsletter for Shopping with a Conscience." This newsletter describes the reasons for national boycotts of particular products and the progress of various boycotts. Available from *The Grapevine,* P.O. Box 1319, Ames, Iowa 50010.

---

9. Do you want to support any? If so, how could you cooperate?
10. How are boycotts an example of national cooperation? What helps to make them successful? What can hurt their chances of success?

COMPLETION A student receives credit for this activity if all group members have contributed to the task at each center as assigned and the group hands in the number of assignments required or contracted for.

Rita's Center: Diary entries, accurate in content and form
Mothers' Center: Radio tape
Young Girl's Center: Creative stories, correct in form.
Union Members' Center: A newspaper article
Priest's Center: Six correct "Meet the Truck" cards
Students' Center: A report, "Boycotts in the U.S. Today"

Update: The Farmworkers

The strategy of the boycott is still used in the 1980s to try to improve the situation of the farmworkers.

Campbell Boycott

Farmworkers in the mid-west, in the early 1980s, made an average hourly wage of $1.96, were sprayed with pesticides as they worked, and had to work and live in unsanitary conditions.

In 1979 the Farm Labor Organizing Committee, based in Ohio, began a national boycott of the Campbell's Soup Company. The cannery signs contracts with growers each year. These contracts determine the farmworkers' wages and working conditions.

In August 1983 the farmworkers marched from the Ohio tomato fields to the Camden, New Jersey headquarters of Campbell Soup. Many other Americans gave support to the farmworkers along the way. For example, people in Johnstown, Pennsylvania collected about $500 so the marchers could leave town in new shoes.

"Those individual victories are what will make the protest successful," said Cesar Chavez. "There is a strong bond between the public and the farmworker. The people know that every time they eat, it was the farmworker who sacrificed most to get the food to their table."

The farmworkers asked consumers not only to boycott Campbell's soup, but also the many other products made by Campbell's, among them: V-8 juice; Franco-American products; Pepperidge Farm baked goods; and Swanson Frozen Dinners. The boycott was also supported by the United Farmworkers.

The boycott succeeded in producing the first three-way labor contract between workers, employers, and the employers' major customer. In early 1986 the union, a group of vegetable growers, and Campbell's Soup Company signed a contract guaranteeing farmworkers their jobs, raised wages, and improved health and working conditions.

Akron Beacon Journal (August 7, 1983),
Dollars and Sense (December 1, 1983),
New York Times (Feb. 24, 1986).

Grape Boycott

In 1984 Cesar Chavez called for a renewal of the boycott of nonunion table grapes in order to get better working conditions for farmworkers. The issues in the current boycott include: spraying of dangerous pesticides which threaten farmworkers and consumers; free and fair elections for farmworkers, and good faith bargaining by growers.

The film, Wrath of Grapes, which depicts the farmworkers' situation is available from United Farmworkers, PO Box, 62, Keene, Calif. 93531.

WHO LABELLED THE DISPLAY ITEMS ?!

Underground Railroad—The 1980s _____

OBJECTIVES
To provide an example of citizens across the United States cooperating to run an underground railroad in contemporary times
To help students understand why the sanctuary movement developed and how it depends on the cooperation of numerous citizens

MATERIALS
Worksheets—"The Links" (cut up, one per group member), "The Sanctuary Movement" (one per person), pages 341–343

IMPLEMENTATION
Explain to students that they will be learning about an underground railroad of our day. This is the sanctuary movement, a cooperative endeavor that shelters Central American refugees fleeing from persecution in their homelands.

Background for Teachers

The sanctuary movement is often called the underground railroad of the 1980s and is compared to that of the 1850s. In both cases American citizens chose, because of conscience, to disobey a law that they believed was immoral. In doing so, they saved people escaping persecution, but risked being arrested themselves.

For background information on the sanctuary movement see:
Sanctuary: The New Underground Railroad, Rennie Solden.
Sanctuary: A Resource Guide for Understanding and Participation in the Central American Refugee Struggle, Gery McCean.

Divide students into groups of four. Give each student a section of "The Links" worksheet. Explain that each student has the role of a person who is a link in the contemporary underground railroad. Each reads silently about her person. Use the dictionary or ask other group members to define difficult words. Then, each group member tells others only enough to figure out the correct sequence of links on the chain of the underground railroad. When that is determined, the group member with the first link tells the group about her person. Students follow in sequence until they have a picture of all the people linking the underground railroad together.

Move around the room and encourage students to help each other clarify difficult words or ideas. When they have shared information, distribute "The Sanctuary Movement" worksheet and have students discuss all the questions together. They divide questions one–four and write a group response. Each student writes her own response to questions five–seven. They check each other's papers for grammar, spelling, and punctuation and turn them in.

DISCUSSION

1. Discuss questions one and two on the "Sanctuary Movement" worksheet.
2. How is the Underground Railroad of 1850 like this contemporary underground railroad? How are they different?
3. As in the 1850s, so in the 1980s, people who served as links on the underground railroad were taking a risk for what they believed in. What values are important to these people?
4. For what reasons do many Americans choose not to support, or participate in, the Sanctuary Movement? What values are important to them?
5. What values are important to you? For what value would you be willing to take a risk now or when you're an adult?

COMPLETION

A student gets credit for this lesson if all group members have written the group's response to one of the first four questions on the "Sanctuary Movement" worksheet and each has written individual responses to questions five through seven.

A City of Shelter

The Berkeley City Council declared the entire city a refuge for Central Americans fleeing right-wing terror Feb. 19, 1985.

The Berkeley resolution forbids any city employees, including police, from co-operating with the Immigration and Naturalization Service (INS) in investigating, locating, or arresting undocumented persons from Guatemala and El Salvador. It also prohibits denial of city services to Central American refugees or to organizations that protect them.

Berkeley Mayor Gus Newport sponsored the resolution and defended it as a modern equivalent of the anti-slavery underground railroad. Newport responded to the INS, saying, "I think it's humanitarian to help victims of oppressive governments. We're not saying we're going to violate any laws. We're saying we're not going to cooperate with the INS."

The Guardian (3/27/85)

Berkeley is one of numerous locales to become a sanctuary from the U.S. government's persecution of refugees. Among the many others are San Jose and Los Angeles, California, St. Paul, Minnesota and the State of New Mexico.

Nonviolent Protest

The Sanctuary Movement is one of many examples of nonviolent protest of what supporters believe are immoral actions of governments or other institutions with power. The Gandhi-led movement for the independence of India and the civil rights movement in the United States are well-known examples of nonviolent struggle.

The philosophy of nonviolence challenges people to consider their ideas about violence. Below are a few quotations that provide food for thought.

> There is a violence that liberates, and a violence that enslaves; there is a violence that is moral and a violence that is immoral. . . . For me violence is profoundly moral, more moral than compromises and transactions.
>
> Benito Mussolini, 1922

> Nonviolence means the largest love. It is the supreme law. By it alone can mankind be saved. He who believes in nonviolence believes in a living God.
>
> Mohandas K. Gandhi, 1939

> Most Americans would say that they disapproved of violence. But what they really mean is that they believe it should be the monopoly of the state.
>
> Edgar Friedenberg, 1966

> America is the greatest purveyor of violence in the world today.
>
> Martin Luther King, Jr., 1966

WE'RE NOT PLAYING COPS AND ROBBERS ...
WE'RE GIVING SANCTUARY!

C. OVERCOMING BARRIERS TO A COOPERATIVE SOCIETY

SUBJECT—SS, LA
FORMAT—GROUP
PROJECT, JIGSAW

Fifth Graders: Friends or Foes? _____

OBJECTIVES
To examine ways in which individuals, communities, and the country as a whole can cooperate to find creative alternatives to competitive individualism
To provide an example of how the country has attempted to deal with the negative effects of competitive individualism in the field of education
To help students understand that what they might see as an individual problem is often a national problem

MATERIALS
Worksheets: "Friends or Foes?" one per student, pages 344–345
"Better Their Chances Program Cards" (cut up), pages 346–347

272

IMPLEMENTATION It is recommended that the lessons "Head Starts: For Some or All" (Chapter 4) and, if possible, "With the Odds Against Them" (Chapter 6) be completed before doing this lesson.

Tell students that they will be examining how individuals, communities, and the nation, have worked cooperatively, and can work cooperatively, to change competitive individualism.

PART 1 Review competitive individualism. Ask students to remember the solar design project activity ("Head Starts for Some or All" lesson) and the "Hurdles of Life Game." If students have not done these activities, explain competitive individualism to them. See page 103.

Divide students into heterogeneous groups of four. Distribute Worksheet "Fifth Graders: Friends or Foes?" to each student. Students follow the directions. Make sure students stop after answering question 2. Check their response. If necessary, reproduce the box below; seeing such information in writing may help the students.

Examples of Competitive Individualism at Aronson School

Competitive Individualism
The students from Rickey School said everyone had an equal chance to succeed.

Reality
Everyone didn't have an equal chance. Most Rickey students had more opportunities to learn at home. In school they had more money spent on their education. They had teachers who challenged them to do their best. They had afterschool programs. They had, in fact, a head start.

Competitive Individualism
Some Rickey School students say they do better because they're naturally smarter than Barnett School students.

Reality
Barnett School students haven't had as much encouragement to learn or as much educational opportunity. If Barnett students had the educational advantages of the Rickey School students, many could achieve well.

Competitive Individualism
Rickey students feel good about themselves and put Barnett students down because they get better grades than Barnett students.

Reality
Their feeling of success is not necessarily deserved. They had a head start. They put Barnett students down to make themselves feel good.

DISCUSSION PART 1
1. Discuss questions 1–3 on the worksheet "Friends or Foes." After students have given their ideas in response to question 3, provide other ideas—such as peer tutoring, described in the box below.
2. Was it their fault that Barnett students didn't do well in school? Why or why not?
3. Discuss questions 4–5 on the worksheet.
4. Ask students to imagine that some of these ideas have been implemented. Pretend that you are students at the Branch Rickey School and don't understand competitive individualism. What might be something you'd say about these special programs?
5. Now become yourself. You understand competitive individualism. How would you answer that comment?

Repeat questions 4 and 5 until ideas are exhausted.

> **Peer Tutoring**
>
> Here's just one example of what students and teachers at Aronson School, or other schools like it across the country, could do to change competitive individualism.
>
> With the support of the teacher, some of the activities during the school day could involve peer tutoring. Students with advanced skills can help others catch up. Students praise each other's accomplishments. Rickey School students feel good about themselves for helping others learn. They are pleased when Barnett students get good grades too. Barnett students feel more confident and competent. Tutors have the added advantage of improving their skills too.

PART 2 Tell students that in the late 1960s and 1970s, some Americans became concerned about the unequal chances that different groups of students had. People asked the government to develop federal programs to help make children's chances more equal.

Children return to groups. Each gets a Better Their Chance Program Card that describes an educational program developed to give students equal educational opportunity. Each student reads the card, learns the information, and teaches it to others.

Based on the information, each student makes up a short quiz for others. Students give the quizzes. They can correct any mistakes and teach the information again so it can be learned correctly. Students may take a quiz over in order to improve. When everyone in the group does well on each quiz, hand them in to the teacher and go on to Part 3.

PART 3 Students work together in their groups to write a new story about fifth graders at the Aronson School. The story will be different than the first account "Fifth Graders: Friends or Foes?" Now students are to imagine that students coming from the Barnett School had the opportunity to participate in Head Start, bilingual education or Title VII projects. They had minority teachers as role models. At the Aronson School, teachers and students cooperated to provide equal chances for all. Their story should describe: (1) what would be going on at the school; (2) what special programs there are; (3) how students get along. When groups finish their stories, they sign them, read them aloud to each other, and hand them in to the teacher. Each student writes a statement describing her contributions to the story. This is then signed by other group members.

DISCUSSION PART 3
1. How were the stories you finished different from the first worksheet? Why was this so?
2. In your story, students who came into the Aronson School had the benefit of national programs and school changes that had given them a more equal chance to learn. How did these experiences affect their feelings? Their skills?
3. In your story were fifth graders friends or foes? Why?
4. If the programs to give all students an equal chance were put into effect in schools across the country, how might that influence how students in American schools get along?

COMPLETION A student receives credit for this activity when:

PART 1 All members of her group take part in thinking about and responding to the worksheet "Friend or Foe?" as indicated by their individual answers and signatures.

PART 2 All members of her group submit a part of the group quiz on educational programs for equality and everyone in the group does well on the quiz.

PART 3 Each member submits a statement describing her contribution to the new version of "Fifth Graders: Friends or Foes?" This must be signed by other group members.

SUBJECT—Math, SS
FORMAT—CLASS
JIGSAW, GROUP
PROJECT

Working for the Community _____

OBJECTIVES

To learn to look at the needs of all people and design institutions and systems to work for all

To design an economic plan for a community so that all people have work and thus, adequate food, clothing, and shelter

To design an economic system that appreciates the value to the community of all members' work

To discuss the implications of such a cooperatively-oriented economic system for people in the United States

MATERIALS

Worksheet: "Community Worker Role Cards" (cut up), pages 348–349, paper

IMPLEMENTATION

Tell students that in an effort to create a cooperative country, people can learn to look at the needs of *all* people and make institutions and systems work for all. They will have practice doing that in this lesson.

Give each student a Community Worker Role Card. Going around the circle one by one, each student says what she does, how much she earns and why that job is important to the community. All students listen carefully and make a list of all jobs and salaries.

Divide students into heterogeneous groups of five as noted below.

GROUP 1   unemployed worker, doctor, farmworker, teacher, bus driver

GROUP 2   unemployed worker, businessperson, child-care worker, teacher, car mechanic

GROUP 3 factory owner, unemployed worker, factory worker, house builder, garbage collector

GROUP 4 unemployed worker, dentist, waitress, religious leader, repair person

GROUP 5 unemployed worker, factory worker, artist, lawyer, road worker

If you have more than twenty-five students, give out extra role cards, and when necessary, make up your own.

Tell students their task is to make a community plan in which all people in the community have a job with pay that provides them and their family money for adequate food, clothing and shelter. The minimal amount needed for a family to do this is $17,000. Assume that everyone's work is important and that cooperation of all is necessary to make the community work. Group members may create new jobs and salaries, and change salaries of any jobs they wish.

A Low Family Budget

According to U.S. Department of Labor statistics, a "low budget family" earns a minimum of $17,000 a year.

Social Graphics

After discussion, each group posts on the Community Plan Bulletin Board their community plan—a list of all the jobs and salaries they've decided on for their community. They should be ready to explain why they developed the plan they did. When all groups are finished, come together for discussion. Each group shares its plan with the others.

DISCUSSION
1. How do you feel about the community work plan your group developed? Why do you feel that way?
2. How do the unemployed feel? Those who already had jobs?
3. What were the hardest decisions you had to make when you were developing your community plan? Why were they hard?
4. How did you decide what new jobs were needed in order to provide work for unemployed people?
5. How did you create money for the jobs? What other alternatives did you discuss?
6. How did you decide what salaries to pay? How did groups differ? What were the reasons for those differences?
7. "If all work is important to the community how should pay be determined? For example you might want to consider factors such as: riskiness of job, appeal/pleasantness of job, educational costs needed to develop skills for job, crucialness of job to the community, popularity of job, emotional stress of job, time of day job needs doing, etc."

You developed a plan for a small community. The United States is like that community only a million times bigger. The economic system of the U.S. is based on competition. In America about 10% of the population is unemployed. Cooperation means thinking about other people. A cooperative economic system takes into account the needs of all people and tries to create jobs for all.

8. If the U.S. developed a more cooperative economic system, how could it make sure everyone had a job that allowed them to support their family? Think about what you learned from your community plan. Do you think this should be done? Why or why not?

9. If new jobs in the U.S. were created to provide jobs for all Americans, what jobs should they be? Why? What kind of training would people need to be able to do those jobs?

The salaries workers began with in your community are like salaries paid to workers in the U.S. All workers contribute to the country but they get very different amounts of money for what they do, and some have no jobs at all. Think back to Rodney's father and Stacey's father in "Team Players" for an example.

10. What are your thoughts and feelings about the fact that workers are paid such different salaries? If the U.S. wanted a more cooperative economic system, how would this be changed?

11. What effects would full employment (jobs for all) and a more cooperative economic system have on Americans' lives? On the employed? Unemployed? Who would lose? How? Who would gain? How?

12. If every worker was sure she could get a job, how would it affect workers' feelings about each other and willingness to work together cooperatively?

13. How would a more cooperatively-based economic system affect the country as a whole? What would be gained? What lost?

COMPLETION

A student receives credit for this activity if each person in her group participates in the development of a Community Plan, indicating agreement with their signatures.

Full Employment

Full employment would give people security, dignity and income. While such a program would be complex, it would be possible.

Despite immense political benefits, the U.S. has not adopted full employment because it would change the way the economy works and threaten those who own and control U.S. corporations.

With full employment, there would be no unemployed workers to use as a wedge for owners to maintain their profits and control. Economic planning—public decision making about what and how much private companies will produce—would be necessary. If corporations won't willingly go along with economic planning, the government would need to nationalize companies or set up new ones.

Thus full employment would make very real the ideal, human need before profit.

"Why Don't We Have Full Employment?"
Dollars and Sense (September 1982).

SUBJECT—SS, LA
FORMAT—GROUP
PROJECT

Splitting Woodcutters

OBJECTIVES

To understand how differences—such as race, sex or age—can be used to keep people who don't know each other and who live in different locations from cooperating
To examine how such people can overcome these barriers to cooperation

MATERIALS

Worksheets—"Splitting Woodcutters" (cut up)—Parts IA and IB and Parts II A and II B, one per group, page 350

IMPLEMENTATION

Tell students that in many places across our country differences—like race, sex and age—are used by others to keep people who don't know each other, who live far apart, but who have something in common, from working together. Today, they will examine a situation where race was used as such a barrier to cooperation. They will consider what that situation can teach many other Americans. Read the following Background Information out loud.

BACKGROUND INFORMATION

In 1971 in the state of Mississippi, 3,900 woodcutters went on strike against the paper companies to which they sold wood because their pay was cut by 20 percent. Most of the woodcutters didn't know each other and were spread out across the southern part of the state. Half of the woodcutters were white and half black. Most were members of the Gulwood Pulpwood Association. Their action was important for a number of reasons.

Mississippi has a history of segregation and racial discrimination. In the past, as well as today, when black and white people worked for the same company, some owners would use racial fears and stereotypes to keep workers from cooperating or from forming unions.

In 1971 the woodcutters decided to stop cutting and selling wood to the paper companies until their pay cut was restored. The woodcutters stood together. The paper companies tried to break the strike by splitting the black and white workers. Let's see how this happened.

GROUP WORK   Divide students into groups of four. Within groups, subdivide them into two partnerships—A and B. Give Part I of the "Splitting Woodcutters" worksheet to each respective partnership. Students work on them separately, as partners.

When finished, each partnership gives their completed Part I to the other partnership in their group. At the same time, pass out Part II to each respective partnership, A and B. First students talk separately as partners and then they work together as a group.

When finished, have groups read their responses aloud to the class. Each writes down her contribution to the group effort, others sign, hand in. Then proceed to the discussion.

Examples: Possible Statements of Company Officials

(Don't give these to students as examples. See if they can come up with them!)

To white workers
1. What kind of Southern white men are you to cooperate with blacks?
2. Why are you cooperating with blacks? We're all white, we will take better care of you than black workers can.
3. We companies won't give you any more work if you strike with blacks.
4. The black workers are cooperating with you now. After the strike is over, those black workers will compete with you and take over your jobs. Then you'll be sorry.
5. If you stop the strike, we'll pay you more for your wood than we'll pay the black workers.

To the black workers
1. White workers are using you to get what they want, but they call you names behind your backs.
2. The white workers are cooperating with you now. After the strike is over, those white workers will compete with you and take your jobs.
3. Before the strike, white workers tried to get the company to pay them more for their logs than black workers.

DISCUSSION   1. How hard or easy was it to think of ways the company would try to separate the black and white workers from each other? What made it hard or easy?
2. Of all the ways the groups came up with, which ones do you think would work in real life? Why?
3. In Part II of the activity, what helped or hindered you, as white and black workers, from understanding each other and working together to respond to the company statements?
4. Do any of the things that helped you work together happen in real life? How? Do any of the things that kept you from working together happen in real life? How?
5. If you wrote a joint statement to the company, how did you feel about it? Do you think you could have stuck together and won the strike? Why or why not?

Explain that, in fact, the black and white woodcutters stuck together in spite of the attempt by the companies to divide them along racial lines. Their pay cut was restored.

The unity of black and white workers surprised the companies and the news media. It encouraged others to work together for common goals.

Ask students if the strategy of splitting groups of people is common in the U.S. Why? Set up a research project to find out more.

6. What have you learned that you could share with other Americans who face this situation?

COMPLETION A student gets credit for this activity if each group member hands in a statement of her contribution to either the joint statement to company officials or a statement from each partnership, explaining why they aren't working together. The statements must be signed by all group members.

SUBJECT—SS, C
FORMAT—JIGSAW,
GROUP PROJECT

Make That Connection! _____

OBJECTIVES To understand how students are connected to other Americans whom they don't know as individuals
To explore how people distance themselves from the knowledge of those connections
To examine ways in which peoples' choices and actions affect others' lives

MATERIALS Worksheet—"Situation Cards," "Questions" (one per student), pages 351–352

IMPLEMENTATION It is helpful if students have first done "Love Canal Treasure Hunt," "United Farmworkers' Boycott," and "Fifth Graders: Friends or Foes?" If they haven't, review the material yourself to provide any needed background information.

Ask students to suggest ways in which they are connected to other Americans whom they don't know. Explain that often, people don't take time to think about those connections and that today we are going to take that time. We are going to examine connections.

Pass out one "Questions" worksheet to each student. Explain that soon they will draw situation cards and will figure out how one person's decision affects others.

As an example, work through this situation with the whole class.

Example

Situation: You are grocery shopping with your father. He tells you to go buy some grapes. You remember that the farmworkers have asked people to boycott grapes. What do you do?

1. How does this situation connect me to other people? How does my choice affect other people?

   Response: My decision will affect farm workers. If I don't buy, I will help the boycott. If I do buy, I will hurt the boycott.

2. How would I feel if I were the other person(s) affected by my action?

   Response: If I were a farm worker, I would feel support and hope if someone helped the boycott. If someone didn't support the boycott, I would feel discouraged.

3. What are all the options I can think of for dealing with the situation?

   Response: I can
   a. buy grapes
   b. buy another fruit
   c. tell my father about the boycott so he'll understand and support the idea of buying some other fruit
   d. ask to change the menu so we don't have grapes
   e. learn how to grow grapes
   f. talk to the store manager and ask her to order grapes from places other than California
   g. tell my father that the store is all out of grapes

4. What do I choose? Why?

   Response: I'll choose
   c. because maybe if he agrees he can support the boycott too
   e. because it will be fun to learn something new
   f. she will learn about the boycott and might decide to support it

---

Divide students into groups of three. Each one draws a situation card and works out the response to each of the four questions on the "Questions" worksheet. Then students share answers with each other and get more ideas from others. Next each student completes her worksheet. All proofread and then sign each other's worksheets, indicating agreement. Come together for discussion.

DISCUSSION

1. Take each situation card separately, having students discuss each of the four questions.
2. In daily life, what keeps us from thinking about our connection to other people? What can help us do that?
3. How hard or easy was it to get into the shoes of the other people in these situations? Why was it hard or easy?
4. In daily life, what can help us get into the shoes of the "invisible others" we often affect by our action, but don't think about?
5. It is called "distancing" when we don't stop to think about how our action affects others. Why is it easy to distance? What can we do about that?
6. In what other choices and actions in our daily lives are there connections to other Americans across the country—connections we don't think about?
7. How can we begin to see these connections and to be aware of all people? How can we help others become more aware of connectedness? What are the advantages to such an awareness? What are the disadvantages?

Talk with students about raising these issues with their parents. It's not helpful for parents to feel guilty or pressured. It is, however, legitimate to ask them to look at the choices they have in life. Often many Americans don't realize that they do make choices that deeply affect other Americans.

COMPLETION A student gets credit for this activity if his group completes three "Make That Connection" worksheets that are thoughtful in content and correct in form and signed by all other group members.

FOLLOW-UP Follow-up with "Connecting Friends: Known and Unknown" in the last section of this chapter. Here students research additional connections and educate their friends about these.

D. STUDENTS NETWORKING FOR A CHANGE

SUBJECT—SS
FORMAT—
COOPERATIVE CARD
GAME

STOP _____

OBJECTIVES To examine how students across America can cooperate, in spite of distance, to work for a common goal
To learn about a national student organization, the Student Organization to Prevent Nuclear War

MATERIALS Worksheets—(1) "Directions for STOP" (one per group), (2) "STOP Cards" (mounted on 3/5 cards, one set per group of four, students mount cards to save time), (3) Information about STOP (see box on page 283); see pages 353–359

IMPLEMENTATION Explain to the class that they will be learning about one of the many ways students from all across America have cooperated, despite distance, toward a common goal.

Give students the following background information. STOP Nuclear War is an educational organization of high school students and teachers committed to reducing the threat of nuclear war. In schools and houses of worship across the country, STOP members and chapters sponsor extracurricular activities to educate themselves and their communities about the nuclear arms race and the possibilities for reversing it. They seek to empower young people and adults by demonstrating that an educated, organized group can make a meaningful contribution to the effort to prevent nuclear war.

Explain to students that they will play a simple cooperative card game to learn more abut STOP. Divide students into heterogeneous groups of four. Give each group a copy of "Directions for STOP" and a set of STOP cards. Students read and follow directions. Answer questions as needed. Play until all groups win.

If some groups finish before others, give them the descriptive information on STOP to read. Remind students that because luck, as well as strategy, will affect the game, some groups may have to play several times before they win.

DISCUSSION First let's talk about the playing of the game, and then about what you learned.
1. What helped you win the card game STOP? What contributed to a group's losing?
2. What were important parts of an effective strategy for winning STOP? How did you figure that out?

3. Why do students join STOP? What are some of the benefits STOP members receive from their work in that organization?
4. What are some of the feelings and opinions that students, teachers, and parents have about STOP? To what extent do you agree or disagree with their ideas?
5. What are some of the projects that STOP students have undertaken across the country? Which ideas did you like? Not like? Why?
6. What other effective projects could students carry out to help prevent nuclear war?
7. STOP is an example of a national organization that tries to coordinate efforts of students all across America. What are some ways it does this?
8. Would you like to become involved in STOP? Why or why not?

COMPLETION A student receives credit for this lesson if her group successfully completes the game of STOP according to the rules.

FOLLOW-UP If students express an interest in STOP, have some students write for material. Students then share material with each other. They discuss feasible small group, class, or schoolwide projects. If interest is strong, they can work with high school students to form a STOP chapter.

Information about STOP

Before doing this lesson, send for descriptive information about the Student-Teacher Organization to Prevent Nuclear War. Write to: STOP, 11 Garden St., Cambridge, Mass. 02138. Also available from STOP, in addition to general information, is:

1. A slide show, "STOP Nuclear War," about this student-teacher organization
2. A video, "Changing the Silence," a high school students' dramatic presentation of their growing awareness of their choices regarding nuclear war
3. A book describing successful STOP projects all over the country

---

Student Action

In conjunction with the June 12 Disarmament March in New York City, I decided to do a unit on disarmament with my fourth and fifth grade class.

I started by telling the class about Hiroshima, reading from the survivors' diaries and giving very basic facts about the power of nuclear weapons and the possible effects of such a war.

Perhaps the most successful activity was involving the class in a writing/poster contest on "World without Weapons" that a local peace education group was sponsoring. The students were to write or draw about issues relating to a world without weapons: nonviolence, disarmament, conflict resolution, etc.

A month after school closed for the summer, I asked the parent of a student who had written a thoughtful essay if the student could testify in front of a City Council Committee on the Jobs and Peace Referendum question. The parent approved and the student was delighted. She enlisted a friend and they both gave testimony that got on all three TV stations.

These children helped organize a group called "Children for Peace," and they are planning a city-wide meeting for this fall. Correspond with the Children for Peace group in Milwaukee through Bob Peterson at 3340 N. Pierce Street, Milwaukee, WI 53212.

CIBC Bulletin, vol. 13, no. 6 and 7

Reprinted by permission, from the Interracial Books for Children. Write the Council on Interracial Books for Children at 1841 Broadway, New York, NY 10023 for a free catalog of anti-racist, anti-sexist materials.

Youth Links, Nationwide _____

OBJECTIVES To provide students an example of a student-led cooperative project that positively affects many others across the country

To work together to develop a cooperative project that will have positive peace-giving effects for others

MATERIALS Worksheet "Creating *The Kids' Book of Divorce*," pages 360–361, whatever materials your class will need to create the project it decides upon, a copy of *The Kids' Book of Divorce,* if possible (New York: Random House, 1982). Order in advance through interlibrary loan.

IMPLEMENTATION Tell students that there are many different ways that they can develop a cooperative project that will positively affect others across our nation. Explain that they will learn about one such project developed by a group of students in Massachusetts. Then they will work together to develop their own plan. Note that the Massachusetts students' project was very intensive and long term. While their own project will probably be much more limited, it still can be effective!

PART A Divide students into groups of three. Give each group one copy of the worksheet, "Creating *The Kids' Book of Divorce*." Take turns reading parts of the worksheet. Discuss the questions. Finally, divide the responsibility for writing the response to the questions. Hand in responses.

DISCUSSION
1. Discuss with students their answers to worksheet questions.
2. Share the copy of *The Kids' Book of Divorce: By, For, and About Kids* if you were able to get it. Ask students how they feel when they realize the book was written by young people ages 11–14. (Leave book in the class for students to look at. Some may want to read it.)
3. What things usually keep us from believing that we can affect or cooperate with other young people across the country? What could help us believe that this is a realistic possibility?

Youth Link

A fine newsletter reporting news of national organizations for young people is "Youth Link." This is a bimonthly publication aimed at being a catalyst for young people who are concerned about the world they are growing up in and want to have an impact on its future shape. It includes reports of related youth activities around the world, children's comments and poems, creative suggestions for students, parents and teachers, and ways to link up with others. Contact Paula DeCosse, 4835 Penn. Ave. S., Minneapolis, MN 55409.

PART B Explain to students that they will now have the chance to generate ideas about how they can work cooperatively to affect others across the country in a positive way. They can now also think of helping to organize a nationwide cooperative project for students.

APPROACH 1   A class project that affects others

Discuss all the things you know about, know how to do, or could learn about, that would be beneficial to other students countrywide. The Fayerweather Street students knew about, and learned a lot more about, divorce. In what areas are you experts?

Examples
- Cooperative games kids play.
- A resource book for parents on ideas of what they can do together, as a family, with their 11–14 year olds that would be appealing and that kids would be willing to do.
- Cooperative themes in popular music.

Next discuss the ways this knowledge and experience could be communicated to students across the country.

Examples
- Slide tape
- Video
- Article in a magazine

Put the two together and see what you come up with.

Examples
- A class in which students knew how to cook dishes from many different cultures might come up with the idea of writing a multicultural cookbook that would include information about the cultures represented, as well as recipes. This could be described in national magazines and the cookbook sold locally and nationwide.
- Another class might write an article for a youth magazine about how to organize a school-wide Cooperation Day.

APPROACH 2   A class project that involves others

Think about the kinds of nationwide efforts that your class could coordinate that would raise awareness about cooperation and peace.

Example

A class might decide to coordinate a History of Peace Calendar. Students would send out a call to other young people through national peace organizations and youth magazines. The students would ask for examples of nationwide community efforts that contributed to peace and cooperation and the dates on which these efforts occurred. These examples would be collected and included in a History of Peace Calendar that could be sold throughout the U.S. The calendar would educate others about the positive efforts for peace made by Americans. Sale of the calendar would raise money for participating schools and peace organizations.

Example

Students might decide to coordinate a Friends of Endangered Animals Campaign. Students would first research endangered animals in their area. Then they would do a write-up about this, including scientific information, addresses to write to, information on what steps can be taken to protect these. They would mail these to students in other parts of the country. Thus different groups could (1) make each other's efforts more effective by joining together and having more folks part of each effort (2) share strategies and thus improve ones own strategy by learning from what others did (3) learn more science and ecology.

Students discuss possible projects and decide on one that they feel committed to and have the time and energy to carry out. An article for a national magazine would take a limited amount of time and energy. Coordinating a History of Peace Calendar for example, would be a more involved commitment. Students organize tasks and responsibilities. Help students structure tasks in small, workable steps. Students might work best in small groups of two or three. Since students often feel very powerless, be assertive in helping them make complete plans that are realistic, so they see they **can** make a difference.

Come together periodically to assess progress and make further plans.

DISCUSSION

(This can be held periodically, or at the end of the project.)
1. What are we learning in our project?
2. What are we learning about working together as a class? What's working well? What could be better? How can we improve that?
3. What are we learning about communicating with other young people across the country?
4. As you complete this project, what feelings do you have about yourselves and the power and potential of students?

COMPLETION

A student gets credit for Part A if each member in his group participates in reading "Creating *The Kids' Book of Divorce*" worksheet and in writing the group's response for a couple of questions. A student gets credit for Part B if each member of the class participates in the project and writes a statement about the importance of his contribution.

A Cooperative across the Country

Another way students can help build links of cooperation across the country is to learn about CO-OP America (a national cooperative) to educate others about it, to join, and to buy and sell products from it.

CO-OP America is a nonprofit, member-controlled, worker-managed association linking socially responsible businesses and consumers in a national network, a new alternative marketplace.

CO-OP America allows consumers to align their buying habits with their values. It also enables businesses, co-ops and nonprofits which put people ahead of profits to expand the market for their goods and services.

CO-OP America brings together individuals and organizations to build a market-place based on social and environmental responsibility and a spirit of cooperation in the workplace. It emphasizes economic democracy, worker participation, responsiveness to members and customers; and it demonstrates that business can be done in an ethical manner.

Address: CO-OP America
2100 M St. NW, Suite 310
Washington, D.C. 20063

Stories with a Vision

OBJECTIVES   For students to imagine ways that young people across the country could work together to solve common problems
To write a story about that possibility
To share their stories with younger students and assist them in writing their own
To think about how some of their stories might indeed become realities and take any appropriate steps to make that happen

MATERIALS   Paper, pencils

IMPLEMENTATION   Tell students that they will participate in a project that involves creative thinking, writing, and action.

PART A   Tell students that there are examples in both fiction and nonfiction of young people across large geographical areas working together to solve a problem or bring about positive change.

Books Where People Work Together across the Miles

The Fragile Flag, Jane Langston.
Freedom Crossing, Margaret Clark.
Winged Watchman, Hilda Van Stockum.
A Swiftly Tilting Planet, Madelaine L'Engle.

As a class, ask students to discuss freely what they see as serious problems facing the nation today, problems that hurt people or deny them or others equality. List those on the board.

Divide students into small groups. Ask students to pick a problem and develop an outline for a story that would describe how young people across the country worked together to solve that problem. Encourage them to use their imaginations and creativity. The story can be either realistic or visionary, but in either case the story should be possible, not based on pure fantasy.

Provide this example. Tell students that in 1984 television programs were "the most violent ever," averaging 914 acts of violence per hour, and with 64 percent of all prime-time programming featuring themes high in violence. Explain that many people believe that such violence on TV is a national problem because it encourages violence in viewers, and is especially harmful to children.

Provide an example of the plot of an inappropriate story: A science student invents a potion that when poured over the TV eliminates all the violence. She distributes it to young people who flood their TVs. Provide an example of an appropriate story—one that is creative and potentially possible. Students start a campaign to stop TV violence. Through articles in magazines young people read and by making a video that students send around the country, the students educate others about the effects of TV violence, and convince them to stop watching violent shows and stop buying products advertised on the shows. While visionary, this plot is potentially possible.

Students work together to develop an outline for a group story. It should have all the characteristics of a good short story. (See box.) Its main characters would be ones students can identify with. Students share ideas for characters, a plot, and an ending.

Characteristics of a Good Short Story

- story develops characters who are interesting and realistic
- plotline is well developed and absorbing
- story is fair to all people, doesn't have stereotypes based on race, gender, age, ethnic group, socioeconomic status, sexual orientation, physical abilities, etc.
- story is told in clear language which readers can understand and enjoy
- spelling, handwriting and English mechanics do not distract from readers' involvement in story
- readers like reading story, become involved, keep reading

Ideally, students can divide up the outline and each write a section. To do this, they must be very specific about what goes in each section and what the characters are like. They come back with rough drafts and read to each other. Students give each other feedback on content and form. If students need a structure for doing this use the Peer Feedback worksheet in Chapter 7, page 493. They work together to make sure the story is sequenced well.

Students can either rework their section of the story or exchange sections and rework a different one. Continue reading and reworking until the story holds together well. They proof all sections for spelling, punctuation, and grammar.

If such cooperative group story writing would be too difficult for your students, have each write a story on his own. Then they give feedback about each other's work.

Students read completed stories to each other. If possible make copies, bind as a booklet, title the collection, and distribute to others.

DISCUSSION PART A

1. What are your feelings about your stories?
2. In writing these stories you were called upon to be visionary—to imagine something that could possibly happen. What helped you be imaginative in this way? What made it hard?
3. Could some of these stories become realities? If so, how? If not, why not?
4. How hard or easy was it to write a cooperative story? What helped make it work? What hindered it?
5. If you were giving others advice on how to work effectively in writing a cooperative story what would you tell them?

PART B
Make arrangements to link student groups in your class to groups of students in a younger grade. Explain to groups that they will be reading their stories to groups of younger students and discussing the stories with them. When feasible, they will then help those students write their own story about how young people across the nation work cooperatively to bring about change, using the same process they went through. Review guidelines for cross-age projects.

Students discuss the tasks involved in reading and discussing their story with younger students. They divide the tasks. They discuss questions about their story and the ideas it raises that can be asked of the younger students.

Students work with younger students. Each group member writes an "I Learned Statement" based on the experience. They proof each other's work and hand in. Return for discussion.

DISCUSSION PART B
1. How did younger children respond to your stories?
2. What did you learn by their responses?
3. How did the questions you asked the younger students help stimulate their thinking?
4. To what extent do you think younger students have a broader vision of what young people can do working together across the country to create change?

PART C As a class discuss which, if any, of your stories could be put into effect in reality. What steps would have to be taken to do that? Discuss whether or not you would like to take on that project. If so, delineate tasks, responsibilities, and a time line.

COMPLETION A student gets credit for this activity if each member of her group (A) writes a section of their group's cooperative story, and (B) hands in an "I Learned Statement" from the cross-age project.

The Bay Area Writing Program

Bay Area is a writing program that utilizes peer teaching. Write to Bay Area Writing Project, Graduate School of Education, University of California, Berkeley, CA 94220 for more information on this excellent program.

Below is a sample of the type of cooperative feedback students learn to give each other. After two students have written a story, they exchange papers and check them both for ideas and mechanics. Then students fill out a feedback sheet and return it to their partner. Questions might include:

I like. . . .
I was wondering. . . .
Things to add. . . .
Things to delete. . . .
Suggestions. . . .

Why not incorporate cooperative peer-feedback into your writing lessons?!

Cooperative Groups: A Solution to Learning Problems

Mary Travis, a fifth grade teacher at the School in Poughkeepsie, NY, was faced with dealing with the difficult behavior of Jim, a boisterous, disruptive student who was known as a joker.

Once Jim was placed in a cooperative learning group he could no longer hide the fact that he had trouble understanding the material. His disruptive behavior had been his public "cover" for so many years. For him, working in cooperative groups was a relief—he didn't have to play that game any more. He had been called on it and now he could get the help he needed.

Connecting Friends: Known and Unknown __

OBJECTIVES
To research ways that students are connected to other people across the nation who need the cooperative efforts of others to improve their lives

To help their friends understand these connections and examine how their actions can affect these "unknown friends"

To plan a cooperative action strategy to support efforts for change in the situation of those "unknown friends"

MATERIALS
Worksheet—"Seeing Connections: Taking Action," page 362

IMPLEMENTATION
It is advisable that students complete "Make That Connection," page 280, to provide them a clear framework for this lesson.

Begin by reminding students that of the people all over America who are hurt by both the competitive norms of our society and the policies of our institutions, many are people of color, women, or poor and working-class people. How we act or don't act, what we do or don't do, often directly affects these persons. We will call these people unknown friends, because our lives are connected, even though they are invisible to us day to day.

Explain to students that they will participate in a three-part activity. In Part 1 they will research current legislation and actions that affect such unknown friends and then determine how their actions as students can support them. In Part 2 they will help their school friends understand more about a particular group of "unknown friends" and help the students understand the ways they are connected to the "unknown friends." In Part 3 students will cooperatively take action to try to positively affect the situation of one group of "unknown friends." If your students need a concrete example before beginning, discuss the example in the box at the end of this lesson.

PART 1

Divide students into research groups of six and within those groups, into partners. The group decides on a group of "unknown friends" it would like to research. Each partnership is assigned one of the following research areas:
1. proposed legislation at the state or national level
2. strikes and boycotts
3. citizens' action groups

Students are to do research to find out what legislation is proposed or what action is in progress that will positively affect a particular group of "unknown friends". Students do research in the library, and also contact knowledgeable people in the community. These might be: journalists, religious leaders, labor organizers, representatives of minorities, feminist leaders or elected politicians.

After completing the research, each student fills out the "Seeing Connections: Taking Action" worksheet. Students then report their findings orally to their group. All members read all worksheets, making suggestions for clarity, grammar, and punctuation. They indicate agreement by their signatures. Students post worksheets on a special bulletin board. Finally, students decide on the most important of these situations and report to the whole class. Tell students that you will call on one group member to describe these "unknown friends." Therefore, all must know the chosen situation well.

DISCUSSION PART 1

1. Randomly call on students from each group to answer the three questions on the worksheet. Continue until all groups are covered.
2. How hard or easy was it for you to get the information you needed? Why was that so? Does that help people see their connections to others across the country? If so, how? If not, why?
3. What approach was most useful in getting the information you needed for the research?
4. As you hear other groups report, do you feel that the groups of "unknown friends" have anything in common? If you do, can you talk about those things?
5. Since you've heard others, can you think of new action students can take to affect the situation of your chosen group?
6. Use consensus to decide which situation of "unknown friends" you'd like to change. You will follow through on this in Part 3 of this activity.

PART 2

Before beginning Part 2 make arrangements for your class to work for about twenty minutes with another class of students their age.

1. Tell students they will now plan to educate other students about a group of "unknown friends." They will also show the ways they, as students, are potentially connected to those "unknown friends." They will have twenty minutes to work with a group of three students from another class. While they could convey the information by telling it, they could also use more creative ways to educate their peers. For example, students could devise a dilemma-situation like that in "Make That Connection." (Reiterate one as a reminder.) They could present the dilemma to the group, have them discuss it, and then provide background information from their research. Move around to help groups as they make their plans.

Interrupt students once in the middle of planning. Ask groups who've developed creative peer-teaching approaches to share briefly with the class. This may stimulate creativity among others.

2. Go over guidelines for peer tutoring, page 43, as a review. Students go to the cooperating classroom and use the peer-teaching strategy they developed to educate their peers about the situation of a group of "unknown friends."

DISCUSSION PART 2

1. How effective was your peer-tutoring approach?
2. How did other students respond to the information you presented?
3. Did other students come to understand their connection to the situation of the "unknown friends" you described? Why or why not?
4. What would you do differently next time?
5. What did you learn from this peer-teaching experience?

PART 3

Tell students they will now focus on what they can do about the situation of the "unknown friends" they chose to support. (See Part 1, Discussion questions 3, 6.)

Have the group that presented that situation review it. They list their ideas for student action. Write these on the board.

As a class, brainstorm additional action ideas. Discuss the pros and cons of the suggestions. Choose one or two suggestions to implement. Develop a class plan of action, delegating various responsibilities to subgroups. Periodically evaluate progress. At the end of the action, evaluate the project.

DISCUSSION PART 3

1. How did our cooperative action strategy help improve the situation of this group of "unknown friends"?
2. How did you feel about the plan?
3. As a class, how well did you cooperate to put the plan into effect?
4. To be even more effective, what would you do next time?

COMPLETION

PART 1 A student receives credit for this activity if:
Each group member completes research on the situation of a group of "unknown friends" in America and the group hands in three worksheets "Seeing Connections: Taking Action," signed by all.

PART 2 Each group member participates in developing a peer-teaching strategy presenting the situation of a group of "unknown friends" in America and each group member takes part in implementing the strategy.

PART 3 Each member of the class carries out his assigned task in the action project.

Example
Group of "Unknown Friends"

Citizens' Action Group—The Gray Panthers

A. Situation of Older People in America

- One-third of all elderly Americans are struggling to feed and house themselves on less than $4,000 a year.
- Forty percent of older Americans are in nursing homes not because of illness, but because they cannot care for themselves and have nowhere to go.
- Health care for the elderly costs four times what it does for other Americans. Many older people avoid medical attention because of the cost.

B. Legislation or Action
 1. Legislation proposed—The President proposes cuts in Medicare funds, which provide health care for older Americans. For millions of older Americans, this is the only health insurance they have.
 2. Action in Progress—The Gray Panthers are a national citizens' group that has 100 Gray Panther communities in 30 states across the nation. Their motto is "Youth and Age in Action." Gray Panthers work for many things that will make life liveable for older Americans. They lobby in Washington, educate other citizens, hold demonstrations, speak on radio and TV, and organize neighborhood meetings. Two of the many changes they work for are:
  a. Health Care
   - Fight cuts to Medicare.
   - Work to limit profit of drug companies, nursing homes and hospitals which often benefit at the expense of the poor.
   - Work for a National Health Service that would guarantee adequate health care to all Americans.
  b. Housing
   - Lobby for rent control and subsidized housing for older Americans.
   - Set up shared living arrangements for older people to live together with younger ones.
   - Fight for alternatives to nursing houses such as home care and adult day care.

C. Student Action
- Get more information on the Gray Panthers and give it to our friends and family.
- Write a petition to Congress asking them not to cut Medicare funding; get friends and community members to sign it.
- Invite a Gray Panther to speak in our school to help educate others about the situation of older Americans.
- Hold a car wash to raise money for the Gray Panthers.
- Write a letter to the President asking support for health care and housing rights for older Americans.
- Ask my parents to encourage my doctor to take Medicare or Medicaid patients.
- Join a Gray Panther demonstration.
- Interview older people in a nursing home. Ask them what the government and local citizens should do to make life better for older Americans. Write an article for the local newspaper about this.
- Collect refundable bottles and donate the money to the Gray Panthers.
- Develop an exhibit showing the problems of older Americans; display it in local places like the library, bank, or community center.
- Start cooperative senior-youth skill exchanges. Here older people teach young people a skill (like braiding a rug) and younger exchange a service (like going marketing for the older persons).
- Analyze reading books for treatment of older people and rewrite stereotypical stories to make them more fair.

Life Hurdle Cards

Life Hurdle Card B—1 You want to gain points by going into state or national politics. It's much harder to get elected because of your race. Your group loses ten points.	Life Hurdle Card B—2 You wanted to get a job that is considered "man's work" . . . like an engineer's job. Your parents and your guidance counselor advised against it. You trained for a job more typical for a woman—a nurse. You are like the average American woman. You make $.59 for every dollar a man makes. (If you work ten minutes to earn $.59, a man has to work only about six minutes to make the same amount.) Lose the points from the last match.	Life Hurdle Card D—1 You are very bright. You speak Spanish. Your school has no bilingual program. You have a great deal of trouble keeping up with your classmates while you learn English. Also, the white school in the district gets more money for materials and has much smaller classes than integrated schools like yours. You don't learn as much as you could. Your group loses fifteen points.
Life Hurdle Card D—2 Your school uses achievement tests that are biased against females. Your reading books provide few career choices for females. Therefore, female students don't develop positive self-images and they don't learn as much as they could. Your group can't count the scores of the next two matches.	Life Hurdle Card F—1 You want to enter a job-training program so you can get a good job. You have two young children. There are not any day-care centers with space for your children, so you postpone plans for job training. Your group must wait thirty seconds before continuing play.	Life Hurdle Card F—2 Your family wants to move to a nearby community where there is better education and recreation than where you live now. You tried to rent several apartments, but when you got there to look at them you were told they were already rented. A white friend went later and was told the apartments were still for rent. There are no low-income housing projects in that community. You stay where you are. Take twenty points away from your group's score.

WITH THE ODDS AGAINST THEM WORKSHEET

Information Sheet—Part A

Life Hurdles in America Today

Directions

The Life Hurdle Game Cards reflect real hurdles that groups of Americans face in our society. Pull out the Life Hurdle Cards from the deck and distribute at least one to a person. (One or two people may have extras.)

One person reads the first Information Item aloud. The person who thinks her Life Hurdle game card relates to that information item reads it aloud. If the group agrees that this is the right choice, the reader of the Information Item marks the correct number on the worksheet. Discuss and try to agree on an answer to the question. The reader writes it down. The next person reads Information Item 2. Continue accordingly until the worksheet is complete. Sign to indicate agreement.

Information Item 1

A report of the U.S. Department of Housing and Urban Development (HUD) indicates that 85 percent of blacks seeking a rental unit will encounter at least one instance of discrimination. For those seeking to purchase, 48 percent will face racial discrimination.

(National Urban League, 1980)

Life Hurdle Card _____
How is this a life hurdle? _____

_____

For whom is this a life hurdle? _____

_____

Information Item 2

a. Over 70 percent of characters on the California, Iowa, and Stanford achievement tests are male. Girls are more apt to get an answer correct if it mentions at least an equal number of girls.

(P. Campbell and E. Scott, 1980)

b. In school books, there are five times as many career choices for males than for females. Mothers and other typical female jobs such as teachers are the most common roles for women.

(G. Britton and M. Lumpkin, 1984)

Information Sheet—Part A—continued

Life Hurdle Card _____

How is this a life hurdle? _____

_____

For whom is this a life hurdle? _____

_____

Information Item 3

a. Students whose native language is not English can much better develop their abilities and potential in schools with bilingual education programs. Children do best in learning environments which respect them, their culture, and language.

(R. Ttoike, 1981)

b. Nationally, about 60 percent of students identified as limited-English speaking or non-English speaking were receiving bilingual education or equivalent services.

(U.S. Department of Education, 1981)

Life Hurdle Card _____

How is this a life hurdle? _____

_____

For whom is this a life hurdle? _____

_____

Information Item 4

All U.S. presidents have been white. In 1981 the Senate had two minority members, both Asian-American, out of 100 Senators. The House had 18 Blacks, 6 Latinos, and 2 Asian-Americans, out of 435 Representatives. In 1980 there were 4,912 Black officials in 50 states, the District of Columbia, and the Virgin Islands, representing 1 percent of the 490,000 elected officials in the U.S.

(Joint Center for Political Studies, 1981)

Life Hurdle Card _____

How is this a life hurdle? _____

_____

For whom is this a life hurdle? _____

Information Sheet—Part A—continued

Information Item 5
Inadequate child care:

a. restricts women from participating in federally-supported education and job employment programs geared to equal opportunity

b. prevents women from taking jobs or advancing in present ones

c. often keeps women in a state of poverty

(U.S. Commission on Civil Rights, 1981)

Life Hurdle Card _____

How is this a life hurdle? _____

_____

For whom is this a life hurdle? _____

Information Item 6
Although there were more than 44 million women in the paid labor force, the majority were restricted to just 20 of the 420 listed occupational categories—mostly retail sales, service, clerical and factory. Of those who found jobs in 1978, only 9.9 percent held well-paid traditionally male jobs.

(*Women Today,* February 1981)

Life Hurdle Card _____

How is this a life hurdle? _____

_____

For whom is this a life hurdle? _____

WITH THE ODDS AGAINST THEM WORKSHEET

Information Sheet—Part B

The Distribution of Wealth

Directions

Read the following information aloud. Then discuss the two questions at the end. Summarize the group opinion(s) in writing.

What is wealth?

Wealth is composed of the assets (or resources) a person or family has. It includes the worth of house, cars, clothes, stocks, bonds, and money in the bank.

Where is the wealth in the United States?

Upper-class people

Top 1 percent of the population has 33 percent of the wealth.

Top 20 percent of the population has 77 percent of the wealth.

Middle-class people

The middle 60 percent of the population has 23 percent of the wealth.

Poor people

The lower 20 percent of the population has no wealth.

1. How does the distribution of wealth in the United States affect the life chances of various people and groups?

2. Competitive individualism is the belief that competition is fair and each person or group has an equal chance to succeed. How do these facts on the distribution of wealth in America affect your thoughts about the idea of competitive individualism?

Signed _____

_____

_____

THE SLIDE, SCREAM, AND SPLASH WATER SLIDE COMPANY WORKSHEET

Group Information Sheet

General Information: Slide, Scream, and Splash Water Slide Company

Slide, Scream, and Splash Water Slide Company is a thriving business. It makes large water slides that are sold across the country to parks and amusement parks. It employs one hundred workers who receive, on the average, $300 a week. There is no union.

The Board of Directors of SS&SWSC make final decisions about the company. Each board member has a salary of $150,000. Profit of the company last year was $800,000. The Board of Directors and their friends are also the owners of the company.

Board of Directors: Slide, Scream, and Splash Water Slide Company

As the Board of Directors of Slide, Scream, and Splash Water Slide Company, you have enough orders to fill so that you need to hire more workers. You have enough work to do to keep fifteen people working hard full-time, but you decide to save money on salaries, and thus make more profit, by hiring only ten. You think that if you push people to work hard, and give bonuses to the fastest workers, maybe you can get close to the same amount of work out of ten people as you could from fifteen.

During this simulation, you have the power to do what you want. You can change decisions that have already been made. You can also make new decisions based on discussions and on what you believe is right.

White Women

In the past, you have not been able to get jobs in the Slide, Scream, and Splash Water Slide Company because you are women. Owners thought women were too weak to make water slides. Furthermore, they thought you should be at home raising children.

You very much want to work at Slide, Scream, and Splash because the jobs pay well and because you believe you are competent to do the work.

Group Information Sheet—continued

White Men

You look forward to getting a job at Slide, Scream, and Splash Water Slide Company. Men like you have worked there in the past and have done an excellent job. Some of you have fathers, brothers, or friends who work there and want you to get into the company.

You very much want to work at Slide, Scream, and Splash because the jobs pay well and because you know you are competent to do the work.

Minority Men

In the past you have not been able to get jobs at the Slide, Scream, and Splash Water Slide Company because you are minority men. Owners thought you didn't have the skills to put together the different parts of the water slide. Yet many of you have had much more complicated jobs than making water slides.

You very much want to work at Slide, Scream, and Splash because the jobs pay well and because you know you are competent to do the work.

Minority Women

In the past you have not been able to get jobs at Slide, Scream, and Splash Water Slide Company because you are minority women. The owners said you weren't qualified and hinted that you would be too aggressive and would intimidate the men. Furthermore, they thought you should be home taking care of your children.

You very much want to work at Slide, Scream, and Splash because the jobs pay well and because you know you are competent to do the work.

THE SLIDE, SCREAM, AND SPLASH WATER SLIDE COMPANY
WORKSHEET

Individual Information Sheet

White Men

White man: You support your five children.

White man: Your father worked for Slide, Scream, and Splash for fifteen years and is a dedicated worker.

White man: You are particularly skilled at welding.

White man: You help support your mother who is very sick.

White man: You are an experienced worker who worked for Slide, Scream, and Splash once before and were laid off.

Minority Men

Minority man: You support your three children.

Minority man: You have excellent recommendations from other jobs.

Minority man: Your father is handicapped and has medical expenses that you help with.

Minority man: You are willing to work overtime as much as the company needs you.

Minority man: You are a very skilled metal-worker.

THE SLIDE, SCREAM, AND SPLASH WATER SLIDE COMPANY
WORKSHEET

Individual Information Sheet—continued

Minority Women

Minority woman: You support your two children.

Minority woman: You have worked for five years in a playground equipment company and just got laid off. You have excellent recommendations.

Minority woman: Your husband is a disabled Vietnam veteran and you support him and your two children.

Minority woman: You are an excellent team leader and know how to motivate people to work hard.

Minority woman: You have worked on a construction crew building a bridge and are not afraid of work that demands strength.

White Women

White woman: You support your three children.

White woman: You have worked before and have excellent recommendations. You never missed a day's work.

White woman: You support your mother who is blind.

White woman: If you don't get this job, you will have to go on welfare. You want to work and don't want to be on welfare.

White woman: You've been enrolled in a job-training program in metal work and want to be able to use your skills.

MOVING WORKSHEET

Dialogues

September 15

Hector: Mom, I'm so excited we're going to move! Did you look at houses in the Lakeview and Parkside parts of the city?

Ms. Morales: The real estate agent didn't want to show me any houses there.

Hector: What's a real estate agent?

Ms. Morales: That's a person whose job is to sell houses. She said we wouldn't like those neighborhoods. She took me to the Greenwood area.

Hector: I wish we would live in Parkside where my best friend Tanya lives. That's where the city pool is and I could walk there from our house.

Ms. Morales: I'll ask the real estate agent again about that. Now let's go out and have a catch.

September 25

Theresa: Dad, why are you so upset?

Mr. Riley: A Puerto Rican family bought the house down the block. I'm afraid we'll have to move.

Theresa: But why?

Mr. Riley: The value of our house will go down.

Theresa: What does that mean?

Mr. Riley: It means that our house won't be worth as much money because Puerto Rican people will be living in the neighborhood.

Theresa: That's silly! It's the same house.

Mr. Riley: It may be silly, but that's the way the world is. Many people don't like living with Puerto Ricans on the block. They think they won't keep their houses nice.

Theresa: Well, I think that's even sillier. Mr. Warren has the messiest house on the block and he's as white as can be. Anyway, I don't want to move. I like it here in Greenwood.

Dialogues—continued

October 13

Ms. Morales: Hector, I asked the real estate agent to take me to Parkside. She said there were no houses for sale there. But I drove through Parkside and saw a "for sale" sign.

Hector: Why didn't the agent show you that house? Doesn't she want us to live there?

Ms. Morales: Maybe that's true. I called and found out it cost $45,000. That's just what we could afford because Aunt Carmen would move in with us and give money toward the mortgage payment every month. I went to the bank to apply for a mortgage.

Hector: What is a mortgage?

Ms. Morales: That's a loan a bank gives to people so they can pay for a house.

Later:

Hector: What's the matter, Mom. You look sad. What happened?

Ms. Morales: They didn't give me a mortgage. They told me to look in the Greenwood area.

Hector: That's not fair. I wanted to live near Tanya!

October 20

Mr. Riley: Theresa, I know you'll be upset to hear this, but we're going to move.

Theresa: Dad, no!

Mr. Riley: Ms. Pope, the real estate agent, offered me $35,000 for our house. She told me to take that money while I could. There will be more Puerto Ricans moving in.

Theresa: But Dad, you bought the house for more than that! You told me you could sell it for $40,000 if you needed to.

Mr. Riley: Theresa, if more Puerto Ricans move in it will be worth even less.

Theresa: I don't want to move away from my friends. Anyway, I will make new friends with the Puerto Rican kids.

Mr. Riley: I've already talked to your friends' parents. They'll be moving too.

Dialogues—continued

Theresa: If everyone who lives here now got together, we could decide to stay and welcome the Puerto Ricans who move in. If new people feel welcomed they'll keep up their houses. I'd like a neighborhood with different kinds of people. I could play with someone like Hector Morales. He was a friend of mine in day camp last summer.

Mr. Riley: No, we're going to save our shirts. I want to get $35,000 before it's too late.

November 1

Ms. Morales: Hector, I have good news for you. I bought a house in Greenwood. It's a nice integrated neighborhood.

Hector: How much did it cost?

Ms. Morales: $50,000

Hector: Wow, Mom, that's a lot of money.

Ms. Morales: Yes, it is. It's the only house I could get that the bank would give me a mortgage for. We'll have to give up everything special for a few years. I'm sorry, but there won't be money for a new bike. It will be a tight squeeze. I hope we can make it.

MOVING WORKSHEET

Dialogues—continued

December 20

Mr. Riley: Get out of bed, Theresa, it's moving day!

Theresa: I don't want to get out of bed and I don't want to move!

Mr. Riley: Don't blame me. If those Puerto Ricans weren't so pushy, we wouldn't be moving.

Theresa: Hmph!

December 29

Ms. Morales: Welcome to our new house, Hector.

Hector: Mom, it's great! Someone left a great tree house in the backyard tree too. The only thing I don't like is that so many houses on the block are for sale.

Ms. Morales: The white people on the block don't want to live near us. I'm sorry about that. I wanted to live in an integrated neighborhood.

Hector: Go talk to them. Maybe you can convince them to stay.

Ms. Morales: It's no use. They won't listen to me.

Hector: Well, Mom, welcome to Greenwood.

MOVING WORKSHEET

Questions

Answer the question from the point of view of the person whose part you read. You answer first. If your group has a different answer, write that below yours.

1. How do you feel about moving? Why do you feel that way?

    a. Theresa

    b. Mr. Riley

    c. Hector

    d. Ms. Morales

2. Below are ways people are sometimes treated unfairly regarding housing. Even though many of these practices are against the law, they still occur. Work together to give an example for each from "Moving."

    a. **Steering:** Real estate agents show only certain neighborhoods to certain people or races of people.
    Example:

    b. **Blockbusting:** Real estate agents scare white people by telling them that minority people are moving in. White people sell their houses cheaply. Then the real estate agents sell those houses to minorities at a high price.
    Example:

    c. **Redlining:** For certain areas, banks refuse loans to minority people.
    Example:

3. In "Moving," white people did not work together with Puerto Ricans. Give an example.

Questions—continued

4. Actions of these bank and real estate agents helped keep white and Puerto Rican people from working together. Everyone lost out by not working together. What did each person lose? Answer the question about the person whose part you read. You answer first. If your group has a different answer, write that below yours.

   a. Theresa

   b. Mr. Riley

   c. Hector

   d. Ms. Morales

5. How could whites and Puerto Ricans have cooperated? How would each person gain?

   a. Theresa

   b. Mr. Riley

   c. Hector

   d. Ms. Morales

6. How much money did the real estate agents make by blockbusting and steering?

7. Mr. Riley blames Puerto Ricans for his decision to move. Who would you blame? Why?

Signed _____

_____

_____

TEAM PLAYERS? WORKSHEET

Dialogue

Stacey: Hi, Rodney! It's ten o'clock on the button. I really like you as a friend because I can count on you!

Rodney: Thanks, Stacey. We don't even have to walk fast to get to the soccer game on time.

Stacey: How's your dad doing?

Rodney: Worse than ever. Ever since he was laid off from this job he hasn't been himself. He feels so hopeless. You know what he said to me today?

Stacey: What?

Rodney: He said, "Rodney, I'm a loser. I've worked so hard all my life and now I'm unemployed. I've tried week after week to get a job and I can't find one." Then he started to cry. I've never seen my dad cry before, except when his brother died.

Stacey: Oh, Rodney, what did you do?

Rodney: I said, "Dad, you're not a loser. You worked for fifteen years on the assembly line making great cars. It's not your fault that you were laid off. I learned in social studies that over 10% of the work force is unemployed. There's nothing wrong with *you*. You were an excellent worker! You're not a loser!"

Stacey: Then what happened?

Rodney: He said, "Thanks, son. I really appreciate your trying to cheer me up." He gave me a big hug. "Out here in the world I do feel like a loser, though."

Stacey: I feel so bad for your dad. You're lucky in one way, though. You and your dad share feelings. My dad is always too busy to share feelings with me.

Rodney: Is that because he's a businessperson?

Stacey: I guess so. He does so much. He's an inventor, a businessperson, and the head of a company that makes and sell robots. He's always so busy we hardly ever get a chance to do anything together, let alone talk.

Rodney: Gee, that's too bad. You should tell him to think twice about making robots. It's robots that put my dad out of work. The company bought robots to do things workers used to do.

Stacey: I told him that already. He said, "Stacey, I can't think about other people's problems. They've got to deal with them themselves. You can't be a winner in life by asking questions like that. I won't make enough to buy that swimming pool for our yard if I get into those kinds of questions."

Dialogue—continued

Rodney: I should try to get my dad to talk to him. Maybe he'd change his mind.

Stacey: I wish you would. My dad is always rushing around. He says he does enough work for three people. He never has time for me.

Rodney: Gee, Stacey, have you tried to talk to him about that?

Stacey: I tried to give him a way to cut down on his work. I told him about your dad being unemployed and how good he is working with electronics and machines. I suggested he hire your dad to test the new robots.

Rodney: What a great idea!

Stacey: I thought so too. But my dad said, "No. I need to do all the work myself. Only if I test and sell the robot alone can I stay in control of the whole business."

Rodney: Is that all he cares about?

Stacey: Sometimes I wonder. Because then he gave me a quick kiss and said, "Bye, Stace, I'll be home late tonight. I'm testing the latest model."

Rodney: That's sad. I'd try to tell him how you feel. Maybe he'd change.

Stacey: I hope so. I worry he'll get a heart attack at the pace he goes. Well, here we are at the field. It's great to have someone to talk to! Now let's play a great game!

Rodney and Stacey played a terrific soccer game. They accepted a ride home with a team member's brother and were in an automobile accident. Each suffered a broken arm. They didn't see each other for a week.

Rodney: Hi, Stacey! Do you want to autograph my cast?

Stacey: Sure, if you'll sign mine! What a mess we're in! How have you been?

Rodney: My arm is ok now, but I wasn't sure there for a while. Right after the accident, Dad came and picked me up. We had to wait for over an hour in the emergency room before my arm got examined and set. There were so many people and so few chairs that I had to stand up. When Dad and I asked if I could be taken next because my arm hurt so much, I was told to wait my turn. Wow, the pain was killing me! What also was so terrible was that there were so many other people in pain and everybody had to wait. Many people were crying. That was such a horrible experience!

Stacey: That sounds awful! When my dad got me, we called our doctor and she met us at the hospital right away. She was so nice to me. I'm going to get special therapy too.

Dialogue—continued

Rodney: What a difference from me! When I went back to the clinic to have my arm checked a few days later, I had to wait two hours. The people there aren't very friendly. My father says they're overworked. Still, it didn't make me feel very good.

Stacey: It doesn't seem fair, does it, that because my father makes a lot of money, I get better medical care than you.

Rodney: It sure doesn't. Let's figure out what we can do about that!

TEAM PLAYERS? WORKSHEET

Questions

1. Why are Rodney and Stacey worried about Rodney's dad?

2. Why does he feel like a loser?

3. Is it Rodney's father's fault that he is unemployed? Why or why not?

4. Why are Rodney and Stacey worried about Stacey's dad?

5. Stacey's dad says he wants to be a winner. What does he do to try to be a winner?

6. The work Stacey's dad does to make money contributes to Rodney's dad losing his job. Yet Stacey's dad says, "I can't think about other people's problems or I won't get ahead." In what ways do you agree? Disagree?

The economic system in a society determines the way work is organized, who does what and who gets what. In our country, it is organized competitively. People compete against each other in order to get ahead. In such a system there are "winners" and there are people who lose even though they may work very hard. There are thousands of people in America today like Rodney's father and Stacey's father.

7. What are some of the prices—the things they lose out on—that Stacey and her father pay because he is trying to be a winner?

TEAM PLAYERS? WORKSHEET

Questions—continued

8. What are some of the prices Rodney and his father pay because Rodney's father is unemployed?

9. Name some of the benefits to Stacey's father if he shared some of his power, status, and money with Rodney's father by hiring him. What would be the benefits to Rodney's father?

10. In a competitive economic system some people get ahead at the expense of others. How does Stacey's family benefit at the expense of Rodney's? How do you feel about this? Why?

11. Compare the health care Rodney and Stacey received. What accounts for the differences? How do you feel about this? Why?

12. Some people believe, "In America the best services go to the most deserving people. This is the way it should be." How do you feel about this? Why?

13. How is the fact that Stacey gets good health care connected to the fact that Rodney gets poor care? What could be done about this?

Language Arts

Remember the stories you heard about the Underground Railroad. Look back at them in order to get more concrete information on the times and events. Look especially for details such as clothing, food, landscape, method of travel, conversation, and so forth. Remember . . . travel took place at night.

Now you are going to work cooperatively, in pairs, to write your own Underground Railroad stories. Write them in the first person as if you were a conductor on the railroad. Check back with your sources as you discover what other information you need. When you are finished, have another pair read your story and help you correct it for grammar and historical accuracy.

Now make a large copy of your story to read aloud with a younger class. Print it out in marker on newsprint so that the younger children can read it with you as you read it aloud. Illustrate your story on large newsprint—again check pictures in history books so you can be sure to make your pictures accurate.

When you go to the younger class, read your stories to them. Go over the information. Then divide them into small groups and take dictation from them on their own stories about being conductors on the Underground Railroad. Print these neatly and give to the students to illustrate.

UNDERGROUND RAILROAD—THE 1800s WORKSHEET

Math

At this center you will work with some math problems from the Underground Railroad. You will then create math problems for the younger class and work with those students to solve the problems.

Work in pairs to do one of the following problems. Check each other's work.

1. Slaves escaping on the Underground Railroad walked at night so they wouldn't be seen. They followed the North Star. If a group walked 12 miles the first night, half as many the second night, 5 more miles the third night than the first, and 9 miles the fourth night, how far did they walk in those 4 nights? What was the average amount they walked each night?

2. The Smyth family had a stop on the Underground Railroad. It was in a cave below their basement. The first year they hid 32 escaping slaves and the next year, as more conductors found out about their stop, they hid three times as many escaping slaves. During those 2 years 89 of the slaves they hid escaped to Canada by rowboat. The rest escaped by canoe. How many escaped by canoe?

3. On her first trip North, Harriet Tubman stayed at 7 homes on the Underground Railroad. On her second trip she stopped at 10 homes, half of which were ones she'd stayed with on the first trip. On her third trip she stayed at 9 homes, a third of which were new. On her fourth trip she stayed at three new homes and 8 she'd already been to. What were the total number of **different homes** Harriet Tubman stayed at during her four trips? Why do you think some homes got used repeatedly and some didn't?

Now you are ready to prepare for work with a younger class. First you must find out the math level of the younger class. Talk with their teacher. Borrow a copy of their math book. Be sure to find out what pages they're on. Get copies of any worksheets they're doing. Now work together to design math problems for them about the Underground Railroad. Keep them on their level.

Puppets

Look back at the information you learned about the Underground Railroad. You are going to make stick puppets of different people in order to be able to tell the story of the Underground Railroad.

Brainstorm as a group the puppets you would need in order to tell the story. Cut these out of thin cardboard and color them. Mount on tongue depressors. You might also need to make pieces of scenery (houses, rivers, stars) on sticks. Remember travel took place at night.

Create a puppet show or series of puppet shows to tell stories about the Underground Railroad. You might use the play about Harriet Tubman in *Listen, Children,* edited by Dorothy Strickland, one of the others available in books, or make up your own. Make sure each person contributes to the show and is responsible for a puppet.

Perform your shows to the younger class. Then help them to make their own puppets and create their own plays.

Vocabulary

First learn the meanings of each of the following words as they relate to the Underground Railroad: fugitive, slave, Underground Railroad, conductor, password, Moses, emancipate, North Star. Add any other words you think of from the reading you've done.

Now work together to make a card game younger children could play in order to learn these words. Use ½ size file cards for the words and definitions. Put each word on one card and its definition on another. Can you come up with a game that can be played cooperatively?

Make sure each student has contributed at least four words and cards. Initial them.

Teach your game to a younger class.

Music

At this center, you will learn three songs about the Underground Railroad. They are: "Follow the Drinkin' Gourd," "Go Down, Moses," and "Harriet Tubman." Form partners. Each learns about one song and teaches the information to others. First read through the words of each song and be sure you understand them. Use history books and the encyclopedia to look up anything you don't understand.

The drinking gourd is the Big Dipper with the North Star at its tip. Most of the words in this song give secret instructions (in code) to slaves about how to escape. "Moses" in "Go Down, Moses" refers not just to Moses from the Bible but to Harriet Tubman and other workers on the Underground Railroad.

After all the students in your group understand the songs, listen to them on the records, then learn to sing them yourselves.

Work in partners to each make a large song chart for one song for the younger class so that they will all be able to see the words. Illustrate the chart to help them understand the meanings. Work out how you are going to explain these meanings to the younger class. Partners give other partners feedback.

Practice singing the songs, then practice teaching them to members of your class.

Message Cards: Scavenger Hunt

Family I—The Hunts (color code red)

The Hunts—Message 1a

You are members of the Hunt family. John and Marie Hunt worked very hard to save money for the house you live in in a residential section of Niagara Falls, New York. You like the neighborhood because people take good care of their houses. Your son Billy likes his school, the 99th St. School.

- Find out what you have in common with other residents of your neighborhood.

- Then get your next clue from the teacher.

The Hunts—Message 1b

Your neighbor, Lois Gibbs, comes to your house. She read articles in the newspaper about toxic (poisonous) chemicals that had been dumped in an old canal—Love Canal. The chemicals were then covered up. The articles say that some of the houses in your neighborhood have been built on top of Love Canal!

Lois' son developed epilepsy and blood problems since he started school. His school was built on top of Love Canal. She wants to know if anyone in your family has been sick. Lois thinks his problems may have something to do with the chemicals buried in Love Canal.

Marie tells her that she was pregnant last year and her baby was born dead (stillborn). No one knows why the baby died. You feel it was an accident.

- Find out about the health of other Love Canal residents.

- Then get your next clue from the teacher.

The Hunts—Message 1c

Residents dig up new facts in the Love Canal case. You learn that from 1920 to 1953 the Hooker Chemical Company, a branch of Occidental Petroleum Company, dumped toxic chemicals in Love Canal. In 1953 they covered the canal and sold the land to the Board of Education for $1. Part of the sales contract said that Hooker would not be responsible if anyone got sick or died because of the buried wastes. Now people are getting sick and some are dying and it may be because of buried wastes.

You decide to join the Love Canal Homeowners Association (LCHA) to try to work together with your neighbors. Both John and Marie go to many meetings to tell others about Love Canal and demand that government officials do something. Most officials say things like, "We'll look into it" or "We'll conduct a study." You keep on pushing for action.

- Find new information about Love Canal from neighbors.

- Find out what other members of the LCHA are doing to push for a change.

- Then get your next clue from the teacher.

Message Cards: Scavenger Hunt—continued

The Hunts—Message 1d

Finally after more than a year of organizing—and because of the action of the people in Love Canal—the government bought your houses. Everyone could finally move to a safe area!

Your action together also helped many other people. You educated people across America about the dangers of dumping toxic wastes. You have given other communities an example of how to do many things that will help them. These things are:

1. getting community people to work together
2. doing a health survey
3. discovering what toxic waste or pollution is present
4. organizing protests
5. working with the media
6. pressuring the government for changes

- Find out what other ways the people of Love Canal cooperated to make changes for all Americans.

- Then get a clue from the teacher.

Family II—The Gibbs (color code blue)

The Gibbs—Message 2a

You are members of the Gibbs family. Harry and Lois Gibbs worked very hard to save money for the house you live in in Love Canal, a section of Niagara Falls, New York. You like the community because people are friendly and they take care of their homes. Michael and Missy have many other children to play with.

- Find out what you have in common with other residents of Love Canal.

- Then get your next clue from the teacher.

The Gibbs—Message 2b

Lois read in the paper about toxic (poisonous) chemicals that had been dumped and covered up in your neighborhood. The dump was called Love Canal. The article said that houses and a school were built right on top of the chemical dump. Michael just began kindergarten at that school.

Since he started school he developed epilepsy and blood problems. You think the chemicals underground may have something to do with his problems. You're very angry and want to do something. You decide to go from house to house to see what health problems other people have. You will ask them to sign a petition to get the school closed.

- Find out what else you have in common with other Love Canal residents.

- Then get your next clue from the teacher.

Message Cards: Scavenger Hunt—continued

The Gibbs—Message 2c

You and other residents have dug up more facts about Love Canal. For example, you now know there are 21 tons of highly toxic waste buried beneath the school. Even so, the Board of Education refuses to close the school and send children to other schools.

You organize the Love Canal Homeowners Association (LCHA). The main goal of the LCHA is to have the government relocate (move to new homes) residents affected by the toxic wastes of Love Canal. Lois is elected President of LCHA.

With other residents, you try to educate the community and nation about the dangers you see in Love Canal. Month after month you work and there is still no government action. You go on the radio and TV, and you talk to Congresspeople in Washington, D.C. They say the connection between toxic chemicals and health problems is unproven.

- Find new information about Love Canal from your neighbors.

- Find out what other members of the LCHA are doing to push for a change.

- Then get your next clue from the teacher.

The Gibbs—Message 2d

Finally after more than a year of organizing—and because of the action of the people in Love Canal—the government bought your houses. Everyone could finally move from the area!

You formed a new organization, the Citizens' Clearinghouse for Hazardous Wastes. It gives information and ideas to other Americans who discover there are dangerous chemicals in their neighborhood or town. The new organization is in Washington, D.C. Lois is the president. You used to think that you were ordinary people who didn't have much power. You have learned that "ordinary" people can get together and make changes that affect a whole nation.

- Find out what other ways the people of Love Canal cooperated to make changes for all Americans.

- Then get a clue from the teacher.

Family III—The Kellys (color code green)

The Kellys—Message 3a

You are a member of the Kelly family. Joan Kelly worked very hard to save money to buy the house you live in. You moved here because you wanted a neighborhood where Paul, Andy, and Theresa could walk to school. The 99th Street School is just two blocks away.

- Find out what you have in common with other residents of your neighborhood.

- Then get your next clue from the teacher.

Message Cards: Scavenger Hunt—continued

The Kellys—Message 3b

Your neighbor Lois Gibbs comes to your house. She read articles in the newspaper about toxic (poisonous) chemicals that had been dumped in an old canal—Love Canal. The chemicals were then covered up. The article says that some of the houses in your neighborhood have been built on top of Love Canal!

Lois' son developed epilepsy and blood problems since he started school. She thinks the buried chemicals may have caused the diseases. His school was built on top of Love Canal. Lois wants to know if anyone in your family has been sick.

You tell Lois that the boy next door had a common childhood disease. All of a sudden his body became swollen. He was taken to the hospital, and he died.

Your family was shocked and very sad. You are very worried about the dangerous effects of the chemicals in Love Canal. You would like to move, but you can't afford it. Your house is worth much less money now because people know it was built on top of Love Canal.

• Find out about the health of other Love Canal residents.

• Then get your next clue from the teacher.

The Kellys—Message 3c

You and other residents have dug up more facts about Love Canal. You learn that of the 200 chemicals buried at Love Canal, 12 are carcinogens (things that cause cancer). You also discovered that the state knew about the danger of some of the chemicals in the early 1970s, but did nothing.

Now the health department has told you that you shouldn't let your children out in your own backyard! Their feet will be burned by leaking chemicals. You used to think that people who protested and held demonstrations were un-American. Now you've learned you sometimes need to push the government to get human needs met.

You join the LCHA and march in picket lines and go to demonstrations. You believe it's your right to live in a safe place and your children should be able to play in their own backyard.

• Find out new information about Love Canal from your neighbors.

• Find out what other members of the LCHA are doing to push for a change.

• Then get your next clue from the teacher.

Message Cards: Scavenger Hunt—continued

The Kellys—Message 3d

Finally after more than a year of organizing—and because of the action of the people in Love Canal—the government bought your houses. Everyone could finally move to a safe area!

Your cooperative action at Love Canal caused the government to create the Superfund, money that goes to cleaning up waste sites that may be dangerous. The EPA (Environmental Protection Agency) has found 500 sites in America to clean up with this money. Your hard work paid off for all Americans!

- Find out in what other ways the people of Love Canal cooperated to make changes for all Americans.
- Then get a clue from the teacher.

Family IV—The Rosatis (color code purple)

The Rosatis—Message 4a

You are members of the Rosati family. Louie and Darlene worked hard for 20 years to buy a house in Love Canal, a section of Niagara Falls, New York. You will both retire soon and you look forward to spending peaceful days with friends and neighbors in Love Canal.

- Find out what you have in common with other residents of your neighborhood.
- Then get your next clue from the teacher.

The Rosatis—Message 4b

Your neighbor Lois Gibbs comes to your house. She read articles in the newspaper about toxic (poisonous) chemicals that had been dumped in an old canal—Love Canal. The chemicals were then covered up. The articles say that some of the houses in your neighborhood have been built on top of Love Canal!

Lois' son developed epilepsy and blood problems since he started school. She thinks the buried chemicals may have caused his diseases. His school was built on top of Love Canal. Lois wants to know if anyone in your family has been sick.

Louie tells Lois that he has lung cancer. He never smoked or worked in industry. Now that you've heard Lois, you're worried that Love Canal might have caused it.

You'd like to move to a safer place. You only have a small amount of money saved and you need that to live on during your retirement. No one will buy your house now that they know about the chemicals in Love Canal.

- Find out what else you have in common with other Love Canal residents.
- Then get your next clue from the teacher.

Message Cards: Scavenger Hunt—continued

The Rosatis—Message 4c

You and other residents of Love Canal have dug up more facts in the Love Canal case. You now know that the chemicals buried in Love Canal can damage the central nervous system. Dioxin, which many studies link to cancer, is also buried there.

Before Love Canal, you had blind faith in the government. You refused to believe that the government would build a school—or allow people to build homes—in a dangerous area.

Now you have the LCHA to fight with others to guarantee your safety.

You talk to other people in your city and ask them to sign petitions supporting people's right to a safe environment. You go on the radio too. You hope that other people who don't live in Love Canal will put pressure on government officials. Maybe then there will be some action.

- Find out other new information about Love Canal from your neighbors.
- Find out what other LCHA members are doing to push for a change.
- Then get your next clue from the teacher.

The Rosatis—Message 4d

Finally after more than a year of organizing—and because of the action of the people in Love Canal—the government bought your houses. Everyone could finally move from the dangerous area!

Because of Love Canal, the Citizens' Clearinghouse for Hazardous Wastes formed. This nationwide group works together to try to have landfills made illegal. Scientists have discovered that chemicals buried in the ground are likely to leak into underground water supplies. This can be very dangerous to people who drink the water.

There are many ways for industries to safely dispose of toxic wastes, but this costs money. They must decide to spend the money to do that. The Citizens' Clearinghouse believes the government should make sure that happens.

- Find out in what other ways the people of Love Canal cooperated to make changes for all Americans.
- Then get a clue from the teacher.

LOVE CANAL TREASURE HUNT WORKSHEET

Message Cards: Scavenger Hunt—continued

Family V—The Johnsons (color code orange)

The Johnsons—Message 5a

You are members of the Johnson family. A year ago you moved into the first house you ever owned. It's in Love Canal, an area in Niagara Falls, New York. You picked this area because of the lovely trees around the small, neat houses. The neighbors are very friendly. You will be having your first baby soon.

- Find out what you have in common with other residents of your neighborhood.
- Then get your next clue from the teacher.

The Johnsons—Message 5b

Your neighbor Lois Gibbs comes to your house. She read articles in the newspaper about toxic (poisonous) chemicals that had been dumped in an old canal—Love Canal. The chemicals were then covered up. The articles say that some of the houses in your neighborhood have been built on top of Love Canal!

Lois' son developed epilepsy and blood problems since he started school. She thinks the buried chemicals may have caused his diseases. His school was built on top of Love Canal. Lois wants to know if anyone in your family has been sick.

You tell her that your baby was just born with a birth defect. She has six toes. You have also heard about two other babies in the neighborhood born with birth defects. One has a club foot. Another was so deformed that it died.

What Lois told you has made you stop and think. Maybe, you hope, this is all happening by chance.

- Find out what else you have in common with other Love Canal residents.
- Then get your next clue from the teacher.

Message Cards: Scavenger Hunt—continued

The Johnsons—Message 5c

You and other residents have dug up more facts about the Love Canal case. You find out that in 1979, only 4 babies out of the 22 babies that were born were normal. The Health Department has told your family not to go into the basement and kitchen of your own house because it is too dangerous.

You are very angry. Imagine you can't even go into the basement and kitchen of the house that you worked so hard to buy! You join the LCHA. All the neighbors have gotten together to demand that the government move residents to other houses in a safe neighborhood.

Month after month, officials say they are "looking into the problem." Nothing has been done. More people are getting sick. You think some people's genes may have been affected. You're afraid that birth defects and other diseases could now spread from generation to generation.

Community members were so angry that they surrounded a building where two government officials were. People wouldn't let them out until the President of the United States decided to do something.

• Find out other new information about Love Canal from your neighbors.

• Find out what other members of the LCHA are doing to push for a change.

• Then get your next clue from the teacher.

The Johnsons—Message 5d

Finally after more than a year of organizing—and because of the action of the people in Love Canal—the government bought your houses. Everyone could finally move from the dangerous area!

Because of Love Canal the Citizens' Clearinghouse on Hazardous Wastes was formed. It works to help other communities that face problems like Love Canal. For example, residents in Centrailia, Pennsylvania have been living for 20 years on the top of an out-of-control mine fire under their homes. Toxic fumes, that may be deadly, leak.

The Citizens' Clearinghouse for Hazardous Wastes works with people like residents of Centrailia to fight for safe lives. Your action in Love Canal has been a model for cooperative citizens' action across America!

• Find out in what other ways people of Love Canal cooperated to make changes for all Americans.

• Then get a clue from the teacher.

LOVE CANAL TREASURE HUNT WORKSHEET

The Class Treasure

You've done a terrific job cooperating as a class!

You've learned about toxic wastes and what can be done. You have helped reach the treasure many people are seeking—safe communities for all Americans.

Here's a special treat for you!

You've done a terrific job cooperating as a class!

You've learned about toxic wastes and what can be done. You have helped reach the treasure many people are seeking—safe communities for all Americans.

Here's a special treat for you!

You've done a terrific job cooperating as a class!

You've learned about toxic wastes and what can be done. You have helped reach the treasure many people are seeking—safe communities for all Americans.

Here's a special treat for you!

You've done a terrific job cooperating as a class!

You've learned about toxic wastes and what can be done. You have helped reach the treasure many people are seeking—safe communities for all Americans.

Here's a special treat for you!

You've done a terrific job cooperating as a class!

You've learned about toxic wastes and what can be done. You have helped reach the treasure many people are seeking—safe communities for all Americans.

Here's a special treat for you!

LOVE CANAL TREASURE HUNT WORKSHEET

Treasure Hunt Key

Family	Hunt (red)	Gibbs (blue)	Kelly (green)	Rosati (purple)	Johnson (orange)
Clues & Messages (clue given by teacher at beginning)	*	**	***	****	*****
Round 1 Hiding Place find	message 1a	message 2a	message 3a	message 4a	message 5a
teacher gives clue	**	***	****	*****	*
Round 2 Hiding Place find	message 1b	message 2b	message 3b	message 4b	message 5b
teacher gives clue	***	****	*****	*	**
Round 3 Hiding Place find	message 1c	message 2c	message 3c	message 4c	message 5c
teacher gives clue	****	*****	*	**	***
Round 4 Hiding Place find	message 1d	message 2d	message 3d	message 4d	message 5d
teacher gives clue	The Class Treasure Message				

Treasure Hunt Summary

At Hiding Place * will be message cards 1a, 5b, 4c, 3d.

At Hiding Place ** will be message cards 2a, 1b, 5c, 4d.

At Hiding Place *** will be message cards 3a, 2b, 1c, 5d.

At Hiding Place **** will be message cards 4a, 3b, 2c, 1d.

At Hiding Place ***** will be message cards 5a, 4b, 3c, 2d.

LOVE CANAL TREASURE HUNT WORKSHEET

Examples of Clues

---

*

Our class was interrupted with a buzzing full of force,

Go to the place where that sound has its source.

**

This place has water, no it's not the sink,

When I'm thirsty I go here for a drink.

***

Here is a place that's supposed to be quiet,

You can read about Harriet Tubman, why don't you try it!

****

John slipped and fell on Paul's book of verse,

Oh dear, his ankle is swollen, please help him to the. . . .

*****

This place reaches 400 degrees,

To find your message, get down on your knees.

******

And now for the treasure. Oh where can it be?

Stand in the center of the room, turn west, take long steps of three.

Key

* office public address system switchboard
** water fountain
*** book in library about Harriet Tubman (change if necessary)
**** nurse's office
***** oven in school kitchen
****** hide treasure in room accordingly when students are finding
   last message

THE UNITED FARMWORKERS' BOYCOTT WORKSHEET

Rita's Diary

Bakersfield, California
June 3, 1965

Dear Diary,

I'm so glad to have you, diary, to talk with. I get so sad and lonesome. I wonder how many other 13-year-olds in America have as hard a life as I do.

Last night we arrived at this farm. There is about three weeks worth of work for us and then we'll have to move on to a new farm. I'm so tired of moving. Dad says we have to follow the crops in order to have work.

The shack we were given here to live in is very dirty. It has no running water and no lighting. I cried when I saw it. My only wish is that the growers would pay us farmworkers enough so we could rent our own house and wouldn't have to keep moving.

Today I worked in the fields picking. We started at 7:00 and worked very hard. We wanted a break in the morning and another in the afternoon, but the owner won't allow breaks. I get so sore and tired! I want to get some other farmworkers together to face the grower and insist that he gives us breaks. Dad told me not to do that. It might get the grower mad and we'd lose our jobs. But, I still want to ask. Do you think I should?

Rita

Bakersfield, California
June 15, 1965

Dear Diary,

Today I worked in the field picking from 7A.M. until 5P.M. The sun was very hot and about noon I thought I was going to faint. I'm so glad I didn't because then I wouldn't have earned enough money to buy dinner.

You might want to know that we did get together last week and asked for breaks in our work. The owner refused our request. He told us to stop being troublemakers or we'd lose our jobs. He said he can find more agreeable workers if we don't listen to him.

I had to skip school today to work. Dad stayed home because of his back. Farmworkers are forced to bend over and use short-handled hoes to work in the fields. This is called stoop labor. We farmworkers want short-handled hoes to be outlawed. Because he has done stoop labor all his life, some days he wakes up with a terrible pain in his back and can't work.

I have a big problem. Tomorrow is the last day of school. We get a big test. It's so hard to do well in school because we have to move from place to place. I never have the same teacher. I have to miss lots of days of school in order to work. But I study so hard and I want to learn. How I wish we were paid a fair wage so we could live in one place and go to the same school all year!

If I pass the test tomorrow I can go on to the 8th grade. I am so afraid Dad's back will still be bad. If he can't work and I don't work, we won't have money for food tomorrow. But if I miss the test, I can't get promoted. What should I do?

Rita

Rita's Diary

Delano, California
August 4, 1965

Dear Diary,

I was so angry today I could have hit the foreman. When we came here, we were promised we would be paid $1.00 an hour to pick grapes. Today is pay day, and we've all worked for a whole week. The foreman said he would pay us $.80 an hour and that's all we're getting. That's so unfair!

I was waiting so long for pay day! I'm always hungry. I hoped this next week our family would have enough to eat. It looks like I'll be hungry again!

But I have some exciting news, too. A man and woman came and spoke to workers tonight at church. They were Cesar Chavez and Delores Huerta. They organized the United Farmworkers Association. This group will get farmworkers together to fight for our rights—fair pay, decent housing, and better working conditions. They are organizing a strike. Farmworkers will refuse to pick grapes until the growers raise wages. Should I join the strike?

Rita

Delano, California
October 1, 1965

Dear Diary,

So much has happened since the last time I wrote. The farmworkers here in Delano went on strike. Our motto is "Huelga"—the Spanish word for strike.

I have a big decision to make in the next week. In addition to the strike, the United Farmworkers Association has decided to begin a boycott. We will travel across the United States and explain to Americans how unfairly farmworkers are being treated. If people want to do something to help us, we will ask them not to buy grapes and to organize their friends not to buy grapes. Then the grape growers won't be able to sell their grapes. They will lose money unless they meet with the farmworkers. As soon as the growers are willing to sign a written agreement, a contract that gives us some rights, the UFWA will stop the boycott.

I have a chance to go to New York City to help organize the boycott there. I would talk to people and explain why it's important for them to stop buying grapes. I would picket in front of grocery stores where grapes are sold and would try to convince shoppers not to buy any food at that store until the owners stopped selling grapes.

What should I decide? If I go to New York City, I will be so homesick for my family and friends. Yet, if I go, I could help make the boycott a success and see a new exciting city. Life for thousands of farmworkers would be so much better!

Rita

Rita's Learning Center

Directions

Each person chooses a diary entry. Order the entries according to the date. The person with the first entry reads it aloud. As a group, discuss possible responses to the question at the end of the account. Try to develop a response all group members can agree with. Continue in the same way with each account.

Each person then writes a diary response to her entry based on the group's discussion. Proofread each other's writing for spelling, grammar, and punctuation. Clip individual entries together and hand in.

The Students' Learning Center

Background

The goal of this center is to find out what boycotts are being held across the U.S. today.

To complete this center, you will work together to do research—find information. You can get information from printed matter or from people.

THE UNITED FARMWORKERS' BOYCOTT WORKSHEET

The Mothers' Learning Center

Directions

Step 1

Read the background information aloud.

Step 2

Read Role Card A. Follow the directions. Then pick two group members to role play the dialogue using the information gathered in the class. Others observe. When finished, give helpful suggestions. Continue with Role Cards B and then C. Change role players for each situation.

Step 3

Plan a tape recording. It should include:

1. A brief introduction—one minute or less—one student
2. Three dialogues
   - a daughter and mother—two minutes—two students
   - husband and wife—two minutes—two students
   - thirteen-year-old son and mother—two minutes—two students
3. Conclusion—one minute or less—one student

Each student participates twice. Make sure everyone agrees with the information on the tape.

Step 4

Make the tape. Play it back. Enjoy your production! Hand the tape in to the teacher. When all groups have finished, you will play the tapes for each other.

Background Information

Mothers' groups helped make the boycott a success. Many mothers across America cooperated with the boycott. They refused to buy grapes. Many others walked on the picket lines at grocery stores. They explained the boycott to other shoppers and asked them not to buy grapes.

Cooperation by the mothers in the boycott was not always easy. Their children sometimes wanted to eat grapes. Sometimes, other members of their family didn't think it was proper that they were on the picket lines. Yet the mothers believed in what they were doing. Again and again, they explained the reason for the boycott to others. They understood that the cooperation of many people was needed to help the farmworkers.

The Priest's Learning Center

Directions

Read the background information aloud as a group.

You are getting information for a priest who has volunteered to organize the truck picketers across the country. Once you tell him what day and time the grapes will arrive in each city, he will call organizers there to set up a picket line.

Work with a partner. Each partnership chooses three "Meet The Truck" cards. Work together to find out:

1. Where the destination city is on the map

2. How many miles it is between Delano, California and that city

3. How many hours it will take to get there
   - Assume the truck goes 55 miles per hour.
   - Allow the truck driver one hour of rest for every six hours of driving.
   - Allow the driver six hours of sleep after every sixteen hours has passed.

4. How many hours gained because of the time change

5. On what day and at what time the pickets would be told to arrive

Work together as a group to answer one "Meet the Truck" card before you meet in partners. If you have a question, call the teacher before you start.

When each partnership has answered three cards, exchange cards and answers. Check each other's work. Remember . . . if there are errors, the pickets will be standing out in the rain, snow or sleet waiting for a truck to arrive!

If checkers find errors, point them out and return problem cards to the partnership to re-do. When all group members know that all problem cards have been answered correctly, turn them in to the teacher. Congratulations!

The Priest's Learning Center

Background Information

Church people also cooperated to support the boycott. Many ministers, nuns, rabbis, priests, and church members helped organize and educate others. In the case presented in this center, a priest takes an important role.

Farmworkers used many approaches to help make their boycott a success. One strategy was to find out at what time a truckload of grapes was leaving California and to what city it was going. United Farmworker volunteers would phone this information to the organizers of the boycott in that city. The organizers would alert U.F.W.A. supporters to come to the picket lines at the time the truck would arrive. Many times, then, grapes would not be unloaded. In other cases, pickets brought public attention to the fact that non-union grapes were coming into the city. This reminded people not to buy those grapes.

Here is one account of that strategy in action:

"One day we got a report that there was a truckload of Guimarra grapes going to Appleton, Wisconsin. We knew what time the truck left, figured out that it would arrive in Appleton sometime between midnight and 5:00 A.M. on the following day, and called the people up in Milwaukee who got to work on it. I got the report the next day.

This truck driver arrived in Appleton at 2:00 in the morning. Waiting for him were about forty or fifty pickets. The truck driver was beside himself.

He said, "You picket me down there when I go in. You picket me when I'm coming out. Now, here in Appleton, Wisconsin, at 2:00 in the morning, here's thirty, forty more of ya!"

And they said, "Well, we're going to be wherever you go."

So he just turned the truck around and took off for Montana. I don't know whatever happened to the grapes after that."

The Young Girl's Learning Center

Directions

1. One group member reads aloud the account below. Cesar Chavez, a leader of the United Farmworkers, describes one of his memories of the boycott. He remembers a young girl who helped the boycott by blocking trucks that would carry grapes.

   "We had sit-ins in warehouses, and there was one beautiful picture of a little girl wearing a poncho sitting on the pavement down in Los Angeles, in the middle of about thirty trucks . . . and over here a line of about fifty policemen."

2. As a group, list as many ideas as possible (one minute on each topic):
   a. Who is the girl?
   b. What could she be feeling?
   c. What events brought her to block these trucks?

3. Each student writes a short story from the point of view of the girl. Be sure to answer the three questions above. Also describe what happens next.

4. Criteria for evaluation of the story are:
   a. It shows an understanding of why a girl would be part of the UFW boycott.
   b. It presents a clear character study of the girl.
   c. It presents thoughtful ideas.
   d. It presents creative ideas.
   e. Grammar, punctuation, and spelling are correct.

5. Once each student has written a draft, exchange papers with another person in the group. Read your partner's story and give suggestions for improvement. Return the story to the author.

6. Think about the comments your partner has suggested. Make any desired changes in your story.

7. Check with your teacher for any corrections you and your classmates may need to make.

8. Read the final stories to each other.

9. Hand in.

10. At the end of the unit some of these will be posted on the United Farmworkers Bulletin Board for other students to read.

THE UNITED FARMWORKERS' BOYCOTT WORKSHEET

Union Members' Learning Center

Background Information

It is the fall of 1965. Unions across the country have taken action to support the boycott of the United Farmworkers. Even though the supporting workers didn't know the farmworkers, they believe in what they are doing and want to help.

Directions

1. Each student chooses a worker card.

2. To yourself, read about the worker you picked.

3. Next, tell your group about the worker you are and how and why you are helping the farmworkers. Do not read from the card or let anyone else read your card. Put cards away.

4. As a group, write a newspaper article about **how** and **why** workers across the country are cooperating with the United Farmworkers to help make the boycott a success. Decide together on a title. Divide writing in such a way that each person is writing a paragraph about a worker **other than** the card she pulled.

5. Put sections of the article together. Read aloud. Make suggestions for changes. Proofread for grammar and spelling. Be sure writing style is consistent between paragraphs.

6. Write "Journalists" at the bottom of the article and sign your names. Hand in. At the end of the unit, these will be posted on a United Farmworkers bulletin board in the school hall so others can learn.

THE UNITED FARMWORKERS' BOYCOTT WORKSHEET

The Students' Learning Center

Directions

1. Discuss the written sources you could investigate to find out what boycotts exist in the U.S. today. Examples are: (1) current newspapers, (2) magazines, and (3) indexes of periodicals in the library. Ask your teacher and librarian for more ideas. Be alert also for relevant information on television.

2. Think of all the people you could ask to find out what boycotts are being held in the U.S. today. Examples are: (1) union members or leaders, (2) clergy (ministers, priests, rabbis), and (3) social studies teachers.

3. Contact the United Farmworkers to find out if the farmworkers are still running boycotts. Write to:

    a. United Farm Workers of America
       Keene, California 93531

    b. Farm Labor Organizing Committee
       714 S. St. Clair
       Toledo, Ohio 43609

4. Divide research tasks among members of your group. Work with partners if you wish.

5. After getting your information, report to the group what you have learned.

6. Write a short report, "Boycotts in the U.S. Today." Describe the boycotts and the reason for each. Divide writing tasks. Hand in.

7. At the end of the unit, join with the whole class to share information. If you wanted to support any of the boycotts, how could you talk to friends and parents about that? What follow-up steps might you take?

Example: During the United Farmworkers' grape boycott, a group of children in Detroit held a block party and mailed their check for $6.41 to the farmworkers.

THE UNITED FARMWORKERS' BOYCOTT WORKSHEET

Family Role Cards

Role Card A

Seven-Year-Old Daughter

Grapes are your favorite fruit. Your mother has come home from the store without any grapes. What might a seven-year-old girl say to convince her mother to buy grapes?

Mother

In what ways could you answer your daughter that would help explain the boycott to a child this age?

Role Card B

Husband

Your wife is a volunteer on the picket line at the Eats and Treats Supermarket. You think it's too risky for your wife to picket. She might become known as a troublemaker and hurt your career. What might you say to convince your wife to stop working on the boycott?

Mother

In what ways could you answer your husband's concerns and also educate him about the boycott?

Role Card C

Thirteen-Year-Old Son

Your mother is a volunteer on the picket line at Eats and Treats Supermarket. You are embarrassed and don't want your friends to see her. What could the son say to his mother?

Mother

What could you say to your son to deal with his embarrassment and also to explain why your activity in support of the boycott is so important?

Meet the Truck Cards

Card 1

Truck leaves Delano on June 11 at 9:00 A.M. for Los Angeles, California.

Card 2

Truck leaves Delano on June 11 at 10:00 A.M. for Detroit, Michigan.

Card 3

Truck leaves Delano on June 11 at 11:00 A.M. for New York City.

Card 4

Truck leaves Delano on June 11 at 12 noon for Milwaukee, Wisconsin.

Card 5

Truck leaves Delano on June 11 at 1:00 P.M. for Toronto, Canada.

Card 6

Truck leaves Delano on June 11 at 3:00 P.M. for Philadelphia, Pennsylvania.

Card 7

Truck leaves Delano on June 11 at 4:00 P.M. for Boston, Massachusetts.

Card 8

Last card. If your partnership finishes early, make up a card and solve it.

THE UNITED FARMWORKERS' BOYCOTT WORKSHEET

Worker Cards

Ralph

You work loading and unloading ships on the docks in San Francisco. You are a member of the International Longshoremans' and Warehouse Union. Members of the United Farmworkers set up a picket on the docks because trucks of grapes have arrived. They are supposed to be loaded on ships. You and other longshore workers decide to walk off the job so the grapes can't be loaded onto the ships. You do this because you want to support the struggle of the farmworkers for their rights.

Walter Reuther

You are the leader of the United Auto Workers Union (the U.A.W.). This is a large organization of workers who make cars. You visit the striking farmworkers in Delano and promise to them $2,500 a month to help support the strike. You do this because you believe it is the right of all workers to have a fair wage and good working conditions.

Leanore

You work on ships in the New York City Harbor. You are a member of the Seafarer's Union. You and your union members have the farmworkers staying in your homes while they lead the boycott in New York. You are glad about this and think it's an important thing to do. You remember when you were once on strike and weren't getting a pay check. You worried about being able to feed your family and were grateful for help from other workers. Now your union is helping other workers in the same situation.

Jesse

You work as a truck driver. You're a member of the Teamsters Union. Supporters of the U.F.W.A. have set up a picket line around the truck depot in Philadelphia, Pennsylvania where you live. In order to give support to the farmworkers, you and other truck drivers decide not to drive the grapes to the grocery stores. Even though you don't know any farmworkers personally, you believe it is important to cooperate with other working people who are fighting for a better life.

The Sanctuary Movement

1. Why do sanctuary workers believe an underground railroad is needed for Central American refugees?

2. How does this contemporary underground railroad operate? In what ways is cooperation necessary for the underground railroad? What would have happened otherwise?

3. For what reasons do people cooperate to make the underground railroad work?

4. What other steps could be taken so that, in the future, there will no longer be a *need* for the underground railroad?

Your Opinion

5. How do you feel about the activity of people like Stacy Merkt, Rev. John Fife, Barb Lagoni and Sam Coleman?

6. What, if anything, do you believe the U.S. government or Central American governments should do to deal with the problems they are creating for the refugees?

7. Do you believe individual Americans should participate in the contemporary underground railroad? Why or why not?

The Links

Stacy Merkt

I am a young white woman. I have met many refugees who are fleeing from persecution in Central America. Many of them are from El Salvador or Guatemala. They were afraid to stay in their native countries because members of the military often shoot and kill people in the streets or in their homes. These refugees want to escape to the United States.

When these refugees get to the U.S. border, I help them get across the border and transport them to a safe place to hide. What I do is dangerous because the U.S. government does not admit these people as refugees fleeing from violence and physical terror. The Immigration and Naturalization Service (INS) calls them "economic migrants." The INS claims they are seeking better economic conditions rather than escaping repression. To recognize them as refugees would be to admit that their governments cannot or will not protect their citizens. The U.S. backs these governments with money and arms.

Reverend John Fife

I am the pastor of the Southside Presbyterian Church in Tucson, Arizona. I was the first U.S. clergyman to declare my church to be a sanctuary for refugees fleeing from violence in Central America. Members of my church receive refugees from people like Stacy Merkt who have helped them cross the border. We keep them in our church and give them food, shelter, and moral support. In several weeks, we will send them on to other cities in the United States where they will finally live.

We are part of the sanctuary movement across the United States. Sanctuary means welcoming of undocumented Central American refugees into the protection and care of the church. We do this publicly to point to the injustice of the current U.S. policy that denies them refuge and the just claim of the refugees for protection from persecution. It is an act of civil disobedience on the part of churches. We are obeying a higher commandment—to love human beings.

In 1985 I was arrested for aiding and abetting illegal aliens. If the choice is protecting people's lives or going to jail, I'd have to choose jail.

The Links—continued

Sam Coleman

I'm 14 years old and I live in Enfield, Connecticut. We don't have any churches in Enfield that provide amnesty for Central American refugees. Yet my friends and I are still part of the sanctuary movement. We raised money and sent it to other churches that are helping these refugees. We try to educate our friends about the problems facing the refugees. We write to our representatives in Congress and write letters to our newspapers.

We want U.S. citizens to understand why refugees are coming to the U.S. Amnesty International and other human rights groups document the repression of the governments of El Salvador and Guatemala toward the civilian populations. We try to inform people about what would happen if these refugees were deported. There would be a good chance many would be killed.

We hope people will see why supporting the sanctuary movement with our money, time, and letters is so important.

Barb Lagoni

I'm chairperson of the church council of the Wellington Ave. Church of Christ in Chicago, Illinois. Our church sponsors Central American refugees who are fleeing their homes. Refugees are transported here from the Southwest where they enter the United States. When they arrive in Chicago, families in our church sponsor these families. Our church provides them food, clothing, and friendship. Then we help them find places to live and a way to support themselves.

We know that what we do is risky. We could be arrested. Yet we believe it is the right thing to do. What may happen to the families in the Wellington Church is small compared to the pain that happens every day to the people of El Salvador and Guatemala.

In 1980, the U.S. Congress adopted as law the UN guidelines on refugees. This says that the United States should give refugee status to persons who cannot return to their country because of persecution or fear of persecution for reasons of race, nationality, or membership in a particular social or political group. Since this applies to the Central American refugees, we believe the U.S. should abide by its law.

Many churches around the country are involved in giving sanctuary. We are part of a national movement.

Friends or Foes?

Directions: Take turns reading the paragraphs in this account. Then discuss each worksheet question, one at a time. Take turns writing the answer on the worksheet. Make sure each student reads once and writes once.

When students enter fifth grade, they come to the Aronson Middle School from two elementary schools—the Ida Wells Barnett Elementary School and the Branch Rickey Elementary School. These two schools are very different.

The Branch Rickey School is mostly white. Parents of children who go there have middle-class incomes. They are able to make enough money to pay for good food, clothing, and shelter. They also have enough money to buy things that help their children learn—books, calculators, and sometimes even a home computer. Many teachers at the Rickey School have high expectations of their students and challenge them to their fullest. The school has nineteen white teachers and one black teacher. The district gives more money to the Rickey School than to the other schools. There are special afterschool programs in art, drama, and reading, and tutoring is available.

The Ida Wells Barnett School is racially-mixed. Students are white, black and Chicano. Many parents of children who go there have low incomes. They are not able to get jobs that pay enough to cover the cost of good food, clothing, or shelter. Many don't have enough money to buy books, calculators, or computers for their children. Some teachers at Barnett School have low expectations of their students. They don't always challenge students to their fullest. There are nineteen white teachers and one black teacher. There are no afterschool or tutoring programs at the Barnett School. Some students speak Spanish. There are no special programs to help them learn English.

When students come together in the fifth grade, most students from the Rickey School get higher grades and have better math and reading skills than most from Barnett School. Students from Rickey make negative comments about those from Barnett. Behind their backs, and even sometimes to their faces, they call them "dumb" or "stupid." They think, or sometimes say, such things as: "Poor people are lazy," or "White people work harder than minorities." Some say, "You Barnett students had an equal chance to learn. You all went through grades one through four like we did. Since you don't do as well as we do, that proves we're smarter."

Friends or Foes?—continued

Questions

1. Pretend you're a student coming from the Rickey School and you don't understand anything about competitive individualism. What are some of your feelings about yourself? What are some of your feelings about students from Barnett School?

2. Now become yourself. You understand about competitive individualism. How do the ideas of the students from the Rickey School show competitive individualism?

   STOP! Check your answer with the teacher to make sure you're on the right track.

3. What happens at the Aronson School happens all over the United States in thousands of cities and towns. Discuss what students and teachers in the school could do to better *all* students' chances for success in school.

4. What could the community do to better *all* students' chances for success in school?

5. What could the nation do to better *all* students' chances for success in school?

Signed _____

_____

_____

Better Their Chances Program Cards

Headstart

There are not enough fair wage jobs for all the people in the U.S. who want to work. Therefore, many parents in the U.S. don't have enough money to buy books or games to help their young children learn. When these children begin kindergarten, they are behind. Other children have had more chance to learn at home.

In order to give children an equal chance, concerned people convinced the government to develop a program called Headstart. Young children who didn't have as much chance to learn at home went to Headstart Centers for their pre-school years. Their mothers were actively involved in the centers and learned methods to better help their children learn. This helped give their children an equal chance.

Affirmative Action

Some schools in the United States hired only white teachers. Minority students didn't have people of their race to look up to. Sometimes minority teachers best understand minority students, take a special interest in them, and help them learn. It is hard for a minority student to believe that she can become a teacher or principal, when there are no minority teachers or principals in her school.

People who wanted to change this situation encouraged the government to develop affirmative action guidelines. These guidelines had schools make a special effort to find and hire good teachers who were minority (or women). With minority teachers in their school, minority students can feel more comfortable and can learn better.

Better Their Chances Program Cards—continued

Bilingual Education

Some Puerto Rican or Chicano students come to school knowing only Spanish. They can't understand lessons which are taught in English and therefore they fall behind in their work. Some people think these students are slow. That isn't true. Many of them are very smart. They just can't speak English yet.

In order to give these children a better chance, concerned people convinced the government to begin bilingual education in schools across the United States. Teachers teach these children in both Spanish and English until they learn English well. In this way they can better keep up with the work.

Title VII of the Elementary and Secondary Education Act

Some schools in the United States discriminated against minority children without knowing it. For example, books and texts that were used had very little about the life of minority people. People now know this keeps minority children from learning as well as they could. They don't score up to their potential on tests. Sometimes there weren't any bulletin boards that displayed minority people or holidays that honored minority leaders. This made minority children feel unimportant. When people feel that they're unimportant, it's hard for them to learn.

Some people saw that this situation didn't give minority children an equal chance to do well in school. They convinced the government to pass Title VII to give money to schools to help with integration. Many schools developed programs to train teachers to see the ways books, tests, and bulletin boards discriminated. The programs helped teachers create changes in their classrooms and schools so everyone would have a better chance to learn.

Community Worker Role Cards

You are unemployed with no salary. You do have skills to serve the community. You can decide what these are.	You are a dentist. You make $80,000 a year. You clean and repair people's teeth.
You are unemployed with no salary. You do have skills to serve the community. You can decide what these are.	You are a farmworker. You make $4,000 a year. You pick apples and vegetables that community members eat.
You are unemployed with no salary. You do have skills to serve the community. You can decide what these are.	You are a teacher. You make $20,000. You educate children.
You are unemployed with no salary. You do have skills to serve the community. You can decide what these are.	You are a teacher. You make $20,000. You educate children.
You are unemployed with no salary. You do have skills to serve the community. You can decide what these are.	You are a bus driver. You make $17,000 a year. You drive the community bus.
You are a doctor. You make $80,000 a year. You serve the community by attending to the people who are ill.	You are a child-care worker making $7,000 a year. You take care of young children at the community day-care center.
You are a factory owner making $150,000. Your factory makes boxes. Some people in the community buy them, but most are sent to other places.	You are a car mechanic. You make $15,000 a year. You fix broken cars.

Community Worker Role Cards—continued

You are a factory worker. You make $8,000 a year. You assemble boxes.	You are a road worker. You make $17,000 a year. You fix the community roads.
You are a house builder. You make $30,000 a year. You build homes and apartments.	You are a theater worker. You make $15,000 a year. You show the movies at the community theater.
You are a garbage collector. You make $17,000 a year. You collect garbage and maintain the community landfill.	You are a lawyer. You make $80,000 a year. You give people legal advice and represent them in court.
You are a waitress. You make $8,000 a year. You serve food at the community restaurant.	You are a youth director making $10,000. You plan programs for children and teenagers for summers and after school.
You are a religious leader. You make $25,000 a year. You give people spiritual help.	You are an artist. You paint and sell pictures. You make $7,000 a year.
You are a repair person. You repair broken appliances—TVs and so forth. You make $23,000 a year.	You are a factory worker. You make boxes in a factory. You make $10,000 a year.
You are a businessperson. You make $30,000 a year. You own a small handmade-toy business.	

Splitting Woodcutters

Part I: Partnership A

Imagine you are a paper company official. List three things you could say to the white workers to try to make them split away from the black ones.

1.

2.

3.

Part I: Partnership B

Imagine you are a paper company official. List three things you could say to the black workers to try to make them split away from the white ones.

1.

2.

3.

Part II: Partnership A

Imagine you are black workers. The company has told you these things. (Read statement of company officials.) Discuss them yourselves. What are your feelings about these statements?

Next discuss them with the white workers in your group. What feelings do you have in common about these statements?

If you want to continue to work together, write a joint response to the company officials. If you don't work together, each partnership write a statement about why you don't.

Part II: Partnership B

Imagine you are white workers. The company has told you these things. (Read statement of company officials.) Discuss them yourselves. What are your feelings about these statements?

Read and discuss them with the black workers in your group. What are your joint (taken together) feelings about these statements?

If you want to continue to work together, write a joint response to the company officials. If you don't work together, each partnership write a statement about why you don't.

MAKE THAT CONNECTION! WORKSHEET

Situation Cards

The Questionnaire

You are a white, English-speaking 6th grader who lives in rural New England. Your family is middle-class. Your parents got a survey letter from your representative in Washington, D.C. She wants to know the voters' opinions on certain issues.

Your mother asks your opinion on one question on the survey. It reads: "Congress should cut off money for bilingual education programs." Your mother says that if national programs are cut, she might get a few dollars off her taxes. Your mother says she is going to consider your advice seriously in responding to the survey.

What is your response?

The Blue Line Bus Strike

This weekend, you are going to take the bus to visit your grandmother in Detroit. You get to the bus terminal and see that the Blue Line Bus workers are on strike. The Blue Line Bus Company wants to cut the workers' pay. The workers are on strike to try to prevent this. They ask customers to support the strike by not riding the Blue Line.

You can take the Green Line Bus to Detroit, but you'll have to wait two extra hours for it and you'll lose that time with your grandmother. Also, you would have to change buses half way.

What do you do?

The Toxic Dump

You live in Austin, Texas. You heard on the radio that people in Williamstown, Vermont, had discovered a toxic waste dump in their community. The residents are asking other Americans to write letters to the company that dumped the waste to demand that dumping be stopped and residents be compensated for damages.

You learned about toxic wastes in school and know how dangerous they are. You have a lot of homework this week and feel very busy.

What do you do?

MAKE THAT CONNECTION! WORKSHEET

Questions

1. How does this situation connect me to other people? How does my choice affect other people?

2. How would I feel if I were the other person(s) affected by my actions?

3. What are all the options I can think of for dealing with this situation?

4. What do I choose? Why?

Signed _____

_____

_____

Directions for STOP

STOP

STOP is a cooperative card game that is a revision of a competitive game called War.

Purpose

The goal of your group is to work together so that every player has five cards of one of the following types—"Quotation," "Benefit," "Project," "Coordination." If you do so according to the rules described below, the group wins.

Types of Cards

Quotation Cards: These cards are quotations from students, teachers, and parents about STOP.

Benefit Cards: These cards describe the benefits gained by students who are STOP members.

Project Cards: These cards describe projects that STOP chapters have implemented all across the country.

Coordination Cards: These cards describe what STOP does to help students across America coordinate their efforts to stop nuclear war.

STOP Cards: These cards have the word STOP written on them in large letters.

Luck Cards: These cards add an element of chance to the game.

To Play

1. Divide into groups of four. Sit around a table or on the floor.

2. Deal one card to each person. Each player reads her card aloud. She tells what type of a card it is. If a group member disagrees, the whole group discusses it and comes to a conclusion about what type of card it is. When in doubt, consult the teacher. If anyone draws a STOP or Luck card, she returns it to the deck and receives another card.

3. Follow step 2 once more until each person has two cards. From then on, a player's cards are held in her hand and not shown to others. Place the remaining cards in a pile in the center of the table.

Directions for STOP—continued

4. Next, one player starts by turning over the top card of the deck to a face-up position, beginning a discard pile alongside the deck. Other players wait with cards ready. Player one reads the card aloud and names the type. The player continues to turn over and read cards until a STOP card appears. At this point, all players try to slap the STOP card. The player whose hand is on the top of the STOP card picks up the STOP card and all cards under it.

5. That player gives one card to each person. First he tries to remember what type of card each player needs. He then reads one aloud and gives it to a player. He does so for each player and for himself. No one may ask for a certain type of card. Extra cards from the discard pile are placed at the bottom of the deck.

6. After receiving cards, each player **may** place one card at the bottom of the deck. At no time may a player have more than five cards.

7. Luck cards can be used only once. Once they are used, they are placed aside.

8. Now the player to the left begins by turning over cards. Continue play in the same manner. When a player gets five cards of one type, she must lay them down in front of her.

9. The group wins if all players complete their sets of five cards within the turning over of three STOP cards after the first person lays down a set. Otherwise, the group loses. In that case, play again until you win!

10. The only talking allowed during the game is the reading of the cards. You may not discuss strategy. You must develop a strategy by being alert to what other people do and by being willing to cooperate. After the game is over, discuss what happened. If you lost, try to work out a more effective strategy for the next game.

Reminders

This is a cooperative game. You win or lose as a group. Therefore, you do what you can to help other players. For example, you may have decided to collect Project Cards, but realize that another person is trying to collect them. Either you or he must decide to collect another type of card. Good luck! By cooperating you can work toward a winning strategy to STOP!

STOP Project Cards

Amherst, Massachusetts—The STOP chapter designed and had printed thousands of pro-disarmament book covers to be sold in schools.	Louisville, Kentucky—STOP students organized a nuclear education outreach to local schools. Dominique David said, "We really got through to a lot of kids. Because we're all kids, there's a ready-made common bond."
Philadelphia, Pennsylvania—STOP students at Archbishop Ryan High School have a peace bulletin board where they put posters and current articles.	Longmeadow, Massachusetts—STOP and the Social Studies Department sponsored a Nuclear Awareness Day at Longmeadow High School. The entire six-hour program was broadcast on local TV.
Chicago, Illinois—Three hundred students, half white and half Black or Latino, attended a conference sponsored by STOP. Students came from private, public, and Catholic schools. They formed a city-wide STOP. Students made 1,000 paper cranes, the traditional Japanese disarmament symbols. They sent half to the U.S. President and half to the USSR Premier, with the wish that these men would get together, combine the cranes to make 1,000, and begin serious efforts for peace. They got the Mayor of Chicago to send them.	STOP

STOP Quotation Cards

Wendy Adams from Cosmos, Minnesota, is a student. "I'm not that important to the world, but the world is important to me, and nuclear war is a way to see it end. I want to help stop nuclear war."

Michael Stanek lives in Pocatello, Idaho. Trains pass through carrying parts for Trident missiles. "It's spooky. I don't like living in fear. Doing something like being in STOP helps me believe in the future. In STOP students discover that the best way to find hope is to act."

Stephanie from New Orleans, Louisiana, is a student. "There is no reason to have dreams if you won't be there to see them come true. The only dream I have is that we get rid of nuclear weapons."

Wally from New Jersey, is a parent— "Kids can get through to adults whether they be parents or politicians. They are adept at surprising adults— making them forget their conditioned responses for a moment."

Gary from Wallingford, Connecticut, is a teacher. "Stopping a nuclear war requires faith, hope and a lot of hard work, and believe me, the students I've worked with have all those things in abundance."

STOP

STOP Benefit Cards

Being part of a national high-school movement gives students the energy to keep going.	It's great for students and teachers to work together in STOP.
By joining STOP, students learn a lot about the nuclear arms race.	STOP shows young people how they can help stop nuclear war.
In STOP, students discover that the best way to find hope is to act.	STOP

STOP Coordination Cards

STOP holds conferences to bring concerned students together to meet each other, talk, and organize. It holds leadership conferences to train young people to be leaders in their communities.	STOP publishes "STOP News" to keep students and teachers informed. This is sent to members all across the country. STOP also networks with other peace groups working toward similar goals.
STOP distributes packets of materials about nuclear war to help students and teachers educate people in their communities. It gives suggestions for talking with people, organizing films, dealing with the media, and so forth.	STOP distributes media. "It's Our Future: Stop Nuclear War" is a color-slide tape show about what students across the country are doing to stop nuclear war. "Changing the Silence" is a video of a student play with the same focus.
STOP produced a book full of successful projects that students working together from all parts of the country carried out as part of an overall effort to bring peace.	STOP

STOP Luck Cards

Pass one of your cards to the person on your right.	Pass one of your cards to the person on your left.
Give any other person one card of yours—either now, or any time during the game.	Change the type of card you're collecting.
Get any card from any other player in the game.	STOP

Creating *The Kids' Book of Divorce*

We are twenty kids between the ages of eleven and fourteen. We live in the Boston area and are part of a class called The Unit at the Fayerweather Street School in Cambridge, Massachusetts. We wrote this book because the issue of divorce has affected each of us in some way. Fourteen of us have actually gone through the whole process of a divorce in our families. The rest of us still live with both our parents, but we have had fears and fantasies about divorce happening in our families or we have friends who have gone through it all.

In the fall of 1978, we started the work which led up to this book. We held regular discussion groups that met twice a week for about six weeks. Each group had nine people.

The teachers facilitated the groups, but we all had a say in what we discussed. We talked about our feelings and thoughts about divorce, our specific living situations, custody arrangements, parents' boyfriends or girlfriends, how we were first told about the divorce, and if divorce changed us. Sometimes, kids whose parents weren't divorced felt different or left out, but we soon realized that even if parents never become divorced, the fear of divorce is a part of every child's life. That's why, today, divorce is an issue for everyone.

The two groups joined together, finally, into one big group, which met over a two-week period. We all talked about some of the things which had come up in the two groups. Our teacher suggested that we read books about divorce. Most of us read a book or two—some fiction, some nonfiction—and wrote reports on what we read.

So our teachers came up with the idea of writing a book about divorce for kids **by** kids. We talked about this idea a lot and we thought about what we'd have to do to write it. After a lot of discussion, we decided to do it. That was right before our winter vacation.

We knew we had to interview people to find out about different perspectives on divorce: kids, parents, marriage counselors, grandparents, rabbis, ministers, lawyers, teachers, divorce experts, psychiatrists. When we finished most of the interviews, we got together as a group and discussed how to organize the book. Then we broke into teams of two or three and each team took a chapter to write. Once the first half of the book was written, parents and friends in the school typed it. We started the second half of the book the same way, though some of the writing groups were different. Everyone in the class wrote some part of the book.

Creating *The Kids' Book of Divorce*—continued

When the book was finished, we edited it and took photographs and drew pictures. We also worked as a class to learn about the way to find a publisher for the book. Once we found our publisher we worked with them to finalize the book, plan the way the book looks, and discuss how to promote the book. The entire process—from writing the book through publishing it— took two years.

1. Describe the students who wrote *The Kids' Book of Divorce.*

2. Why did they write it?

3. Describe how they organized themselves to write the book.

4. What do you feel is the value of students writing a book for other students?

5. How do you imagine the process of working together on a book about divorce affected the students writing it?

6. What influence do you imagine the book had on other young people across the country?

Seeing Connections: Taking Action

Description of your group of "unknown friends"

Describe here the situation of people in another part of the country who are negatively affected by competitive policies in our society and to whom we can be connected by positive action.

Legislation or Action

What legislation or action is proposed or in effect that would help the situation of this group of "unknown friends"?

Student Action

List the various ways students' actions or choices could positively affect the situation of these "unknown friends."

Signed _____

_____

_____

7 WORKING TOGETHER FOR WORLDWIDE INTERDEPENDENCE AND PEACE

> It is as if we are riding on a bus headed up the wrong side of a divided highway. From time to time the good-hearted driver may swerve to avoid a collision, turn on the stereo, hand out goodies to the passengers or remind us to fasten our seat belts. But unless we discover we are going the wrong way and insist on reversing directions, we are doomed.
>
> David Dellinger,
> *More Power Than We Know.*

Chapter 7 gives students the chance to think about our interdependent world and to examine the potential of cooperation for fostering global awareness and world peace. Students learn what positive contributions they can make to create that peace. The lessons transpose the ideas and values of cooperative learning—democracy, respect for diversity, and responsibility for self and others—to the international arena.

Excessive international competition affects all of us. These effects are examined in Section A. Lessons provide opportunities for students to explore how reliance on violence, and use of the threat of violence, affects the hope for peace. We also examine the ways that competition undergirds the arms race. Students consider the way the United States government's effort to maintain a superiority in the world, together with multinational corporations' competitive practices, can affect people internationally and hinder equitable global relationships.

Exemplary models of cooperation within other countries, and between nations, provide examples of the potential for international cooperation. Cases of effective international networks, such as the Universal Postal Union, offer students models of the possibilities for such cooperation which benefits all nations. Students then examine examples from other nations of cooperation among people and cooperation within the political, economic, and social system itself. Finally, case studies of international cooperation are considered. These case studies present alternatives to war.

"Removing Roadblocks to Global Interdependence," Section C, contains lessons that teach students to recognize, and potentially change, ideas and policies that block international cooperation. Students examine how they learn to see people of other countries and cultures as "different" from themselves, and thereby threatening or untrustworthy. They consider the consequences of the nationalism and militarism that often results. Also explored are the ways in which feelings of insecurity block cooperation and cause citizens to project their fears onto other peoples and nations. Finally, lessons provide perspectives and materials for students to look at the ways they are connected to peoples of other nations. Students learn how these connections can benefit some people and hurt other people. Since most students studying these materials are U.S. citizens, there is a special focus on how U.S. institutions can block worldwide cooperation, as well as on the responsibility and opportunity they have for creating change. The responsibility for international peace is, of course, a collective one and citizens of all other nations must assess their country's policies and similarly catalyze change.

Finally, "Think Globally: Act Locally," Section D, contains projects and activities that students complete as contributions to global cooperation. From putting on plays, to developing international people-to-people projects, students work with their peers to contribute to global awareness and international peace.

Some lessons in this chapter expose students to a perspective seldom presented to them in standard educational materials—that is, that the competitive stance of the United States in the world mitigates against international peace and justice. Since critical thinking necessitates a broad range of ideas from which to develop an analysis, these activities provide students with an important additional perspective about international affairs. For any of these lessons, a teacher may ask some students to present the societal assumptions or governmental policy statements that favor a more competitive stance and ask others to further research the ideas presented in these lessons. By discussing both, rich critical thinking can ensue.

The lessons in Chapter 7 are the most complex in the book and are particularly applicable to the secondary level. Since the ideas presented, while sophisticated, are also extremely thought provoking, it is better to choose a few lessons and do them well than to do many superficially. The lessons are ultimately empowering and give students awareness, skills, and hope for building a just and peaceful world.

> A human being is a part of the whole called by us *Universe,* a part limited in time and space. He experiences himself, his thoughts and feelings as something separated from the rest, a kind of optical delusion of his consciousness. This delusion is a kind of prison for us, restricting us to our personal desires and to affection for a few persons nearest to us. Our task must be to free ourselves from this prison by widening our circle of compassion to embrace all living creatures and the whole of nature in its beauty.
>
> Albert Einstein

A. CONSEQUENCES OF INTERNATIONAL COMPETITION

SUBJECT—SS
FORMAT—GROUP
PROJECT

Being #1: In Anyone's Best Interest? _____

OBJECTIVES
To examine the ways nationalism and militarism fuel international competition and hinder international cooperation and peace
To explore ways the U.S. government's efforts to maintain superiority in the world can block a global perspective toward international cooperation

MATERIALS
Worksheets—"Questions—To Stay #1: On the Court" (one per group, cut up); and "To Stay #1: In the World" (one per group), pages 434–436; Chart, "Nationalism and Militarism: Are There Alternatives?" (Based on information in box on the next page.) Have some students make the chart before you teach the lesson.

IMPLEMENTATION

This activity has three interconnected parts. The activity can be extended over a three-day period if necessary.

Explain to students that they are going to examine some of the effects of international competition. They will begin with a personal example close to home, and then compare it to the international situation.

PART 1

Divide students into heterogeneous groups of four. Tell them that you are going to read them an account about Rick Wallace, a high school basketball star. Tell them it is important that they listen carefully because, when you are finished, you will give each person in each group a question to answer.

Read the account "To Stay #1: On the Court." Then distribute "Questions—To Stay #1: On the Court," a different question to each student in every group. Students respond in writing. Allow about five minutes. Then allow another five to ten minutes for reading answers, for discussion, and for correcting spelling, punctuation, and grammar. All sign and hand in.

TO STAY #1: ON THE COURT

Rick Wallace is on the varsity basketball team. He's an outstanding player.

Being a very good player and a valuable team member is not enough for Rick. He wants to always be number one in points scored, no matter what!

Rick sees that some of the other players are improving, so he practices constantly. He loses sleep, lets his schoolwork slide, and spends less time with his friends. He doesn't want anyone to be better than he is.

A new student, Dwayne, joins the team. While Rick pretends to be friendly, he is really very suspicious of Dwayne. Dwayne is a very good player and Rick doesn't trust him. Rick doesn't teach Dwayne anything he knows because he is afraid that Dwayne might score more points than Rick does.

During basketball games Rick keeps as many shots as he can for himself. Sometimes another player might be closer to the basket and Rick knows that player would have a better chance to get a basket but Rick doesn't pass the ball; instead he shoots. The coach has talked to Rick about this but hasn't put him off the team because Rick scores so well.

Rick doesn't understand that criticism is something that could help him improve his game. He sees it as an attack. If anybody criticizes his game he gets angry and then he's out to get the person.

Rick finds other ways to defend himself from others and keep his number one status. He "accidentally" tripped Joe, another good player, during a practice, causing Joe a sprained ankle.

Rick never stops to consider whether being number one is worth all the time and energy he is putting into it. He keeps himself from thinking about what it does to other people. Some of the other players believe the team would win more games if Rick passed the ball more often. But Rick doesn't listen to that because being number one is the only thing on his mind.

DISCUSSION

1. Discuss each of the four questions on the worksheet, "Questions—To Stay #1: On the Court."

2. What were the benefits to Rick in trying to stay #1?

3. What prices did he pay?

Tell students to remember the account of Rick because they will compare it to what happens internationally.

Pride and Security

It is one thing to be proud of our nation. There is much to be proud of! It is another to be so nationalistic as to believe that the U.S. is superior to other nations and has the right to determine their destinies.

Similarly it is natural to want to feel secure. We have been brought up, however, to equate national security with military power, without learning other alternatives to national security, such as nonviolent conflict resolution and civilian-based defense.

For excellent background reading that further explores these issues see the special issues of *The Bulletin of the Council on Interracial Books for Children* on Militarism and Education.

PART 2

Ask students why people often perceive people from other countries as very different from themselves. Ask them what kinds of results this has for the world. Build on the discussion by suggesting to the students that nationalism is one of the causes of our seeing people of other nations as different from ourselves. When governments see themselves as different or as better than others, they often protect by military means what they define as their national self-interest. Militarism can block worldwide co-operation and peace. Explain that students will now examine these terms and these ideas.

Pass out the worksheet "To Stay #1: In the World." Students read it and complete it as a group. Tell them to remember the account of Rick Wallace in "Staying #1: On the Court" when they think about these issues.

	Nationalism and Militarism: Possible Benefits and Costs	
	Rick's Desire to Stay #1	**U.S. Nationalism and Desire to Stay #1**
Helps Self	Gave him good feelings about self	Provides good feelings about the country
Helps Others	Convinced self he was best	Gives feeling U.S. is best
Helps Others	Motivation to practice a lot	Motivation to work hard
Hinders Self	Loses sleep, grades suffer, less time for friends	Less time, energy, and $ to put into ongoing internal needs of the nation—e.g., environment, housing, recreation, health care, etc.
Hinders Others	Others may be resentful, angry	Other nations may be resentful, angry
	Motivates other players to greater competition	Stirs other governments' nationalism
	Blocks cooperation	Blocks cooperation
	Ways Rick Acts to Defend His Position and Protect His "Interests"	**U.S. Militarism and Efforts Of U.S. to Protect Its "Interests"**
Helps Self	Feels safe from threats from others (on one level) as long as #1	Feels safe from challenges from other nations (on one level) as long as #1
Helps Others	If go along with Rick, get favors	If friendly to U.S., may get favors (military, economic aid, treaties, etc.)
Hinders Self	Constant anxiety (at another level) What if someone else becomes #1?	Constant anxiety (at another level) What if someone else becomes #1?
	Always defending self against other people—creates need to think of more ways to defend interests	Fear of other nations, creates need for more and more military
	Never sees others as potential friends or allies	Little focus on positive aspects of nations different from U.S. which could be basis for cooperation
	Makes enemies At certain point people may join together against him	Makes enemies At certain point nations may join together against U.S.
	Never know how good you really are	Never know how effective U.S. policies and ideals really are
	Other players never had a chance to do their best	Other nations kept from developing theirs to the fullest, in their own ways
Hurt Others	Not given a chance to develop own talents and get recognition	Nations seen as threat to U.S. and aren't given chance to develop in own self-determining way U.S. may intervene, withdraw aid, supply money & arms to one group, etc.
Hurt Both Self and Others	No chance to try real cooperation to see if all players can be successful and create a more skilled and satisfied team	No chance to try real cooperation where all nations are self-determining and sharing ideas and power in a reciprocal way

DISCUSSION

1. Discuss each worksheet question in full.
2. In what ways does nationalism help or hinder worldwide cooperation and peace? Why? How?
3. In what ways does militarism help or hinder worldwide cooperation and peace? Why? How?
4. Rick never stopped to see his alternatives. If he stopped worrying about being #1, he could have worked together with other team members to try to create a more effective, cooperative team. If the U.S. government was concerned less with superiority, how do you think it could work with other nations to create an even more cooperative world?
5. Would this be a good idea to try? Why or why not?

Explain to students that an alternative to nationalism is internationalism, or taking a global perspective. Post chart "Nationalism and Militarism—Are There Alternatives?" using information in box below. Inform them that an alternative to militarism is nonviolent conflict resolution. Discuss briefly.

Tell them they will learn more about those ideas soon!

Nationalism and Militarism: Are There Alternatives?	
Nationalism	**Internationalism**
Devotion to interests of one's nation as separate from interests of other nations	The principles of cooperation among nations to promote the common good
One's nation is seen as different, and often better than, other nations	Differences among nations are appreciated and commonalities sought
National perspective	Global perspective
Often assumes there will be conflicts between nations	Assumes nations of the world can live together in cooperation
Militarism	**Peaceful Cooperation**
Principles and practices of maintaining military efficiency as a supreme goal of a nation	Principles and practices of maintaining peace among nations with differences resolved without recourse to war
Military threats and wars are the most effective ways to solve international conflict	Nonviolent strategies are the most effective and humane ways to solve international conflict
Maintaining a large military establishment	Maintaining a militia with a system of civilian-based defense
Assumes the necessity of defending one's national interest against others by use of the military	Assume nations can cooperate and work to solve conflicts without military force
Other national needs are less important than the military	Meeting peoples' needs within a nation contributes as much to national security as the military does
The military is glorified	Peace and cooperation are valued

COMPLETION

A student receives credit for this lesson if her group: (a) completed "Questions—To Stay #1: On the Court" with each member completing a part; and (b) completed "To Stay #1: In the World" as evidenced by a clear, coherent response representing the views of the group, when called upon in class discussion.

Un-American?

As noted in the Introduction, the lessons in *Cooperative Learning, Cooperative Lives* stimulate critical thinking in students by providing them perspectives on various issues that are not typically represented as choices for students to consider. These perspectives reflect the idea of cooperation in the international arena.

Cooperative Learning, Cooperative Lives is based on the assumption that the strength of a democracy lies in citizens' abilities to ask critical questions about their government and to advocate for changes when changes are necessary. While some see such critical thinking as unpatriotic and Un-American, the premise of this book is that the opportunity for people to be exposed to a wide range of perspectives, to think critically about them, and act collectively to influence government is a strength of the United States. Schools must take responsibility for teaching this process to students.

If parent or administrator criticizes the ideas in these lessons, discuss with them the roots of our democracy.

GOING FURTHER Have students examine a current international issue or a series of contemporary international events. Ask them to document ways the United States is cooperating with other nations to encourage a global perspective. Ask them to note ways nationalism, militarism, or the U.S. desire to maintain superiority is affecting the events or issues. Discuss the findings.

SUBJECT—SS

The Towers

OBJECTIVES To enable students to understand better the dynamics and causes of the arms race, by participating in a simulation game

To provide students a chance to share their feelings and reactions to the effects of the arms race on their lives and the lives of others

MATERIALS A set of blocks with at least the number of students in your class plus twelve. The blocks should lend themselves to building a strong, stable tower.

Role tags: two large signs ("Big Bear" and "Mighty Eagle") for leaders; four tags shaped like rockets—for block builders; four 3″ × 5″ cards with two stars on each—for military officials; four 3″ × 5″ cards with a government building on them—for legislators.

Worksheets: "Eagle Roles," "Bear Roles," pages 437–438, cut

Also a box of star stickers, straight pins, at least forty pennies, and a box marked "Food, Clothing, and Shelter." Ten chips (cut up pieces of cardboard or construction paper) of the same color for each group member. Make enough sets of ten chips of different colors so that only two players have the same color.

Worksheet: "America and the Arms Race: A Closer Look" (one per group), pages 439–440

IMPLEMENTATION
1. PREPARATION

To make the simulation game most effective, build up to it a few days before. Give some mysterious and enticing information or pose questions about the game. For example, write on the board "Will the towers stand?" When students ask about it just say, "When you play The Towers activity in a few days, you'll find out." This builds suspense and interest.

2. SET UP

There are two groups in the game—the Bears and the Eagles. Have an equal number of students in each. If there is an extra student, she can be your assistant. Groups sit on opposite sides of the room. Draw or place a line down the middle of the room, dividing the groups. Each group begins with blocks equal to the number of people in each group minus two. The leader of each group builds a strong, sturdy tower with the blocks on its side of the room, but close to the line. The leader sits close to the tower.

Tell students they will play a simulation game called The Towers. Explain that there will be two groups—the Bears and the Eagles. Divide students and send to opposite sides of the room. Explain that each person will have a role. Ask for volunteers or assign: one Bear leader, one Eagle leader; one Bear member of legislature, one Eagle member of legislature; one Bear military official, one Eagle military official; one Bear design head, one Eagle industrial head (known as block builders); one Bear favoring disarmament, one Eagle disarmament advocate. Give name tags to these students. All others are Bear citizens or Eagle citizens.

3. DIRECTIONS TO STUDENTS

Purpose

Tell students the purpose of the game is for each player to try to meet her goal. If, at the end of the game, you have met your goal, you are a winner.

Role Cards

Distribute role cards. Students read them to themselves. They are not to share the information on their cards with others. Tell students that they are to play the roles as if they are the person described. A player may change his feelings or goals only if convinced to do so in the course of the game.

Tower

Tell students that each group already has a tower. The leader and military officials set up the group's tower.

Each block has the power to wipe out a person in the other group. When a block falls, a member from the other group is destroyed. When you have the number of blocks in your tower equal to the number of people in the other group, you have enough blocks to destroy that other group. There is no need to add more blocks to the tower except to make the tower taller.

There are two ways a tower may fall: (1) By accident; (2) By a leader's action. A leader may pull the block from the bottom of the other group's tower. If a tower is destroyed this way, the leader of that group has five seconds in which to pull the bottom block from the other's tower, if he chooses to do so. When a tower falls, any previously-gained programs for the people are wiped out.

Play

Tell students that the simulation game consists of a series of three-minute rounds. During each round, members of the military, block builders, and members of the legislature may speak to the leaders of their government. The citizens of each government may write letters to their leader.

Each citizen gets ten chips of mixed color each round. Each gets to keep them by trading chips with other citizens in his group to get ten of the same color. A player might say, for example, I'll give you a white if you give me a green, and so forth. After this happens, chips can be used. In order to live, each citizen must put six chips in the food, clothing, and shelter box. Each citizen must pay four chips to the government by the end of the round. Two go to support basic programs to maintain the group, like postal service, parks, and highways. The remaining two are needed for a block for the tower.

At the end of each round, the government leader of both Eagles and Bears is offered a block. He has three choices: (1) to take the block and add it to the tower; (2) not to take a block and to apply the chips to programs for the people; (3) to do #2 and remove one or more blocks from the tower. Describe typical programs for the people.

Examples of Possible Programs for the People

- Calm background music in class for one period (30 chips)
- A healthy snack for all for tomorrow (60 chips)
- A special guest speaker, musician, magician, etc. (90 chips)
- A period of cooperative games (60 chips)
- Other items/events which you know your class would enjoy

If all blocks are removed from a tower, the block builder becomes a citizen and the military official becomes a conflict negotiator. If both teams take down all their blocks, each person knows the towers can't destroy her anymore. In addition, members of both groups can cooperate to choose a program for the people.

Play continues for six rounds, unless towers are knocked down or taken down before then. Remind students before beginning that each should work hard to reach the goal on her card. If students ask to talk with players from the other group, tell them that their leader and one or two citizens may do so.

4. INSTRUCTIONS TO THE TEACHER

Since this is a simulation, there are many possible directions the game may take. Be flexible.

Prepare for each round by giving each player on a team ten chips of different colors. Give government leaders, military officials, and block builders ten chips of the same color. When everyone has chips, announce "The round begins." Time it for three minutes. Citizens will be trading. Encourage Bear officials to discuss what their plans are for their tower and what they will do if the other group knocks their tower down. Encourage the disarmament activist to try to organize the citizens. Suggest Eagle officials do the same. Coach students who have key roles, if they are having trouble playing their roles. After all players have ten chips of the same color, remind each to put six into the food, clothing, and shelter box and to pay four to you (the government) for services.

At the end of each round, offer a block to each leader. If he accepts it, he adds it to the tower. In that case give that group's military officials a star to stick on their 3" × 5" cards and give each block builder a penny. Take two chips from each citizen.

If a leader does not ask for a block, take one chip from each citizen. Citizens then have three minutes to decide together which programs to use. Play until six rounds are over or the towers are knocked over.

If players knock down each other's towers, discuss the game and have them play again. They may choose different alternatives the second time.

DISCUSSION

THE GAME

Tell students that we will first discuss the game and then compare it to the real world.

1. What were some of the feelings you had while you played The Towers? What made you feel that way? (Spend plenty of time on this question and give each person an opportunity to respond.)
2. In which roles did players feel most satisfied? In which did you feel most frustrated? Why?
3. How did the leaders decide which choices to make—to add a block, not add a block, or take blocks down? How did players in other roles feel about these choices?
4. Who influenced the leaders' decisions? For what reasons? Which players had most influence?
5. How did different players feel about those decisions? Which players gained, and which players lost, from having a block added? Which players gained, and which players lost, from the block being substituted for programs for the people? Which gained and lost from removing a block?
6. What hindered players from influencing the leaders? What, if anything, did you do to change that? What did you think of doing, but didn't carry out? Now, looking back, what could you have done, but didn't try?
7. Who won The Towers activity? What did "winning" mean to the winner? How did other players define winning? How would you, personally, define what winning is?
8. Was the game set up in a fair manner? Why or why not? How could it be changed to make it more fair?
9. If you were to play The Towers again with the same rules what, if anything, would you do differently? Why?
   (If the class knocked The Towers down immediately, you might want to play the game again.)

THE WORLD

Now let's compare the game to the world today. If your students aren't knowledgeable about the arms race, have them now do the worksheet, "America and the Arms Race: A Closer Look." Otherwise assign it after the discussion.

10. Who might the Bears represent? Who the Eagles? Why?

11. What could the towers be compared to?
    Remind students that in the game, when each side had enough blocks equal to the number of people in the other group, they had the power to destroy the other group. Explain that this is true in the arms race today. Both the U.S. and the U.S.S.R. have many more than enough weapons to destroy each other's total populations.

12. Using what you learned from the game, why do you think more and more arms are developed each year? To what extent do you agree or disagree with our leaders' decisions about this?

13. What organizations or groups benefit from the arms race? How?

14. How does the average citizen benefit in her life because of the arms race? How does he lose?

In the game citizens were kept busy trading chips. In real life that could be compared to working day to day, trying to earn a living.

15. Why is it hard for the average citizen in the U.S. to think about, or do anything about, the arms race? What can be done to change that?

16. In the U.S., who influences our leaders when they make decisions about the arms race? What must citizens do to have effective influence? What methods do they have to get their voices heard?

17. How do you feel about the great power that the leaders of the U.S. and the U.S.S.R. have regarding decisions about the arms race and starting a nuclear war? Are there alternatives to this situation? What?

18. Sometimes when playing The Towers, the blocks fall down by accident or someone who isn't the leader pushes them down. What is this like in the world today? Can you give an example?

19. In the game if chips weren't spent on a block they went to programs for the people. In the United States today, if money was taken from the arms race, what programs should the money be spent on—to help people meet their needs?

Dollars for Which Kind of Defense?

- Every gun that is made, every warship launched, every rocket fired signifies . . . a theft from those who hunger and are not fed, those who are cold and not clothed. This world in arms is not spending money alone. It is spending the sweat of its laborers, the genius of its scientists, the hope of its children.

  Dwight Eisenhower, April 16, 1953

- Each year 327,000 American babies are born prematurely, shrinking their survival chances and increasing their rate of birth defects. The President and Congress say we can't afford the $120 million needed in 1984 to provide their mothers pre-natal care. They say we can afford to spend $120 million **each** for 226 MX missiles.

- Each school lunch costs $1.20 in federal subsidy. Each federal executive dining hall meal costs $12.48 in federal subsidy. Just the $1 million annual subsidy for the Pentagon's four executive dining rooms would buy 800,000 school lunches.

  Children's Defense Budget:
  Reprinted with permission from An Analysis of the President's FY 1985 Budget and Children, 1984, Children's Defense Fund, 122 C St. NW, Washington, DC 20001.

20. Military officials and some government leaders say the arms race gives our country security. What is security? What do you believe will make our nation secure?
21. Some people say the U.S. must win the arms race. How do they define "win"? What does "winning" mean in a world where nations have the weapons to destroy it?
22. What changes do you believe should be made to create a more peaceful world?

Unless you assigned the worksheet "America and the Arms Race: A Closer Look" after question 9, divide students now into heterogeneous groups and distribute worksheets. When completed, come together, and discuss answers to the final questions.

COMPLETION A student gets credit for this activity if each group member contributes to sharing information from the worksheet "America and the Arms Race: A Closer Look" and to his group's answers to the questions, as evidenced by signatures on the worksheet.

Oakwood School: A Nuclear Free Zone

A nuclear free zone is a place that has been declared off limits to the nuclear arms race. In 1984 the students and staff of the Oakwood School in Poughkeepsie, New York decided, by consensus, to declare their school a nuclear free zone.

"Oakwood was founded with the objective that the school and the individuals which comprise the community should make a positive contribution in the world. There would be no world as we know it if nuclear weapons were ever to be used."

Nuclear free zones offer people a clear way to protest the nuclear arms race. Over 14,611,000 Americans lived in 132 Nuclear Free Zones in America by February 1987. "The New Abolishionist," the newsletter of Nuclear Free America lists nuclear free zones worldwide. Nuclear free zones include Takomo Park, Maryland; Marin County, California; Durham, North Carolina; Greenfield, Massachusetts; Iowa City, Iowa; and many more.

Congers New York
March 13, 1985

Dear Mr. President

My name is Christopher Fragale and I am 10 years old. Mr. President, I would like to know why we have nuclear missiles. I would also like to know what nuclear missiles are good for? Mr. President I would like to say something. We don't like the Russian government so if we fire nuclear missiles we're going to kill the citizens of the Sovet Union and there innocent; they didn't do anything, only the goverment did. And if we fire the missels we'll be just as bad as them.

Respectfully
Christopher Fragale

Do We Have the Right? _____

OBJECTIVES

To understand how other people in the world can experience the effects of the United States' efforts to maintain its economic, military, and political superiority in the world

To examine the effects of these efforts on a particular nation, Nicaragua

MATERIALS

Worksheet: "Marta and the People of Nicaragua" (one per group), Worksheet: "Marta and the People of Nicaragua—Cards," cut up (one set of each kind of card per group), pages 441–446. Mount cards. Number the backs with #1 for "Life in Nicaragua Cards," #2 for "The Somoza Family," and #3 for "U.S. Ties to Nicaragua." (Remember students can do this preparation with you!)

IMPLEMENTATION

This lesson presents a perspective that is critical of the U.S. government's support of the former Somoza regime in Nicaragua. You may wish to have students research the U.S. government's rationale for its action and discuss both perspectives in class. (See the next box.) Tell students they will be learning about the people of Nicaragua and the effects of U.S. ties to that country, before the Sandinista revolution through a fictional case study representative of real experiences and perspectives of thousands of adolescents in Nicaragua.

Explain to students that very often Americans have been afforded few opportunities to see the effects of U.S. policies on other peoples of the world, especially from those peoples' points of view. Explain that an inability to get into others shoes is a significant barrier to international cooperation. This lesson will begin to enable them to do that.

The U.S. Government Rationale

Among the reasons the U.S. government put forth to justify its position supporting the Somoza regime, and similar governments, are the following:

1. The Somoza regime would maintain a stable government and keep Communists from taking over.
2. A stable capitalist government is necessary for American businesses there to prosper.
3. The Somoza regime is a friend of the U.S. government and supports it in international organizations, like the UN.

Students can be encouraged to use newspapers, magazines, and government documents to further research this position.

Divide students into groups of three or four. Distribute one copy of "Marta and the People of Nicaragua" worksheet and one set of the three types of cards to each group. Students take turns: (1) reading Marta's accounts; (2) reading cards; and (3) discussing and then filling in answers to the questions. Continue with each section. Remind groups to make sure that each student participates equally. Move around the room as students begin to make sure they have the right idea.

Resources for Teachers

Here are useful books on Nicaragua that describe both the Somoza regime and life after the 1979 revolution. Students with good reading skills can use *Now We Can Speak*, an excellent resource. These books broaden the reader's perspective in that they are critical of the Somoza regime and document a positive picture of revolutionary Nicaragua.

- **Especially useful for the classroom**
  Now We Can Speak: Journey through the New Nicaragua, Francis Moore Lappe and Joseph Collins.
  Bulletin of the Council on Interracial Books for Children—Special issue: "Central America: What U.S. Educators Need to Know," vol. 13, nos. 2 & 3, 1982.
- **Good background reading for teachers**
  The Politics of Intervention: The U.S. in Central America, Roger Burback and Patricia Flynn.
  Triumph of the People: The Sandinista Revolution in Nicaragua, George Black.
  The Ends and the Beginning: The Nicaraguan Revolution, John Booth.

DISCUSSION

1. Go over the questions on each section of the worksheet. Spend enough time on the latter questions; they raise complex and important issues.
2. Who in the U.S. benefited from the economic and military ties the U.S. had to the Somoza regime? Who in Nicaragua benefitted from the ties to the U.S.? How do you feel about this?

Human Rights in Nicaragua

Amnesty International investigated human rights violations in Nicaragua in 1976. Many union and political activists were detained for crimes of conscience. Normally prisoners were held incommunicado. Torture techniques employed in the Model Prison at Tipitapa included beatings, electric shock, near drowning, abuse of the genitals, and hooding for periods of months.

John Booth, *The End and The Beginning.*

3. How would you feel if Nicaragua was more powerful and richer than the U.S. and decided to use its power to control our government? What would you advocate the United States to do?

4. One U.S. teenager recently wrote, "I think we should support **anything** our government does to keep us #1!" Do **you** believe the U.S. government and U.S. corporations have the right to stay number one in the world by intervening in other countries? Why or why not?

U.S. and the World's Hungry

A myth exists about the national security that pits the U.S. against the hungry around the world. The myth is that the Soviet Union (or Cuba) instigates every conflict or revolutionary movement in the Third World. If we accept this myth, then every movement for change in the third world must be combatted as part of a Soviet plan for domination.

But the facts are otherwise. Of the 105 major wars documented since World War II, virtually all have been caused by such factors as economic injustice, colonialism, ethnic conflict, nationalism and border disputes. What these conflicts often have in common is a struggle for the right to eat by people living in poverty and hunger.

Institute for Food and Development Policy, 1984,
"Biting the Bullet: Hunger, Intervention, and the Threat of Nuclear War."

COMPLETION

A student gets credit for this lesson if each group member contributes to the worksheet "Marta and the People of Nicaragua" as evidenced by their written responses and final signatures.

GOING FURTHER

Tell students that in 1979, as Marta had hoped, there was a revolution that overthrew the Somoza regime. The new government developed programs to help the majority of the people. More people had access to better health care, basic food, land and education.

Students should research the specific effects of the revolution on the Nicaraguan people. *Now We Can Speak* is one excellent resource written at a level many students can read. Get it on interlibrary loan or order direct (see bibliography).

After the revolution, the U.S. government continues to intervene in Nicaragua—not to support the government, but now to attempt to overthrow the new government. Among many steps, it: suspended aid to Nicaragua; blocked loans from international agencies; gave money to groups trying to overthrow the government; defied U.S. law by illegally funding the contras and illegally mining Nicaraguan harbors; and turned a blind eye to camps in Florida where ex-Somoza guardsmen were trained for counterrevolution; and promoted a policy of terrorism. Students can research these and any other policies, and present their findings and thoughts to the class. Be sure they use a variety of sources in addition to the standard media.

Then return to the theme of the lesson, "Do we have the right?" in a final class discussion.

What Is the U.S. Afraid Of?

Two American educators who visited Nicaragua write, "Nothing we have learned about Nicaragua—during Joe's ten visits and the journey we made together or from the piles of documents and interviews in Washington—indicates Nicaragua is a threat to the United States.

So why do Reagan administration officials feel so threatened?

Perhaps the U.S. government realizes that the potential threat of Nicaragua is . . . that of a good example which could inspire the majority in so many countries throughout the world who still suffer impoverishment and tyranny similar to that under Somoza.

Now We Can Speak

SUBJECT—SS, M
FORMAT—GROUP
PROJECT

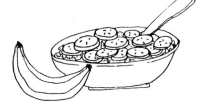

Banana for Breakfast: Healthy for Whom? —

OBJECTIVES

To examine how some policies and practices of U.S. corporations and multinational corporations hinder cooperation among nations

To consider how these practices contribute to world hunger

To study this pattern through a particular case, the banana industry, and its effects on the Honduran people

MATERIALS

Worksheets—"Jill's Dialogue" (three copies), "Elisa's Dialogue" (two copies) and "Connecting the Lives of Jill and Elisa" (one per student), pages 447–449

IMPLEMENTATION PART 1

Before the class, ask for five volunteers who will participate in reading two different dialogues to the class. Give one group of three, "Jill's Dialogue" and the other group of two, "Elisa's Dialogue." Have them practice together so they can make a convincing presentation.

Explain to students that in order to understand some of the effects of U.S. corporations on the world's hungry, they will examine accounts of two thirteen-year-old girls, who, while fictional case studies, are representative of many Honduran and American girls.

Tell students to listen very carefully to their classmates who will read two dialogues aloud. Tell them they will then be asked to answer questions based on what they heard. Begin with Jill's dialogue and follow with Elisa's.

Tell students to number off from one to four. Distribute "Connecting the Lives of Jill and Elisa" to all students. Person 1 reads question 1 aloud and the group discusses it. Person 2 reads question 2, and so forth. After all questions have been discussed, each group member will write, on a separate piece of paper, the group's response to the question she read. If there are differences of opinion, the writer makes sure those are represented. The group decides who will write answers to numbers five and six. Possible criteria for that decision might be: (1) who finishes first; (2) who has the least complex questions; (3) who writes most quickly and easily. When all members are finished writing, they read their answers to the group to assure agreement and then exchange with another member for proofreading. All group members sign a cover sheet and turn in.

DISCUSSION

1. As a class, discuss questions one through six on the worksheets.
2. Jill doesn't think she's connected to the hunger of the Hondurans. How would Elisa respond to that? How do you think Jill is connected to the poverty of the Hondurans? How do you think she is not?

Background Information

For Teachers
Read *Bread and Justice: Toward a New International Economic Order*, by James McGinnis, for clear and detailed information on effects of international economic competition on the lives of the peoples of the world, particularly in the Third World.

For Students
The *Food First Curriculum* is an excellent resource for further exploring the roots of hunger here and abroad and how to act locally on a global program. Have some, or all, of your students use it as a follow-up.

Media
Controlling Interest, a useful film for advanced students or adults, provides excellent background on the influence of multinational corporations on poverty in the Third World.

PART 2

Students return to groups of four for a role play. Someone plays the role of Jill. Review with the group what you know about her. Someone plays the role of Elisa. Review with the group what you know about her. The other two students are observers.

Elisa comes to meet Jill to explain to her the effects of the J and J Box Company involvement in the banana industry. She wants to convince Jill to help work for a change that will allow Hondurans to be more self-sufficient and reap more benefits from the banana industry.

Tell students to role play for five minutes and see if they can come up with a joint agreement as to what to do. Observers watch for things role players do that help or hinder them from coming up with a plan.

Tell students to role-play for five minutes and see if they can come up with a joint agreement as to what to do. Observers watch for things role players do that help or hinder them from coming up with a plan.

DISCUSSION

1. How did it feel to play Elisa? What did you learn?
2. How did it feel to play Jill? What did you learn?
3. Observers, what did Jill or Elisa do to come to an understanding?
4. What helped or hindered their coming up with ideas about how they could help change practices that hurt the Honduran people?
5. Role players, how did you feel about the understandings you had or the action plans you developed?
6. How effective might these ideas be?

Now go on to discuss the broader issues raised by this dialogue.

7.
   a. What other products do we get from Third World countries?
   b. Who owns the companies that bring us these products?
   c. How does this affect Third World countries?

8.
   a. What are alternatives to the current patterns?
   b. Who then would control the processing, transportation, and distribution of materials?
   c. How would that affect the Third World country?

If students have little information on this topic, you can explain the following and have them do follow-up research. In addition to the banana industry, there are many more U.S. corporations contributing to world hunger by keeping Third World countries dependent on them. These corporations often get raw materials from other countries without enabling those countries to share in the benefits of processing, shipping or transporting the products. Among many examples are cocoa, jute (used in fabrics) and coffee.

Put the following chart on the board.

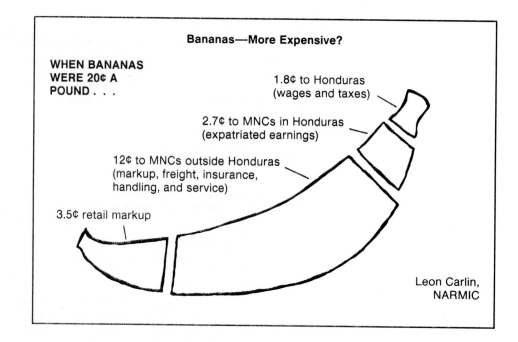

If Hondurans could get some of the 2.7¢ and 12¢ going to the multinational corporations out of every 20¢ of bananas, the price of bananas would not have to be raised and Third World incomes would increase.

Explain that these policies maintain vertical interdependence with the multinational corporations controlling the economies of the other countries. This type of interdependence is based on inequality and contributes to hunger in the Third World.

vertical interdependence

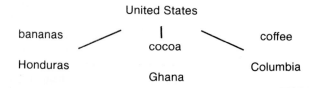

The alternative is horizontal interdependence where Third World countries have more autonomy over their own resources and where countries share in decision making and benefits. This type of interdependence is based on equality and mutual cooperation.

horizontal interdependence

United States ⎯⎯⎯ Honduras

To put this simply, the United States depends on Third World countries for resources, but it has all the control. An alternative would be for the United States to depend on Third World countries for some things, Third World countries to depend on the United States for others, and the control to be shared.

PART 3 Consider with students the action steps they could take to bring information about the connection between policies of some multinational corporations and world hunger to others. Students could take the example of the bananas or another product (such as a candy bar) that they can personally identify with. For background information consult *Bread and Justice* or have an interested group of students do research and present their information to the class.

To Be Active: A Student's Decision

In this lesson, or any, students can choose to take action if they agree to speak up about a particular issue. It's okay not to take action, if they want to leave doing so to adults. Also, they might not want to act if they have an opinion that isn't very strong, they don't feel ready, or if their parents disapprove. In these cases, they can wait to be active until they're older.

Possible ideas are:
1. **Inform other students**

   Provide other students with information about the connection between themselves, policies of some multinational corporations, and world hunger. On a day that your school serves bananas for lunch:
   a. Put on a skit, followed by discussion, for other classes.
   b. Make a bulletin board to put in a prominent place in the school.

2. **Carry out projects with other students**
   a. Plan an "International Hunger Awareness Day." Have students who are willing to participate eat only a small bowl of beans for lunch. This is what a typical Honduran child might eat. Contribute the remainder of their lunch money to a program supporting economic self-sufficiency for the Honduran people.
   b. Support Honduran—or other Third World people—who are attempting self-sufficiency by selling products that they make. As a class or school project, sell the products and return the proceeds to the people.

Mexican Women's Cooperatives

One group to contact if your class decides to sell products is CED (The Centro de Encuentrosy Dialogos). This group is the contact organization for Mexican Women's Cooperatives that make skirts, blouses, baby shirts and scarfs that can be sold in the U.S. See their address in the Resources section.

---

3. **Carry out projects with family and churches**

   Some families and churches have stocks in corporations that contribute to hunger in the Third World. Students can educate their family members and churches. The Interfaith Center for Corporate Responsibility has excellent information. With other families/churches, they can use their influence to help change corporate policy.

COMPLETION

Students receive credit for this lesson if their group (1) turns in a "Connecting the Lives of Jill and Elisa" worksheet on which each member has written one or two responses and has signed; and (2) participated in discussion about the role play.

GOING FURTHER

Students investigate other products that are familiar to young people (such as a candy bar) and how the controlling corporation operates by unequal competition—and so, contributes to world hunger. Students make a bulletin board to raise the awareness of other teachers and students. Put it in the hall so people can see it.

A good poster that shows the worldwide interdependence necessary to make a chocolate bar is "The World in a Chocolate Bar" from the U.S. Committee for UNICEF.

Bananas—$1.00 a Pound?

Some people think that the only way to make trade more just for Third World countries is to raise the prices on imports from those countries. This is not necessarily so if: (1) the profits multinational corporations controlling the banana industry didn't "have to" increase and (2) more of the profits made on boxing, labeling, and shipping bananas, went to Honduras.

Bread and Justice

Cecil Rhodes 1895

I was employed in the East End of London yesterday and attended a meeting of the unemployed. I listened to the wild speeches, which were just a cry of "bread! bread!" and on my way home I pondered over the scene and I became more than convinced of the importance of imperialism. . . . My cherished idea is a solution for the social problem, i.e., in order to save the 40,000,000 inhabitants of the United Kingdom from a bloody civil war, we colonial statesmen must acquire new lands to settle the surplus population, to provide new markets for the goods produced in the factories and mines. The Empire, as I have always said, is a bread and butter question. If you want to avoid a civil war, you just become imperialists.

B. COOPERATION WITHIN AND BETWEEN NATIONS

SUBJECT—SS,
SCIENCE
FORMAT—JIGSAW,
GROUP PROJECT

International Cooperation: To Benefit **All** the World's People

OBJECTIVES

To give students the opportunity to learn about a long-standing model of international cooperation, the Universal Postal Union

To design a plan for international cooperation in a situation needing attention today—the use of the world's oceans

MATERIALS

Worksheets—"The Universal Postal Union" (jigsaw sections—cut up), "Issues and Problems Concerning the World's Oceans (jigsaw sections—cut up), "The Oceans: Common Heritage of Humankind," pages 450–452

IMPLEMENTATION

This lesson is comprised of two parts. In Part 1, students will learn about a model of international cooperation, the Universal Postal Union, that has served the peoples of the world for over 100 years. In Part 2, they will contribute to a more challenging task that actually faces the nations of the world today: designing a model of international cooperation regarding the world's oceans—a model of cooperation that will benefit **all** the peoples of the earth.

PART 1

Tell students that they will learn about one organization fostering international cooperation that benefits them. Divide students into heterogeneous groups of five. Pass out the jigsaw sections of the "Universal Postal Union" worksheet. Group members read the sections in numerical order and make sure all others understand the material. Tell students you will spot check their understanding by coming to their group when they are finished reviewing, and asking a question about the UPU. Their group will get credit for Part 1 of the lesson if that member answers correctly.

Discuss with the whole class how they benefit from the UPU. Students with relatives, pen pals, or friends in other countries can make particularly relevant contributions.

PART 2

Explain to students that a current problem facing the world is the use of the oceans. Explain that the world's oceans are the greatest potential natural resource that has yet to be explored and developed. Because the oceans don't belong to any one country, representatives from many nations of the world have recently worked together to try to determine how different nations will benefit from the oceans. The use of the oceans could be regulated to benefit some nations more than others. Or a plan could be devised whereby all nations would share the oceans' benefits. Just as international cooperation in mail service was an issue 100 years ago, so international cooperation regarding the oceans is an issue today. Explain that students will now devise a plan to bring about international cooperation regarding the world's oceans.

For Background

Useful background reading for this lesson is the section on "Ocean Management" in *Reshaping the International Order,* edited by Jan Tinbergen. Nobel Laureate Tinbergen brought together experts from around the world in 1976 to examine ways to work together as a global community to bring more equality among nations of the world. The section on ocean management offers principles and plans for preserving the oceans as the common heritage of all humankind.

Divide students into groups of five. Tell them they are representatives from different countries meeting to draw up an International Law of the Seas. Distribute jigsaw sections of the worksheet "Issues and Problems Concerning the World's Oceans"—to each member. Have each learn the information or problem presented on her card and teach that to her group. If there are different words or ideas, group members help each other understand them. Group members discuss their problems briefly.

Next tell students that each group will design an international agreement to regulate the seas. Remind them that they should think of the needs of **all** nations equally: the underdeveloped, as well as the developed countries; the poor as well as the richer nations, and the landlocked, as well as the maritime countries. Distribute worksheet, "The Oceans: Common Heritage of Humankind." After each group has formulated its plan, bring everyone together for discussion.

DISCUSSION   Each group shares its plan for international regulation of the seas to benefit all peoples and nations. Each group member explains one section of the plan.

After each group presents its plan, ask:
1. What are the strengths of this plan?
2. What, if any, are its weaknesses? Are there any ways it doesn't uphold the five principles of preserving the oceans for the common heritage of all humankind? If so, how could that be changed?
3. After all plans have been read and discussed, ask: In your proposals for ocean use, what were the most creative examples for sharing between nations with unequal money, technology, or access to the sea?

Benefits of the Ocean:
A Means to a New International Order

A suggestion (from *Reshaping the International Order*) for using the oceans to help benefit the poorer nations and reshape the international order is: All nations using the oceans would make contributions to an International Ocean Institute, based on the amount of their use of the oceans and its resources. Some of these monies would be returned to the poorer nations of the world.

---

4. What were some of the hardest problems to resolve while you were making your plans? Why? What issues did these problems raise?
5. To what extent do you think your plan could be put into effect by the nations of the world today? Why? What could be explained to people to make it more possible for nations to accept your plan?

COMPLETION   A student gets credit for Part 1 if the member of her group called on by the teacher answered correctly the question about the UPU.

A student receives credit for Part 2 if each person in her group contributed to the group plan for preserving the ocean for the common heritage of humankind, wrote a section for that as evidenced by a signed plan handed into the teacher, and presented clearly, in class, a part of the plan.

FOLLOW-UP   Have students write letters about their project and send them to appropriate officials, for example—the U.S. Ambassador to the U.N., the U.N. Coordinator for the Law of the Seas, the U.S. President.

Advanced students can write to the U.N. Department of Public Information and request the Press Release of April 30, 1982, describing the Convention on the Law of the Seas and giving other relevant information. They can trace the role of the U.S. in developing and voting on the convention and present their findings to the class.

Law of the Seas Convention

In April 1982, after nine years of negotiation, the UN Conference on the Law of the Seas adopted a Convention on the Law of the Seas.

The Conference failed to meet a goal it had set for itself—to adopt the Convention by consensus. Instead, in a vote requested by the United States, it adopted the text by a vote of 130 in favor to 4 against, with 17 abstentions. Voting against were Israel, Turkey, the United States, and Venezuela.

During the final stages of the Conference, efforts to achieve consensus focused on the deep seabed. Hard bargaining failed to close the gap between a group of major Western industrialized countries, led by the United States, and a group of 77 developing countries—over the future system for sharing resources of the international seabed area which the General Assembly, and the Conference, have declared to be the common heritage of humankind.

International Cooperation in Science

There are many other examples of international cooperation which students can research, particularly in the sciences. International cooperation to solve health problems, combat disease and protect the environment are all exciting areas for investigation.

Rescue in Denmark: A Choral Reading ____

OBJECTIVES

To examine an example from another country of cooperation across the nation, and between people unknown to each other

To learn specifically about the rescue of the Danish Jews from the Nazis during World War II

To think about this example of massive, nonviolent resistance as an alternative to military resistance

MATERIALS

Worksheet—"Rescue in Denmark: A Choral Reading," pages 453–457, cut up into parts

IMPLEMENTATION

Tell students that they will be participating in a classwide cooperative activity—a choral reading. Then they will work with a younger class to help them present the reading. The focus of the reading is cooperation—specifically, the rescue of Jews by the people of Denmark.

Background Information

Harold Flender's *Rescue in Denmark* is an excellent book for both teachers and advanced students. It provides a very readable account of the Danish peoples' cooperative rescue of the Danish Jews.

Facing History and Ourselves is a valuable curriculum on the holocaust and useful in providing a context for this lesson.

PART 1 **The Choral Reading**

The activity is designed for twenty students. If you have more students in your class, you can easily divide longer readings into two parts to accommodate all your students. The reading is divided into four sections: (1) Background (1–4); (2) The Warning (5–9); (3) Hiding (10–15); and (4) Escape (16–20).

Before distributing roles, take time to discuss anti-Semitism and the Nazi extermination of the Jews during World War II. Draw upon student knowledge. See bibliography for other sources. Answer additional questions. Begin when you believe students have a clear historical context for the reading.

Divide students into the four basic groups (Background, Warning, Hiding, Escape). Pass out readings. While you might want to help students with pronunciation of Danish names, remind them that accurate pronunciation is not important for the activity. Don't belabor it. Ask students to read their parts silently. Then pair up in twos or threes to practice reading aloud. Tell them that their goal is to read in a clear, strong voice and with feeling. They are recreating feeling in the classroom!

When students are prepared, bring them together. If possible, sit in a circle, in proper numerical sequence. Reader 1 stands, reads her part, and others follow in order.

DISCUSSION

1. How did you feel being part of this choral reading?
2. What words would you use to describe the actions of the Danes?
3. What risks did they take in helping the Jews?
4. How do you feel about the actions of the Danes?
5. What do you think you would have done if you were a Dane who wasn't a Jew? Why?
6. How does anti-Semitism exist in our own society? What can we do to deal with that?
7. The action of the Danes is an example of many people working together in non-violent resistance to oppression. What do you think of this alternative to military power? What are other examples of the use of this alternative? Cite examples from U.S. history and from the history of other countries.

GOING FURTHER

Have students research ways in which anti-Semitism exists in our society today and what people have done to change that. When students present their findings to the class, you might invite a guest speaker from a Jewish organization or synagogue to add additional information and to share feelings.

PART 2 **Cross-Age Project**

Make plans for your class to work with a younger class. Prepare students by telling them that they will: (1) work with younger students to give them background on the Rescue in Denmark; (2) help them learn their choral-reading parts; (3) present the reading; and (4) lead discussions about the rescue and the information raised. Review with students the attitudes and behaviors that help or hinder cross-age projects (see pages 120–121). In groups, (Background, Warning, Hiding, Escape), have students plan discussion questions to be used after the reading. Review these together to make sure they're thoughtful and age-appropriate.

Organize the procedure carefully before bringing the two classes together. When they do come together, pair students with the same roles, across grades. The older student helps the younger one learn her role. Younger students then present the class choral reading. Then divide into the four groups of younger and older students. Older students lead a discussion. Rotate around the room to help if needed.

When they return, have groups discuss their experiences. Each student writes a statement about something she learned during this project.

DISCUSSION

1. How did you feel about your role in helping the younger students present "Rescue in Denmark"?
2. What did you do that was helpful?
3. What would you do differently next time?
4. What did you learn by doing this project? What did the younger students learn?

COMPLETION

A student gets credit for this lesson if she participates in the choral reading and if each member of her group hands in a statement of what she learned by doing the project.

GOING FURTHER

1. Present the choral reading for other classes, a school assembly, or the PTA.
2. The U.S. did not seem to care about the Jews as much as Denmark did. The Wagner-Rogers Bill, which would have saved 20,000 Jewish children, was undermined in Congress. See *Facing History and Ourselves* for materials for students on the U.S. response. This resource also contains descriptions of courageous individuals in Europe who risked their lives to save the Jews. Assign interested students follow-up research on these topics or assign advanced students Flender's entire book.

SUBJECT—SS
FORMAT—
RESEARCH, JIGSAW

Cooperation: The Swedish Way of Life ____

OBJECTIVE   To learn about a nation—Sweden—in which the economy, the political system, and the culture are all based on the value and practice of cooperation

MATERIALS   3 × 5 cards, supplementary books on Sweden

Background Reading on Sweden

Teacher and advanced students will profit from books about Sweden. Two clear, well-organized and relevant books are: *The New Sweden: The Challenge of a Disciplined Democracy*—Frederic Fleisher, and *Sweden: The Welfare State*—Wilfrid Fleisher.

Students can read: *Sweden: A Good Life for All*—Kari Olsson.

IMPLEMENTATION   Tell students that they will study a country that bases its economy, political system, and culture on cooperative values. That country is Sweden. Give students the following introduction to their research on Sweden.

Sweden is a democracy with several political parties. Sweden has always had a commitment to mutual aid. In this century, Sweden developed a special welfare system that guarantees that no one will go hungry or be homeless. It assures medical care for all.

Sweden is a socialist country. This means the government takes a very significant role in planning the economy. Its goal is to assure jobs for everyone and usually that goal is met. Sweden is often called the middle way between capitalism and communism. Sweden allows private enterprises to exist, but businesses and corporations don't have significant control of the economy as they do in capitalist societies.

Reiterate to students that Swedish life is based on cooperation—everyone working together for the common good of all. This is reflected in a variety of aspects of Swedish life. They will research this.

Divide students into groups of three or four. Tell them that as a group they need to research information about Swedish life, focusing on cooperation—caring for the common good and for peace. Write these areas of Swedish life on the board: (1) Housing (2) Health care (3) Maternity benefits (4) Retirement pensions (5) Unemployment benefits (6) Education (7) Vacations (8) Child-care centers (9) Percent of people employed (10) Labor unions (11) Cooperatives (12) Political system (13) Foreign affairs.

It is ideal if students have access to three different encyclopedia sets at school and/or in the public library—preferably *World Book* (easiest), *Encyclopedia Americana,* and *Encyclopedia Britannica.* If working with groups of three, assign each group member, (according to ability) the gathering of relevant information in the encyclopedia assigned. If students do not have access to three different encyclopedias, two students could use the same one at different times. When group members pool their information, they can then select the most relevant information.

Use groups of four if there are enough additional resources for the fourth student in each group to use. If the resources available are advanced, the fourth student in each group should be advanced. If they are basic resources, the least-skilled students could be assigned them.

Give students guidance regarding using the encyclopedia. Since there is much information on Sweden, remind them to skim the topic headings and read only sections that are relevant to the areas above (unless they have the time and motivation to read more for background!) Remind them, too, that each encyclopedia doesn't cover all areas of research. It will only be by pooling their information that they will be able to find examples in all areas.

If you feel it would be helpful, suggest the following topic areas for each encyclopedia.

• *Encyclopedia Britannica:* Labor Unions, Living Conditions, Welfare Services, Education

• *World Book:* Introduction, Social Welfare, Education, and Sweden Today

• *Encyclopedia Americana:* Standard of Living and Social Welfare, Education, Labor Force, Political Parties, Pressure Groups, Defense

```
┌─────────────────────────────────────────────────────────────────────┐
│                        Summary for Teachers:                          │
│              Effects of Cooperative Values on Swedish Life            │
│                                                                       │
│     1. Housing                                                        │
│        Good quality, government-subsidized housing available to all   │
│        Housing costs (including fuel and electricity) 10–15 percent of family budget │
│        Rent control and rent subsidies                                │
│     2. Health care                                                    │
│        Health insurance and health care for all                       │
│     3. Maternity benefits                                             │
│        Free prenatal care and delivery, six months leave at two-thirds the former salary │
│     4. Retirement pension                                             │
│        Two-thirds of earnings from the fifteen years of highest pay   │
│     5. Unemployment benefits                                          │
│        Almost equal to former earnings                                │
│     6. Education                                                      │
│        Free school lunches and books                                  │
│        Tuition in all schools, colleges, graduate schools free        │
│        Adult education programs                                       │
│     7. Vacation                                                      │
│        Four weeks paid-vacation for all workers                       │
│     8. Child care                                                    │
│        State supported, inexpensive child care                        │
│     9. Full employment                                               │
│        Job training, free moving expenses for those whose jobs replaced by auto- │
│           mation or who are out of work                               │
│        It's a national priority to work toward this goal.             │
│    10. Labor unions                                                  │
│        Very strong, 95 percent of all workers are in unions           │
│        Workers in same industry are all in same union, irrespective of the work they │
│           do                                                          │
│    11. Consumer and producer cooperatives                             │
│        Many strong, well-organized cooperatives                       │
│        20 percent of country's retail sales through cooperatives      │
│    12. Political system                                              │
│        Politicians skilled in the art of compromise                   │
│        No bill introduced without advanced consultation of all interested groups—goal │
│           to reach agreement                                          │
│    13. Foreign affairs                                               │
│        No wars since 1812, no intervention in other nation's affairs   │
│        Government actively works for international peace—e.g., Nobel Peace Prize, │
│           participation in UN peacekeeping forces                     │
└─────────────────────────────────────────────────────────────────────┘
```

When students complete their individual research, have them gather as a group to pool information relating to the areas of research. They should take one area at a time—for example, housing—and pool their information. Group members then pick out one or two examples of cooperation in the area of housing. Remind students that cooperation means that everyone is working together for the common good of all. For example, there is good quality housing for all Swedes. There is rent control, and there are rent subsidies. Students go on to the next area—health care—and repeat the process. Once there are three or four (depending on the number of students in the group) agreed-upon examples (from two, three, or four areas), students stop discussion and each titles a 3 × 5 card and writes the example.

HOUSING Example of Cooperation

The government provides rent support for people who are in need.

Students then proceed with pooling of information on the next areas investigated and when there are three or four examples, stop again to write. They continue this process until they have pooled all their information. They proof each other's notecards for correct grammar, spelling and punctuation.

When groups have finished, join together as a class to discuss research findings about each area. Number each group. Begin with group one regarding housing. A spokesperson shares her group's example of cooperation reflected in the housing policies of Sweden. Group two continues with another example, **if it is different,** and so on. When all groups have had a chance to share an example, ask for student comments or questions. Bring out important information that students have neglected. Then go on to the next area, and begin by having group two start. Be sure spokespersons rotate. Continue through all areas of research.

Heterogeneity: The Swedish Norm in Schools

In Sweden, students are not grouped by ability. This is specifically prohibited by statute. Swedes believe such grouping strongly reflects class background and is detrimental to poorer students who have developed lower morale and who learn less quickly.

It is important to point out that Sweden is more homogeneous than other nations, including the United States. Race and class distinctions are less apparent than elsewhere.

DISCUSSION

1. How do you feel about cooperation in Swedish life?
2. What do you think you'd like about living in Sweden? What do you think you wouldn't like? Why?
3. In order for all people to have jobs and in order for people to have their basic needs met, the government takes a very strong role in planning the economy and in providing social services. What do you feel are the strengths in this approach? The weaknesses?
4. In order to support the many government services offered to all the people, workers in Sweden pay high taxes. What are the benefits of raising taxes to meet the needs of the people? The losses?
5. In Sweden there is no poverty. Since people don't have to struggle for their basic needs, some people are afraid that individuals will lose their initiative. Do you agree? Why or why not?
6. What can Americans learn from the Swedes? What might be changed in our country to build in more cooperative policies? Who would these policies help? What can the Swedes learn from Americans? How would that affect Sweden?

COMPLETION

A student receives credit for this lesson if her group hands in a set of notecards, completed by all group members, with an example of cooperation for the areas of research.

GOING FURTHER

Have interested students volunteer for a Bulletin Board Committee to make a bulletin board, "Cooperation in Sweden," for a prominent place in the school. Students select one or two notecards as examples of cooperation in each area of Swedish life. They draw or find pictures to illustrate each area of information. Have other interested students research positions of those critical of the Swedish and present their findings to the class.

SUBJECT—SS
FORMAT—BOARD
GAME, RESEARCH

Wisdom of Native Peoples _____

OBJECTIVES

To understand how the Hau De No Sau Nee (The Iroquois Confederation) cooperated among themselves as nations, and also with the earth
To examine how such cooperation fostered peace and justice
To research other examples of Native American's interdependence with each other and the earth, and learn from them

MATERIALS

Part A—cardboard for game boards, "Iroquois Game Cards," cut up (one set for each group of three), one die per group, Worksheet: "Cooperative Beliefs and Customs of Native Peoples" (one per group), "Directions—The Iroquois Game" (one per person), pages 458–461
Part B—Several weeks before the lesson, order books with accurate information on Native American culture. See box later in this lesson. A second copy of Worksheet: "Cooperative Beliefs and Customs of Native Peoples," page 461

IMPLEMENTATION PART A

The Iroquois Game*

In preparation for the Iroquois Game, cut game cards and mount on 3 × 5 cards. On the back, number half of the Belief Cards 1, and the other half 2. Do the same for Practices/Customs Cards. The day before the lesson, ask students to bring in pieces of shirt cardboard or other cardboard pieces that size. Have some yourself in reserve.

Tell students they will learn about the Hau De No Sau Nee—the Six Nation Iroquois Confederation on Native Americans. Explain that the Hau De No Sau Nee existed on this land way before the Europeans arrived. Their culture is among the most ancient continuously existing cultures in the world. Explain that sometimes the Iroquois were called People of the Longhouse because they lived in longhouses.

Divide students into groups of three. First ask them to make the boards for the Iroquois game by drawing fourteen squares in any shape. Label as below.

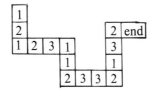

Give each group a brown envelope containing game cards, a die, and "Directions—The Iroquois Game." Have students put the pile of 1 cards and the pile of 2 cards next to the game board. Have students go over directions in their groups. Answer questions if necessary. Students begin play.

After completing the game, the group members review the list of beliefs and practices of the Iroquois. Each group then picks one belief and two practices that they think are most interesting. Distribute worksheets "Cooperative Beliefs and Customs of Native Peoples." **Together** group members discuss the questions on the worksheet regarding the one belief and two practices they chose.

Next group members divide the three beliefs and customs among members so each takes one. Each member writes the group's answers for that belief or custom on her worksheet. They proof each other's worksheet for content, grammar and spelling. They attach worksheets, sign, and hand in.

DISCUSSION

Tell students that first we will talk about the game itself and then what they learned.
1. Did your group win? What helped or hindered that from happening?
2. What strategy, if any, did you plan cooperatively to help you win?

Now let's talk about what you learned.
3. What beliefs of the Hau De No Sau Nee did each group find most interesting? Why?
4. Discuss the questions on the worksheet for the beliefs and customs the students chose. Take enough time to go into detail.
5. Which changes in our nation and world, discussed above, do you think would be most helpful to all people? What steps can individuals, groups, and nations take to bring those about?

*Adopted from a game devised by Kenneth Seltman and Judith Reynolds.

Background Reading

Background information on the Hau De No Sau Nee is available in:

Basic Call to Consciousness, Akwesasne Notes (see bibliography).
The White Roots of Peace, Paul Wallace.

If your students hold typical stereotypes about Native Americans, use the excellent lessons in *Unlearning Indian Stereotypes* from the Council on Interracial Books for Children.

PART B Research

Tell students that they will do research to find out about beliefs and practices of other Native American nations that fostered cooperation among themselves and with the earth.

Because some books in our libraries still reflect stereotypical views of Native Americans or are not written from a Native American perspective, it is wisest to order a selection of books with accurate information. Do this through the interlibrary loan several weeks in advance of this lesson.

Authentic Books on Native Americans for Students

And It's Still That Way: Legends Told by Arizona's Indian Children, Byrd Baylor.
Corn is Maize: The Gift of the Indians, Aliki Brandenberg.
The Mishomis Book, Edward Banai.
I Am Eskimo—Aknik My Name, Paul Green and Abbe Abbott.
Tonweya and the Eagles and Other Lakota Indian Tales, Rosebud Yellow Robe.
I Am Fire of Time: Voices of Native American Women, Jane Katz.
Tales of the Iroquois, Tehaneturens.
Yucayeque (Life of the Teino Indians), Luis Nieves Falcon.
Owakage: Activities for Learning about the Plains Indians.
The Mamook Book: Activities for Learning about the Northwest Coast Indians.

Also encourage students to do people research—that is, to interview Native American people. Try to invite someone to your class for this purpose.

Make books available to group members. Each group decides on a native people to research. Over the course of a week they take turns using the resources to take notes. Distribute new copies of the worksheet "Cooperative Beliefs and Customs of Native Peoples." Students use the questions for guidelines for research and note taking.

When research is complete, groups join together. They share the information they gathered. They cooperatively decide on responses to the worksheet questions. Each organizes the material to present a three-minute report to the class. Each group member takes a part. Presentations may be made over several days. When all reports are given, come together to draw conclusions.

Students' stereotypes of Native Americans may be that they were "savage" and fought all the time. It is certainly true that, in addition to fostering cooperative beliefs and practices, native Americans engaged in warfare. Among some nations this was more common than among others.

It is important for students to understand, however, that some of this warfare was to protect their lands from being taken over by whites.

For a useful classroom activity to help students understand the Native American's perspective, see Jane Califf's "Role Playing in the Classroom: An Antidote to Stereotyping" in *Unlearning Indian Stereotypes,* cited previously.

It is also true that there is a high rate of alcoholism and suicide among Native Americans today. This can be attributed, in part, to the racism, cultural alienation, and poverty Native Americans have had to face because of policies of the U.S. government.

COMPLETION
PART A

A student receives credit for Part A if each member of her group finished one of the three worksheets "Cooperative Beliefs and Customs of Native Peoples" with agreed-upon content and correct spelling and grammar, evidenced by signatures.

PART B

A student receives credit if each member of his group participated in the research and oral presentation on the native people they studied.

GOING FURTHER

Make a "Cooperation among Native Peoples Bulletin Board" for a school hall. Using true, not stereotypical images, have each group make a bulletin board section depicting cooperation by the Indian nation the group researched. Include the group's report.

If your class did not do Part B, or if the class prefers, your bulletin board could be completely about the Iroquois.

SUBJECT—SS, LA
FORMAT—JIGSAW,
GROUP PROJECT

Alternatives to War _____

OBJECTIVE

To examine international, nonviolent settlements of disputes as alternatives to war among nations

MATERIALS

Worksheets—"Nonviolent Resistance: Historical Examples" (cut up), "Nonviolent Resistance—Questions" (cut up), and "The People Defend Their Nation," pages 462–465

IMPLEMENTATION

Ask students why people grow up thinking that violence is the ultimate weapon in the settlement of disputes. Children on the playground get into fist fights and nations fight wars. Ask students to review what they have been studying about alternatives to fist fights. Tell them that in this lesson they will examine alternatives to war.

Ask students to think about "human nature." Note that some people believe that human beings, by nature, are competitive. Note also that many others feel "human nature" to be essentially cooperative. Many people feel that our values, culture, and experiences are what shape us and that people learn to be competitive because they live in a competitive society. Just as humans can learn to be cooperative, so too they can learn alternatives to war and violence—peaceful alternatives which can resolve conflict throughout the world.

Tell students that they will now study some methods of international, nonviolent settlement of disputes as an alternative to war. One method is through international organizations, like the United Nations, which are very important in promoting worldwide cooperation and peace. Explain that since most students have studied the U.N. before, we will focus here on less well-known strategies and examples.

Background Reading

An excellent, short pamphlet that provides a clear overview of nonviolent alternatives is "Making the Abolition of War a Reality" by Gene Sharp.

PART 1

Explain to students that the political power of governments depends on the obedience and cooperation of their subjects. Many peoples throughout history have resisted powerful invaders and rulers through cooperative, nonviolent action. A recent example was the nonviolent resistance of the Filipino people to Ferdinand Marcos. Discuss this with the students. Then tell them they will now learn about three other such examples.

Divide students into groups of three. Give each one part of the worksheet, "Nonviolent Resistance: Historical Examples." Have them study their material and teach it to the other students in their groups.

When the students have learned the information, give them the section of "Nonviolent Resistance—Questions" about a situation **other** than the one they read. Each student answers the questions. After all have finished, they can check their answers with their group members. Hand in.

DISCUSSION

1. What are your feelings about these examples of nonviolent resistance to domination or attack?
2. What are the benefits of nonviolent resistance compared to violent, international conflict? What are the prices?
3. Can you think of other examples of people using nonviolent resistance to oppression or attack? (Students might think of the colonists' resistance to the British in the prerevolutionary years or the Danes' rescue of the Jews.)

Now tell students they will continue their learning about alternatives to war. One alternative to defending a country with military arms is "civilian-based defense." People cooperate to resist an attacker. This resistance to an attacker is sometimes called noncooperation. An attacker finds domination impossible because of massive, nonviolent noncooperation by the population and its institutions.

Noncooperation can involve schools, newspapers, radio, television, churches, government and the general population. These groups can resist the ideas of the attackers and struggle for democratic principles. People can organize boycotts and strikes. Noncooperation by transport workers, managers, and experts can keep attackers from making economic gains.

The police can refuse to arrest people who resist the attackers. Journalists can refuse to submit to censorship and can publish papers illegally. Free radio programs can continue from hidden transmitters. The clergy can preach the duty of refusing to help the invader. Politicians and judges can ignore the enemy's illegal orders. Teachers can refuse to introduce propaganda into the schools. Workers and managers can call strikes and work delays.

PART 2 Have groups of three join together to make groups of six. Tell them they will be dealing with a hypothetical situation. Discuss that word. The hypothetical situation they will be dealing with calls for them to develop a plan for civilian-based defense. Distribute worksheet, "The People Defend Their Nation." Go over any difficult words. Then students work on their own.

Come together as a class. Have each group explain its plan.

DISCUSSION

1. How hard was it to think of a plan for a civilian-based defense to the situation posed? Why was it hard or easy?
2. How effectively did you work together to develop a group plan? What helped or hindered that process?
3. How was cooperation needed in your plan for civilian-based defense?
4. How effective do you think your plan would be in real life? Why?
5. What are some advantages of a system of civilian-based defense?
6. What are some of the disadvantages? How could some of the disadvantages be dealt with?
7. Some people might think that civilian-based defense is impossible. Can you think of an idea or event that people once thought was impossible, and now is possible? How could you use that to help people rethink their ideas about civilian-based defense?

COMPLETION A student gets credit for: Part 1 if each group member hands in a section of the worksheet "Nonviolent Resistance" on a case study that he didn't read about; Part 2 if his group hands in a complete plan for civilian-based defense that includes at least one step written by each group member.

But. . . .	
War is inevitable. You can't change millions of peoples' minds about that.	One hundred years ago most people thought slavery was inevitable. Few people do today. Millions of people's minds were changed.
If people used civilian-based defense, everybody could get killed.	One of the most valuable resources of a nation is its people. An attacking nation wants to control people for its own ends. This is impossible if people are dead.
Civilian-based defense is useless in a nuclear age because in a full-scale nuclear war everyone will be killed.	Yes, civilian-based defense is useless in nuclear war. Yet nations that defend themselves by civilian-based defense would be less likely targets of a nuclear attack. A country would not be afraid of a nuclear attack by a nation that didn't have any weapons.
Our government might not like people being trained in civilian-based defense. Then people would be more able to cooperate to confront problems and possibly challenge policies of the government, as well as being able to resist an attacker.	Good point. Our government would have to want an educated, thoughtful population that could act together to deal with problems and press for change.

GOING FURTHER Have interested students do more research on nonviolent alternatives to war as a means of settling international conflicts. Some students could research historical examples of civil disobedience. Others could research current examples.

Advanced students could read sections of the following books: Gene Sharp, *The Politics of Nonviolent Action,* vols. 1–3. Other students can read more basic sources about some examples described in this lesson. Have students present their findings to the class.

A Contemporary Example: Nonviolence Wins the Philippines

When the National Assembly supported altering of the 1985 election results by proclaiming Ferdinand Marcos the winner, Corazon Aquino called for a nonviolent struggle of rallies, vigils and civil disobedience.

When two top military leaders defected to Aquino with a handful of soldiers, Marcos prepared for a showdown. But government troops sent to attack the rebels were met by hundreds of thousands of unarmed citizens marching in the streets, singing and praying. When fighter planes sent to bomb the rebel camp saw it surrounded by masses of people, the pilots defected to Aquino. One of the defectors, Colonel Alimonte exclaimed, ''This is something new. Soldiers are supposed to protect the civilians. In this particular case, you have civilians protecting the soldiers.''

The people would not be denied. Facing the rapid collapse of all his support at home and abroad, Marcos and his family fled the country and the world hailed Corazon Aquino, president of the Republic of the Philippines.

Fellowship of Reconciliation

C. REMOVING ROADBLOCKS TO GLOBAL INTERDEPENDENCE

Us/Them, War/Peace: Sources of Our Assumptions

OBJECTIVES
To better understand how students, and other Americans, learn nationalism and militarism

To examine students' preconceived ideas about Americans and Russians

To explore how, without direct contact, we learn to see people as "other" (as different from ourselves)

To examine the consequences of this provincialism on our attitudes regarding international cooperation

MATERIALS
Part 1: Worksheets—"The Visitors," Story A and Story B (half the class gets Story A and the other B), "National Traits Checklist" (half the class gets Typical American Youth and the other half, Typical Soviet Youth), pages 466–467

Part 2: Worksheets—"Task Cards, I, II, III, IV, V" divided among small groups, pages 468–472 (This works out to one task card per student.)

Take It Slowly!

Ideas in this lesson, as others in this chapter, are important for students to grasp if they are to understand the implications for cooperation toward worldwide interdependence and peace. At the same time, the ideas are difficult and therefore the lessons can be time-consuming.

Since our goal is to empower students to feel confident, it is important to take the time needed to discuss these ideas in depth. It's better to do a few lessons and do them thoughtfully than to do many lessons superficially.

IMPLEMENTATION PART 1
Begin by telling students that they will examine their ideas about themselves and others, first through creative writing.

a. Divide students into groups of four. Distribute to half of the groups the worksheet "The Visitors—Story A." Distribute "The Visitors—Story B" to the other half. Have students spread out and working quietly so they don't overhear each other's work. Give students about ten minutes to finish the story.

b. Distribute the worksheet "National Traits: Typical American Youth" to half the class and "National Traits: Typical Soviet Youth" to the other half. Individually they fill it out, fold it, and keep it at their desk. While they are working, make a composite chart on the board. Don't put the titles in until students are finished.

Traits	National Traits Typical American Youth	Typical Soviet Youth
1		
2		
3		
4		
5		
6		
7		
8		

c. Have the groups that had Story A read their stories to the class. Then groups with Story B do the same.

If Students Challenge the Stereotypes

If students "catch on" to this lesson early on, encourage them to complete it in any case. They will still learn. In addition, you can discuss how their sensitivity to stereotypes clues them in to the purpose of the activity.

DISCUSSION

1. For those of you who had Story A, how would you describe Uri? Why did you decide to portray Uri in the way that you did?
2. For those of you who had Story B, how would you describe Peter? Why did you decide to portray Peter in the way you did?
3. As you see, the beginnings of Story A and Story B are the same. How was the ending of Story A the same or different from Story B? Why do you think that was so?

Now let's look at the "National Traits Checklists." Some of you had "National Traits: Typical American Youth" and others of you had "National Traits: Typical Soviet Youth." Write "Typical American Youth" and "Typical Soviet Youth" at the top of each of the columns you drew on the board. Read each adjective aloud and ask for a show of hands for those who checked that trait for Americans. Mark down the appropriate number. Do the same for Russians.

1. What generalizations can we draw from looking at this chart?
2. Why do we imagine, if we did, that Russian young people are different from ourselves? If you didn't imagine that, why not?
3. How do we learn that?

Explain to students that sometimes when we think of the Soviet people we are really thinking of the Soviet government. Remind them that there is a big difference. Millions of people in the United States might not agree with the policies and practices of the current government of the U.S., and their personalities might be very different from those of the government officials. The same is true for the Russian people.

4. Has anyone here met young people from the Soviet Union? If so, what were they like? If not, how did you decide what they were like for your story?

5. What are some of the ways we learn to think of ourselves, as Americans, as different or better than people of other nations?
6. Does this help or hinder worldwide cooperation? How?

GOING FURTHER Use materials from The Elementary School Educational Package on Soviet Geography, Language, Culture, and Children to provide students concrete information on the Soviet Union and its people. See the bibliography for details.

Kids Meeting Kids Can Make a Difference

"Kids Meeting Kids" is a group that coordinates pen pals for American and Soviet young people. It is their hope that these letters can do much to replace mistrust and fear with understanding and friendships. This, in time, could make for meaningful changes in the relationships between our countries. At the very least, children will learn a great deal about each other and life in one another's country.

Young people 7–15 can participate by sending a first letter to "Kids Meeting Kids Can Make a Difference," Box 8H, 380 Riverside Dr., New York, NY 10025. Teachers can gather individual letters from their classes and send them as a group.

Pen pals are also available from Ground Zero Pairing Project.

PART 2 It is wise to do the previous lesson, "Being #1: In Anyone's Best Interest?" (page 365) before this one.

There are five possible group tasks in this activity. Review them before assigning the lesson. Assess the feasibility of Task II, depending on TV programming at the time, and assign or delete accordingly.

Begin by asking students to redefine nationalism and militarism. (See boxes on pages 368–369.) Tell them they will be explaining how they learn nationalism and militarism and how that affects their thinking and their perceptions.

Divide students into heterogeneous groups of three to four and give different groups different tasks. Two or three groups may, however, do the same task.

Tell students to read Part A of their Task Card and make sure everyone understands the task and how they will go about accomplishing it. Set a date by which tasks should be completed.

On that day, students move on to Part B. Tell members of each group to discuss the questions on Part B of their Task Card. Each student then writes a response that represents the ideas **of the group.** Reiterate to students that what each will hand in is not simply their own thought but the information and viewpoints of the group—whether consensus was reached or varying opinions retained.

Now, if more than one group worked on a particular task, have them join together, compare findings, and draw conclusions about their task. They will report to the class.

Have each group prepare a five-minute presentation in which they will explain to the whole class:
1. The task
2. The results of their investigation
3. Their conclusions

Encourage them to divide the responsibility so various group members have a role in the presentation.

DISCUSSION

1. Have the groups who investigated nationalism present first. (Groups I, II, and III) After each group's presentation, go over the questions on the task card with the entire class.
2. Based on these surveys, what can we conclude about some of the ways Americans learn nationalism?
3. How does this affect our thinking and perceptions about the U.S. and other countries?
4. Redefine internationalism with students. (See box on page 369.) How would peoples' thinking change if they had a more internationalist perception? How might such change affect the world?
5. Have the groups who have investigated militarism present next. (Groups IV and V) After **each** group's presentation, discuss the questions on the task card with the entire class.
6. Based on these surveys, what can we conclude about some of the ways Americans learn militarism?
7. How does this affect our thinking about how conflicts should be resolved?
8. Redefine antimilitarism. (See box on page 369.)

How would people's thinking change if they had a more antimilitarist perception? How might this affect the world?

COMPLETION

A student receives credit for this lesson if (a) each group member participated in completing "The Visitors Story" and (b) each member of his group handed in a worksheet that accurately reflected the ideas of the group members and if the group made a satisfactory presentation to the class which included the task, findings, and conclusions.

DO YOU HAVE A FEMALE *ACTION FIGURE* THAT SPEAKS OUT AGAINST *DISCRIMINATION AND WAR!?*

Playing War?

An estimated 10,000 adult persons play the National Survival Game each weekend, shooting each other in a grown-up version of "Capture the Flag." People are "killed" by pellets that raise welts, hurt, and sting.

"It gets the blood boiling," says developer John Evangeliste. "It lets you live out a fantasy of being Mike Mercenary in Angola."

The National Coalition on Television Violence polled twelve nationally recognized experts on aggression and violence, all of whom agreed the game was very dangerous.

The Coalition's chair, Dr. Thomas Radacki, said, "At the very moment that U.S. soldiers are getting more deeply involved in wars in El Salvador, Nicaragua, Lebanon, and Chad, college fraternities and normal American businessmen are rehearsing declarations of war and duels to the death."

Times Herald Record,
Middletown, NY (September 1, 1983).

Jobs with Peace _____

OBJECTIVE

To examine the commonly held assumption that if we were to limit the worldwide arms race by cutting down on weapons production, Americans would lose jobs and the quality of life in America would suffer

MATERIALS

Worksheets—Graphs A, B, and C and Questions (**one** worksheet **section** of graph and questions for each student), pages 473–477

IMPLEMENTATION

Explain to students that one roadblock to increased international cooperation, by reducing or freezing the arms race, is the fear that a cutback in military spending would increase unemployment and hurt the quality of life in America. Some believe that the U.S. must keep building weapons in order to have enough jobs for Americans. Tell students they will examine this common assumption.

Divide students in groups of three, heterogeneously grouped by mathematical ability. The worksheet, Graph A and its questions are the easiest. Give these to the least-skilled student in each group. Graph C and its questions are the most difficult. Give these to the most-skilled student.

Have each student work individually on his worksheets for five to ten minutes (depending on how much time they seem to need).

Then form "expert groups" of students having the **same** graph. If your class is small and you think they can manage it, let all students with Graph A join together, and so forth. Most classes will be too large for this. In that case, form small expert groups of three to four students.

The purpose of the expert group is to allow students to go over individual worksheets, to help others understand the ideas, and to correct errors. Each member of the expert group makes sure that other members understand, and can explain, their graph and the answers to the questions.

Next, expert group members go back to their original groups. Each explains the graph to the others. She then reads and answers the questions on her worksheet. She checks to make sure other group members understand. Tell students that, in the large discussion, you will ask them for information taught to them by their peers; therefore, they should be sure to ask questions if they don't understand.

Students sign a cover sheet indicating agreement with the group's work, attach the three sets of worksheets together, and gather for class discussion.

DISCUSSION

1. What was the area of increase in federal spending from 1982 to 1986? Name some areas in which federal spending decreased. (Ask someone who was not an expert on Graph A to answer.)
2. How much of each American's tax dollar in 1987 went to military spending? (Ask for a volunteer who was not an expert on Graph B to answer.)
3. What seems to be the relationship between unemployment and military spending? (Ask someone who was not an expert on Graph C to answer.)
4. Do **you** feel it's important to maintain, or even increase, the amount of military spending even though it risks higher unemployment? Why?

5. If someone said to you, "Oh, I'd support international cooperation by freezing the arms race, but I know Americans will lose jobs if we do that," how could you reply?
6. What is your opinion about spending more money on the arms race as compared to spending money for programs for people, like job programs, health services, recreation, transportation, and so forth? How can you justify your opinion?

Explain to students that people working in defense industries and in the military worry about losing their jobs if the U.S. should cut back on military spending, freeze the arms race, or move to more of a peacetime economy. Explain that plans called "Conversion Plans" have been made that would convert (change) industries that make products for war to those that make products for peace. Even people whose jobs depend on military spending wouldn't have to lose their jobs. (See Going Further.)

The average American family will spend $25,000 in military related taxes between 1982 and 1986.
- A five-year housing program costing the same amount as the B-1 bomber would produce 30,000 more jobs than the Pentagon project.
- Each time the military budget goes up: blacks lose 1,300 jobs, women lose 9,500 jobs, teachers lose 2,000 jobs.

CIBC Bulletin, vol. 13, nos. 6 and 7.
Reprinted by Permission.

COMPLETION

A student gets credit for this lesson if each group member hands in a correct section of the worksheet and if group members called upon in class discussion can answer the question posed.

Power

Bob Peterson's fourth and fifth grade class in Milwaukee had completed a unit on disarmament. A student who had written a thoughtful essay, with a friend, gave testimony before the City Council Committee on the jobs with Peace Referendum question. This was broadcast on all three local TV stations.

These children then helped organize a Milwaukee group called Children for Peace. For more information contact Bob Peterson at 3340 N. Pierce St., Milwaukee.

GOING FURTHER

If you and your students are interested in knowing more about "Conversion to Peace Plans," assign student groups to gather information and present a report to the class.

Sources of Information about Peace Conversion

Background Information for Teachers
The Permanent War Economy, Seymor Melman

Background Information for Students
Jobs With Peace

Children's Defense Budget, 1985: 55.
Reprinted by permission: Tribune Media Services

To Be Secure _____

OBJECTIVES   To understand how feelings of insecurity can be a roadblock to cooperation and cause people to project their feelings of fear and inadequacy onto others both at the personal and international levels

To examine ways of thinking and organizing society that are premised on competition and that foster feelings of inadequacy

To consider how insecurity contributes to fears about the "spectre of communism" and how this blocks accurate information-gathering and potential cooperation among peoples and nations of the world

MATERIALS   Part 1: One copy of "To Be Secure" worksheets (Situations B and C) for each group, ("Did You Consider? Cards" cut up, mounted, and numbered on back), pages 478–481

Part 2: A copy for each student of a recent speech or extended statement by a U.S. government official or politician linking American security with confronting the spectre of Soviet communism in the world. One copy of "Examining the Threat" worksheet for each group, page 482

IMPLEMENTATION   Tell students that they will examine how competition can stimulate peoples' feelings
PART 1   of insecurity and how this can block cooperation among peoples of the world. Explain the following as background for their work and discussion.

Feelings of security, at the personal and international levels, are tied to peoples' definitions of security and power. When people feel powerful or secure inside themselves, they have less need to have control over others or be "better than" others.

To be powerful does not have to mean to be in control of others. It can be a feeling of inner strength combined with the ability to influence others. Power does not have to be power **over** others; it can be power **with** others. This can apply to nations as well as individuals.

When people or nations act competitively they can do so, in part, because of insecurity or a desire to have power over others. When people or nations act cooperatively they can do so, in part, because they feel secure in themselves and want to share power with others.

Competitive ways of thinking and of organizing society can breed insecurity in people and nations. We will try to understand how this can happen to Americans and how such insecurity can be a roadblock to cooperation.

Many common ways of thinking and ways of organizing society can keep Americans from feeling secure. The idea that people must compete and that society must be organized competitively is one example. The constant struggle to keep up with others and be like others can make people feel insecure. If they're not on top, some people think they're not good enough. This undermines a feeling of security.

There are alternatives to these ways of thinking, but usually people haven't considered them carefully. Often people feel insecure, but don't talk about their feelings or examine the causes of these feelings. Instead, people might project these fears and insecurities onto others. They might join with others like themselves for protection against those who are different. This sometimes helps people convince themselves they're secure, but it is a false sense of security.

As background, let's see how this happens in our daily lives and then we'll apply what we learn to international cooperation.

Students will examine three situations—in order to explore some causes and results of peoples' insecurity and some alternatives to this problem.

In each situation they will respond to the following questions:

1. What ways of thinking or ways of organizing society keep a person from feeling secure?
2. What are the results of this insecurity?
3. How could the insecurity be lessened?
4. What might result if these changes came about?

Work together with the class on Situation A so students get the idea. They will work together in small groups on Situations B and C.

Read Situation A, ask the first question, and discuss ideas. Suggest possible responses if students don't. Continue with all questions.

Before class, cut worksheets along line. Then cut "Did You Consider Cards," mount (if desired), and number the card on the back.

Next, divide students into groups of four. Distribute worksheet "To Be Secure," Situation B, to each group and distribute one "Did You Consider Card" to each person in every group. One student reads the situation and asks question 1. Students discuss a possible answer. After discussion, the student with "Did You Consider? Card 1" reads it. If they have not considered that idea, they discuss it. Continue with all questions. When a group finishes Situation B, give them Situation C, worksheet and cards. Tell students to discuss the questions carefully, because when you come together for class discussion and when you call on a member of their group, only if that person can present the group's ideas in a clear way will the group members get credit.

"I'M TOO FAR AWAY FROM THE PENTAGON TO PURCHASE THE $2070 WASHER I NEED... GIMME THOSE 3 FOR 69¢ REPLACEMENTS."

Situation A

John Leder is twelve. He loves dancing. He wants to join the dance troupe at school. He starts to feel scared and insecure because boys who join things that are typically for girls are called sissies or faggots. He's scared to talk to anyone about his feelings.

John decides to join the J.V. football team instead. Guys on the football team are looked up to in his school. He doesn't play much, but at least he's on the team. He wants to be part of the group, so he joins the other "guys" in calling other class-mates "sissies." This hurts others' feelings, but it helps John feel good and "se-cure."

---

1. **What way of thinking or way society is organized keeps John from feeling secure?**

   One example: The sexist way of thinking that proposes that there are certain things that are okay for boys to do and certain things that are okay for girls to do contributes to John's insecurity. Another way of thinking does this too—the idea that if you do something the opposite sex likes you are a homosexual. The fear of homosexuality is called "homophobia."

2. **What were results of this insecurity?**

   John joined the football team not out of free choice but out of fear of joining the dance troupe. On the football team, he would be safe in a group that was respected. Then he wouldn't be looked down on. He called others names like "sissie" or "faggot" and hurt others so he could feel better about himself.

3. **How could the insecurity be lessened?**

   People could help John examine sexism and homophobia. They could help him consider that it's okay for boys and girls to do **anything** and there aren't "boys" and "girls" activities. He could learn that no person or group is better than another because of what they like to do. They could point out that to do some things that more people of another sex participate in does not mean a person is homosexual and that, anyway, feeling love for a person of your own sex—is normal and okay.

4. **What might be the result if those changes came about?**

   John would feel secure doing dance. He would develop his talents to their fullest. He wouldn't feel the need to call other people names because he would be secure in himself.

Hopefully you will feel comfortable raising the issue of homophobia with your students. If you wish additional background information, see: Letty Pogrebin, "The Secret Fear That Keeps Us From Raising Free Children," and other articles in the special issue of the *Bulletin* of the Council on Interracial Books for Children on "Homophobic and Education." This example of John can be used by talking about challenging traditional sex roles in and of themselves.

DISCUSSION

1. Discuss questions on the "To Be Secure" worksheet Situation B, and then Situation C, with the class.
2. Who can describe a situation when they felt insecure or afraid and projected their fears onto others? How, instead, could you have examined the way of thinking or organizing society that made you feel insecure? What would have been an alternative for dealing with the situation?
3. Why is it hard to talk about feelings of insecurity? How do competitive ways of thinking and organizing society contribute to this?
4. When some government leaders talk about the threat of Soviet communism, how can Americans clearly examine how accurate the threat really is? Can you think of an example?

5. Who benefits when some government leaders reinforce Americans' insecurities by promoting the way of thinking that Soviet communists want to take over the world? How do they benefit? Who loses? How?

6. When a person feels secure, he doesn't need to feel power over others, but can share power with them. How might American policy be different if the United States government gave more respect to each nation's desire to be secure and powerful on its own terms?

Welcome to the world of strategic analysis, where we program weapons that don't work to meet threats that don't exist.

Ivan Selin, Head of Strategic Forces Division,
Office of the Assistant Secretary of Defense, 1966.

Concerned Catholics

. . . in recent years, U.S. policy toward development in the Third World has become increasingly one of selective assistance based on an East–West assessment of North–South problems, at the expense of basic human needs and economic development. Such a view makes national security the central policy principle. Developing countries have become largely testing grounds in the East–West struggle; they seem to have meaning or value mainly in terms of this larger geopolitical calculus. . . .

. . . in 1985 the United States alone budgeted more than 20 times as much for defense as for foreign assistance, and nearly two-thirds of the latter took the form of military assistance (including subsidized arms sales) or went to countries because of their perceived strategic value to the United States. Rather than promoting U.S. arms sales, especially to countries that cannot afford them, we should be campaigning for an international agreement to reduce this lethal trade.

In short, the international economic order, like many aspects of our own economy, is in crisis; the gap between rich and poor countries and between rich and poor people within countries is widening. The United States represents the most powerful single factor in the international economic equation.

U.S. Bishops, *Economic Justice for All:*
Catholic Social Teaching and the U.S. Economy
(Washington, DC: United States Catholic Conference, 1986),
paragraphs 262, 289, 290.

PART 2   While Part 2 is very useful for students to complete, it can be difficult. It takes effort on your part to get primary source materials. Also you may need to work more closely with students because analyzing the material can be difficult for some.

Find, or help students find, a recent statement by a U.S. government leader or politician that links American security with confronting the threat and spread of Soviet communism in the world. For example, see President Reagan's speech on Central America in May of 1984. The *New York Times* often prints texts of such speeches. (See excerpts in box on page 412.) If you use the statements in the box rather than finding your own, assign them to the student, in each group, most able to understand them. Maybe you'll want to work with these students to assure comprehension. These students can then work with their groups to insure that everyone understands the statements and the assumptions and implications of the statements.

Students remain in their groups. Distribute one copy of the statement (if you decide to use it) to each student and one copy of the worksheet, "Examining the Threat" to each group. They work together to answer the questions on the worksheet. For some questions, students will need to do research. Help them identify sources that will give them varied pieces of information and points of view. Advanced students may be able to read magazines like *The Nation, The Progressive,* or *Mother Jones.* Some students can do people-research and interview representatives of local religious, peace, or political groups that question the idea that the spread of Soviet communism is the greatest danger to national security. National organizations listed in the Resources section can often provide names of local resource people. Help groups divide research tasks so each person has a specific responsibility commensurate with her ability level.

When research is complete, come together for further discussion.

DISCUSSION

1. Discuss questions on the worksheet, "Examining the Threat." You can share information in the following box for background. Help students be specific, especially with question 5. Refer back to lessons "The Tower," and "Do We Have the Right?" If you haven't done those lessons, discuss the benefits to the military, defense contractors, and multinational corporations of U.S. intervention in the Third World.

2. Who did different group members talk with to get information? What written material did you use?

3. How hard or easy was it to find information from different points of view? What made it hard or easy?

4. How hard or easy is it for the average American to find information? What should be done, if anything, about this?

5. How can we help ourselves and others see the idea of the threat of worldwide Soviet communism as **one** way of thinking about international events and not necessarily the only way?

6. If Americans felt secure in themselves and had access to information from different points of view on international affairs, what might be some effects on co-operation among nations of the world?

COMPLETION

A student receives credit for Part 1 of this lesson if the group member(s) called on in class discussion, to answer a question from the "To Be Secure" situation worksheets, clearly represented the group's answer.

A student receives credit for Part 2 of this lesson if her group completes "Examining the Threat" worksheet to which each member has contributed research, as indicated by signatures.

The Spread of Soviet Communism or "A Threat to U.S. National Security?": Two Points of View
Reagan Speech on Central American Policy, May 9, 1984

Excerpted from *New York Times* text of the speech, May 10 issue: 16.

I asked for this time to tell you some basic decisions which are yours to make. I believe it is my constitutional responsibility to place these matters before you. They have to do with your national security, and that security is the single most important function of the Federal Government. In that context it is my duty to anticipate problems, warn of dangers, and act so as to keep harm away from our shores.

. . . In the last 15 years the growth of Soviet military power has meant a radical change in the nature of the world in which we live.

. . . (The Soviet leaders) are presently challenging us with a different kind of weapon: subversion and the use of surrogate forces—Cubans, for example. We have seen it intensifying during the last 19 years as the Soviet Union and its surrogates moved to establish control over Vietnam, Laos, Cambodia, Angola, Ethiopia, South Yemen, Afghanistan, and recently closer to home, Nicaragua and now El Salvador. . . .

Central America is a region of great importance to the United States. And it is so close—San Salvador is closer to Houston than Houston is to Washington, D.C. Central America is America; it is at our doorstep. And it has become the state of a bold attempt by the Soviet Union, Cuba, and Nicaragua to install Communism by force throughout the hemisphere. . . .

We can and must help Central America. It's in our national interest to do so, and morally, it's the only right thing to do. But helping means doing enough—enough to protect our security and enough to protect the lives of our neighbors so that they may live in peace and democracy without the threat of Communist aggression and subversion. . . .

Communist subversion is not an irreversible tide. We have seen it rolled back in Venezuela and, most recently, in Grenada.

. . . Let us show the world that we want no hostile, Communist colony here in the Americas: South, Central or North.

More than 80% of U.S. military expenditures are for conventional warfare, much of it designed for intervention in the third world. To win support for massive military expenditures . . . the Reagan administration is trying to make us accept three myths about our national security. . . .

Myth 1: Soviet expansionism is the cause of conflicts in the third world.

In this myth, the U.S. and Cuba are seen as instigating every conflict or revolutionary movement. If we accept this myth, then every movement for change in the third world must be combatted as part of a plan for domination.

But the facts are otherwise. Of the 105 major wars documented since World War II, virtually all have been caused by such factors as economic injustice, colonialism, ethnic conflicts, nationalism and border disputes. What these conflicts often have in common is a struggle for the right to eat by people living in poverty and hunger. . . .

Myth 2: Revolutionary movements in the third world are hostile to the U.S. and so are our enemies.

Yet the record has been different. Revolutions against the status quo by the poor and their allies often bring national, even socialist, governments to power. Seeking to "diversify their dependence" these governments often seek diplomatic and aid relations with the Soviet Union, as well as the United States and other countries. . . . But virtually every revolutionary government has tried to maintain or expand its trade with the United States. . . .

(U.S. embargos of revolutionary governments often force them to depend more on the Soviet Union than originally intended.)

Myth 3: Military intervention is required to safeguard U.S. national security. . . .

After $252 billion in military aid and arms sales since World War II, are we more secure? . . . .

We have set ourselves an impossible task by defining U.S. national security to mean that we must control political change in the third world. By defining our security in this way we set ourselves up for defeat, because no military power is capable of sustaining indefinitely dictatorships which exclude the majority of people from participation in national life.

But what if we took the side of these movements seeking economic justice and abandoned instead the dictatorships? What if we stopped seeing third world countries as ours to "win or lose"? What if the U.S. defined its national security differently?

Instead of making us more secure, our country's massive arms buildup is making us even less secure, militarily and economically. American soldiers are being shot at from Lebanon to Central America. And the more we intervene in third world conflicts, the greater the risk of nuclear confrontation. . . .

SUBJECT—SS
FORMAT—JIGSAW,
GROUP PROJECT

Where Is My Money Going?

OBJECTIVES

To see the connections that exist between the lives of Americans and other people throughout the world, to understand the ways we *keep* from seeing those connections, to look at the benefits Americans receive from those connections, and the harm others receive

To examine an example of how American institutions can support injustice abroad—the connections between U.S. banks and South African apartheid

To explore opportunities that individuals and groups have to examine these connections and cooperate with other people who are fighting for justice around the world

MATERIALS   Worksheets—"Facts about Apartheid Cards" (cut up), one per group, "Connections to Apartheid," one per person, pages 483–484

IMPLEMENTATION   Tell students that they will be examining how Americans often don't think of their connections to others around the world, how that happens, and what we can do about it.

PART 1   Begin on a more personal level, closer to home. Relate these anecdotes to students.
1. Jane is sailing down the school hall at the end of the day, hurrying to softball practice. She unwraps a candy bar and, not wanting to go back to her classroom to throw away the wrapper, she throws it on the floor.
2. Paul is putting the juice back in the refrigerator and knocks over a glass of milk. No one sees him do this. Rather than wipe it up, he goes to watch TV.

Ask students if these situations sound familiar. Have they, their friends, or family members ever done things like this?

Ask students—Who will most likely pick up Jane's candy bar wrapper? Clean up Paul's milk? Is this fair?

Explain to the class that when we throw a paper like Jane did, we usually don't think about the custodian who will have to pick it up. We don't think that the custodian might have a bad back or how he might feel as he sees the thoughtlessness of kids. Jane's act of throwing the paper is directly connected to the custodian's bad back, tiredness and feeling of being unappreciated. Jane didn't stop to think of those connections. Jane benefits, the custodian pays a price.

Explain also that when we make a mess and leave it, like Paul did, we often don't think about the other person who will have to clean it up. We don't think that a parent might be very tired of cleaning up after us and aggravated that we don't clean up after ourselves. We don't consider that our parent might feel resentful and less willing to do things for us—like play catch after dinner. Paul's act of ignoring the mess is directly connected to his parents' weariness and lack of motivation to do things with him. Paul didn't stop to think about these connections. Paul benefits from not thinking of the connections and his parent pays a price.

Summarize by telling students that our personal actions often affect other people, but we don't take time to stop and think about these connections. So too, acts of individuals, organizations, and countries have direct effects on people around the world. We often don't stop to examine those effects.

PART 2   Divide students into groups of four. Give two "Facts about Apartheid" cards to each student. Have students read the cards in numerical order to the group. Have students discuss the material.

Then distribute one copy of the worksheet "Connections to Apartheid" to each group. Have students take turns reading the questions. When they've discussed all questions, students divide the questions and each writes, on a separate paper, the group's response to one or two questions. When there are several opinions, those should be summarized. Students proofread each other's answers, sign, and turn in.

DISCUSSION   As a class, discuss all questions on the worksheet.

COMPLETION   A student gets credit for this lesson if each member of the group has participated in the discussion and worksheet, "Connections to Apartheid," as indicated by written responses to questions, and signatures.

Have students do further research on unexamined connections—connections that enable Americans to benefit at the expense of other peoples. Sources of information include:

Interfaith Center for Corporate Responsibility
American Friends Service Committee (see bibliography)
Advanced students can read *Women in the Global Factory* by Barbara Ehrenreich and Annette Fuentes.

From Another Perspective

Some Americans believe that the U.S. banks and other institutions should not sever connections with South Africa. They argue such actions would hurt the South African economy, which would hurt blacks. They also believe the U.S. should keep its foot in the door as a kind of leverage. If students are not familiar with these arguments, have a few students research them and present them to the class.

Banks Act

In response to public pressure, some banks have already stated that they will not lend money to South Africa or its agencies in the future. The First Pennsylvania Bank, Maryland National Bank, and Central National Bank of Chicago are among them.

SUBJECT—SS
FORMAT—JIGSAW,
CLASS PROJECT

The Message in Our Texts _____

OBJECTIVES

To have students investigate one source of their assumptions about war, nuclear weapons, and the struggle for peace—by analyzing history textbooks
To have students share their findings with others

MATERIALS

Worksheet—"Textbook Analysis,"* pages 485–486
American history textbooks (one per student). It is ideal, but not necessary, to have four different books per group.

Militarism in Textbooks

Before doing this lesson it is wise, though not essential, to obtain and read "Militarism in Textbooks: An Analysis" by Sharon Wigutoff and Sergiu Herscovia in the "Bulletin of the Council on Interracial Books for Children," vol. 13 (1982). It provides information on their study of eleven widely-used junior high and high school textbooks. It also provides very valuable supplementary information and commentary. See Bibliography for ordering information.

IMPLEMENTATION

Begin by telling students that textbooks often teach students more than meets the eye, what some people call the "hidden curriculum." By virtue of what's included or not included, stressed or underrepresented, textbooks influence students' perceptions, at-

*Adopted from "Militarism in Textbooks: An Analysis," see above.

titudes, and values. Explain that they will be analyzing textbooks for information about war, nuclear weapons and the struggle for peace, and will then share their findings with others.

PART 1

Divide students into groups of three or four. It is ideal to have three or four different American history textbooks, including one that students do use or have used. If that is not possible, use the same book.

Distribute a "Textbook Analysis" worksheet to each student. Initially, students brainstorm ways of going about analyzing the books—using the index, finding particular topic headings in the text, and so forth. If each group member has a different textbook, each works on her own to answer the questions. If students are all using the same book, they divide up questions or possibly work in partners to answer questions. Students then share their findings with others in their group. Other members must be convinced that the information given supports the conclusions.

If students have been using different books, students group together with all others who analyzed that same text. They share findings and come up with a composite analysis sheet. In either case, the next step is to come together as a class for discussion. Then sign worksheets and hand in.

DISCUSSION PART 1

1. Cover each question on the worksheet. Discuss the specific examples students give to back up their points. After students have reported, you might compare their findings to those of the educational researchers, Wigutoff and Herscovici.
2. Given your findings, what conclusions can you draw?
3. What do students learn, or not learn, about war?
4. What do students learn, or not learn, about nuclear weapons?
5. What do students learn, or not learn, about the struggle for peace and organized anti-war movements?
6. What additions or subtractions to what the texts now present do you think are important?
7. What effect do you think the textbooks have had, if any, on the way people think about international cooperation and peace in the world today?

PART 2

As a class, discuss ways you can share your findings with others. For example, small groups or the whole class could write a report on findings regarding what is learned about war, nuclear weapons, and the struggle for peace—for each textbook. These could be distributed to teachers who use those textbooks and then possibly to students in those courses as well. Or students could write letters to the editors of the texts, include their findings, and suggest any revisions, if needed. Students present other ideas. When the class decides on an approach to use, divide tasks and responsibilities, and devise a plan to carry them out.

When the project is complete, students regroup for a discussion.

A valuable book presenting an inclusive view of American history is *A People's History of The United States* by Howard Zinn. Order it for your classroom. Both you and your students will benefit.

DISCUSSION PART 2

1. What did you learn by sharing your findings with others?
2. What kinds of questions did others have about your findings? How did you answer them?
3. What do you think will be the effect of your project?
4. What would you do differently next time to make it an even more effective project?

416

Each student writes a short statement indicating how her work contributed to the class project. Share with a partner for feedback. Correct as needed. Both sign. Hand in.

COMPLETION A student gets credit for this lesson if: in Part 1 each group member contributed information to the "Textbook Analysis" worksheet and checked other members' work as indicated by signatures, and if in Part 2 each group member took part in class project and submitted a statement of the importance of her contribution to the success of the project, signed by a partner.

**The Hidden Curriculum
Conclusions of One Study**

After examining the newest editions of these eleven widely-used history textbooks, we have concluded that the information they present about nuclear weapons and the danger of nuclear war is inadequate, misleading, and irresponsible. At worst, texts completely avoid reference to nuclear arms and concentrate on the use of nuclear power as an energy source. At best, they acknowledge the existence of an arms race and the need for arms limitation, but they uniformly fail to provide the background necessary for informed discussion about the consequences of the arms race, nor do they ever make clear that limiting arms does not eliminate the threat of nuclear war.

We believe textbooks can—and must—do better. We recommend that textbooks:
• Include past and current criticism of wars as legitimate tools for conflict resolution, as well as criticism of particular wars.
• Include information on the growth and power of the military-industrial complex.
• Include comparative expenditures on armaments and social services.
• Include information about the ideas and activities of important peace activists.
• Include substantive information about nuclear-related issues.
• Convey to students the grave consequences of war in the nuclear age.
• Challenge students to think critically about nuclear issues.

Sharon Wigutoff and Sergiu Herscovia
in "Militarism in Textbooks: An Analysis,"
CIBC Bulletin, vol. 13 (1982).

D. THINK GLOBALLY: ACT LOCALLY

SUBJECT—LA, A
FORMAT—GROUP
PROJECT, CROSS-
AGE PROJECT

Sadako and the Thousand Paper Cranes ___

OBJECTIVES To learn and share the story of *Sadako and the Thousand Paper Cranes*
To use literature and art as a bridge for communication with others in the fostering of worldwide interdependence and peace
To involve students in actively sharing their global awareness with others

MATERIALS Copies of the book *Sadako and the Thousand Paper Cranes*. See first paragraph under Implementation below.
Worksheet: "Sadako and the Thousand Paper Cranes" (one per group), page 487
Materials for making paper cranes—origami paper or gift wrap, scissors, rulers, art book with directions, if needed (see page 419)

IMPLEMENTATION
PART A   Literature

In advance of this lesson, get copies of *Sadako and the Thousand Paper Cranes* by Eleanor Coerr (a Yearling Book, New York: Dell, 1977). This short, excellent book tells the story of Sadako, a Japanese child whose courage and spirit made her a heroine to children in Japan and across the world. It is available in an inexpensive paperback edition. Ideally, buy a copy for each student in your class to use for this lesson and in future years. If school district funds are not available, approach a local church, peace, or international group for possible donations. If this is impossible, use interlibrary loan to get one copy for each group. As a last resort, buy or borrow one copy of the book and read it aloud to the class. Tell students that a relatively easy book has been chosen so they can use it effectively with younger students.

Divide students into groups of four or five. Tell them that they will be reading the life story of a girl who lived in Japan at the time the U.S. Air Force dropped an atom bomb on her city of Hiroshima. Ten years later, she died as a result of radiation from the bomb. Tell students that parts of the book are sad and that it's perfectly okay for them to show sad feelings or to cry. Have a discussion with the class, if necessary, of the feelings in their peer group about showing sadness or crying. Discuss the importance of sharing feelings and respecting each other's feelings.

Group members take turns reading *Sadako and the Thousand Paper Cranes* aloud to each other in their small group. The book is easily divided, chapters 1–4, 5–9, if time in one day is short. When students finish, have them discuss together their feelings about the story. Then distribute the worksheet: "Sadako and the Thousand Paper Cranes." They discuss the questions as a group. When discussion is complete, they divide the responsibility for writing the group's answers. At that time, they can cut questions into strips in order to facilitate writing. They proof each other's work. When students are finished, come together as a class for discussion.

DISCUSSION A

1. First discuss each of the questions one through four on the worksheet "Sadako and the Thousand Paper Cranes." Make sure to take enough time to discuss each question fully. Then proceed.
2. What gifts did people think of to give Sadako? Why did you choose those gifts? Why would she appreciate them?
3. What ideas can you come up with to help prevent an atom bomb from ever being dropped again?
4. Which of these ideas that contribute to world peace are people already working on? What do you know about these projects?
5. Which ideas for bringing about world peace haven't been tried? How could people start trying them?
6. What do we need to think about before we read this story to small groups of students in another class?

Arrange for students to visit another class or classes to read *Sadako* to small groups of students, perhaps over a period of several days. Divide students in partners. Have them plan how they will divide the reading and the leadership in the discussion.

PART B   Art

Tell students that there are many different ways that they can use the story of Sadako to contribute to world peace. One traditional way has been through the making of cranes.

Invite the art teacher to your class to teach paper crane making or collaborate with the art teacher so students learn to make cranes as part of an art class assignment. The process for making paper cranes is described in a number of books, including *The World of Origami* by Isao Honda and *Paperfolding for Fun* by Eric Kenneway. Also see example below.

ORIGAMI—BIRD   Start with a perfectly square sheet of light-weight paper.

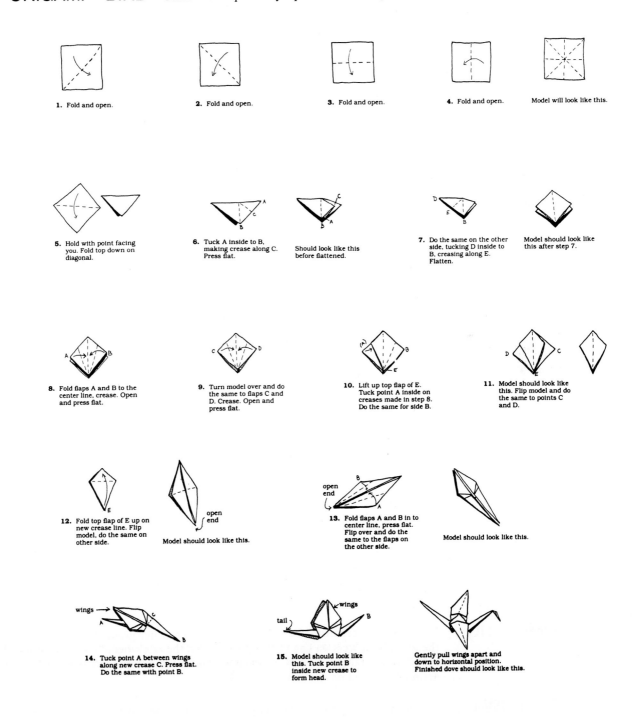

1. Fold and open.

2. Fold and open.

3. Fold and open.

4. Fold and open.

Model will look like this.

5. Hold with point facing you. Fold top down on diagonal.

6. Tuck A inside to B, making crease along C. Press flat.

Should look like this before flattened.

7. Do the same on the other side, tucking D inside to B, creasing along E. Flatten.

Model should look like this after step 7.

8. Fold flaps A and B to the center line, crease. Open and press flat.

9. Turn model over and do the same to flaps C and D. Crease. Open and press flat.

10. Lift up top flap of E. Tuck point A inside on creases made in step 8. Do the same for side B.

11. Model should look like this. Flip model and do the same to points C and D.

12. Fold top flap of E up on new crease line. Flip model, do the same on other side.

Model should look like this.

open end

13. Fold flaps A and B in to center line, press flat. Flip over and do the same to the flaps on the other side.

Model should look like this.

wings

14. Tuck point A between wings along new crease C. Press flat. Do the same with point B.

tail   wings

15. Model should look like this. Tuck point B inside new crease to form head.

Gently pull wings apart and down to horizontal position. Finished dove should look like this.

Paper cranes are somewhat difficult to make. One approach is to teach one student from each group to make cranes during recess or at another free time. They then can help you or the art teacher instruct their group members when the whole class is learning to make cranes.

Another approach is to teach each person in each small group a few of the steps in the paperfolding. Each student can then help the others, as together they make the paper crane.

Describe to students the four possible art projects listed below. These use the story of Sadako and the making of cranes to educate others about the importance of world peace. Add other possibilities that you or your students think of. Discuss the projects and decide if you will work on one project as a group or if different groups will take on different projects.

1. **Cross-Age Projects**
   Visit another class. Each group tells another small group in the class the story of Sadako. Teach others how to make cranes. Help others develop a plan for displaying the cranes in their room.

2. **Sharing with Friends and Family**
   Work in your group to make more cranes. Write the story of Sadako in your own words. When a group story is agreed upon by everyone, design it so that it can be folded as a pamphlet, copy onto a ditto, and run off. Give a crane and pamphlet to friends and family. Then discuss their responses with them.

3. **Bulletin Board Display**
   Make a bulletin board that tells the story of Sadako. Put it in a prominent place in the school. Make mobiles of paper cranes to fly over the bulletin board.

4. **Crane Mobiles**
   Make crane mobiles. Sell them to family, at library fairs, or at the PTA bookfair with copies of the book, *Sadako and the Thousand Paper Cranes*. Donate profits to an organization working for world peace.

Once students have finished projects, come together for discussion.

DISCUSSION B

1. What was your experience working with others by using the story of Sadako and by making cranes?
2. How did others respond?
3. What do you think others learned?
4. What did you learn about trying to educate others concerning the need for world peace?
5. In this project you used literature (the story of Sadako) and art (the making of cranes) to try to communicate. What are other examples of the use of art and literature to help others feel the urgency of worldwide cooperation for peace?
6. If you were to do this project again, what would you do differently?
7. What were the most successful things you did—things you wouldn't change?
8. What other kinds of projects could our class participate in to contribute to world peace?

COMPLETION

A student gets credit for Part A if each member of her group hands in a summary of the group's answers on one of the questions on the worksheet "Sadako and the Thousand Paper Cranes," Part B—if each person in the group or class contributes to the art project based on the story of Sadako.

FOLLOW-UP

If students are interested in going further, have them discuss more ideas for class, group, or individual projects.

A Sampler: Student Contributions to World Peace
More Ideas

A World Peace Mural
The class cooperatively plans, designs, and paints a large world peace mural to hang in the cafeteria, the entrance to their school, or in another public place.

World Peace Organizations
Students gather information about local groups working toward world peace—e.g., disarmament groups, international exchange projects. Study the information and share it with others. Invite speakers for school assemblies.

T-Shirts
Design artwork about world peace and have it screened onto T-shirts. Wear the shirts, and discuss your ideas about world peace with others. In addition, students can make a lot of shirts and sell them. Give money to organizations working for world peace.

Letter Writing
Write to your congresspeople and share your views with them about what should be done to bring about world peace.

Peace Symbols
Research the evolution of peace symbols in other cultures, particularly African and Native American. Report to the class or make a display for the bulletin board.

Student Letters

April 9, 1986

Dear Mr. President,

I believe that testing bombs is uncalled for. Especially since Russia stopped testing bombs for now.

The reason why I am writing this letter is because my teacher just read a book called "Sadako and the Thousand Paper Cranes." The book is about a little Japanese girl that was alive when the atom bomb was dropped in Hiroshima. She was a healthy young girl with a bright future until the atom bomb was dropped. Then she developed leukemia as a result of radiation.

This was such a needless death. I am young and healthy and I want to live a long life. I don't want it to end because of a nuclear bomb.

So please, Mr. President, think about all the children in the world who want to grow up. So please try to pass laws in favor of peace.

Sincerely yours,
Karl Vucich
Arlington Elementary School
Poughkeepsie, N.Y. 12603

April 9, 1986

Dear Mr. President,

Recently, our teacher read us the story called "Sadako and the Thousand Paper Cranes" which is about a little Japanese girl that lived in Hiroshima, Japan. She eventually died because we dropped bombs on her city. I think it's just terrible that we have to keep testing bombs for no reason.

I personally think that we should stop testing bombs and spend our money on other things besides buying bombs so that we can kill people.

I just started to think of her and it made me feel so sad. Should we really keep on testing bombs?

Sincerely,
Bryan Nicalek
Arlington Elementary School
Poughkeepsie, N.Y. 12603

SUBJECT—SS, SCI
FORMAT—
RESEARCH
PROJECT, GROUP
PROJECT, CLASS
PROJECT

For Every Child a Tree: The Tree Project ___

OBJECTIVES To learn about an international effort of youth cooperation toward solving one of the pressing problems of the world
To organize a Tree Project in the community and/or school

MATERIALS Worksheet—"Research Group Tasks: Tree Project" (one section to each group), page 488

IMPLEMENTATION Tell students they will be participating in a project based on international cooperation. Explain that the United Nations proclaimed 1985 as International Youth Year. During 1985, young people around the world began a project. It is continuing today and is called "The Tree Project." The goal of the project is to plant a tree for **every child in the world.**

PART A **Background Information**

Explain to students that one of the biggest environmental problems facing the world today is deforestation. Pressures of increasing population, demands of urbanization, overuse of limited natural resources, and expansion of agricultural lands have diminished the world's tree resources. One of the earth's most useful renewable resources is now in serious danger.

Ask students to discuss the uses of trees. If they don't mention the following, be sure to suggest them: food, fuelwood, timber, medicine, paper products. Ask them to discuss how trees help our environment. Add any of the following that they leave out: soil conservation, oxygen production, shade and beautification, wildlife protection.

Tell students that the Tree Project is a global reforestation program implemented by youth in their home communities. Its purpose is to increase awareness of the effects of deforestation and spur action to reverse current trends. The goal of the project, to plant close to 1,000 million trees in 1985, one for every youth in the world, is continuing through the following decade. Share an example of what young people are doing in other parts of the world. (See box on page 423.)

Tree Projects around the World

Youth in more than 50 countries are participating in the Tree Project. One example is the Youth Association of Risso in Meckhe, Senegal. There for four years over 160 young people have planted 3,000 trees. They have also provided trees to two local villages and shown people how to plant them properly. Young people watered the trees during the dry season and protected them from animals.

In the summer of 1985 youth participated in the Walk Norway Project. Young people walked 2,600 km across Norway bringing with them Trees of Friendship to be planted in villages and towns along the way. Money from the trees that are sold will be donated to a reforestation effort in Nepal.

December 1 is National Tree Day in Zimbabwe. Youth across the country plant thousands of trees. Students devise many creative ways to protect the small seedlings they plant.

Fourteen million students and 500,000 teachers in schools in Vietnam are involved in tree planting efforts. Their goal is "to cover the plains, highlands and mountainous areas with green leaves."

Youth in China planted 2.6 billion trees in 1984 alone.

Tree Project, United Nations

PART B   Implementing the Tree Project in the Community

Possible ways to implement the Tree Project suggested by the U.N. include:
1. Planting trees in rural areas as flood and windbreaks to protect farmland from topsoil loss and crop destruction.
2. Developing a planting program to replace every tree that is cut down in a given community.
3. Plant trees in urban and suburban areas to create recreational space and to reduce traffic noise and air pollution.

Explain to the students that they will be doing research to determine the best ways to implement the Tree Project in their community. Give each group a task from worksheet "Research Group Tasks," if appropriate. Otherwise, make up tasks based on your community needs.

Have group members determine ways they can do the research needed to answer the questions for their topic. Move from group to group and assist as needed.

After several days for research, come together as a class and share information. Together, make any class decisions that need to be made. Allow time for any invited guests to speak.

Groups then become action groups, doing what needs to be done to implement their part of the project. For example, the *Contributions* group would organize a plan for getting contributions of trees and money needed or the *Community Education* group would write up educational pamphlets or plan talks.

Make plans for the actual tree planting and public educational programs. Focus throughout on the worldwide nature of the project. When all is completed, come together as a class to discuss the project.

Have each student write a statement describing what he did to contribute to the successful completion of his group's task. These statements must be signed by others in the group.

DISCUSSION

1. How did you feel participating in an international project—one that other youth around the world are also participating in?
2. What did you learn about worldwide deforestation?
3. What did you learn about the trees in your community?
4. Share some of your learnings about the process of educating others about a worldwide problem.
5. If another class was going to implement the Tree Project, what advice would you give them?
6. How do you feel about yourselves now that the project is complete?

A Student's View

Rory Becker, an eighth grade student, participated in the Tree Project in 1984 in Highland, New York. He commented that as a result of the project students had gained great insight into the problems of deforestation in the world. He dedicated the energy of his group to working together with other young people throughout the world to solve this problem. Those who participated in the events were enthusiastic about their importance in the world community. They are looking forward to continuing their participation in this project on an international level.

Highland Post (6/6/84)

PART C **Implementing the Tree Project in Your School District**

You and your class could organize a Tree Project for your school district. A wonderful model is the Highland Tree Project in Highland, New York. (Write to Madeline Labriola at the Highland Middle School, Highland, New York 12528 for a packet of information and curriculum ideas.) The week before Arbor Day, all teachers can take part in an interdisciplinary curriculum effort to educate students about the Tree Project that culminates in tree-planting ceremonies on school property on Arbor Day.

1. **Interdisciplinary Curriculum**—Below is one idea, of the many possible, for various subject areas.

Language Arts—Students write poems about trees. Use "cinquain" for example.

"Cinquain" (pronounced Sin-cane) comes from a French and Spanish word meaning five. A cinquain is a poem that has many descriptive words in it but it has only five lines. Each line has a specific number of syllables.

Listed below are some suggestions for writing a cinquain.
Write two words that describe how a tree looks (4 syllables).
Write three words that describe tree action (6 syllables).
Write four words that tell how you feel about trees (8 syllables).
Write one word that sums up what you have written (2 syllables).
Now, go back and give your poem a one-word title (2 syllables).

Science—Students learn how to plant a tree and what is needed to take care of trees after they are planted.

Social Studies—Students study the history of Arbor Day. They study the problem of worldwide deforestation and why and how trees are dying or being cut down without replacement.

Math—On the computer, students make up a quiz game that uses the information learned in social studies.

Art—Make posters about the Tree Project.

Gym—Dig the holes for the upcoming tree planting.

2. Arbor Day Tree-Planting Ceremonies

In Highland Middle School, students adopted an elementary class. Consider that model. Middle School shared information with elementary students on international cooperation and the Tree Project. They helped elementary students with tree-planting ceremonies, and the tree planting itself. Older students can also make a plan with younger students for taking care of the trees.

Then teach elementary students words and motions to the Planting Song:

From our hearts (touch hearts)
With our hands (hold hands out)
For the earth (touch earth)
All the world together (circle arms around)

If you want to expand the interaction, older students can help younger ones learn more about trees and write poems for the tree-planting ceremony.

Middle School Ceremonies and Tree Planting

Students write a ceremony that focuses on international cooperation for their tree-planting ceremony. Below is part of the ceremony used in Highland, New York.

Dedication

We dedicate these trees to all the children of the earth. May their lives grow in beauty and peace. Let us strive to protect and care for them so that they may be enjoyed by all people. We dedicate them to all those who work for a better world and for a new harmony between children and adults of all nations of the earth.

Closing Words

It is the children who will bring peace and harmony to all the earth. For they have a natural vision of a whole unified earth.

As we plant these trees, this Arbor Day, we are also reminded of our place in the worldwide family. We shall always remember that:
The earth is one organism and it is my home.
All the people on the earth are one family. They are my brothers and sisters.
All parts of the earth are interconnected.
All parts are in my care.
It is the work I do with my hands that makes the world grow.
It is holding hands with each other as brothers and sisters that makes us grow, that brings us harmony and peace.

COMPLETION

A student gets credit for this lesson if each member of her group contributes to the group's task and hands in a statement signed by all group members describing those contributions.

GOING FURTHER

Write to the United Nations Tree Project Office and ask to be put on the mailing list to receive the Newsletter of the Tree Project. Then arrange for students to become pen pals with other students described in the newsletter who are actively implementing tree projects in their nations. In this way, students can feel part of a worldwide network of youth working toward a common goal.

SUBJECT—LA, CW
FORMAT—GROUP
PROJECT, PEER
TEACHING

Poems for Peace _____

OBJECTIVES

To appreciate and utilize poetry as a bridge for communication with others in the fostering of worldwide interdependence and peace
To write poetry about creating peace for the world and sharing those poems with others
To write peaceful poems which are, themselves, gifts of peace

MATERIALS

Worksheets—"Communicate through Poetry!" (one per student), "Peer Feedback" (one per student), pages 489–493

IMPLEMENTATION

Reiterate to students how the arts can touch people's feelings in ways that can motivate them to act for worldwide cooperation and peace. Explain to students that they will examine poetry in that light.

A. READING POETRY

Discuss with students the use of poetry to promote world peace. Discuss ways it can sensitize people to the experiences of all human beings and can highlight the dangers and absurdity of war.

Divide students into groups of three. Pass out worksheet "Communicate through Poetry!" Tell students the first two poems were written by middle-school students in Wappingers Falls, New York. The first poem alerts people to the danger of nuclear war by communicating the horror of it. The second poem awakens readers to the threat of nuclear war. It also portrays some reasons for that threat and some alternatives to it. Explain that the third poem was written by a well-known German playwright and poet, Bertolt Brecht. The poem tells of the power people have to stop war.

Tell students to take turns reading each poem aloud. After one group member reads the first poem, discuss the questions together. Then go on to poems B and C, repeating the process. After the last poem has been discussed, each member takes a poem and writes out the group members' answer to the worksheet questions. Check each other's work, sign, and turn in.

DISCUSSION

1. Discuss answers to questions about "What If?", poem A.
2. What effect, if any, does this poem have on the reader's motivation to work for world peace? How does the poem motivate?
3. Discuss answers to worksheet questions about "What If?", poem B.
4. Do you agree with the poet's suggestion that the American government blames the Russians for trouble that sometimes the United States starts? Give examples to back up your answer.
5. Do you agree with the poet's suggestion that if ordinary, everyday people made up governments we'd have a more peaceful world? Why or why not?
6. Discuss the answers to worksheet questions about "General," poem C.
7. The poet makes the reader stop and think about people's power to stop war. What are your thoughts about the poet's ideas? What are some examples from history of ordinary civilians and soldiers stopping a war?
8. How can these poems, and others like them, be used to help people think about the threat and horror of war and to encourage them to take action for world peace?

B. WRITING POETRY

Tell students that they will now have a chance to communicate some of their feelings and thoughts about creating a peaceful world for all people. Ask students, as a small group, to list all the barriers to worldwide interdependence and peace that they've talked about this year. Ask them then to write together their vision of a peaceful world. Finally have them discuss and list what people are doing, and can do, to create that peaceful world. Then encourage each student to write a poem that includes some of these ideas—and communicates the feelings of the writer.

If students need a more structured format for writing, or if you want them to write a group poem, use the "What If?" format that Greg Holden used in his poem. This idea comes from Educators for Social Responsibility's curriculum, "Dialogue." Students list weapons and then transform them into needed and useful objects in our society. For example:
    "What if" tanks became tractors,
    "What if" grenades became chickens,
    "What if" uniforms became dresses, shoes?
Expand it to include other ideas:
    "What if" bombs became balloons?

When students are finished writing, each trio joins another to form groups of six. Each student chooses a partner. Pass out "Peer Feedback" worksheet. Explain the worksheet. Point out that "Things I Wondered" section is a place to make suggestions, for example, "I wonder if you could include more feelings in your poem." Partners read each other's poems, fill out the "Peer Feedback" worksheet, and return it to their partner.

Each student shares his poem with members of his small group. Then come together as a class. Encourage students to read their poetry to everyone!

C. USING POETRY TO REACH OUT TO OTHERS

Have the class discuss the ways they can share their poetry with others. For example, they could make a class booklet of their poetry to distribute to families, libraries, other classes and community organizations. They could give a poetry reading for parents, other classes, at a nursing home, or to a community organization or church. They could send their poetry for possible publication, to various magazines for youth or to national organizations that promote world peace.

Generate all the possible ideas and decide as a class which one(s) is appropriate for them to do. Divide responsibilities and carry it out!

When students have completed the project, come together and discuss what they've learned about themselves, others, and poetry as a way to communicate about world peace.

COMPLETION

A student gets credit for this lesson if (Part A) every group member contributes to the completion of "Communicating through Poetry" as evidenced by signatures; (Part B) if each member writes a poem, gives feedback to a partner on the "Peer Feedback" worksheet and, in turn, revises her own; and (Part C) contributes to implementing a class plan for sharing their poetry with others.

The Beginnings of Peace

Neve Shalom is an Arab-Jewish cooperative village in Israel, a School for Peace, a growing community of families and singles; the outstanding example of interfaith and intercultural cooperation between Arabs and Jews in the Middle East today.

The purpose of Neve Shalom and its activities is to develop a partnership and sense of responsibility among all of Israel's citizens. Since 1980, over 5,000 young people and 1,000 adults in mixed groups from the Arab and Jewish communities have attended its programs.

The cooperative is supported by donations from abroad, and each member of the community pays a monthly share of rent and other expense.

As a jointly planned and fully democratic community, Neve Shalom provides a model of Arab-Jewish coexistence based on equality and mutual respect. All members are encouraged to maintain their separate identities with pride in a spirit of true cultural and religious pluralism.

The Neve Shalom School for Peace serves as the main training facility for those interested in Arab-Jewish cooperation, reconciliation, and coexistence.

American Friends of Neve Shalom
225 W. 3rd St. Room 918
New York, NY 10122

SUBJECT—SS
FORMAT—GROUP
PROJECT, CLASS
PROJECT

Acting as Global Citizens _____

OBJECTIVES

To consider projects that the class, the school, or individuals can do to live as global citizens
To carry out one or more of these projects

MATERIALS

Information Sheets—A: "Live Simply So Others May Simply Live," B: "Third World Products," C: "Pairing Project," D: "Boycott" (one different information sheet for each group), pages 494–497

IMPLEMENTATION Explain to students that many people around the United States are engaged in projects that build positive connections with, or are supportive of, peoples around the world. Tell them that they will be learning about some of these projects and deciding which one or ones they might want to participate in. The class can decide on one project, different groups can carry out different projects, or the class might want to develop its own project(s).

Divide into groups of about five. Give each group an information sheet. If you have more than 20 students give the same worksheet to two groups. (In this case they will need to work together at the point of planning the class presentation.) Explain that each group has information about one possible project. They are to take turns reading parts of the information sheet aloud within their group and then discuss the project. Group members then discuss and list things they like and things they don't like about that particular project. Next they discuss and list aspects of the project that would make it possible to implement and aspects that would make it difficult. Finally group members decide upon a way of dividing among themselves: information about the project; likes and dislikes; possibilities and difficulties. They share that with the whole class in a five- to seven-minute presentation.

Come together as a class. Each group makes a presentation.

DISCUSSION
1. What responses do you have to each of the project ideas?
2. Have you heard of some of these ideas being implemented in our community or the nation? Have you participated? How?
3. What are the similarities and differences between the different project ideas?
4. What project or projects do you like the best? Give reasons.
5. As a class let's decide on one project to do together or let's decide on several and work together as groups. Which way of proceeding will be best? Why?

After a project (or projects) has been agreed upon, divide into subcommittees to work on specific tasks if one project was chosen, or groups if different projects were chosen. Group members list steps that must be taken to do the project and divide up responsibilities.

If possible, invite someone from the community who has participated in the type of project students have chosen to come speak to the class and give suggestions and support. As the project(s) progresses, meet periodically in groups and as a class to share information, accomplishments and problems. When the project(s) is complete, evaluate it (or them) together as a class.

DISCUSSION
1. What did you learn from this project about acting as global citizens?
2. What did you learn about other people here? Others abroad?
3. What did you learn about yourself?
4. If you were to do the project again, what would you do differently? Why? How?
5. What would be a logical follow-up to this project? What steps could we take to begin it?

> . . . we find the disparities of income and wealth in the United States to be unacceptable. Justice requires that all members of our society work for economic, political and social reforms that will decrease these inequities.
>
> The fulfillment of the basic needs of the poor is of the highest priority. Personal decisions, policies of private and public bodies and power relationships must all be evaluated by their effects on those who lack the minimum necessities of nutrition, housing, education and health care. In particular, this principle recognizes that meeting fundamental human needs must come before the fulfillment of desires for luxury consumer goods, for profits not conducive to the common good and for unnecessary military hardware.
>
> U.S. Bishops, *Economic Justice for All:*
> *Catholic Social Teaching and the U.S. Economy*
> (Washington, DC: United States Catholic Conference, 1986),
> paragraphs 185, 90.

COMPLETION A student gets credit for this lesson if each member of his group makes a clear and accurate presentation during their group's report on the project it examined, and each class member writes a statement regarding her contribution to the class project(s).

> ### Iowa Children Take Action
>
> Fourteen children, who range in age from fourteen through eighteen and are members of Children Acting for Nuclear Disarmament (CAN-DO) made a 1984 trip to Washington, D.C. They participated in a march for peace. The children put on their play, "Crickets in a Nuclear Bomb Patch," which presents a hopeful message about peace through activism. They also read their declaration of peace to legislators on Capitol Hill.
>
> What did the children think? "I think what we did is going to help a lot," said Mary Martin, age eight. "I hope we do get peace."
>
> *Youthlink* (July/August 1984).

Let the Whole World Sing! _____

OBJECTIVES   To learn songs about international friendship, peace and worldwide cooperation
To share those songs with others through concerts, song festivals, tapes, or songbooks

MATERIALS   Worksheets: "Songs for World Peace," pages 498–503

IMPLEMENTATION   Talk with students about the power of songs to inspire and motivate people. Why do people sing? Why do people sing together? Have students list as many reasons as possible, giving their examples in as wide a range of settings as they can. What happens to a group when they sing? How does that influence the mood of the group? Their strength? Explain to the class that they will be learning some songs about world peace and friendship and then sharing those songs with others.

If appropriate, cooperate with the music teacher on this leasson by having him teach the songs or by eliciting his help in finding additional songs.

PART 1   **Singing Songs**

Pass out worksheets, "Songs for World Peace" and either you, interested students, or the music teacher teach them to the class. "It Could Be a Wonderful World," "Dona Nobis Pacem," "Shalom Chaverim," and "Study War No More" are easy to learn. The "United Nations Song" and "Song of Peace" ("Finlandia") are somewhat more difficult. They are very appropriate for a school chorus performance.

DISCUSSION   1.   What feelings do you have as you sing these songs?
2.   What vision of a peaceful world do the songwriters present?
3.   Some of the songwriters suggest ways we can move toward that vision. What are some of these ways toward peace?

Resources

Songbooks
Friendly Songs for a Small Planet, Pricilla Prutzman, et. al., from *World Around Songs,* Burnsville, NC 28714—a source of many other related songbooks.
Songs That Changed the World, Wendy Wilson, Crown Publishers, 1969.
Winds of the People, available from Food for Thought Bookstore, Amherst, MA 01002.

Cassette Tapes
"Two Hands Hold the Earth," Sarah Pirtle.

PART 2   **Researching More Songs**

This can be done by the whole class, or by one small group as a special project. If the whole class does it, divide into groups of four to five. Tell students that you want their group to do research to find other songs about international cooperation, global awareness, and world peace. When possible, they should find background information about the song. As a class, list possible resources—for example, the music teachers in the district, the school and public libraries, local chorus members, international peace groups, and so forth. Either within the groups, or within the class, divide up areas for research.

After groups return with songs, have them decide on three or four which are the most singable and spirited, and which reflect the themes of international cooperation and world peace. Share titles among groups to avoid overlap. Students then write the words to their chosen songs on a ditto. Run enough for everyone. If students are willing, have each group teach their songs to the class. If they are self-conscious, you, or an invited guest, could teach the songs. In either case, students share background information about their songs.

DISCUSSION

1. What was your experience in searching for songs about international cooperation, friendship and world peace?
2. What did you learn by doing this?

Drama
Another Bridge to Cooperation and Peace

Putting on a play is a fine way for young people to experience cooperation. Dramatic presentations can be an inspiring medium for young people to communicate a vision of a cooperative and peaceful world.

A particularly wonderful play is Peace Child. This musical depicts how an American boy and Russian girl become friends and bring together other children of the world to persuade their leaders to end the arms race. With the script and music comes a curriculum, making the play excellent for school-wide or community use. It involves many young people and several adult resource people.

Materials are available from the Peace Child Foundation (see bibliography).

PART 3 Sharing with Others

As a class, consider ways to share these songs with others. Examples might include writing and distributing a small songbook, holding a songfest, making a cassette tape to sell, and so forth. Together choose the project that is workable for your class. Organize needed tasks, divide responsibilities, and carry out the project.

DISCUSSION

1. How did others respond to our Songs for International Friendship and Peace Project? What effect did it have on them?
2. What did you learn from doing this project?
3. What might we do differently next time, to communicate more effectively with others? Work together more effectively among ourselves?

Singing Strengthens

Two examples of singing fostering group cooperation and increased spirit and energy in our nation's history are in the civil rights movement and in labor organizing and workers' strikes. In both these examples, songs served to keep up people's spirits and to bring a group together. Often songs got some of those not part of the group or even those in opposition to hear pieces of the messages. Students can examine songs throughout the black liberation movement, starting with those sung by slaves and then by workers in the Underground Railroad. Some good examples are: "Follow the Drinking Gourd," "Harriet Tubman," "Ain't Gonna Let Nobody Turn Me Around," "It Isn't Nice," "Hold On." Students can also examine songs sung by strikers when picketing. Some of these are particular to a specific strike or time in history; others have been sung repeatedly. Some good examples are: "Union Maid," "Which Side Are You On?" "Bread and Roses." All of the songs listed above can be found in *Winds of the People.*

BEING #1: IN ANYONE'S BEST INTEREST? WORKSHEET

Questions—To Stay #1: On the Court

1. How did Rick's effort to stay #1 affect **his view** of other people?

2. How did Rick defend himself against other people he perceived as threats?

3. How did Rick work to convince himself and others that he was #1?

4. How did Rick's actions to stay #1 affect other people? How would you feel if you were one of those people?

To Stay #1: In the World

Directions—Take turns reading the paragraphs aloud. Discuss questions. Try to develop a group answer for each. If there are different viewpoints, be sure each member of your group can express them. In discussion your teacher will call on a member of your group to give the group's response. Your group will receive credit if the response is thoughtful and clear, and if it represents the ideas of your group.

Governments of nations can be compared to individual people. Many government leaders think of their own interests first. In addition, they often feel threatened by other governments and find ways to defend themselves. Since we're citizens of the United States, let's look at how the United States government does this. You can compare this government behavior to the individual behavior of Rick Wallace.

Many American government and business leaders believe that it's important for the United States to be #1 in the world and to do what's necessary to maintain that position. This enables the government to keep military advantages and corporations to make more profits. Nationalism helps them accomplish this.

Nationalism is the devotion to the interests of one's own nation as separate from the interests of other nations or the common interests of all nations. One's nation is seen as different, and often better than others.

For example:
- Some students have worn T-shirts that say "U.S.A., #1."
- Many Americans don't learn other languages, or schools offer them to students late in their educational careers. We often expect people from other nations to learn English, however.
- Covertly or overtly, the U.S. government intervenes in other nations if it decides U.S. "interests" are threatened, limiting the right of self-determination of that other nation. Vietnam, Chile, Grenada, and Nicaragua are a few of many examples.
- The U.S. spends billions of dollars to compete with other nations and be "superior." The arms race and space exploration are a few of many examples.

Rick's feeling that "I'm the greatest," and his desire to look out for himself at the expense of others, can be compared to nationalism.
1. How does nationalism help Americans? People of the world? (Think back to Rick Wallace. How did his efforts to be better than others help him? Help others?)
2. How does it hinder Americans? People of the world? (Again think back to Rick. How did his efforts to be better than others hurt him? Hurt others?)
3. What are some ways Americans learn to accept nationalism? (Think back to Rick and the ways he kept convincing himself he was the best.) How does our society, our schooling, our media help convince Americans we are best and that America's self-interest comes first?

To Stay #1: In the World—continued

4. When someone tried to give Rick criticism that might help him improve, he got angry and defensive and turned on that person. Sometimes when groups of people or other nations make criticisms of the American government that might help it improve, some government officials get angry, see them as attacks and "are out to get" those groups. Can you think of some examples? What is helpful about doing this? Not helpful?

Just as with Rick, when the U.S. tries to stay #1, other governments are often perceived as threats to its economic, military, and political advantage in the world. Like Rick, the U.S. government officials can mistrust other governments, look for the worst motives and defend its interests against them. Governments defend through military might what they define as their interests in the world today. Like Rick, the U.S. also takes aggressive steps to stay #1. It uses, or threatens to use, its military and its weapons, including nuclear weapons, to do this.

Militarism is maintaining a large military force and using the military to defend a nation's interests against others. Other national needs are seen as less important. The military and war are glorified. Militarism assumes that military power and war are the most effective ways to solve international conflicts. Our socialization as young people can contribute to our acceptance of militarism as adults.

For example:
- Some children like to play war and pretend to kill other children.
- Some young people wear military-type clothes to school.
- Every two weeks, the world spends 17 billion dollars on military arms.
- Over 50% of the U.S. taxpayers' dollars go to military related expenditures.

Rick's strategies to defend himself and protect his interests can be compared to militarism.
1. How does militarism help U.S. citizens? Other people in the world? (Think back to Rick. How did the actions he took to defend his #1 position help him, help others?)
2. How does it hinder U.S. citizens? Other people in the world? (Think back to Rick. How did the actions he took to defend his #1 position hurt him, hurt others?)
3. How does our culture teach people that nations must show power by military means? How does our schooling teach us the same thing? Our media?

THE TOWERS WORKSHEET

Eagle Roles

---

1. **Military official in the Eagle government**

   You feel good about yourself when you feel tough and strong. You like to feel like a winner. The more gold stars you have, the more like a winner you feel.

   Your goal is for the Eagle nation to have the highest tower. You tell others that the tower will make the nation secure.

---

2. **Head of an industry that makes blocks in the Eagle nation**

   You feel good about yourself when your company makes high profits. This happens when the government uses your blocks. The more pennies you make, the better you feel.

   Your goal is to make as much money as possible. You tell others that blocks will make the nation secure.

---

3. **Leader of the Eagle government**

   You feel good about yourself because you are head of the Eagles. You like having the power you do, although many groups use *their* power to push you to make decisions *they* like. You feel good when your government is powerful in the world.

   Your goal is to keep your position as leader of the government.

---

4. **Citizen disarmament advocate in the Eagle nation**

   You feel good about yourself when you feel secure. You do not feel secure with the two towers standing. You feel good about yourself when you work with others to take action that leads to peace.

   Your goal is to have the towers taken down.

---

5. **Citizen in the Eagle nation**

   You feel good about yourself when you have adequate food, clothing, and shelter, and a meaningful job. You also feel good when you have a voice in decisions affecting your life.

   Your goal is to live out your life in peace.

---

6. **Member of legislature, Eagle government**

   You feel good about yourself when you are elected to be in the legislature. You like having the power to influence decisions about your country.

   Your goal is to keep your position in the government. Money and support of important people helps you do this.

Bear Roles

1. **Military official in the Bear government**

   You feel good about yourself when you feel tough and strong. You like to feel like a winner. The more gold stars you have, the more like a winner you feel.

   Your goal is for the Bear nation to have the highest tower. You tell others that the tower will make the nation secure.

2. **Head of a block "design group" in the Bear nation**

   You are head of a "design group" that plans blocks. You feel good about yourself when the government decides to use a block designed by your group. This brings you status, power and privileges which are represented by a penny. The more pennies you have, the better you feel.

   Your goal is to have as many pennies as possible. You tell others that blocks will make the nation secure.

3. **Leader of the Bear government**

   You feel good about yourself because you are head of the Bears. You like having the power you do, although many groups use their power to push you to make decisions they like. You feel good when your government is powerful in the world.

   Your goal is to keep your position as leader of the government.

4. **Citizen, favoring disarmament in the Bear nation**

   You feel good about yourself when you feel secure. You do not feel secure with the two towers standing. You feel good about yourself when you move government policies in the direction of peace.

5. **Member of legislature, Bear government**

   You feel good about yourself when you are chosen to be in the legislature. You like having the power to influence decisions about your country.

   Your goal is to keep your position in the government. Support of important people helps you do this.

6. **Citizen of the Bear nation**

   You feel good about yourself when you have adequate food, clothing and shelter, and a meaningful job. You feel good when you have a voice in decisions that affect your life.

   Your goal is to live out your life in peace.

THE TOWERS WORKSHEET

America and the Arms Race: A Closer Look

Let's look at some questions and answers about the arms race. Remember that this is only a small amount of information about the arms race. Why not gather other information and do more research yourselves?!

Take turns reading each question. If any group member can give information in response, she should do so. Then the reader reads the section of information. When you finish all questions, answer the questions at the bottom of the page. Try to come to consensus. If there are different points of view, list them all.

---

1. In the game, when a group has the number of blocks equal to the number of people on the other side, it has enough blocks to destroy the others. Nevertheless, sometimes groups keep adding blocks to the tower. How is that like the real world? (Stop reading. Can a group member answer?)

Less than 2 percent of all the firepower of the world's nuclear powers could destroy all the large and medium-sized cities in the entire world. Yet the nuclear nations continue to build more weapons. For example, in the next decade the U.S. plans to build 17,000 new nuclear weapons.

Children's Defense Budget

---

2. In the game, someone could accidentally knock down—or almost knock down—the tower of the other team, which would destroy the other team. How is this like the real world? (Stop reading. Can a group member answer?)

There have been many accidents that could almost start a nuclear war. For example:
   a. The United States mistook the rising of the moon for a missile attack (mid 1960s).
   b. A computer with a practice Soviet missile attack tape on it accidentally was introduced into an approaching missile warning system (1979).
   c. A microchip failed to compute in a Strategic Air Command headquarters in Omaha and the B52s almost took off (1980).

Roger Molaner, *New York Times* (1984)

America and the Arms Race: A Closer Look—continued

3. In the game, people in the military and war industries benefited from the arms race. In what way is this like real life? (Stop reading. Can a group member answer?)

The military and war industries in the U.S. often collaborate to benefit from the arms race. For example, the Department of Defense (DOD) offers contract proposals to weapons manufacturers with prices far above what it would cost in the store. Defense industries make big profits at the expense of the average taxpayer. A few examples follow.

   a. Allen wrench for Air Force F16 jet: DOD price $9,606, market value $12
   b. Nut, used by Navy for F-18 jet: DOD price $2,043, market value $13
   c. Antennae motor, Air Force for F16 jet: DOD price $7,417, market value $13

Senator William Roth in *Children's Defense Budget*

4. In the game, money not used for blocks could be used for programs for the people. How is this like real life? (Stop reading. Can a group member answer?)

Much money that goes to weapons could support our people. For example, every day thirty American children die from poverty. One-third of President Reagan's proposed military **increase** for 1985 could lift every American child out of poverty. Similarly, the poor standard of living of people in the Soviet Union could be greatly enhanced with changed priorities.

Questions
   1. What are some of your feelings about the arms race?

   2. What should be done about the arms race? How could that happen?

Signatures _____

_____

_____

_____

Marta and the People of Nicaragua

Marta

My name is Marta and I'm nine years old. I live in Nicaragua, a country in Central America. The year is 1976. I'd like to tell you about life in my country.

Please draw the "Life in Nicaragua Cards" (cards numbered 1) one at a time. Read them aloud to each other and then, as a group, discuss them and answer the questions below.

1. How would you describe the life of most people in Nicaragua?

2. Imagine that your class was like our country.
    a. How many students make up 5 percent of your classroom? _____
    b. About how much space is 58 percent of your classroom? _____
    c. Imagine that only 5 percent of students could use that 58 percent of the classroom. How would you feel if you were one of the other 95 percent?

    d. What is about 23 percent of the classroom? _____
    e. Imagine only one special student could use all of that. How would you feel if you weren't that student?

_____

Marta—1976

When you imagined so few students having so much space in your classroom, you could imagine how most of us in Nicaragua feel. Without land many of us can't grow food to eat and we go hungry.

You may think that life in Nicaragua is so hard because the people are lazy, backward, or don't try to improve things. That is not the case! We want a better life! The problem is that a small group of people—and especially one family—have most of the land, money, and power. They keep it for themselves and don't allow others to have a better life. I'd like you to know more about that one family—the Somoza family.

Marta and the People of Nicaragua—continued

Please draw the "Somoza Family Cards" (cards numbered 2) one at a time. Read them aloud to each other and then, as a group, discuss them and then answer the questions below. If you don't know the meaning of some words, please look them up in the dictionary.

1. How would you feel if you were living in Nicaragua under the Somoza regime?

2. What would you try to do to change things?

Marta—1976

Did you come up with many ways to change things? We've tried a lot of the ideas you probably suggested. However it is very difficult because many people have been killed or imprisoned for challenging Somoza.

You might wonder why it's important that Americans learn about Nicaragua. It's important because the U.S. government helps keep the Somozas in power. That's why it's important that the people of Nicaragua talk to the people of the U.S. Then maybe you can influence your government.

Draw the "U.S. Ties to Nicaragua Cards" (cards numbered 3) to see how this happens. Read them aloud, discuss them, and then answer the following questions.

1. How do you feel about the U.S. government's support of the Somoza government? Why do you feel the way you do?

2. Do you think the U.S. should give money and support to countries with military dictators, like the Somozas? Why or why not?

3. Do you think the U.S. corporations should do business with the Somoza government, or governments like them, when the businesses help the dictators and the corporations more than the people of Nicaragua? Why or why not?

Marta and the People of Nicaragua—continued

Marta—1976

We Nicaraguan people want to be friends with the American people. But now maybe you see why some Nicaraguans say "Yankee, go home." It is because the U.S. government and corporations have ties to our government that hurt the Nicaraguan people.

The taxes Americans pay to their government help train the National Guard that kills people who oppose Somoza. The corporations that Americans work for put my parents' small company out of business. The trade policies of the U.S. government help you get all the sugar, coffee, and cotton **you** need, but keep us from developing businesses to make the products **we** need.

I'll tell you why I think the U.S. government leaders protect Somoza. They're afraid a new government wouldn't be as supportive of the U.S. They're afraid that a new government might limit U.S. businesses in Nicaragua. They're afraid it might not support the U.S. in world organizations like the U.N. That may happen with a new government, but it may not.

Also, I think they're afraid that if there is a revolution here (that means an overthrow of the government) it will be Russians who are responsible for it. But that's not true! There are all different people who want a revolution—peasants, teachers, priests, factory workers. Some are communists—people who want all property to be held in common by the state. Most people aren't communists, and those who are aren't controlled by Russia. The most important thing to know is that the majority of people here in Nicaragua want a big change.

But, anyway, should the U.S. tell us how to run our government just because it's more powerful and richer than we are? Should the U.S. use its power in Nicaragua to keep the government in the hands of leaders the U.S. wants rather than the leaders we want?

Now that you understand this, maybe you can work to change the policies of your government and U.S. corporations. That's how you can help us! Here in Nicaragua people are joining the FSLN, the Sandinista National Liberation Front—to fight the Somozas. We will fight together to create a country that gives justice and hope to **all** the Nicaraguan people.

Marta and the People of Nicaragua—continued

1. How would you answer Marta's questions in paragraph five? Give a reason for your answer.

2. How can people try to change such policies of their government and corporations if they decide they want to do so? What, if anything, would you want to try?

Now check your answers for correct spelling, punctuation and grammar.

Signatures _____

_____

_____

Marta and the People of Nicaragua—Cards

1. Life in Nicaragua It's 1976. Our country, Nicaragua, is controlled by one wealthy family—the Somoza family. They have been in power since 1933.	1. Life in Nicaragua 1976 Eighty percent (80%) of the houses people live in have no running water. Fifty-nine percent (59%) have no electricity.
1. Life in Nicaragua 1976 Five percent (5%) of the population owns 58% of the arable land. (Arable land is land that can produce crops.) The Somozas own 23% of it.	2. The Somoza Family 1976 The dictator of Nicaragua—Anastasio Somoza—is the ninth richest man in the world. Much of his money was obtained in unfair ways. Some was supposed to be for the people of Nicaragua, but the Somozas kept it for themselves.
1. Life in Nicaragua 1976 Half of the people of Nicaragua make less than $100 a year.	2. The Somoza Family 1976 In 1972 there was a terrible earthquake in Nicaragua. People from around the world sent money for food, housing, and medicine to the suffering people. The Somoza family took a lot of this money for themselves and never gave it to the people in need.
1. Life in Nicaragua 1976 Over 60% of the people are affected by unemployment each year.	2. The Somoza Family 1976 The Somoza family controls many industries and keeps others from setting up businesses. For example, the Somozas owned the only milk pasteurizing plant in Nicaragua. The sale of milk that is not pasteurized is forbidden.

Marta and the People of Nicaragua—Cards—continued

2. The Somoza Family 1976 The Somoza family built the National Guard to work for them. The Somoza family and the National Guard constantly violated human rights. People who oppose the Somozas are put in prison, tortured, and sometimes executed.	3. U.S. Ties to Nicaragua 1976 From 1950–1975, 4,897 National Guardsmen passed through U.S. military training. The U.S. provided aid to the National Guard, including training and equipment, such as helicopters and cargo planes.
2. The Somoza Family 1976 Somoza uses the Guard to keep the people from challenging him. In 1967 many people demonstrated against Somoza in Managua. Somoza directed the National Guard to open fire with machine guns and tanks. Six hundred people were killed.	3. U.S. Ties to Nicaragua 1976 Many U.S. companies moved into Nicaragua. Some took over or pushed out local businesses. Some U.S. companies cooperate directly with the Somoza regime. For example, U.S. Steel operates a plant jointly with Somoza.
3. U. S. Ties to Nicaragua 1976 U.S. ties to the Somoza regime have been very close. The U.S. has provided moral support, economic aid, and military aid.	3. U.S. Ties to Nicaragua 1976 U.S. trade policies have made Nicaragua dependent on the U.S. The U.S. gets what it needs instead of allowing Nicaraguans to produce things they need. In one U.S. development plan, credits were only for agricultural exports, not for Nicaraguan industries.
3. U.S. Ties to Nicaragua 1976 From 1946 to 1975 the Somoza government received over 23 million dollars in military assistance from the U.S.	

BANANA FOR BREAKFAST: HEALTHY FOR WHOM? WORKSHEET

Elisa's Dialogue

Place: Honduras
Date: September 17
Characters: Elisa, age 13; her father

Father: Good morning, Elisa.

Elisa: Good morning, Papa.

Father: You seem very sad.

Elisa: Oh, Dad, I'm still so upset about Carmen. She was only three years old. I still can't sleep at night.

Father: I can't either. To have your own cousin die of hunger is horrible.

Elisa: I still don't understand why.

Father: I don't really understand either. Your uncle, Roberto, was laid off at the box factory where he worked because the factory didn't have enough work. He tried to find another job but couldn't. He had no money to feed his family. I only wish we could have helped, but we too go hungry many days, even though I work twelve hours a day.

Elisa: But, Dad, there should be plenty of work at Roberto's factory. Look at all the boxes of bananas shipped out of Honduras. Someone must be making all those boxes.

Father: Someone at Roberto's factory told him they're being made by U.S. companies, like the J and J Box Company, the company that makes the boxes bananas are shipped in.

Elisa: Why can't Honduran companies make the boxes?

Father: Roberto's been asking that ever since he's been laid off.

Elisa: It just doesn't seem fair.

Ask another student, or your teacher, to read the following information to the class.

- Big U.S.-based multinational corporations, like United Brands, who sell bananas, control the banana industry.

- Other companies tied to the banana trade, like the hypothetical J and J Box Company, are subsidiaries of United Brands.

- If boxes were made by Honduran companies, more Hondurans would have jobs.

BANANA FOR BREAKFAST: HEALTHY FOR WHOM? WORKSHEET

Jill's Dialogue

Place: United States
Date: September 17
Characters: Jill, 13 years old; Jill's father

Father: Good morning, Jill.

Jill: Good morning, Dad.

Father: What are you getting for breakfast?

Jill: Bananas on cereal, of course! Do I ever go a morning without bananas?

Father: Never! Did you get that social studies reading done last night?

Jill: Of course, Dad, what do you think? It was interesting. I was reading about Honduras. There's so much hunger and poverty there.

Father: Yes, it's a hard life. But the people can't seem to change their ways. They're not into working as hard as we are.

Jill: It's too bad. At least Americans don't contribute to their suffering. Isn't there anything we can do to help them?

Father: Well, our government gives them plenty of economic aid. . . . Speaking of money, I want to tell you some really good news. I was reading the stock pages before you got up and our stock in J and J Box Company has gone up a lot. That means we'll be able to take that winter vacation we were talking about.

Jill: That's great, Dad!

Connecting the Lives of Jill and Elisa

1. Compare the lives of Jill and Elisa. How were they alike? How were they different?

2. Jill's father says that if only Hondurans worked harder they'd be better off. Do you agree? Why or why not?

3. What do you believe is needed to help Hondurans have a better standard of living?

4. Jill says that, "at least Americans don't contribute to the suffering" (the hunger and poverty of the Hondurans). To what extent do you agree with her statement? Why?

5. What is stock? How does Jill's family benefit from the J and J Box Company's involvement in the banana industry?

6. What would you recommend to the multinational corporations that profit from this banana trade? Why?

Signatures _____

_____

_____

_____

The Universal Postal Union (Jigsaw Sections)

1   Imagine yourself living in the United States in the middle of the 19th century. If you wanted to mail a letter to a country in Europe, you might face a very expensive and complicated matter.

2   You would hope that the United States has a treaty with the country to which you were mailing the letter; otherwise, your letter wouldn't get there. There would not be a fixed rate for your letter. Many different issues would determine the final cost. They would be:

1. Postage of the country from which the letter was sent.
2. The rate charged by the ship carrying the letter (sea-postage).
3. The rate charged by each country the letter passed through.
4. The domestic postage of the country in which the letter was delivered.

The sea-postage would vary according to the route or nationality of the ship.

3   Today almost all the nations of the world are members of the Universal Postal Union. Now all member nations are regarded as one big postal district. Postage is paid in the country from which the letter is sent and delivered without charge in the country to which it is addressed. Each member country pays a fee and then has the right to use the postal systems of all countries through which the mail travels.

4   How did this happen? In 1874, representatives of nations around the world met in Berne, Switzerland to form a Universal Postal Union to bring international cooperation to the mails. From this conference developed an international mail service that we now take for granted.

5   The Universal Postal Union promises freedom of transit for all letters. It helps settle disputes between member countries. Recently, it has provided special programs to help developing countries expand and modernize their postal services. Thus for over 100 years, through peace and war, peoples of the world have been able to maintain communication because of this organization based on international cooperation.

Issues and Problems Concerning the World's Oceans (Jigsaw Sections)

---

1 The world's oceans are a very special resource because they are an interconnected whole. What one nation does in an ocean affects other parts of the ocean as well. The oceans, therefore, need international regulation.

---

2 International cooperation is needed among all countries not only to protect the environment of the oceans, but for international air flights, ship navigation, and for scientific research.

---

3 One current problem is that toxic wastes and other forms of pollution are being poured into the world's oceans by many nations. If this continues, it can negatively affect the ecological balance, the climate, and all life on earth. An international organization is needed to deal with this problem.

---

4 A problem exists now because there is little international regulation of the oceans. Weaker nations along the oceans, and landlocked nations, are concerned that they might not be allowed to benefit from the oceans. Therefore, they will be tempted to go out and claim ocean space. This will bring about greater conflict among nations.

---

5 A serious problem today is the trend toward dividing up the world's oceans and giving rights to the oceans to nations next to them. If this continues, it would make world tensions greater. Twenty nations, mostly the richer ones, would have two-thirds of the world's ocean space. This would make greater inequality between the nations of the world.

The Oceans: Common Heritage of Humankind

Your task as a group is to design a plan for international use of the oceans—a plan that will safeguard the interests of all peoples and nations. Work toward a plan of cooperation and shared development so that all nations, especially the less developed and the landlocked, would benefit equally from the oceans.

There are five principles that underlie the belief that the oceans are the common heritage of all humankind:

1. Oceans may be used by individual nations but not owned by them.
2. The oceans need a system of management in which all users of the ocean must share.
3. All nations can actively share the benefits from the sea.
4. The oceans are to be reserved for peaceful purposes and are to be areas of disarmament.
5. The oceans are the heritage of future generations and the environment of the oceans must be protected.

Think about the potential of using the resources of the sea to create a new international order that is more fair for all nations.

Now work together to develop a plan for the preservation and shared use of the seas. Here are some questions you may want to consider. Don't limit yourself to these questions.

1. What organizations will regulate the seas? Who will be represented in these organizations?
2. Who will be able to use the seas?
3. What rights do ocean-bordering nations have?
4. By what means will landlocked nations benefit from the seas?
5. How can poor nations share in the benefits of the seas?
6. What laws could be made to assure that the seas are used for peaceful purposes?
7. What regulations would be set to protect the environment of the seas?

Once you have developed a plan, divide it into sections. Distribute sections. Group members will each write a section. Be ready to present your plan to the class with each group member presenting a section **other than** the one she wrote. Then hand in your plan to the teacher with all group members' signatures.

Rescue in Denmark: A Choral Reading

A. Background

1. Introduction

   Denmark had been occupied by the Nazis in 1940. It was not until October 1943, however, that the Nazis decided to round up Denmark's eight thousand Jews for shipment to death camps. Many people throughout the country acted together as an underground movement to warn Danish Jews, hide them, and then help them escape to Sweden.

2. This type of action was not typical for most of the countries the Nazis occupied. In many other countries, local populations didn't protest the murdering of the Jews. In some cases, they even collaborated with Nazis in the genocide.

   In Denmark, however, people risked their lives to save their Jewish neighbors. Some Danish people died to save Jewish people. Through a choral reading, we will discover how and why they did this. The time is fall, 1943.

3. October 29

   I am George Duckwitz, a German. I had been living and working in Denmark for fifteen years. After the German invasion of Denmark, I had been given a post in the German Embassy in Copenhagen as head of shipping. I learned that several German transport ships would arrive in Copenhagen on September 29. They would transport Jews, to be arrested in a raid October 1, to German concentration camps. I risked my life to warn Jews of the coming raid.

4. I am Inge Barfeldt. I work as a secretary. I got word that the Germans planned to round up the Jews. I couldn't warn people on the phone because the phones might be tapped by the Germans. It was almost the curfew time on the night of September 29. If I was caught outside after the curfew, I could be arrested. Nevertheless, I went out with the message to the house of Rabbi Melchior, rabbi of the Copenhagen Synagogue. I knew he would warn his congregations the next day.

Rescue in Denmark: A Choral Reading—continued

B. Warning

October 30

5. Introduction
The word of the planned German raid spread quickly and secretly. Throughout the day Christian policemen, postmen, taxi drivers, shopkeepers, doctors, teachers, and students took time off from their work to give warning to their Jewish friends and acquaintances. Being caught hiding a Jew could mean arrest and imprisonment.

---

6. I am Jorgen Knudsen, a young ambulance driver. When some student friends rushed up to me with the news, I had to do something. I ripped the telephone directory from the phone booth nearby. I opened the directory and circled Jewish names. I didn't report for ambulance duty that day. Instead, I drove through Copenhagen calling on total strangers to give them the warning. When people were frantic because they had no one to turn to, I piled them in my ambulance and drove them to a hiding place.

---

7. I am Dr. Ege, a professor. When a friend told me the news, I took off my laboratory smock and put away my coat. I went to warn all my Jewish friends. Whenever anyone didn't have a place to go into hiding, I offered my big apartment above the laboratory at the school where I worked.

---

8. I am Mrs. Ege. When my husband brought me the news, I went out and began contacting all my Jewish friends. When asked why I did it, I explained that it was exactly the same as seeing your neighbor's house on fire. Naturally I wanted to try to do something about it. We hid many Jews disguised as doctors, nurses, and patients at the hospital. We helped Jews because, for once in your life, you felt you were doing something worthwhile. It was a terrible time. Nevertheless our activities gave us a special feeling of oneness. We were together.

---

9. My name is Mr. Carstensen. I am a conductor on a train. On September 29 a man who rides my train to work came home early. I didn't know his name, but I knew he looked sick. I asked him what was the matter. He said he just learned that the Germans were going to round up the Jews and he had no place to hide with his wife and small children. I said bring them all to my house.

Rescue in Denmark: A Choral Reading—continued

C. Hiding

10. Introduction

   In the early weeks of October, many Danes helped Jews hide. Since the Germans controlled the police, radio, and newspapers, Danes didn't know what other Danes across the country were doing. It was only through word of mouth that people could communicate.

11. I am Pastor Ivan Lage. I read a proclamation of the Danish Lutheran bishops in support of the Jews. Part of it said, "Not withstanding our separate religious beliefs, we fight to preserve for our Jewish brothers and sisters the same freedom we ourselves value more than life." Even though politics aren't supposed to be discussed in church and I could be punished, I added that I would rather die with the Jews than live with the Nazis. I wanted to give my congregation courage to help the Jews.

12. My name is Christian Kisling. At first I didn't believe that the Germans would arrest the Jews. But on the night of September 30 I was wakened by screeching trucks outside our apartment. The Germans broke into the apartment of our Jewish neighbors. Luckily they weren't home. I knew we had to do something. There was a large attic above the garage of the company that I worked for. By the next night we had helped forty Jews hide there.

13. My name is Gethe Kisling, Christian Kisling's wife. Feeding the refugees in the attic was a problem because I didn't want to arouse suspicions by suddenly buying huge quantities of food at stores where I shopped. So I traveled from store to store making normal-size purchases. I would make sandwiches and coffee and sneak them to the refugees at night. My husband and I sat up most of the night trying to help them keep their spirits up. These were terrible days. It wasn't easy to be cozy in one's own warm bed at night knowing our countrymen were frightened or uncertain about what was going to happen to them, not knowing where to escape, where to turn.

Rescue in Denmark: A Choral Reading—continued

14. I am Dr. Karl Koster, a doctor at the Bispebjerb Hospital in Copenhagen. I arranged for over 2,000 Jews to pass through our hospital on the way to Sweden. Toward the end of October the Germans started to raid the operating room in the hospital. When a doctor was found performing surgery on a Jewish patient, the Germans would machine gun to death the patient, doctor, and anyone else in the operating room. I had to escape to Sweden and I couldn't return to Denmark until the end of the war. Because the entire medical profession stood together as a single unit in opposition to anti-Semitism, our efforts on behalf of the Jews were much easier. We knew the Germans couldn't arrest all of us.

15. My name is Signe Jansen. I am head nurse at Bispebjerb Hospital. I convinced our nursing staff to share their nurses' quarters with Jewish refugees. We shared our 130 apartments and donated money to help the refugees. Despite risks, raids, and murders, the nurses continued to help rescue the Danish Jews.

Rescue in Denmark: A Choral Reading—continued

D. Escape

16. Introduction

    Many Danes risked their lives helping Jews to get out of Denmark. Many were part of an underground network that hid Jews and transported them to safety. Many people were strangers helping strangers, united in a common effort.

17. My name is Peder Hansen and I'm a fisherman. I was approached by a stranger during the first week in October and asked if I could take his two sons to safety in Sweden. I said I would. I also took the fifty other Jews hiding with him. Over the next month, I took many Jews to Sweden.

18. I am Ina Haxen. I was a housewife before October 1943. Then I joined underground activities to help Jews escape to Sweden. I acted as a courier. I contacted Jews in hiding and accompanied them to a central point where they would be taken to the boats.

19. I am Erling Kaiser. Before October 1943 I was a bookbinder. After that I became a sailor. I never had sailed a boat before in my life. Four friends and I got together and bought a speedboat. I made many secret trips carrying Jews across to freedom in Sweden. I was captured by the Gestapo and tortured, but I gave no information about our secret operation. I was put in a German concentration camp and made a slave laborer. I was lucky to live to the end of the war. Many of the other Danes imprisoned with me died.

20. My name is Ellen Nielson. I sell fish on the docks in Copenhagen. Two brothers who sold flowers next to me on the docks asked if I could help them find a boat to Sweden. I hid them in my house. Since I knew fishermen, I arranged for boats to transport them. My sons guided them to the boats at night. I did this for many other refugees. I was caught by the Gestapo and sent to a German concentration camp. The day I was in the line to go into the gas chamber to be killed, word came that Danish prisoners were to be shipped to Sweden. I was saved.

Iroquois Game Cards—A (Belief Cards)

The Hau De No Sau Nee believed that humans have minds which enable them to come to peaceful resolutions of conflict.	The People of the Longhouse assumed that no one had a right to a greater share of wealth than anyone else. The Peacemaker, a great leader, taught that if absolute justice were established in the world, peace would follow.
The Iroquois people held the conviction that governments should be formed not to establish law and order, but peace and universal justice.	The Hau De No Sau Nee remembered the original instructions of the Creators of Life. They were told that human beings who walk the Earth have been provided with all things necessary for life. They were told to love one another and show great respect for the earth.
The Hau De No Sau Nee believed that the world does not belong to humans, but to the Great Creator. Therefore all people have a right to things they need to survive.	The People of the Longhouse believed in strict conservation. One principle was to think about the welfare of seven generations in the future.
The Iroquois thought that a peaceful society can come about by eliminating causes of conflict between individual peoples.	

Iroquois Game Cards—B (Practices and Customs)

The Hau De No Sau Nee developed a government under the Great Law. Everyone had direct participation in the workings of the government.	In the Iroquois Confederacy, councils of women appointed the male leaders who were to do the will of the people.
The People of the Longhouse formerly were five countries each of which guarded hunting lands. A great leader, called the Peacemaker, convinced the people to abolish the idea of separate territories. After that, people could hunt and occupy lands of any other nation.	The People of the Longhouse lived in harmony with the earth. They used only what they needed to live. They didn't waste the earth's resources.
Before it became a Confederacy, the Iroquois were five nations. Each gave up part of their power to others in the Confederacy. The Peacekeeper, a great leader, thought this system could go beyond the Confederacy to other peoples of the world.	The Iroquois didn't do anything that would cause suffering in the future. For example, they only killed the number of animals needed to meet their basic needs.
If they were attacked, the five nations defended themselves together. They would unite to carry on war in the invader's country until they won. What they demanded of the attacking nation was that it put away its weapons of war and stop attacking others. They did not seize their territory, force their religion on them, or collect tribute.	The leaders of the Iroquois were both political and spiritual leaders. The leader had to be generous with material goods. Ceremonies were held where the leaders would give away things to others.

Directions—The Iroquois Game

1. The goal of the game is to get all players to the end of the game path and to learn about the cooperative beliefs and practices of the Native American nations of the Iroquois Confederation. All game cards must be read before the group can win.

2. Each player chooses a mover—a penny, paper clip, and so forth.

3. Using a piece of paper with a line down the middle, a group member makes a group chart, one side titled "Beliefs" and the other "Practices and Customs."

4. Each player rolls the die and moves the number shown. If she lands on a 1, she takes a #1 card and reads it aloud. She decides if it is a "belief" or a "practice or custom" of the Iroquois. If they disagree, two other group members give their opinions and the group comes to a consensus.

5. The reader of each card lists, in shortened version, the belief or practice/custom on the correct side of the game chart. The card is set aside.

6. If a player lands on a 3, one of two choices must be made:
    a. The player may roll the die again and move ahead the number shown. No card can be chosen for this free turn.

    −or−
    b. The player may roll the die again, but give the free turn to the player who is furthest behind on the board. That player **may** pick a card. The free turn does not interfere with that player's regular turn.

7. During play, the group must decide the best way for all players to be at the end of the game circle and have all clue cards read. A player who got to the end of the game may decide to start over again to make that happen.

Cooperative Beliefs and Customs of Native Peoples

1. Belief or custom

2. How does this belief or custom show cooperation of Native Americans with each other or with the earth?

3. What can we learn from that belief or custom?

4. What would our nation and the world be like if we put the belief or custom into practice today? How would things be different than they are now?

ALTERNATIVES TO WAR WORKSHEET
Nonviolent Resistance: Historical Examples

India 1930–31

Indian leader Mohandas Gandhi led the Indian people in nonviolent resistance against British domination of their country. The Indians' goal was independence from Great Britain. In 1930 Gandhi and his followers began a twenty-six day march to the sea in order to commit civil disobedience by making salt. Civil disobedience is to break a law because you believe it is immoral and unjust. The British had a government monopoly on the making of salt and charged a high tax as well. The march was a signal for mass nonviolent revolt throughout the country.

There were mass meetings, parades and strikes. Students left government schools. Government departments were boycotted. People refused to pay taxes.

Many people, including Gandhi, were arrested. The resisters suffered greatly and many people were killed. Their efforts, however, affected the government; it could not function normally.

These actions forced the British government to negotiate with the Indians. These actions were an important step on the road to Indian independence.

Nonviolent Resistance: Historical Examples—continued

Norway 1942

In 1942, Norway was occupied by Nazi Germany. The fascist Minister-President, Vidkun Quisling, set out to make the educational system a tool to promote fascist propaganda. Fascism is a system of government that has a strong centralized government that permits no opposition. It controls all aspects of the nation. It promotes aggressive nationalism and is often anticommunist.

The underground called on the teachers to resist. The underground were people secretly working to free Norway. About 10,000 of the 12,000 teachers wrote letters to Quisling's education department. All signed names and addresses. They said they would not assist in teaching fascism in the schools and would not join the fascist teachers' organization.

The government closed the schools. The teachers held classes in private homes. Protests from parents against the government poured in.

About 1,000 teachers were arrested and sent to concentration camps. Some died there. Nevertheless, the teachers did not give in. They insisted students should learn to think freely and critically. Schools reopened. Teachers who were still free held firm and did not teach fascist education.

After eight months, Quisling had to release the teachers from the camps. The Norwegians were getting too angry. His new organization for teachers never got members. The schools never taught fascist propaganda because teachers were courageous and cooperated with each other. They won an important victory.

Czechoslovakia 1968

In 1968 Russia invaded Czechoslovakia. The Russians expected that with a half million troops they would overwhelm Czechoslovakia in several days. It didn't happen.

Masses of citizens blocked the streets, stopping huge Soviet tanks. A secret radio network called a general strike. All workers stopped their work. The network called together the National Assembly which opposed the invasion. The radio kept areas of resistance throughout the country in communication. The police refused to help the invaders.

The legitimate government remained in power for eight months, much longer than it would have if it had fought by military means.

ALTERNATIVES TO WAR WORKSHEET

Nonviolent Resistance—Questions

1. India

   a. What was the goal of the Indian people?

   b. What event in 1930 spurred the people to action? Why did it motivate so many people?

   c. What types of nonviolent actions did they use to work toward that goal?

2. Norway

   a. In 1942, what were the fascist plans for the education system in Norway?

   b. How did the Norwegian teachers use nonviolent action to resist that?

   c. What were the results of this nonviolent resistance?

3. Czechoslovakia

   a. What did the Russians expect when they invaded Czechoslovakia in 1968?

   b. How did the Czechs use nonviolent resistance to confront the Russians?

   c. What was the result?

The People Defend Their Nation

Hypothetical Situation

(This is truly a hypothetical situation because the U.S. and Canada have, for centuries, had a history of very peaceful relationships!)

Canada has just invaded the United States with conventional (tanks, infantry, planes) military forces. The Canadian government announced that the newly elected U.S. President and Congress were unacceptable to Canada. The Canadian government reported that it was too dangerous to Canada to allow a government to take office that was committed to greatly increasing taxes on corporations and the wealthy and lowering taxes for low and middle-income people. They said such policies aren't democratic. Therefore, they are invading the United States to try to overthrow that government and restore stability to America. The U.S. population is committed to civilian-based defense.

Write the following roles on a piece of paper. Teacher (male), newsreporter (female), mayor (female), bus driver (female), automobile factory worker (male), student (male). Each student draws a role. Take five minutes alone to plan what steps you would take to paticipate in a plan of civilian-based defense. Then share your ideas with group members and get feedback and suggestions from them. Finally, coordinate your efforts to make a united group plan. Each person writes down the steps in her part of the plan. Proofread each other's work. Clip together to hand in.

Stories

The Visitors: Story A

Uri and his family are visiting the United States. They are Russian citizens. They have been sightseeing in Washington, D.C. Included in the visit was a trip to a school.

Peter's dad is working late at his government office building in Washington, D.C. Peter goes in the building to meet him because they're going to go out to an evening movie together. The building is very quiet since almost everyone has gone home. As Peter gets in the elevator to go up to his dad's office, he is surprised to see Uri getting out. He remembered he was a Russian who had visited his school. Uri is carrying a big bag.

Be creative and work together to finish the story.

The Visitors: Story B

Peter and his family are visiting Moscow. They are American citizens. They have been sightseeing in Moscow. Included in the visit was a trip to a school.

Uri's dad is working late at his government office building in Moscow. Uri goes in the building to meet him because they're going to go out to an evening movie together. The building is very quiet since almost everyone has gone home. As Uri gets in the elevator to go up to his dad's office, he is surprised to see Peter getting out. He remembered he was an American who had visited his school. Peter is carrying a big bag.

Be creative and work together to finish the story.

US/THEM, WAR/PEACE WORKSHEET

National Traits Checklist

Typical American Youth

Put a check next to all characteristics that are typical of American youth.

1. kind

2. gets in fights

3. friendly

4. sneaky

5. dishonest

6. clean

7. good sense of humor

8. pushy

Typical Soviet Youth

Put a check next to all characteristics that are typical of Soviet youth.

1. kind

2. gets in fights

3. friendly

4. sneaky

5. dishonest

6. clean

7. good sense of humor

8. pushy

US/THEM, WAR/PEACE WORKSHEET

Task Card I

Task I

Part A

Interview two adults who have a strong influence on your life.

Explain that you will give them a situation and would like their reaction. It has been proposed that scientists and engineers of the U.S. and the Soviet Union begin to work together on joint space exploration. This would save the U.S. money that then would be spent on domestic programs. The new knowledge and the recognition for new discoveries would be shared equally by the U.S. and Soviet Union. Do you support this proposal? Why or why not?

Write down each person's response on a separate piece of paper.

Part B

1. For the people who opposed the program, what reasons did they give? Did those reasons reflect nationalism? If so, how?

2. For the people who favored the proposal, what reasons did they give? Did they support internationalism? If so, how?

3. One potential source of learning nationalism is from adults who are important to us. How true is this for you? How do you feel about what you learn?

US/THEM, WAR/PEACE WORKSHEET

Task Card II

Task II

Part A

Watch an international sporting event on TV. The Olympics are an excellent example if it's an Olympic year. Compare the time and type of coverage given to U.S. athletes and those of other nations.

Part B

1. How much time, coverage, interviewing, and so forth was given to U.S. athletes? To others? What was the difference?

2. It has been said that the media is the source of learning nationalism. Do your findings support or refute this in terms of sports coverage? How?

US/THEM, WAR/PEACE WORKSHEET

Task Card III

Task III

Part A

Each student gives the following short survey orally to three students and three adults.

How do you think the U.S. ranks among the nations listed in the following areas? (Be careful not to read the answers by mistake!)

Doctors (number of people/ doctor)		Hospital Beds (number of people for each hospital bed)		Infant Mortality (number of deaths of infants under 1 year in 1,000 live births)	
	answer		answer		answer
Belgium	3 (570)	France	5 (180)	Denmark	2 (10.7)
Sweden	4 (600)	Japan	2 (80)	France	4 (13.6)
U.S.A.	5 (620)	Sweden	1 (70)	Japan	3 (10.8)
USSR	1 (360)	U.S.A.	4 (120)	Sweden	1 (8.3)
W. Germany	2 (530)	USSR	3 (100)	U.S.A.	5 (16.1)

Write down their guesses on a separate piece of paper, then tell them the correct rankings. Make a note of their responses when they hear the correct answers.

Part B

1. How close were the guesses (of the persons surveyed) to the correct answers? How do you account for this?

2. How, if at all, did people's feelings of nationalism affect their answers?

3. How does nationalism affect our view of our nation? Other nations?

Task Card IV

Task IV

Part A

1. Go to a department store that sells toys and games. Make a list of any toys or games that have to do with making war—for example, toy tanks, battleship game, and so on. Make a list of toys and games that have to do with peace or solving conflicts through cooperation.

2. Do the same for the toys and games you have at home.

Part B

1. What toys and games were on your war list? Which on your peace list?

2. Which was longer? By how much?

3. Some people believe that one way American children learn to accept militarism is through toys and games. Does your survey prove this to be accurate? How or how not?

4. If so, what should be done about it?

Task Card V

Task V

Part A

Go to an arcade where there are video games. As people play, do a survey and get the following information. What is each game about? What is the goal of the game? Note if games are: (1) competitive or cooperative; (2) focus on war or peace; (3) are violent or nonviolent.

Part B

1. Of all the games you surveyed, how many are competitive? How many are cooperative?

2. How many games involve acts and strategies of warfare? How many involve people working for peace?

3. How many games involve violence? How many involve solving conflict by creative, peaceful means?

JOBS WITH PEACE WORKSHEET

Graph A

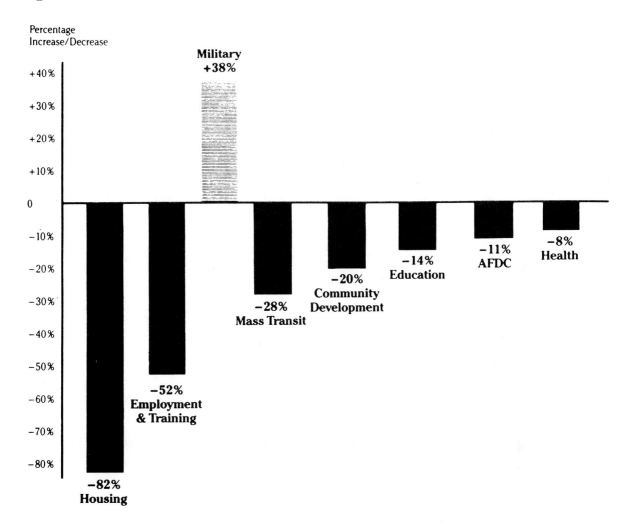

Percentage
Increase/Decrease

Military
+38%

+40%

+30%

+20%

+10%

0

−10%

−20%

−30%

−40%

−50%

−60%

−70%

−80%

−8%
Health

−11%
AFDC

−14%
Education

−20%
Community
Development

−28%
Mass Transit

−52%
Employment
& Training

−82%
Housing

This chart measures how much spending has changed as a result of federal budget policies from fiscal years 1982–86.

Sources:
Military figure based on Department of Defense data, December 1986.
Domestic program estimates, except housing, from "The Republican Record, FY 1982–86," prepared for the American Federation of State, County and Municipal Employees by Fiscal Planning Services, September 1986. All figures based on current service estimates of budget outlays.
Housing figure from the Low Income Housing Information Service based on budget authority data contained in the FY 1987 Budget of the U.S. Government.

Jobs with Peace Campaign,
76 Summer St., Boston, MA 02110.
Copyright © 1987. Used by permission.

Graph B: Your 1987 Federal Income Tax Dollar

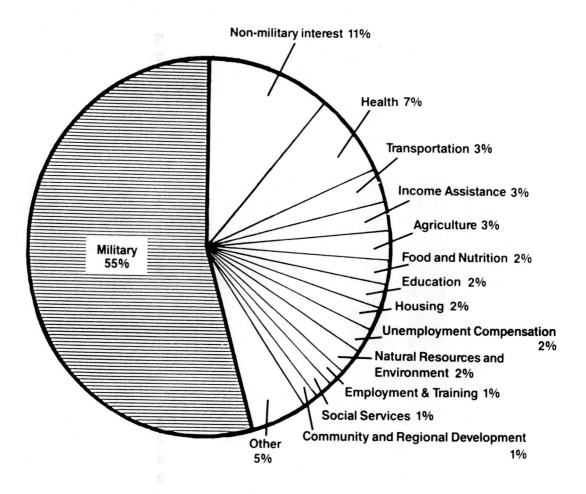

Non-military interest 11%

Health 7%

Transportation 3%

Income Assistance 3%

Agriculture 3%

Food and Nutrition 2%

Education 2%

Housing 2%

Unemployment Compensation 2%

Natural Resources and Environment 2%

Employment & Training 1%

Social Services 1%

Community and Regional Development 1%

Military 55%

Other 5%

This "pie chart" reflects the true division of your 1987 federal income tax dollar. This division looks different than the government's for two reasons:

1. Many military-related costs which are usually kept in separate categories are combined here to reflect the costs of total military spending. These costs include the National Defense Function 050 (37%), military related interest on the debt (13%), veterans (3%), and International Securities Assistance (1%).

2. Revenue from Trust Funds, such as Social Security, has been excluded from the calculation because these are paid for by taxes separate from the income tax.

Source: Calculations based on data contained in FY 1987 Budget of the U.S. Government and FY 1987 Mid-Session Review of the Budget, Office of Management and Budget; Military Spending Research Services.

JOBS WITH PEACE WORKSHEET
Graph A—Questions

1. Between 1982 and 1986 what area has received increased federal funding? Which areas have been cut?

2. What area has received the biggest cut in federal funding? By what percentage?

3. Bob's father is a teacher. He wants to know what percentage increase or decrease there has been in federal funding of education from 1982–86. What can you tell him?

4. Jaime hopes there will be new job training programs so her mother can learn new skills to get a more rewarding and better paying job. If the trend from 1982–86 continues, will Jaime's mother be likely to get new opportunities for job training through federally-funded programs? Support your answer with data.

JOBS WITH PEACE WORKSHEET
Graph B—Questions

1. What percent of each American's tax dollar in 1987 went to support: (a) the military budget, (b) education, (c) food and nutrition, (d) housing?

2. Delores' mother, Ms. Morales, earned $18,000 in 1987. She paid $3,158 in federal income tax. What amount of Ms. Morales' wages went to the military budget? How much went to education and housing combined?

Graph C

This chart examines the relationship between military spending, productivity, and unemployment in six countries from 1960–1978.

"Military Expenditures in GNP" means how much of what a country produces is for the military.

"Annual Rate of Growth in Manufacturing Productivity" means how much increase there is in a country from one year to the next in making products of all kinds.

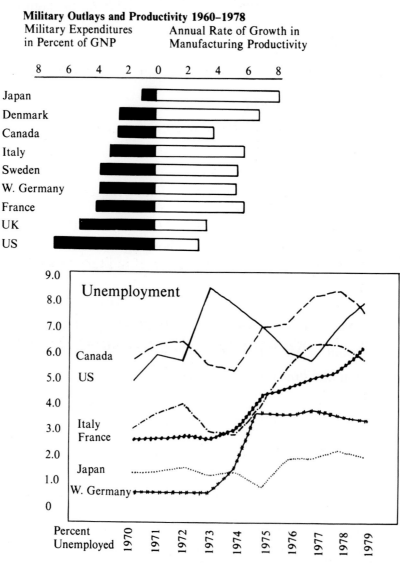

Military Outlays and Productivity 1960–1978
Military Expenditures in Percent of GNP — Annual Rate of Growth in Manufacturing Productivity

From *Guilty and Liking Nuclear War*, 1983.

JOBS WITH PEACE WORKSHEET

Graph C—Questions

1. Which country shows the greatest productivity rates for the years 1960–1978?

2. Which country shows the lowest productivity rate for these years?

3. Which country spends the greatest percentage of its gross national product on the military?

4. Which country spends the lowest percentage on military costs?

The following questions focus on the graph on unemployment statistics for these same countries.

5. Which countries had the lowest rate of unemployment?

6. Which countries had the highest rates of unemployment?

Compare the unemployment rates to the bar graph of military expenditures and rate of productivity growth.

7. Do you see any relationships among the three rates among the six countries? If so, what?

TO BE SECURE WORKSHEET
Situation B

For eight years Morris Leder worked in a factory that made automobiles. A year ago he was laid off and he hasn't been able to find work since. Morris feels scared and insecure because he's afraid he won't be able to support his family. He believes that a real man is a good breadwinner. He feels he's a failure. He doesn't talk to anyone about his feelings.

Morris spends a lot of time with other white men who are out of work. They talk a lot about people of color and women. They blame them for invading the job market. They tell racist and sexist jokes. These hurt other people, but it makes Morris feel better about himself.

1. What ways of thinking, or ways society is organized, keeps Morris from feeling secure?

2. What is the result of this insecurity?

3. How could the insecurity be lessened?

4. What might be the result if these changes came about?

Situation B—continued

1. Did you consider?

The sexist idea that he is a failure if he doesn't have a job keeps Morris from feeling secure. In addition, the way the economic system is organized does this. A competitive, capitalist economic system always has unemployment. There are not enough jobs for all, and people are afraid of losing their jobs and of others who compete with them.

2. Did you consider?

Morris blamed himself for his unemployment and felt terrible about himself. Morris spent a lot of time with other unemployed workers. He took out his frustration at being unemployed on minorities and women.

3. Did you consider?

People could help Morris challenge sexism. They could help him understand that to have—or not have—a job doesn't affect his worth as a man or value as a human being.

People could help Morris stop blaming himself for the fact that he's unemployed. People could help him see that a competitive economic system doesn't provide enough jobs. They could help him and his friends join together to work for changes that would lead to a cooperative economic system that would provide jobs for all people.

4. Did you consider?

Morris would feel secure as a person. He would know he would get a job that would enable him to support his family. He would no longer need to scapegoat women and minorities. He could work together **with** them to bring better conditions for all.

TO BE SECURE WORKSHEET

Situation C

Morris Leder found a job, but it doesn't use his skills and the pay is poor. Deep down, he still feels like a nobody. He's been angry a lot with his wife and kids.

The news of the world is confusing too. Some national leaders talk about the threat of Soviet communism. They say that the communists are trying to take over the world and that America has to protect the "free world." They say that some Americans who want changes in the U.S. are communists.

The fear of the communists taking over makes Morris feel insecure. If that happened, he is afraid he might lose the little he does have. Even if he personally feels like a failure, he can feel proud and worthwhile as an American. He feels Americans are the best people in the world. He feels safer when he supports government leaders who want to make America "secure" by building missiles and intervening in other countries to oppose communists. In fact, he doesn't know much about these communists or the people in the countries the U.S. intervenes in. Nevertheless the feeling that America is tough and strong in the world makes Morris feel a lot better about himself.

1. What ways of thinking or ways society is organized keep Morris from feeling secure?

2. What are the results of this insecurity?

3. How could the insecurity be lessened?

4. What might result if these changes came about?

TO BE SECURE WORKSHEET

Situation C—continued

---

1. Did you consider?

   The way of thinking that says communists are trying to take over the world keeps Morris from feeling secure.

---

2. Did you consider?

   Morris identified with other citizens of a powerful country in order to feel better about himself. He convinced himself Americans were better than other peoples.

   Without clear information, he was willing to blame communists for wanting to take over the world. To make himself feel more secure, he was willing to support some government leaders' programs to build more missiles and intervene in other countries.

---

3. Did you consider?

   Morris could reexamine the idea that communists are trying to take over the world. He could ask how accurate that idea really is. He could examine how that way of thinking can be used to frighten people and make them feel insecure. Morris could learn more about people who are often labeled communists. He could learn more about the kinds of changes they are fighting for, and why.

   If Morris had a job in which he felt dignity, was paid a decent wage, and knew he could keep, he would feel less insecure.

---

4. Did you consider?

   If Morris felt more security and respect in his life and job, he would have less need to feel that Americans are "better than" others. He would have less need to want America to be the nation controlling others. He would be comfortable in a nation that worked cooperatively with others.

   He could feel safe to get more information about peoples in other countries. He could determine where and why communism might be a threat to freedom and where people who wanted justice and equality were simply labeled "communists" so that their efforts toward justice and equality would be blocked.

   Morris might feel less fearful and might think more carefully about a big arms buildup and U.S. intervention in other countries.

TO BE SECURE WORKSHEET

Examining the Threat

1. To what extent does the speech or statement you are examining appeal to peoples' insecurities?

2. What is accurate, and what not accurate, about the threat of the spread of Soviet communism? How does all of that relate to "American Security," or does it?

3. In the statement you examined, who *are* the communists? What do they want to change in their society? Who will these changes help? Who will they hurt?

4. What action is the threat of communism being used to justify? What possible action might be justified by using the threat of communism?

5. Which Americans benefit from such statements and actions? How? Which lose? How?

Signatures _____
_____
_____
_____

WHERE IS MY MONEY GOING? WORKSHEET

Facts about Apartheid Cards

1. The Republic of South Africa is a country where the legal, social, political and economic rights of its citizens are determined by race.

2. If you are black in South Africa, you are not allowed to vote for any member of parliament or play a part in any of your country's national political institutions. The government in your country is mainly white and for whites, even though whites comprise less than 20 percent of your country's population.

3. If you are black in South Africa, you are ineligible for a large number of jobs because they are reserved solely for whites. On the average, you earn one-twelfth the wages that a white person does. You, along with about 85 percent of your fellow blacks, live below the basic starvation level, earning less than $170 a month.

4. If you are black in South Africa, you live under a government that maintains its power by using some of the most severe and brutal forms of police and military repression in the modern world. For example, you may not go into white areas without permission. If you do, you are subject to arrest. You are not allowed to move freely in your own country.

5. There is one doctor for every 455 white people, but if you are black in South Africa, you share your doctor with nearly 50,000 other blacks.

6. More than 350 North American corporations do a booming business in South Africa with investments of more than 1.6 billion dollars. They are attracted by the results of the apartheid system. Apartheid provides cheap labor and has traditionally made possible a profit return of nearly 20 percent compared to a worldwide average of 11 percent.

7. North American corporations like Mobil, General Motors, IBM and Goodyear play a crucial role in maintaining apartheid by providing products and services from North America to South African agencies, including the army and police.

8. Banks lend money not only to corporations for their operations in South Africa, but also directly to the South African government and its state-owned enterprises.

9. One reason South Africa, a rich nation, must borrow millions of dollars is its need to maintain a police and military designed to protect the apartheid government.

WHERE IS MY MONEY GOING? WORKSHEET

Connections to Apartheid

Juan Vega is fifteen and has earned money for the past two summers. He put that money in a bank account in the Metropolitan Bank. Juan Vega now learns that his money is being used by a bank that gives loans to South Africa.

1. What connection is there between Juan Vega and apartheid in South Africa?

2. What do you think Juan should do about this?

3. What would you do if your bank was using your money in ways you thought were wrong?

4. Some American people put pressure on banks to withdraw their money from South Africa. They:
   - write letters to the bank to urge "divestment"—which means that the bank takes its money out of South Africa
   - withdraw deposits from banks that loan money to South Africa
   - organize demonstrations at banks to call attention to the bank's policy
   - organize, or take part in, boycotts of the bank by asking other people and groups to remove their deposits from that bank

   How do you feel about these ideas? Which do you believe might be most effective? Why?

5. What keeps people from seeing the connections between their own money, U.S. banks, and apartheid in South Africa?

6. Who benefits from this "blindness"? Who pays a price?

7. How could our actions regarding American bank policies build cooperation between Americans and the oppressed black people in South Africa? What changes might come about?

THE MESSAGE IN OUR TEXTS WORKSHEET

Textbook Analysis

Name of Text _____

Analyze the text and try to answer these questions. Give examples to support your analysis.

Conventional War

1. Does the text challenge the legitimacy of war as a way of resolving disputes?

2. Does the text suggest that public funds spent on arms reduce funds for human needs?

3. Does the text glamorize acts of war and U.S. war leaders?

4. Does the text explain the military-industrial complex? If so, how is it portrayed?

Nuclear War

5. Does the text convey the devastating effects of the Hiroshima and Nagasaki bombings?

Textbook Analysis—continued

6. Does the text comment on the fact that the first use of the atomic bomb was against people of color?

7. Does the text justify the bombings of Hiroshima and Nagasaki?

8. Does the text report on and question U.S. threats—since Hiroshima—to the use of nuclear bombs?

9. Is the buildup of nuclear overkill arsenals by the U.S. and the U.S.S.R. presented?

10. Does the text show the nuclear buildup as connected to increasing threats of nuclear war?

11. Does the text discuss arms limitation agreements?

Anti-War and Anti-Nuclear Movements

12. Are the anti-war and anti-nuclear protest movements presented in the text? If so, how?

Sadako and the Thousand Paper Cranes

1. What were some of the feelings you felt while you read the story of Sadako?

2. If you were Sadako, or one of the many other children who suffered from leukemia, how would you have felt knowing you had leukemia caused by the atom bomb?

3. How would you have felt as one of Sadako's friends? How would you try to be supportive of her?

4. How did the cranes help Sadako in her fight with leukemia?

5. Sadako died in 1955. What gifts can you give her now?

Research Group Tasks: Tree Project

---

1. Information Gathering

Who in your community knows where trees are being lost or deforestation is taking place? What kind of trees are best to plant in these areas? Do research in the library. Then talk to informed people and gather needed information.

---

2. Beautification Sites

What public places—like your school, other schools, the district's offices, town hall, etc.—have need for more trees on their land? Are there town open spaces or parks in need of trees? Talk to appropriate people and research needed information.

---

3. Network Building

What other groups or individuals in your community are concerned with tree planting? Can you get their help? What other organizations might be interested in supporting the Tree Project?

---

4. Contributions

What individuals, organizations or businesses might contribute trees to the Tree Project? How else can you get contributions to buy the trees you need?

---

5. Community Education about the Tree Project

How can you explain to people why you are implementing the Tree Project? How can you best educate them about the problem of worldwide deforestation?

---

6. Community Education about the Importance of Trees

How can you make people aware of the importance of trees in your community? What kinds of publications, talks, school programs could be planned?

POEMS FOR PEACE WORKSHEET

Communicate through Poetry!

A. "What If?"

What If . . . they dropped the bomb?
What If . . . they hit the ground?
What If . . . the people screamed?
What Scars . . . the fallout leaves

What If . . . the people cried?
What If . . . they started to die?
What If . . . they rebuilt towns?
What Dreams . . . these people have

What If . . . the meager few?
What If . . . the remaining two?
What If . . . the standing two?
What Ways . . . they spent their last days?

Greg Holden,
Poughkeepsie, NY,
Arlington Middle School.

1. What are your feelings after you read this poem?

2. What does the poet believe would be the effect of a nuclear war? How do you know?
   Give examples from the poem.

Communicate through Poetry!—continued

B. "What If?"

What if, all countries went to war,
would we live, would anyone live at all?
What if we did live,
how long could we survive?
Would we really want to?
I don't know.
War is such an ugly word,
full of hate and fear,
fear of dying, fear of the unknown,
fear of future years.
What if it was an accident?
How could we know?
Would we be able to stop it,
or would all the cities go?
Russians, those dirty commies,
always starting trouble,
Americans, on a moments notice,
they are there on the double.
At least, that's what our government
wants us to believe.
That we don't start any of the trouble.
What if ordinary everyday people
made up the governments,
People rich and poor, middle class,
and many more,
Would we get more done,
Would people have more fun,
enjoying life a little more,
All because there is no threat of a
nuclear war?
The threat is there,
very much alive,
Is everyone waiting for the moment to die?
The threat of nuclear war is like a cancer,
it grows and grows and grows,
If you look closely you can see
it in the crystals of a new fallen snow.
It is everywhere, hanging over our
heads, just waiting,
waiting to be shed.

Rae-Ellen Gardner,
Poughkeepsie, NY,
Arlington Middle School.

Communicate through Poetry!—continued

1. What thoughts and feelings do you have after reading this poem?

2. What does the poet suggest as one of the causes of the threat of nuclear war?

3. What does the poet suggest as a way to lessen the threat of nuclear war?

Communicate through Poetry!—continued

C. "General"

General, your tank is a mighty vehicle.

It shatters the forest and crushes a hundred men.

But it has one defect:

It needs drivers.

General, your bomber is awesome.

It flies faster than a hurricane and bears more than an elephant

But it has one defect,

It needs mechanics.

General, a man is quite expendable.

He can fly, he can kill.

But he has one defect:

He can think.

Bertolt Brecht
(translation by Boykin Reynolds
from *Gedichte,* vol. 4).

1. What feelings and thoughts do you have after you read this poem?

2. In society, generals have a lot of power. Who, according to the poet, has even more power? How?

3. What is the poet's answer for dealing with the threat of war?

Peer Feedback

Author's Name _____

Title _____

Your Name _____

_____

Things I liked about this piece of writing:

I liked _____

I liked _____

I liked _____

_____

Things I wondered about this piece:

I wondered _____

I wondered _____

I wondered _____

_____

My suggestions:

Things to add _____

Things to delete _____

Things to strengthen _____

Information Sheet A: Live Simply So Others May Simply Live

If Americans lived more simply, other peoples of the world could have more. Dr. Paul Erlich has noted that the average U.S. citizen has roughly fifty times the negative impact on the earth's non-renewable resources as the average citizen of India.

A group of people who wanted to live more simply decided to live together in a reconstructed Shaker village in Harrodsburg, Kentucky. They described that, "A number of us were personally moved by the global poverty/ecological crisis we saw all around us and we covenanted together to reduce our levels of consumption, to share our personal wealth with the world's poor, and to work for a new social order in which all people have equal access to the resources they need."

Their agreement became known as the Shakertown pledge. A few parts of the pledge are described below.

1. I declare myself a world citizen. Citizens should develop a generous and loyal devotion to their country, but without any narrowing of mind. In other words, they must always look simultaneously to the welfare of the whole human family, which is tied together by the manifold bonds linking races, peoples, and nations.

    As world citizens they committed themselves to some of the kinds of projects described in this lesson.

2. I will choose my work with care and avoid jobs that cause harm to others.

3. I commit myself to leading a life of creative simplicity and share my personal wealth with the world's poor.

For this project students can decide on ways to live more simply. The money saved can then be donated to an organization working to help people of the world. One such organization is Oxfam American (115 Broadway, Boston, MA 02116), a group that provides resources to help the world's hungry become more self-sufficient.

Some ideas are:

• Cutting down on snacks. Calculate how much students spend each week, month, year on snacks. What's the result?

• Creating inexpensive entertainment rather than going out and paying for a movie or other entertainment

• Buying a record or tape as a group and sharing it, rather than each person buying one

Generate ideas yourself and pick the best ones to suggest to the class.

Information Sheet B: Third World Products

Handicrafts and clothing that are made by self-help producer cooperatives and families in the Third World can be sold by individuals and groups in the U.S. The money from the sales is then returned to the people who made the goods. This is different from a typical store where products are bought very cheaply and most profit goes to companies involved.

These handmade items are "labor intensive" which means they take little or no tools to produce and can provide those who have the greatest need with a meaningful and dignified way to earn an income.

The United States Union of Third World Shoppes is a group that coordinates such sales. All products sold through them are researched carefully to insure that the producers receive fair prices for their labor. They buy from producer cooperatives around the world, directly importing items for sale here. The Union of Third World Shoppes has members in towns and cities across the country. Write to them at 611 West Wayne St., Fort Wayne, Indiana 46802 for a list. Another source of Third World items is Alternatives, P.O. Box 539, Ellenwood, Georgia 30049.

For this project you can write to the groups above and get a list of shops and products. You will decide what to buy and how to sell the products. You will want to try to get information about the people who made the products you sell. You'll design a flyer to distribute with the product, containing information about your class project, why you are supporting Third World products, and details about the lives of the people who made the products.

Information Sheet C: Pairing Project

This project is based on the assumption that people across the earth are part of one global family. What many people lack are concrete experiences to help them remember that fact. Through this project you will have the opportunity to create a pairing project with a group of people in a Third World nation who are working for social justice. When people have a deep feeling that they belong to a global family they will be more likely to take risks and work to support members of that family.

A useful resource for this project is a booklet, "Solidarity with the People of Nicaragua and Peru," by James McGinnis. Write to the Institute for People and Justice (4144 Lindell, #400, St. Louis, Missouri 63108) if you decide to do this project. In this booklet you will learn about six groups of people in Peru or Nicaragua who are working for change. For example, some of the groups are youth groups working in the neighborhoods to improve their communities.

For this project, you will select a group of people with whom you can be paired. See the McGinnis book or make other contacts in your community. You will gather materials about yourselves to send to that group. You will write letters, send pictures, and share what you learn about your Third World friends with others in your community through talks, the newspaper, and so forth. You might write letters to U.S. government officials to give them accurate information about the situations of these Third World partners and ask for support for policies that will support their rights to self-determination. The correspondence and support involved in this project would be long-term. You might also want to share resources with the people with whom you're paired. If you choose to implement this project, you'd want to make a commitment to continue after the end of the school year.

ACTING AS GLOBAL CITIZENS WORKSHEET

Information Sheet D: Boycott

One way to support our global neighbors is to participate in boycotts of products and companies that are harmful to people in other parts of the world.

For example, in a previous lesson, you learned that many U.S. banks lend money to the South African government. This helps support their racism and their apartheid regime. This is wrong. Many Americans boycott these banks by withdrawing their money. When enough people and institutions do this, the pressure can encourage such banks to stop lending to South Africa.

Other examples have included: (1) A 1984–85 national boycott of Coca-Cola in support of Guatemalan workers. Coca-Cola deliberately let one of its Guatemalan plants go bankrupt because workers were trying to organize a union. (2) National boycotts of companies that have huge Pentagon contracts, especially those companies that make nuclear weapons. The national boycott of General Electric is one such example. (3) A U.S. and international boycott of Nestles Chocolate Company stopped that company from selling more infant formula to people in Africa. The formula was harmful to their babies' health.

Write for the newsletter *Grapevine* (P.O. Box 1319, Ames, Iowa 50010) for a listing of the current boycotts in the U.S. Check the newspaper, church groups, and local labor organizations for other sources of information about current boycotts.

If you choose to do this project, you will select a boycott that is supportive of people, in other parts of the world, who are being hurt by products or policies of U.S. companies and organizations, and/or by policies of the U.S. government. You will gather information about the boycott and write information sheets to distribute to friends and neighbors. You can write articles for the local newspapers. You can talk to local stores and institutions that use or sell the boycotted product and ask them to join the boycott until the unjust practice ceases.

Songs for World Peace

It Could Be a Wonderful World

Lyrics by HY ZARET

Music by LOU SINGER

2. If there were no poor and the rich were content;
   if strangers were welcome wherever they went;
   If each of us knew what true brotherhood meant;
   it could be a wonderful world. (Refrain)

Songs for World Peace—continued

Dona Nobis Pacem

Source Unknown
Moderato

3-part Canon

Do - na no - bis pa - cem, pa-cem; do - na

Translation: Give to us peace.

no - bis pa - cem. Do - na no - bis

pa-cem; do - na no-bis pa - cem. Do - na

no - bis pa-cem; do - na no-bis pa - cem.

Shalom Chaverim (Glad Tidings)

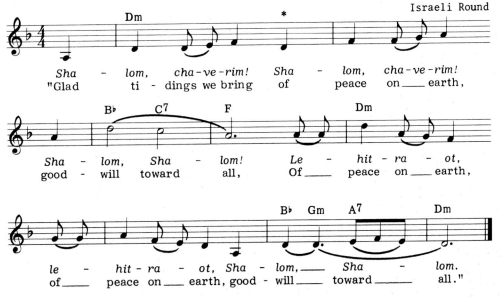

Israeli Round

Sha - lom, cha-ve-rim! Sha - lom, cha-ve-rim!
"Glad ti - dings we bring of peace on earth,

Sha - lom, Sha - lom! Le - hit - ra - ot,
good - will toward all, Of peace on earth,

le - hit - ra - ot, Sha - lom, Sha - lom.
of peace on earth, good - will toward all."

Traditional Hebrew round.
English lyric and New Music arrangement by Paul Campbell.
TRO—© Copyright 1951 and renewed 1979.
Folkways Music Publishers, Inc., New York, N.Y.
Used by permission.

Songs for World Peace—continued

Study War No More

I'm gonna lay down my burden, down by the riverside....
I'm gonna walk with the Prince of Peace, down by the riverside....
I'm gonna join hands with everyone, down by the riverside....

Negro spiritual.
Choral arrangements by Al Moss.

Songs for World Peace—continued

Last Night I Had the Strangest Dream

1. Last night I had the strang - est dream, I
nev - er dreamed be - fore. I dreamed the world had
all a - greed to put an end to war, I
dreamed I saw a might - y room, The room was full of
men. And the pap - er they were sign - ing
said, They'd nev - er fight a - gain.

2. And when that paper was all signed,
And a million copies made;
They all joined hands and bowed their heads,
And grateful prayers were prayed.
And people in the street below
Were dancing round and round.
And guns and swords and uniforms
Lay scattered on the ground.

Words and Music by Ed McCurdy.
TRO—© Copyright 1950 (renewed 1978), 1951 (renewed 1979) and 1955 (renewed 1983)
Almanac Music, Inc., New York, N.Y.
Used by permission.

Songs for World Peace—continued

Song of Peace

Lloyd Stone

FINLANDIA

Jean Sibelius

1. This is my song, O God of all the na-tions,_____ A song of
2. My coun-try's skies are blu-er than the o-cean,_____ And sun-light

peace for lands a-far and mine;_____ This is my
beams on clo-ver-leaf and pine._____ But oth-er

home, the coun-try where my heart is,_____ Here are my hopes, my
lands have sun-light, too, and clo-ver,_____ And skies are ev-'ry-

dreams, my ho-ly shrine;_____ But oth-er hearts in oth-er lands are
where as blue as mine._____ O hear my song, thou God of all the

beat-ing_____ With hopes and dreams as true and high as mine._____
na-tions,_____ A song of peace for their land and for mine._____

Songs for World Peace—continued
The United Nations

The sun and the stars all are ringing,
With songs rising from the earth.
The hope of humanity singing,
A hymn to a new world in birth.

Refrain:
United Nations on the march with
    flags unfurl'd,
Together work for victory, a Free New World.
(*Repeat.*)

Take heart all you nations swept under,
By powers of darkness that ride,
The wrath of the people shall thunder,
Relentless as time and the tide.—*Ref.*

As sure as the sun meets the morning,
And rivers go down to the sea,
A new day for mankind is dawning,
Our children shall live proud and free!—*Ref.*

Refrain:
United Nations on the march with
    flags unfurl'd,
Together work for victory, a Free New World.

Music by Shostakovich and words by Harold Rome. From the songbook of Highlander
Folk School, Monteagle, Tennessee.

RESOURCES

TEACHING FORMATS FOR COOPERATIVE LEARNING

These teaching formats describe various approaches for structuring cooperative learning. Lessons using each of the formats can be found in the activity chapters of this book. By becoming familiar with the variety of formats, and the advantages and disadvantages of each, you can choose or develop cooperative lessons appropriate for your students and your educational goals.

1. PARTNERS

COOPERATION HO!

a. Description
One student works with another to accomplish a joint task.

b. Teacher Preparation
Minimal preparation and materials are needed, as materials are those for a normal lesson.

c. Advantages
- Partnership is a very effective way to introduce students to cooperative learning. It is a simple, manageable format.
- Partners can be used at one time for all students or partners can work together at any time during the day.

d. Disadvantage
Students gain the expertise and support of only one other student.

2. PEER TEACHING

a. Description
A student works with another to teach a skill or review material. Students are divided carefully to assure that the peer teacher is competent in both understanding and conveying the skill or information being taught. This format may also be used with small groups.

b. Teacher Preparation
Minimal preparation and materials are needed, as materials are those for a normal lesson.

c. Advantages
- Peer teaching can be structured at one time for all students or can be flexibly used by partners at any time throughout the day.
- It builds skills that are part of the standard curriculum.
- Self-concept enhancement and inherent satisfaction are developed by investing in another person, especially by students who are perceived as poor students.
- Both students make academic gains, since by teaching, students better learn the content itself. A variety of student skills can be affirmed.

d. Disadvantage
If not planned with care, academically-skilled students will do all the teaching; therefore, vary topics and approaches so **all** students are in the teaching role.

3. GROUP PROJECT

a. Description
Students work cooperatively in small groups to create a project or complete a task by pooling their skills and knowledge. The activity is structured so all participate by virtue of division of tasks or roles.

b. Teacher Preparation

Collect materials or information and prepare clear instructions.

c. Advantages

- Better ideas and a higher order of thinking and creativity come from a group.
- It's possible for everyone to play an important role and share the result.
- Usually students have worked in groups before, so they're used to it.
- Results are often visible and can be shared with others and remembered.

d. Disadvantages

- Without careful processing and task or role assignment, one person could take over or "sit out."
- Students with more skills in the area or more knowledge of the topic may take more responsibility than others.

4. CLASS PROJECT

a. Description

Students work together as a class to create a project or complete a task by pooling their learning and labor.

b. Teacher Preparation

Collect materials and have a very clear plan for organizing a large group.

c. Advantages

- Results are usually very impressive and can be shared with others and looked back on.
- Students develop a feeling of cohesion as a class.

d. Disadvantages

- Without careful organization or a clear process for division of labor, it can become confusing and overwhelming.
- Without a plan for student responsibility for each other, some students can get lost.

5. JIGSAW

a. Description

Students are divided into groups and each is assigned information that is necessary for the group to complete its task. Everyone must contribute for the group to be successful.

b. Teacher Preparation

Preparation is significant; the teacher must divide up or make up packets of material. In some cases, rewriting may be involved if material is too difficult for some students.

c. Advantages

- Shy students are involved, and dominant students can't take control of the group.
- A lesson can be structured according to academic levels of the students.
- The jigsaw is particularly appropriate for heterogeneous classes.
- The fact that the whole group is accountable is very clear.
- Once materials are prepared, they can be used year after year.

d. Disadvantage

If the material isn't structured so all students can succeed, some students will be unable to take their responsibility for the group. Therefore, it is important that a teacher know the skill level of each student.

6. CROSS-AGE PROJECTS

a. **Description**

Students in an upper grade plan and implement projects or activities to do with students in younger grades. Activities may also involve teaching skills.

b. **Teacher Preparation**

Some time is needed training older students in order to make it a positive experience.

c. **Advantages**
- Older students gain satisfaction and pride, younger ones feel special.
- Cross-age projects can become ongoing.
- Cross-age cooperative projects and activities are valuable for enhancing schoolwide cooperation.

d. **Disadvantages**
- Scheduling can present some problems. Work out well in advance.
- If older students are not well-trained, their impact on younger students may not be helpful.

7. LEARNING CENTER

a. **Description**

Students move in groups to complete cooperative tasks at various learning centers.

b. **Teacher Preparation**

There is substantial initial time and material investment in preparing centers and task cards. Once prepared, they can be used again and again.

c. **Advantages**
- Different learning styles of students can be reflected in different centers.
- There is a wide variety of activities.
- Since students can be expected to complete only some of the centers, the centers can be assigned or chosen according to the needs of student groups.
- Students physically move around the room, stimulating both body and mind.
- This format is particularly well-suited to interdisciplinary lessons.

d. **Disadvantages**
- Noise level can be high.
- If the task at each center doesn't take approximately the same amount of time, some students will be frustrated if they finish first and others annoyed if they have to move on before they are done.
- The teacher can't be in more than one place at a time, so directions must be very clear.

8. BOARD GAMES

a. **Description**

Students work together to play a cooperative board game on subject matter they are studying. They win or lose as a group.

b. **Teacher Preparation**

Substantial time and thought goes into preparation of cooperative board games. Once prepared, they last for many years.

c. **Advantages**
- Board games provide a different way of looking at something familiar. They appeal to students with learning styles that are visual and interactive.
- Board games can be picked up and re-used during the year as free-time activity. They are fun and creative.
- Different sets of cards can be substituted for different subject matter areas while using the same board and rules.
- Students can make up their own cards and create their own games.

d. **Disadvantages**
- Stimulating, cooperative games that are played again and again take creativity to design. It helps if they contain an element of humor.
- If the game is open-ended rather than having correct answers, a teacher is needed to monitor it (for example, rhyming work).

9. COOPERATIVE CARD GAMES

a. Description

Rules for card games that students know can be adapted to various subject matter areas and structured cooperatively. Adaptable games include Concentration, Card Couple, Rummy, Double Solitaire.

b. Teacher Preparation

Substantial initial time is needed to prepare the cards.

c. Advantages
- The same card game directions can be used with different content.
- A few students can play when an individual activity is needed in the school day.
- Card games can be assigned according to what students need practice in.
- Students can make up new games for different subject areas.
- Rather than having individual winners, the group wins. For example, using Concentration rules, the group wins when all cards are matched or the group times itself to see how quickly it can make all matches.

d. Disadvantage

It is difficult to make up cooperative card games that motivate older students.

10. TREASURE HUNT

a. Description

Teams working independently of each other follow a series of clues involving use of subject matter being studied. The final clues of each team are pooled or a puzzle using each group's final clue is solved to gain a "treasure" for all.

b. Teacher Preparation

Substantial preparation goes into preparing clues and hiding them in the right place. Be especially clear on which clues follow which. The process of preparation can be creative, if you're not overly pressured for time.

c. Advantages
- This is a novel, involving format.
- It is highly motivating for the individual, the teams, and the whole group.

d. Disadvantages
- Unless structured carefully, it's easy for one person to take over.
- Noise

11. RESEARCH PROJECTS

a. Description

Students work cooperatively on a research project using either the library or human resources for the research. Tasks are sometimes assigned in a jigsaw manner. The compilation of results and analysis is a comprehensive group effort.

b. Teacher Preparation

Preparation involves assuring the availability of adequate materials.

c. Advantages
- Research projects can appeal to different skills if designed well. Both in-depth library research, and "people research" can be used.
- Research projects are educationally-challenging to students with different learning styles and skills.
- Problem solving in this manner can be synergistic and creative.
- Students learn skills that can be applied to their later schooling.

d. Disadvantages
- If topic is not chosen well and groups assigned carefully, students with more knowledge on the topic can take over.
- Lack of appropriate resources can hamper the research with difficult topics or in small districts.

EVALUATION FORMATS FOR COOPERATIVE LEARNING

A. CONTENT FORMATS _____

Content formats are ways to evaluate learning of the subject matter or the substantive material of the lesson. Also, when grading is desired, content formats can be used. These formats are distinguished from the four broad models of cooperative learning described in Chapter 2. These more specific approaches for structuring a lesson, delineated by the authors, are often used within the framework of one or more of the more generic models.

CATEGORY I— GROUP PRODUCT— GROUP GRADE

GROUP PRODUCT OR ANSWER—GROUP GRADE

Description

Students work together as a group to learn content or to develop a project. There is one group result: such as a worksheet, report, or project. As with all methods of evaluation, and especially important for this one, clear criteria for the evaluation are stated at the outset.

Advantages

- Students gain motivation from being part of a group effort.
- It is a low-threat method for students lacking confidence.
- Students with poor skills or low self-confidence take risks to learn and they become more confident when successful as part of a group.
- It's an effective method for students who learn least well under pressure.

Disadvantages

- The learning task should be one that is structured for individual involvement and accountability; otherwise, it is possible for students to "drop out" and not participate fully.
- This evaluation format doesn't **guarantee** individual accountability for each other's work. The task structure of the learning activity must do that.

Example

Step III in the lesson, "Competition and Cooperation: What's to Gain? What's to Lose?" (Chapter 4, page 88) contains an activity culminating in a worksheet.

Students are told at the outset that the worksheet they hand in will be evaluated. The criteria considered will be that: (1) It is complete; (2) It has correct information; (3) It contains thoughtful responses; (4) It includes creative alternatives; (5) All group members have rotated writing worksheet answers; and (6) The worksheet is correct in terms of spelling, punctuation, and grammar.

The teacher evaluates the worksheet either with a ✓, ✓+, ✓− system or a standard letter grade. Each student in the group receives the group grade.

CATEGORY II— CONTRACT GRADING

Contract-grading enables groups to contract for a grade based on the amount of work accomplished. Students get credit for **completing** the assignment in line with specific criteria spelled out in advance. They are not evaluated for specific content information. Since students in one group can do varied tasks, this is a jigsaw approach to grading. It is particularly useful for projects.

a. GROUP CONTRACT—INDIVIDUALIZED WORK

Description

The group **as a whole** contracts for a grade. Within the group, tasks are divided according to interest and ability. Group members check each other's work to make sure it is correct, imaginative, thoughtful, or says what they want to say. The group receives the grade for which it contracted when each group member has satisfactorily completed his or her part of the task and other group members have given feedback.

Advantages

- This allows for individual differences in skills and interests.
- High energy and motivation are typical because of the variety of tasks from which to choose.
- Work can be divided according to ability.
- Knowing that an activity won't be accepted unless it's well done motivates students to do satisfactory work.

Disadvantage

- There is less cooperation than in other methods.

Example

The lesson "Bread and Roses" (Chapter 5, page 168) lends itself to this format. This lesson contains five learning-center projects. Each project is worth ten points.

a.	"Letters from Angelina" worksheet (All students must complete this.)	_____ 10 points
b.	"Bread and Roses" picket sign	_____ 10 points
c.	"Prices and Profit" math problems	_____ 10 points
d.	"News Tonight" tape recording (All students are needed to work on this activity.)	_____ 10 points
e.	"Solidarity Forever" stanza	_____ 10 points

Students decide as a group on the grade to contract for. 50 points = A; 40 points = B; 30 points = C. All students must begin with task A. All students are needed if the group chooses to work on task D. Otherwise, students divide up the other projects. Students must work with one other person on each project. The group receives its grade based on the number of points earned. Each member receives the grade of the group.

b. INDIVIDUAL CONTRACT—GROUP WORK

Description

Students are grouped heterogeneously to complete a project or task. As individuals, they contract to complete a certain amount of work for a particular grade. All students' work, whatever the amount, contributes to the group project. Students check each other's work to make sure it is correct, thorough and thoughtful. Each student must complete her part of the assignment in order for the group to receive its grade.

Advantages

- Students work to their potential while contributing to the efforts of a heterogeneous group.
- This method respects individual choice.
- When working in partners, students may be encouraged to strive for a higher grade than they would on their own.

Disadvantages

- Students who contract for a lower grade contribute less to the final group product.
- It doesn't encourage as much group cohesiveness as other methods.

Suggestion

If the contract grade is determined by quantity of work, materials can be individualized to different levels so slower students can contract for a high grade.

Example

This format applies to "Check Out Those Books" (Chapter 5, page 159). The group task is to complete a report on cooperation and competition in books. For an A, a student analyzes eight stories; for a B, six stories; and for a C, four stories. All work together to complete a project which includes individual analyses.

As an alternative, students can work together in heterogeneous partnerships. For example, a strong reader reads to a weak one and both do the analyses. They contract as partners for a grade. Since all students have the same amount of time, those contracting for a higher grade may need to take work home or use free time in school.

This example has all students doing the same type of work. Work can be individualized depending on the student. The quantity or type of analysis could, for example, be different.

CATEGORY III— INDIVIDUAL ACCOUNTABILITY FOR GROUP RESULT

Those evaluation formats build in accountability to the group for an individual's own learning and for each of the other group member's learning. These formats are particularly useful for assessing specific content-learning. Such formats incorporate significant academic and peer pressure. They add an element of comparison to the evaluation since one group member's learning is compared to others.

a. INDIVIDUAL QUIZ—GROUP GRADE

OPTION 1: Average of Individual and Group

Description

Students work in small groups to learn content information. When the group is satisfied that everyone knows the material, a quiz or worksheet is given to each individual. Those grades are averaged to determine a group grade. An individual's final grade is an average of the group grade and his own grade.

Advantages

- It encourages hard work by skilled, but unmotivated students.
- It provides information about the skill level of each student when you need to assess that for educational reasons.
- There is strong incentive to help others learn the material.

Disadvantages

- It can put undue pressure on a low-skilled student who is motivated, doing her best, and nevertheless does poorly, if the task is not structured to meet her academic level.
- It encourages comparison of grades.

Suggestion

Use larger groups with this method so if one low-skilled, motivated student pulls the group down, it won't affect the group as much.

Improvement Scores

An even fairer way to grade individual quizzes is through the use of improvement scores, advocated by Robert Slavin and others. Student individual quiz scores are compared to the student's own pre-quiz average and points are given based on improvement. This can be integrated into any evaluation method that uses quizzes. Its main disadvantage is it demands time on the part of the teacher to do periodic averaging.

OPTION 2: Group Average

Description

Students work together as a group to learn content material. When they are sure that everyone understands, each person is given an individual quiz or worksheet. The scores are averaged. The group average is the grade for each person in the group.

Advantages

- Advantages of Option 1 plus:
- A slower student has a better chance of doing well and building confidence.

Disadvantages

- Disadvantages of Option 1 plus:
- Students might rely on other group members to pull up their scores.

OPTION 3: Lowest Grade

Description

Students work together to learn common material. The grade of all individuals in the group is the lowest grade received by any member.

Advantages

- Advantages of Option 1 plus:
- Particularly strong motivation for able students to help less able. Often there are very dramatic results in the learning of the less able.

Disadvantage

- This method places a great deal of pressure on students with significant learning problems. Therefore use this method judiciously.

Example

The lesson, "New Ways to Work" (Chapter 5, page 161) could be evaluated with this format. Assume groups of four students. Students would be told that after they complete the lesson they would take a quiz. The quiz will have questions both on the factual information presented on "A Woman's Factory Worksheet" and on the specific items on the "Question Worksheet."

A Sample Quiz

1. Where is McCaysville Industries located?
2. Who owns McCaysville Industries?
3. Why did McCaysville Industries start?
4. Who is the janitor at McCaysville Industries?
5. What happens if a worker's child is sick?
6. How is the profit divided at McCaysville Industries?
7. What are two feelings women at McCaysville have about their workplace?
8. 9. 10. Name three examples of cooperation at McCaysville Industries.

Quiz grades would be averaged in one of the following ways.

OPTION 1: Average of Individual and Group

Individual grades are averaged and each student receives the average of the group's grade and her own.

Sally—100	group average = 92.5	Sally's grade—100
Bob—80		group average—92.5
Jose—90		Sally's grade—96.25
Liana—100		

OPTION 2: Group Average

Each student receives the average grade of the group.
Sally's grade—92.5

OPTION 3: Lowest Grade

Each student gets the lowest grade received by any group member.
Sally's grade—80

b. ORAL RESPONSE—GROUP GRADE

Description

Students work together as a group to find an answer to a problem or to complete a project. When the group feels confident that they have a solution or have successfully completed a worksheet, they make sure that **each** group member understands how they came to those answers and that each is able to explain the answers to someone else. The teacher chooses any group member to explain the group's answer. This may be done in small groups or in the large class discussion. The group is evaluated according to that response.

Advantages

• It provides motivation for students to make sure that everyone understands the lesson well.
• It encourages communication between group members.
• It encourages students to ask when they don't understand something.

Disadvantages

- It is difficult for the teacher to monitor all students' learning.
- If the teacher doesn't stress that it's the group and not the individual who's responsible if someone doesn't know the answer, the individual who gets the information wrong can be scapegoated by the group.

Example

In the activity "Moving" (Chapter 6, page 255), a group of four students has read a dialogue and completed a worksheet. Tell them to review the information on the worksheet to make sure everyone knows the answers well enough to speak for the group.

The teacher tells students she will ask five questions of each group. The questions will be based on the worksheet. Scoring is as follows: five correct response = ✓+ or A; four correct responses = ✓ or B; three correct responses = ✓− or C; and fewer than three correct = unsatisfactory or F. After five responses, the group score is tabulated and each member receives that grade.

c. INDIVIDUAL WORK—GROUP FEEDBACK—GROUP GRADE

Description

Students work individually on a task. They exchange papers with other group members and give each other feedback according to stated criteria. Individuals revise their own work based on the feedback. Grades of individuals are averaged into a group grade that each person receives.

Advantages

- Students get practice being constructively critical of each other's work.
- It encourages students who aren't normally motivated to rewrite their work to do so.

Disadvantage

- Students may feel pressure to make changes in their work that they wouldn't ordinarily choose to make.

Example

In the lesson, "Freedom Farm Cooperative" (Chapter 5, page 162), students have individually answered a question about Fannie Lou Hamer and the Freedom Farm Cooperative. Students exchange papers with a partner and each checks the other's work for content and spelling, punctuation, and grammar. They return papers to each other. Individuals may revise their own work if convinced to do so. Individual papers are corrected and a group average determined. Each student receives that grade.

B. PROCESS FORMATS _____

Process formats are methods to evaluate student progress on cooperative skills used in a lesson. Process formats can also be used to grade students.

**CATEGORY I—
PROCESS
OBSERVER**

Process observer formats use a student observer's notes of member behavior to evaluate group improvement on a cooperative skill.

a. PROCESS OBSERVER—SKILL IMPROVEMENT AS A GROUP

Description

A process observer is a student who watches the group interaction. She makes notes of a cooperative skill the group is working on, and reports her observations back to the group. Talk with students about the cooperative skill the process observer is watching for so they concentrate on that during their group task.

Advantages

• Conscious attempts at new group behaviors, even if initially only for a grade, often lead students to internalize these behaviors.
• Process observer gains skill in observing the group.

Disadvantages

• The process observer doesn't get to participate.
• Students may give the process observer a "hard time" if they are very much concerned with high grades.

Example

Students have been assigned a cooperatively-structured activity that involves group discussion. The cooperative skill the students are working on is—not interrupting others. A process observer is chosen. Each time someone in the group interrupts, the process observer makes a check on her chart. The group gets one point each time someone interrupts. At the end of the discussion, the group is graded—0–1 points A, 2–4 B, 5 or over C.

b. PROCESS OBSERVER—SKILL IMPROVEMENT AS INDIVIDUALS

Description

A process observer makes a list of all persons in the group and observes and notes a specific behavior for each. The easiest method is to observe the same cooperative skill for all—for example, giving an opinion. For the group to receive certain grades, each person must show that behavior a specified number of times. Using a more individualized method, the observer lists a different cooperative skill for each member. These are also recorded on a checklist. The group grade reflects each member's use of the skill.

Advantages

• Quiet students feel special incentive to participate.
• Vocal students encourage others to take part.

Disadvantages

• Students may contribute "for the sake of contributing."
• It may produce stilted conversations.

Suggestions

Use this format when the task is one in which all students can make informed suggestions or one that is creative enough so anyone's idea is okay. Set up the point system so the good grades are achievable, especially the first time you use this method. Subsequently, make the grading scale more difficult.

Example

Students have been assigned a cooperatively-structured activity. The cooperative skill being practiced is "sharing ideas and opinions." A process observer in each group writes down the names of the members and checks off each time (up to five) that a person gives an idea or suggestions for the project. The group grade for cooperation is as follows.

> If everyone gives an idea or opinion once or twice—C
> If everyone gives an idea or opinion three or four times—B
> If everyone gives an idea or opinion five or more times—A

c. PROCESS OBSERVER—CHANGING UNHELPFUL SKILLS THROUGH FEEDBACK

Description

In this method, helpful group behaviors are defined as **making changes** in unhelpful behaviors that the group has defined for itself. The group grade reflects their effectiveness in avoiding or changing unhelpful behavior.

Advantages

- In a structured setting students are learning to give each other feedback.
- Students are being encouraged to **change** a nonproductive behavior.
- Students are very interdependent in watching for and developing cooperative skills.

Disadvantage

- Sometimes it's hard for the process observer to define a behavior and/or clearly label it. Perceptions sometimes differ.

Example

A group has been assigned a cooperatively-structured activity. Members decide that they want to eliminate "put downs." They agree on what specific behaviors are involved in "putting another person down." A process observer evaluates the group during the activity.

1. Not helpful behaviors
    - Puts another person down

2. Helpful behaviors
    - Giving feedback by politely pointing out to a person when she has put someone down
    - Changing unhelpful behavior that another group member points out to you

The group begins at 0 and the process observer adds a +1 for each helpful behavior and a −1 for an unhelpful behavior. Since helpful behaviors can be made only in response to unhelpful ones, the group is not attempting to accumulate points, but to remain around 0. At the end, if the group score is between −2 and +2, they receive an A, between −2 and −5 a B, and below −5 a C. Set the scoring system based on your knowledge of the group.

CATEGORY II— TEACHER ASSESSMENT

The teacher is responsible for observing and noting changes in the cooperative skills of group members.

TEACHER SPOT CHECK

Description

The teacher and class members have defined a cooperative skill that all will try to practice. As students do a task, the teacher mills around the class giving each group a mark on her checklist when she sees the cooperative skill. Initially the method can be used for feedback, and once everyone is accustomed to it, for grades.

Advantages

- All students have a chance to participate in the activity because the teacher, and not a group member, is process observer.
- Students receive teacher feedback, which may be different from what they get from each other.

Disadvantages

- The teacher can't catch all aspects of the group process with a spot check.
- Inaccuracies may occur due to the random nature of the observation.

Example

Students are assigned a cooperatively-structured activity. The teacher and class decide on a cooperative skill that the teacher will check for. Example:

Giving "I-messages" as feedback

With the advice of the students, the teacher sets up a grading scale. Using a checklist, the teacher mills around the room as the students are working, checking each time she sees that cooperative skill being used.

To get an A, each group must have 8 checks.
To get a B, each group must have 6 checks.
To get a C, each group must have 4 checks.

At the end of the class, the teacher shares the checklist with each group, discusses areas for improvement, and determines the grade.

CATEGORY III— STUDENT SELF ASSESSMENT

Students themselves are responsible for recognizing and evaluating the progress of other group members and themselves on a particular cooperative skill.

a. PROCESS PARTNERS

Description

Students work cooperatively to help each other with individualized cooperative skills. Either the teacher pinpoints a cooperative skill for each student to work on, or she decides with a student on a skill to improve. A contract is written for each student.

Partners are assigned within groups. Partners talk about their contracted skills and each makes a copy of the other's contract. Students also share it with the whole group, so other members can be supportive. During the activity, a student checks each time her partner uses the skill and, at the end of the activity, determines a grade based on the contract. Individual grades are averaged and each student receives the group grade.

Advantages

- Students are concentrating on cooperative skills that are most relevant to them.
- There is partner-support within the context of a group effort.

Disadvantages

- It's difficult to concentrate on process and content at the same time. Use only with students who have had practice looking at group process while they're working.
- It's risky for some children to admit there's an individual skill they need or want to change.
- If the teacher assigns the skill and the student doesn't see it as an area for concern, the student may not be motivated to work on that skill.

Example

Students work in small groups on an assigned cooperative activity. A "Cooperation Contract" is given to each. (Make a ditto of the format to save time.) Make sure contracts can be fulfilled with relative ease.

Cooperation Contract

(Student's name)

We've agreed that you'll work on _____

Grading

For a C _____

For a B _____

For an A _____

For example:

John

We've agreed that you'll work on encouraging others in your small group.

For a C—encourage others once

For a B—encourage others two times

For an A—encourage others three or more times

Students form partnerships, share contract within the group, and copy their partner's contract. Partners check each other's behavior during the activity and evaluate progress at the end.

b. GROUP SELF-EVALUATION

Description

When students have had experience observing and evaluating cooperative skills, they may be ready to evaluate themselves. Before beginning a cooperative task, the group decides on a skill they want to improve. They develop a rating scale—for example, a checklist, or an open-ended sentence, or a continuum by which to assess their progress. After the task, students rate themselves and assign a grade. At any point, they can ask the teacher for advice.

Advantages

- Students are committed to working on the skill because they've chosen it and will evaluate it.
- Skills can be individualized to group needs.
- Threat level is low.

Disadvantages

- Students may have difficulty deciding on a skill and criteria for rating.
- Students may polish an easy skill.
- Students may not be objective in their rating.

Example

A group is working on a week-long cooperatively-structured project. Members decide that the cooperative skill they want to improve is the sharing of leadership. They ask, "How will we know if we have shared leadership?" and then develop criteria.

Criteria

1. Each day a different person will lead the group discussion and coordinate group tasks.
2. No one will dominate the discussion by speaking a lot more than others or telling others what to do.
3. In presenting the project to the class, each person will have a part.

The group decides that items 1 and 3 are best evaluated at the end of a project on a continuum from

1	5	10
poor	okay	great

For item 2 each person will fill out a continuum at the end of every day

1	5	10
one person dominates	some people tell more than others	equal sharing

Why I rated the group this way is _____

At the end of the project, they review the continuums and give themselves a grade.

c. INDIVIDUAL SELF-CHECK

Description

Each student chooses a cooperative skill that she wants to work on. The student decides what amount of improvement will be equivalent to what grade and shares her contract with the group. The contract includes a continuum on which each student checks: (1) her starting point; and (2) daily progress. Finally she measures the change.

Advantages

- Students are motivated because they've chosen the behavior they want to change.
- Each student works on a cooperative skill, thereby becoming more self-aware.
- This builds the feeling of being able to change ones own behavior.

Disadvantages

- It's hard to watch cooperative skills and work on a task at the same time. Use after students have had practice processing group behavior.
- Some students find it hard to grade themselves.
- It's possible for students to mark themselves higher than their skill-use warrants.

Example

Students are working on a week-long project. Each student chooses a cooperative skill and makes a personal contract, with a copy for the teacher. The teacher talks with any student who's not challenging himself.

John contracts to share materials with others. He makes the following continuum:

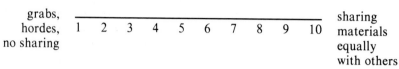

grabs,   1   2   3   4   5   6   7   8   9   10   sharing
hordes,   materials
no sharing   equally
                                                 with others

His contract:

> A—if between points 9–10 average for week
> B—if between points 6–8 average for week
> C—if 5 or below points average for week

He checks himself each day and evaluates himself at the end of the week.

C. CUMULATIVE GRADING

Description

Several sets of group and individual evaluations are combined at the end of a specified period to determine a student's grade. The time might range from a week to a marking period. This combines evaluation of content material and progress on group process skills.

Advantages

- A variety of individual/group, content/process criteria is used to determine a grade.
- There is the incentive to see the whole class as part of one effort.

Disadvantages

- So many criteria can be confusing for some students. Use only at an appropriate time in the year.
- Most students under fifth grade have difficulty with the concept of percentage. For them, it can be explained in simpler terms.
- It takes a great deal of teacher-time to calculate the final grade—unless students do the calculation, which is recommended!

Example

A class is working in heterogeneous groups on a three-week unit. Each person's grade will be a combination of the following:

1.	The individual's average score on quizzes	20%
2.	The group's grade on its project	20%
3.	The whole class's score on a final teacher-made game that uses all the material	20%
4.	Group score on cooperative skills based on process observation records	40%

Students keep group records on scores for different parts and complete and check final calculations.

WHAT WOULD YOU DO IF . . . ?

1. Vera likes to fool around or sit back and doodle rather than contribute to the work of her group . . .

   - Give Vera an assigned role, such as organizer—where she feels important and gets a lot of attention.
   - Put Vera in a group of students who will encourage her. Talk to students privately and ask them to do this.
   - Use an evaluation procedure where the group is judged according to everyone's work.
   - Use cooperative groups in Vera's strongest academic area. Others may feel, "Oh, we're happy to have Vera in our group!"

2. Jose's parents call and complain that Jose is being slowed down academically by having to work together with less-able students . . .

   - Make sure you use cooperative activities that have enough content that stretch the most-able students.
   - Encourage Jose to do independent work which he then teaches to his classmates.
   - Give the parents materials to read that point out the significant cognitive gain for all students who learn cooperatively. (Especially see Slavin and Johnson and Johnson.)
   - Work together with parents to provide Jose with enrichment activities; for example, enroll him in an evening course at a local high school.

3. Ellen has a limited concentration span and gets restless in her group . . .

   - When you notice some people becoming restless, interrupt with a "cooperative energizer."
   - Within a group project, give Ellen the task that has the most variety.
   - Extend a cooperative lesson or project over several days. Stop at a high point on one day, so students will look forward to going back to the project.
   - Where possible, modify the task when you see restlessness. Continue the same task in a new way; for example, go to the library to do research.
   - Make sure that the task is one that Ellen can do successfully.

4. Your principal and colleagues ask, "How can students be learning anything with all that talking going on?" . . .

   - Invite them to spend a free period with you, or to team teach with you to see how you teach and what students learn.
   - During a teachers' conference day, give an in-service workshop on cooperative methods.
   - Share with colleagues books and studies on cooperative methods.
   - Display work that students have done in cooperative groups. Place on bulletin boards or in display cases in the school.
   - Have students do a cooperative project that can be shared with, or used by, other classes.

5. The noise level gets very high because of student communication and motivation . . .

   - Explain to the teachers next door what you're doing and invite them to contact you if it gets too noisy.
   - Develop a signal for reminding students to lower their level of talking, for example, a flash of the lights.
   - Everyone is resigned to the fact that there's noise when work is done in cooperative groups. This is a small price to pay for cooperative learning!

- Have some activities where some people work in groups and others work alone.
- Help students develop a self-monitoring mechanism to deal with noise. For example, one person takes the role of noise barometer and reminds the group when the noise is excessive.

6. Jackie complains that she needs quiet in order to think. She just can't concentrate in a group . . .

- Design or redesign some cooperative activities where students work individually on a task first and then work together as a group.
- If this is a "beginning of the year" problem, give it time.
- Pick a topic Jackie knows well and have her group brainstorm about it. This will give her the positive experience of thinking aloud in a group activity.
- Allow Jackie to work by herself for a while, then with the group.

7. Stephen complains, "Why do I have to work with people who aren't my friends and who aren't as smart as I am?" . . .

- Explain and re-explain your rationale for cooperative groups. For example, "Everyone in this class is a special person with unique talents to offer to others. I want all of you to have a chance to discover that for yourself."
  —or—
  "Throughout your whole life, you'll be working with a wide variety of people and it's important to learn ways to cooperate and to begin doing so now."
- Plan a cooperative activity where low-skilled students excel.
- Encourage Stephen to watch to see how much the less-skilled students in his group really are learning! This learning comes, in part, from his cooperative efforts. Encourage him to feel proud of this!

8. When projects have different tasks, students always tend to take the same ones. Robin takes notes, Chris illustrates projects, Beven does research. They seem content with these roles . . .

- Discuss with the group the importance of taking different tasks so everyone can develop new skills. Ask them voluntarily to rotate tasks in their group.
- Assign the tasks yourself.
- Write various tasks on small pieces of paper and put them in a hat. Have students choose from the hat.

9. Ms. Garcia, a colleague, is excited by the possibility of trying cooperative learning, but is worried that too much of her time will be spent preparing materials for lessons . . .

- Cooperate with other teachers and prepare materials together.
- Remind her that, as in all teaching, once materials are prepared they can be used again and again.
- Choose activities that involve lesser amounts of preparation.
- Involve students and parents in getting materials ready for cooperative lessons.

10. Mr. Wipple, your school principal, insists on seeing your lesson plans every Friday for the next week. He's not enthusiastic about "new-fangled" ideas . . .

- Consult ideas listed under 4.
- Start interspersing cooperative activities, here and there, among your routine plans.
- Give him copies of the educational research that points out the value of cooperative learning.
- Show him evidence of your students' cognitive and skill development resulting from the use of the cooperative activities that you have been able to try so far.

11. Mr. Jackson, a parent, is afraid that if students work cooperatively they won't have practice taking standardized tests . . .

- Remind Mr. Jackson that students work cooperatively for only part of the school day.
- Develop a cooperative unit on "Improving Skills for Individualized Tests."
- Take individualized tests for practice. Have students work together to help each other in areas they don't do well in.
- Show Mr. Jackson how your students are gaining skills and knowledge by working in cooperative groups, thereby enabling more to do well on individualized tests.

TEACHERS AND STUDENTS SAY . . .

The words of a wide variety of teachers and students, veterans of cooperative learning, provide support and inspiration to others.

Teachers Say

"The basic premise of cooperative learning is so simple and so obvious that it comes as a pleasant surprise. If students need each other in order to succeed at a learning task, then they must either cooperate or fail."

"It's interesting that on our report card, and those of many pupils across the country is the criteria 'Student works cooperatively with others.' Yet how many teachers really help students learn how to do that?"

"I find that cooperative learning allows much more time for me to spend with individual children who need help. While each group is working on its assigned task, I can go around and check progress. Because of the ways the groups are structured, I know that all students who require extra support or re-direction will get it from others in their group if I can't get to them right away. I know that they are not sitting around waiting for me to help and thereby wasting their own learning time."

"One angry student was having major personal and academic problems in the class. In one cooperative activity she understood the material and finished first. When students came to me to ask questions, I just said 'I don't know' and sent them to her. She felt great and began integrating herself well into the class."

"I get kicks out of hearing students say 'I understand. Now I want to see if you understand.' "

"A teacher reported that one of her students insisted that his dad bring him to school to participate in class. Immediately after class, he went back home to elevate the plaster-encased leg that he had broken playing football the evening before. He couldn't miss class, he said, 'because his team needed him.' "

"Cooperative work is less scary for my students. All of my students really **like** cooperative work."

"We were working on a weaving project and the L.D. student in my class learned it well. Another student came in late. I said, 'Go ask Ned' and Ned taught it to him! That not only made Ned feel great but also keeps me from having to explain things all the time."

"The training I have received in cooperative learning has had a tremendous impact on my teaching style. I have found I am able to plan more difficult concepts because support systems built into the cooperative lessons provide the student with confidence that success is within his or her range. Furthermore, the students have begun to recognize areas of exceptional interest or ability in their classmates and use each other as a resource in areas where they may need more information."

"It is a reflection of the values in my society that I should approach cooperation with caution, like something not to be trusted. One wonders if there has been a conspiracy to keep people working against each other in order to keep them powerless."

Students Say

"I always liked school . . . but I never looked after anybody else and nobody looked after me. This [class] was really something."

"What I like about cooperative learning is that you don't get in trouble for asking another kid something."

"When you have to explain why something's wrong or something's right, you really have to understand."

What should you do if you're "stuck"? "You should ask for help. It's OK to say you don't know something."

"It's nice to work with somebody different and not my own friends all the time."

"I never realized how differently people think about words. You know, it's one thing when a teacher says 'change this or this.' But it's something else when somebody in your own class, your own age, says it."

"What helped our cooperative group do a good job is that we all gave our ideas and each person had special, and different, ideas."

One student had come to the teacher and said, "We finished first because we worked most cooperatively." The teacher reported this to the class. Another fourth grader responded, "That's not the point. It's not who finishes first. That doesn't matter at all. All that matters is that you work together and all help each other learn."

"It was like having three pairs of eyes instead of one."

BIBLIOGRAPHY

BOOKS AND ARTICLES ABOUT COOPERATIVE LEARNING

Aronson, Elliot. *The Jigsaw Classroom.* Beverly Hills: Sage, 1978. An excellent, practical book that provides necessary information for implementing the jigsaw method in the classroom.

Burns, Marilyn. "Groups of Four: Solving the Management Problem." *Learning Magazine,* vol. 10, no. 2 (September 1981): 46–51. Short, protocol description of the "groups of four approach to cooperative learning."

Cohen, Elizabeth. *Designing Groupwork: Strategies for the Heterogeneous Classroom.* New York: Teachers College, 1986. Useful book integrating theory and practice to help teachers implement groupwork in their classes.

Deutsch, Morton. "An Experimental Study of the Effects of Cooperation and Competition on Group Process." *Human Relations,* 2 (1945): 199–231. A well-known study on the effect of goal structure on group process.

Dishon, Dee and Pat Wilson O'Leary. *A Guidebook for Cooperative Learning: A Technique for Creating More Effective Schools.* Holmes Beach, Florida: Learning, 1984. A well-written, clear guide to implementing cooperative learning in the classroom with a focus on teaching cooperative skills.

Ellis, Susan. "Introducing Cooperative Learning Groups: A District-Wide Effort." *Journal of Staff Development,* vol. 6, no. 2 (October 1985).

Graves, Nancy and Theodore Graves. "Cooperative Team Learning: A Resource Guide." 136 Liberty Street, Santa Cruz, California 95060. Comprehensive and up-to-date bibliography of materials for teachers on cooperatively-structured learning.

Graves, Nancy and Theodore Graves. "Reflecting." 136 Liberty Street, Santa Cruz, California 95060. Useful, short pamphlet on helping students reflect on the **process** of working together in cooperative groups.

Healy, Mary. *Using Student Writing Response Groups in the Classroom.* Bay Area Writing Project, School of Education, University of California, Berkeley, California. A short monograph describing the use of student groups in the teaching of writing.

Henry, Jules. "In Suburban Classrooms." In *Radical School Reform,* edited by Ronald and Beatrice Gross. New York: Simon & Schuster, 1969. A classic account of the effect of competition on students.

Johnson, David, and Frank P. Johnson. *Joining Together: Group Theory and Skills.* Englewood Cliffs: Prentice Hall, 1982. Basic text in group dynamics with attention paid to cooperative goal structuring—numerous experiential activities.

Johnson, David, and Roger Johnson. *Cooperation in the Classroom.* Interaction Book Co., 162 Windsor Lane, New Brighton, Massachusetts 55112. Practical book with strategies for implementing cooperative learning in the classroom.

Johnson, David, and Roger Johnson. *Learning Together and Alone.* Englewood Cliffs: Prentice Hall, 1975. An excellent, basic resource that provides teachers a rationale and methodology for implementing cooperative learning in the classroom.

Johnson, David., *et al. Circles of Learning.* Washington, D.C.: Association for Supervision and Curriculum Development, 1984. A short, practical introduction to cooperative learning especially useful for in-service teacher education.

Johnson, David., *et al.* "Effects of Cooperative, Competitive and Individualistic Goal Structures on Achievement: A Meta-Analysis." *Psychological Bulletin,* 89 (1981): 47–62. Results of an analysis of 122 studies comparing the effects of these three different goal structures.

Johnson, David, Roger Johnson, and Geoffrey Maruyama. "Interdependence and Interpersonal Attraction Among Heterogeneous and Homogeneous Individuals: A Theoretical Formulation and Meta-Analysis of the Research." *Review of Educational Research,* 53 (1983): 5–54. An analysis of all existing research on the relative impact of cooperative, competitive and individualistic learning experiences on interpersonal attraction among students.

Kagan, Spencer. "Cooperation-Competition, Culture, and Structural Bias in Classrooms." In *Cooperation in Education,* edited by Shloma Sharan, *et. al.* Brigham Young University Press, 1980. An examination of the values of various cultures regarding cooperation and competition and the connection of those values and the structure of the classroom to student learning.

Kagan, Spencer. *Cooperative Learning: Resources for Teachers.* Riverside, California: University of California, 1985. A useful resourcebook that presents a variety of detailed approaches for implementing cooperative learning.

Kopple, Hank. "Competition, Cooperation and Individualization in Title I Classes: Which is Most Effective?" *Affective Education Newsletter* (Feb. 1976). Examination of effects of the various goal structures on student learning in the Philadelphia Public Schools.

Lignori, James. "Just for Kicks: Developing Cooperative Based Alternatives for the Teaching of Competitive Sports or Save the Children." Unpublished paper, 1977, S.U.N.Y., New Paltz. An excellent account of a community-based, parent-led, cooperative approach to coaching soccer.

Male, Mary, *et al. Cooperative Learning and Computers: An Activity Guide for Teachers.* Education Apple-Cations, 194 Wedgewood Avenue, Los Gatos, California 95030, 1985. A practical sourcebook of cooperatively-structured activities for the computer.

May, M. and L. Doob. *Competition and Cooperation.* New York: Social Science Research Council, 1937. A classic study of cooperation and competition in education.

Moorman, Chick and Dee Dishon. *Our Classroom: We Can Learn Together.* Englewood Cliffs, Prentice Hall, 1983. A concise book of ideas for elementary school teachers to help them create a cooperative classroom.

Nelson, Linden and Spencer Kagan. "Competition: The Star Spangled Scramble." *Psychology Today* (Sept. 1972): 53–6, 90–1. Popular, well-written article reporting the research on the effect of competition on American children.

Pentecoste, Joseph. "From Competition to Cooperation: Toward a New Methodology in Education." *Negro Educational Review,* vol. XXVI, nos. 2 and 3 (April–July 1975): 110–115.

Pepitone, Emmy A. *Children in Cooperation and Competition.* Lexington, Massachusetts: D.C. Heath, 1980. A fine collection of research studies detailing the effects of cooperation and competition on students.

Reid, Jo-Anne, *et al. Small Group Work in the Classroom.* Education Department of Western Australia, 23 Miles Road, Kewdale, W. A. Australia, 1984. Useful, concise book to support implementation of cooperative learning.

Rhoades, Jacqueline, and Margaret McCabe. *Sample Cooperation in the Classroom: A Beginner's Guide to Establishing Cooperative Groups.* ITA Publications, P.O. Box 1599, Willers, California 94490, 1986. A very basic book with practical suggestions for the teacher just beginning to implement cooperative learning.

Roy, Patricia, Shirley Laurie, and Diane Browne. "Cooperative Learning: Training and Follow-up in Two School Districts." *Journal of Staff Development,* vol. 6, no. 2 (Oct. 1985).

Schmuck, Richard and Patricia Schmuck. *Group Processes in the Classroom.* Dubuque, Iowa: William C. Brown Company Publishers, 1983. Application of theory of group dynamics to the classroom for creating a climate that encourages cooperation.

Schniedewind, Nancy. "Cooperatively-Structured Learning: Implications for Feminist Pedagogy." *Journal of Thought—Special Issue on Feminist Education,* University of Oklahoma, vol. 20, no. 3 (Fall 1983). Discussion of use of cooperatively-structured learning in feminist education with a focus on teaching women's studies at the college level.

Selman, Robert and Diane Byrne. "A Structural-Developmental Analysis of Levels of Role-Taking in Middle Childhood." *Child Development,* vol. 45 (1974): 803–806. An article that helps understand relationship between students' developmental stage and role-taking activities.

Selman, Robert. "Taking Another Perspective: Development in Early Childhood." *Child Development,* vol. 42 (1971): 1721–1734. Relationship between ability to take on another's role and development stages in early childhood.

Sharan, Shlomo and Rachel Hertz-Lazarowitz. "A Group-Investigation Method of Cooperative Learning in the Classroom." In *Cooperation in Education,* edited by Shlomo Sharan, *et al.* Short account of the group investigation approach to cooperative learning.

Sharan, Shlomo and Yael Sharan. *Small Group Teaching.* Englewood Cliffs: Educational Technology, 1976. Presentation of group investigation approach to cooperative learning, particularly applicable to projects and research for advanced students.

Sharan, Shlomo, *et al. Cooperation in Education.* Provo, Utah: Brigham Young University Press, 1980. Proceedings of the first International Conference on Cooperation in Education. Describes current research and practice regarding cooperation in education.

Sherif, Muzafer. "Superordinate Goals in the Reduction of Intergroup Conflict." *American Journal of Sociology,* vol. 63 (1956): 349–56. Classic study of effects of superordinate cooperative goals on existing competition among groups.

Slavin, Robert. *Cooperative Learning.* New York: Longman, 1983. A thorough overview of the research on cooperative learning.

Slavin, Robert E. *Cooperative Learning: Student Teams.* Washington, D.C.: National Education Association, 1982. A short pamphlet describing approaches to cooperative learning, with a focus on the student team learning approach.

Slavin, Robert, *et. al. Learning to Cooperate—Cooperating to Learn.* New York: Plenum, 1985. A collection of research papers presented at 1982 IASCE international conference.

Slavin, Robert. *Using Student Team Learning.* Baltimore: Center for Social Organization of Schools, Johns Hopkins, 1980. Practical manual that describes how to implement the various team learning models developed at Johns Hopkins—STAD, TGT, and Jigsaw II.

Spino, Michael. "Athletics: The Competition for Community Love." In *Demystifying School,* edited by Miriam Wasserman. Prager, 1974. Personal look at effects of competition on experience of an athlete.

Stanford, Gene. *Developing Effective Classroom Groups: A Practical Guide for Teachers.* New York: Hart, 1977. A superb, practical book that uses group process theory to help teachers understand their classrooms as a group and help it, and smaller groups within it, function effectively.

Staub, E. "Helping a Person in Distress: The Influence of Implicit and Explicit Rules of Conduct on Children and Adults." *Journal of Social Psychology,* vol. 17 (1971): 137–44. Effect of the competitive socialization of American children on their willingness to help others.

Tutko, Thomas and William Burns. *Winning Is Everything and Other American Myths.* New York: Macmillan, 1976. A thoughtful book that examines the competitive nature of sports for youth and poses alternatives.

Weigel, Russell, Patricia Wiser, and Stuart Cook. "The Impact of Cooperative Learning Experiences on Cross-Ethnic Relations and Cultures." *Journal of Social Issues,* vol. 31, no. 1 (1975): 219–244. Effect of cooperative learning on cross-ethnic relationships.

BOOKS AND RESOURCES FOR EDUCATORS AND OTHER ADULTS ABOUT COOPERATIVE LIVING

Also included in this section are books that provide background information about some of the specific topics of lessons in *Cooperative Learning, Cooperative Lives*.

Akwesasne Notes, *Basic Call to Consciousness.* Akwesasne Notes, Mohawk Nation, Rooseveltown, New York 13683. A statement of the historical, political, and spiritual roots of the Hau De No Sau Nee (Iroquois Confederacy)—manifesting examples of cooperation among nations and with the earth.

Albert, David H. *People Power: Applying Nonviolence Theory.* Philadelphia: New Society Publishers, 1985. Guide to understanding the dynamics of nonviolent action and using them in ongoing social change struggles.

Aldridge, Robert C. *First Strike: The Pentagon's Strategy for Nuclear War.* Boston: South End, 1983. A detailed analysis of current nuclear strategy and weapon systems by a former technician in the system.

Axelrod, Robert. *The Evolution of Cooperation.* New York: Basic Books, 1984. A game theory analysis of the conditions for cooperation using a prisoner's dilemma problem as the model. Makes frequent analogies to comparable real-world situations.

Bahro, Rudolf. *Building the Green Movement.* Philadelphia: New Society Publishers, 1986. An analysis of the Green Movement in Germany, written by a leading figure in the Movement.

Baxandall, Rosalyn, Linda Gordon, and Susan Reverby, eds. *America's Working Women: A Documentary History—1600 to the Present.* New York: Vintage, 1976. A fine anthology of primary source materials regarding women's work in America and women's efforts to work together for change.

Beer, Jennifer E. *Peacemaking in Your Neighborhood: Reflections on an Experiment in Community Mediation.* Philadelphia: New Society Publishers, 1986. An optimistic evaluation of "Community Dispute Settlement Project" outside of Philadelphia. The Project works for genuine alternatives to the criminal justice system.

Benello, C. George and Dimitrios Roussopoulos, eds. *The Case for Participatory Democracy.* New York: Viking, 1972. An excellent collection of essays on the components of a new society based on decentralist, cooperative principles as well as strategies for social change.

Bergman, Arlene Eisen. *Women in Vietnam.* People's Press, 2680 21st Street, San Leandro, California 94110. A moving account of the way in which women cooperatively struggled for personal and national liberation in Vietnam.

Berman, Katrina. "The Worker-Owned Plywood Cooperatives." In *Self Management in North America: Thought, Research and Practice,* edited by Jeroslav Vanek. Ithaca, New York: Cornell University Press, 1975.

Bernstein, Paul. *Worker Ownership and Community Redevelopment.* ICCR Brief (March 1981). Interfaith Center on Corporate Responsibility, 475 Riverside Drive, New York, New York 10115. A short account describing worker-owned companies with particular emphasis on implications for communities whose plants are being closed.

Black, George. *Triumph of the People: The Sandinista Revolution in Nicaragua.* London: ZFD, 1981. Account of the struggle for national liberation in Nicaragua.

Bodner, Joan, ed. *Taking Charge of Our Lives: Living Responsively in the World.* American Friends Service Committee, Harper and Row, 1984. Values clarification activities to help readers look at issues of time-use, food, shelter, community and work, among others. A classic.

Bookchin, Murray. *Post Scarcity Anarchism.* San Francisco: Ramparts Books, 1971. The vision and critique of anarchism as expressed by a leading contemporary exponent.

Booth, John. *The End and Beginning: The Nicaraguan Revolution.* Boulder, Colorado: Westview, 1982. A history of the origins and dynamics of the Nicaraguan revolution.

Bowles, Samuel and Herbert Gintis. *Schooling in Capitalist America.* New York, Basic, 1976. Scholarly examination of how the competition in schools and the capitalistic economic system affect students and reinforce the societal status quo.

Brecher, Jeremy. *Strike.* Greenwich, Connecticut: Fawcett, 1974. An excellent overview of the history of strikes in America.

Brown, Michael. *Laying Waste: The Poisoning of America by Toxic Chemicals.* New York: Pocket Books, 1981. Account of the Love Canal toxic waste story with additional information about toxic waste problems across America.

Burbach, Roger and Patricia Flynn. *The Politics of Intervention: The U.S. in Central America.* New York: Monthly Review, 1984. An excellent overview of U.S. economic, military, and cultural ties to Central America, ties that maintain U.S. superiority and Third World dependence in that region.

Burton, Cynthia. *Women Taking Charge: New Ways to Economic Power.* Washington: D.C.: Strongforce, 1985 (o.o.p.). A collection of articles describing cooperative and collectively-organized work situations that women have organized.

Chavez, Cesar. *Cesar Chavez: Autobiography of La Causa.* Jacque Levy. New York: W. W. Norton, 1975. A history of Chavez and the development of the United Farm Worker Association until 1975.

Cheatham, Annie and Mary Clare Powell. *This Way Daybreak Comes: Women's Values and the Future.* Philadelphia: New Society Publishers, 1986. Interviews with more than one thousand American women about their transformative visions.

Cockburn, Andrew. *The Threat: Inside the Soviet Military Machine.* New York: Random House, 1983. An analysis of the Soviet military machine, showing how it works and why it doesn't work, and questioning how much of a threat it really is.

Cockcroft, Eve, John Weber, and Jim Cockcroft. *Toward a People's Art: The Contemporary Mural Movement.* New York: Dutton, 1975. An illustrated account of the history and power of the mural movement.

Cooney, Robert and Helen Michalowski, eds. *The Power of the People: Active Nonviolence in the United States.* Philadelphia: New Society Publishers, 1986. A pictorial encyclopedia of the struggles of women and men working cooperatively for peace and social justice through nonviolent action.

Coover, Virginia, *et al. Resource Manual for a Living Revolution,* 2nd edition, 1984. Movement for a New Society, 4722 Baltimore Avenue, Philadelphia, Pennsylvania 19143. An excellent resourcebook of cooperative activities from the personal to the political. Focus on group dynamics, conflict resolution, building community, consciousness raising and organizing for change.

Dellinger, David. *More Power Than We Know: The People's Movement Toward Democracy.* Garden City, New York: Doubleday, 1975. A visionary book describing the power of people working together cooperatively for social change.

Deming, Barbara. *We Are All Part of One Another: A Barbara Deming Reader.* Edited by Jane Meyerding. Philadelphia: New Society Publishers, 1984. Essays, speeches, letters, stories and poems on issues of women and peace, feminism and nonviolence.

Egerton, John. "Workers Take Over the Store." *New York Times Magazine* (11 September 1983). Account of a worker-owned and operated supermarket in Philadelphia.

Ehrenreich, Barbara and Annette Fuentes. *Women in the Global Factory.* Boston: South End Press, 1983. Clearly-written booklet describing the connection of U.S. corporations and government to the oppression of women worldwide, particularly in Third World countries.

Ehrlich, Howard, *et al.,* eds. *Reinventing Anarchy.* London: Routledge & Kagan Paul, 1979. An excellent anthology of essays by contemporary grass roots democrats seeking to address political and social issues of major concern.

Emergency Response Network. *Basta! No Mandate for War: A Pledge of Resistance Handbook.* Philadelphia: New Society Publishers, 1985. A brief guide to the situation in Nicaragua and El Salvador. Includes training materials for nonviolent action.

Everett, Melissa. *Bearing Witness, Building Bridges: Interviews with North Americans Living and Working in Nicaragua.* Philadelphia: New Society Publishers, 1986. Interviews with seventeen North Americans who have lived and worked in Nicaragua since the revolution.

Fenton, Thomas, and Mary Hoffman. *Third World Directory.* Orbis Books, 1984. Valuable directory of organizations, books, periodicals, and audiovisual material on issues related to the needs of Third World people.

Fine, Melinda and Peter Steven. *American Peace Directory.* Cambridge, Massachusetts: Ballinger, 1984. Comprehensive directory of national and local organizations working for peace.

Fischer, Roger and William Ury. *Getting to Yes: Negotiating Agreement Without Giving In.* New York: Penguin, 1983. A useful process for coming to mutually-acceptable agreements in conflict situations.

Fleisher, Frederic. *The New Sweden: The Challenge of a Disciplined Democracy.* New York: David McKay, 1967. A comprehensive account of a democratic country that has cooperative values and practices in all aspects of national life.

Fleisher, Wilfrid. *Sweden: The Welfare State.* Westport, Connecticut: Greenwood, 1973. Clear, concise account of the institutionalization of cooperation in all areas of a modern, industrial nation, what the Swedes call "The People's Home."

Flender, Harold. *Rescue in Denmark.* New York: Schoken, 1963. Book-length account of the successful effort of the Danish people to help Denmark's 8,000 Jews escape Nazi persecution.

Freire, Paulo. *Education for Critical Consciousness.* New York: Seabury, 1973. A practical account of the applications of Paulo Freire's educational ideas and methods—including learning groups or "circles of culture."

Freire, Paulo. *Pedagogy of the Oppressed.* New York: Herder and Herder, 1968. A provocative book presenting the theory of this Brazilian educator who uses learning groups as the context for adult literacy and social change.

Freundlich, Paul, Chris Collins, and Mikki Wenig, eds. *A Guide to Cooperative Alternatives,* 1979. Community Publications Cooperative, P.O. Box 426, Louisa, Virginia 23053. A resourcebook describing examples of cooperative alternatives in the U.S.—in the areas of health, work, food, housing, energy, communication, education and so forth.

Gibbs, Lois Marie. *Love Canal: My Story,* as told to Murray Levine. Albany: State University of New York Press, 1982. Lois Gibbs recounts the cooperative effort that involved neighbors in fighting for a community free of toxic wastes and that eventually educated a nation.

Gilligan, Carol. *In a Different Voice: Psychological Theory and Women's Development.* Cambridge: Harvard University Press, 1982. Gilligan critiques standard developmental theory for its male-oriented bias and posits the need for redefinition based on women's experience and values, in which cooperation and interdependence are paramount.

Ginsburg, Helen. *Full Employment and Public Policy: The United States and Sweden.* Lexington, Massachusetts: D. C. Heath, 1983. Excellent comparison of the philosophical, political, and economic assumptions and the resulting effects of U.S. and Swedish values and policies regarding full employment.

Golden, Rennie. *Sanctuary: The New Underground Railroad.* Tarrytown, New York: Orbis Books, 1986. An account of the Sanctuary Movement, the cooperative effort to aid Central American political refugees.

Gordon, Suzanne and Dave McFadden. *Economic Conversion: Revitalizing America.* New York: Harper & Row, 1985. Thorough book detailing theory and practice of turning business production into peaceful uses.

Hunnins, Gerry, David G. Garson, and John Case, eds. *Workers' Control: A Reader on Labor and Social Change.* New York: Vintage Books, 1973. An anthology of leading essays on the theory and practice of workplace democracy in the contemporary world.

Institute for Food and Development Policy, "Biting the Bullet: Hunger, Intervention, and the Threat of Nuclear War," 1983. Food First: Institute for Food and Development Policy, 1885 Mission Street, San Francisco, California 94103. A very useful pamphlet documenting world hunger and correlating it with U.S. intervention in the Third World, and the threat of nuclear war.

Jackins, Harvey. *Guidebook to Re-Evaluation Counseling.* Seattle: Rationale Island Publishers, 98111. The basic tenets of re-evaluation counseling, a cooperative, community-based peer-counseling approach, with local groups throughout the U.S. and abroad.

Johnson, Carol. *Self Management in Action: Workers' Owned Sewing Machine Company.* ICCR (Interfaith Center on Corporate Responsibility) Brief, vol. 12, no. 12, 1983, from *The Corporate Examiner,* 475 Riverside Drive, New York, New York 10115. Account of the Workers' Owned Sewing Company owned and managed by black women in rural North Carolina.

Joseph, Paul and Simon Rosenblum, eds. *Search for Sanity: The Role of Nuclear Weapons and Disarmament.* Boston: South End, 1984. A current anthology of a wide range of crucial issues concerning the nuclear arms race.

Katz, Neil and John Lawyer. *Communication and Conflict Resolution Skills.* Dubuque, Iowa: Kendall Hunt, 1985. Activities for basic skill development in interpersonal communication.

King, Martin Luther, Jr. "Nonviolence and Social Change," Lecture on CBC, November 1967. *Win Magazine* (August 1983): 10. A powerful statement of the connections between domestic injustice, international oppression and the potential for revolutionary nonviolence.

"Knock on Wood." *Win Magazine,* vol. 8, no. 1, (January 1972): 20–24. Account of the cooperative effort between black and white loggers in Mississippi to provide better working conditions for all.

Kohn, Alfie. "How to Succeed Without Even Vying." *Psychology Today* (September 1986): 22–28. Well-researched article describing how cooperation, rather than competition, produces successful outcomes in education, business, and living.

Kohn, Alfie. *No Contest: The Case Against Competition.* Boston: Houghton Mifflin, 1986. A provocative critique of the competition embedded in our culture, institutions, and society at large.

Kovel, Joel. *Against the State of Nuclear Terror.* Boston: South End, 1983. A superb integration of the political, economic and psychological components of the nuclear crisis with approaches for collective strategies for building a peaceful world.

Kreiger, Sherman and Andrew Larges. "Worker Ownership: Keeping Apace." *Win Magazine* (4 May 1983): 4–5. Account of the worker-owned and operated businesses in Philadelphia, Pennsylvania.

Kropotkin, Peter. *Mutual Aid.* Boston: Extending Horizons Books, 1979. A classic theoretical statement on the key role of mutual aid or cooperation in the evolution of animal and human society.

Lappe, Frances Moore and Joseph Colins. *Now We Can Speak: A Journey Through the New Nicaragua,* 1982. Food First: Institute for Food and Development Policy, 1885 Mission Street, San Francisco, California 94103. A very readable book in which Nicaraguans describe the changes in their lives after the revolution of 1979. Photographs.

Levine, Adelaide. *Love Canal: Science, Politics and People.* Lexington, Massachusetts: 1983. Description and analysis of the struggle against toxic waste hazards by the residents of Love Canal.

Lynd, Staughton. *Nonviolence in America: A Documentary History.* Indianapolis: Bobbs Merrill, 1966. Primary reference source of nonviolent movments in the U.S. from the early Quakers to the Civil Rights Movement.

MacEan, Gary. *Sanctuary: A Resource Guide for Understanding-Participating in the Central American Refugees' Struggle.* New York: Harper, 1985. Good background and practical information on the Sanctuary Movement.

Macy, Joanna Rogers. *Despair and Personal Power in the Nuclear Age.* Philadelphia: New Society Publishers, 1983. Analysis and activities to help us explore our despair and the connections which can help us feel empowered in the face of global threats.

Marin, Peter. "The New Narcissism." *Harpers* (Oct. 1975). Marin explores the cult of the individual, prevalent in the nation.

Matthiessen, Peter. *Sol Si Puedes: Cesar Chavez and the New American Revolution.* New York: Random House, 1969. A history of Chavez and the development of the UFW Association until 1969.

McAllister, Pam, ed. *Reweaving the Web of Life: Feminism and Nonviolence.* Philadelphia: New Society Publishers, 1983. Book of essays and personal statements stressing the connection between patriarchy and war, and the power of nonviolence.

McGinnis, James. *Bread and Justice: Toward a New International Economic Order.* New York: Paulist, 1979. A clear description of the causes of world hunger and poverty and of the global changes and new approaches to interdependence necessary to bring bread and justice to all the world's people.

Mead, Margaret. *Cooperation and Competition Among Primitive Peoples.* New York: McGraw-Hill, 1936. A classic anthropological study of cooperation and competition in a variety of primitive cultures.

Melman, Seymor. *The Permanent War Economy.* New York: Simon & Schuster, 1984. Documentation that our modern defense system, far from ensuring prosperity, has drained American industry and the American economy.

Miller, Jean Baker. *Toward a New Psychology of Women.* Boston: Beacon, 1982. Fine analysis, among other things, of the way women have learned cooperation, how it can be valued as a strength, and its potential for personal and social change.

Oglesby, Carl and Richard Shaull. *Containment and Change.* New York: Macmillan, 1967. See particularly Part I— "Vietnamese Crucibles: An Essay on the Meanings of the Cold War"—which provides an historical overview of American foreign policy from the nineteenth century to 1960s and explains the roots of contemporary policy toward the Soviet Union.

Piercy, Marge. *Woman on the Edge of Time.* Greenwich, Connecticut: Fawcett, 1976. Compelling novel in which the oppressive effects of living in a competitive society on a poor, Hispanic woman are contrasted to her experience in a futurist cooperative, humanistic society.

Read, Herbert. *Anarchy and Order: Essays in Politics.* Boston: Beacon Press, 1971. A collection of moving and lucid essays by a leading English philosopher on the nature and relevance of a social order based on free human cooperation.

Roberts, Ron. *The New Communes: Coming Together in America.* Englewood Cliffs: Prentice Hall, 1971. Historical and contemporary survey of intentional communities in the U.S. and discussion of key issues concerning their functioning.

Rose, Stephen. *Social Stratification in the U.S.,* 1983. Social Graphics, 1120 Riverside Avenue, Baltimore, Maryland 21030. Booklet and chart showing income and wealth distribution in the U.S. according to race, sex, and occupation.

Ryan, William. *Blaming the Victim.* New York: Vintage, 1983. Analysis of how persons discriminated against by a competitive system often get blamed for "their problem" rather than our seeing that system as the problem and changing it to be a more cooperative one.

Ryan, William. *Equality.* New York: Pantheon, 1981. Examination of how the cherished myths of upward mobility, fair play, merit and individual advancement deny most Americans access to a genuine fair share of the social pie.

Sale, Kirkpatrick. *Human Scale.* New York: Perigee Books, 1982. A critique of the dehumanizing effects of large social institutions and an analysis of our potential for developing cooperative non-alienating social, economic and political relations which are fulfilling to human beings.

Sanders, Bob. " 'Boycott Campbells': Ohio Farm Workers Take It to the Top." *Dollars & Sense* (Dec. 1983): 16–18. Account of efforts of the farmworkers in the 1980s to use the boycott to improve their working conditions.

Schutt, Randy. *The Military in Your Backyard: How to Determine the Impact of Military Spending in Your Community.* Center for Economic Conversion, 222 View Street, Mountain View, California 94041. Practical guide to the examination of your community relative to military expenditures.

Seifer, Nancy. *Nobody Speaks for Me: Self-Portraits of American Working-Class Women.* New York: Simon & Schuster, 1976. First-person accounts by working-class women of their lives and their cooperative attempts to create change.

Shannon-Thornberry, Milo. *The Alternative Celebration Catalogue.* New York: Pilgrim, 1982. Rich resource for alternative ways to celebrate holidays, give gifts, and live our lives—ways that value simplicity, meaning, social justice, and cooperation.

Sharp, Gene. *Exploring Nonviolent Alternatives.* Boston: Porter Sargent, 1970. Brief overview of the philosophy of nonviolence and the history of nonviolent alternatives.

Sharp, Gene. *Making the Abolition of War a Realistic Goal,* 1980. World Policy Institute, 777 U.N. Plaza, New York, New York 10017. Short, readable, provocative pamphlet that presents a credible methodology for abolishing war.

Sharp, Gene. *The Politics of Non-Violent Action* (vol. I— *Power and Struggle,* II—*Methods of Non-Violent Action,* III—*Dynamics of Non-Violent Action*). Boston: Porter Sargent, 1973. Comprehensive analysis of the potential for nonviolent action as an alternative to war. Historical background and political implications.

Sidel, Ruth. *Women and Children in China.* Baltimore: Penguin, 1982. An account of the effect of cooperative values and educational policies on women and children in China during the Cultural Revolution.

Simple Living Collective of AFSC. *Taking Charge.* New York: Bantam, 1977. This book documents opportunities for personal and political change through simple living.

Slater, Philip. *The Pursuit of Loneliness.* Boston: Beacon, 1976. Slater studies the pervasive individualism in American society.

Sloan, Douglass, ed. *Educating for Peace and Disarmament: Toward a Living World.* New York: Teachers College Press, 1983. For educators, an excellent anthology of articles giving the rationale for teaching international cooperation and peace and including ideas of how to do that.

Smedley, Agnes. *Daughter of Earth.* Old Westbury: Feminist Press, 1973. Powerful novel depicting the effects of a competitive economic system and of sexism on a poor white woman and telling of her fight for personal and social change.

Stanford, Barbara. *Peacemaking: A Guide to Conflict Resolution in Individuals, Groups and Nations.* New York: Bantam, 1976. An anthology of short accounts, fiction and nonfiction, that focus on causes of conflict and on nonviolent alternatives. Useful for the secondary level as well as for teachers.

Steiner, Claude. *Scripts People Live.* New York: Bantam, 1975. Transactional analysis is the framework for examining the scripts—or roles—people are socialized to live out. Competition and cooperation are examined.

Taylor, Ronald. *Chavez and the Farm Workers.* Boston: Beacon, 1975. A history of Chavez and the development of the UFW Association until 1975.

Tinberger, Jan, ed. *Reshaping the International Order: A Report to the Club of Rome.* New York: E. P. Dutton, 1976. International experts report on the need for a new strategy to ensure the meeting of the individual and collective needs of all peoples of the earth, with more equitable distribution of resources.

Vanek, Jaroslav. *The Participatory Economy: An Evolutionary Hypothesis and a Strategy for Development.* Ithaca, New York: Cornell University Press, 1971. The theory of participatory economics combined with analysis of its practice, reality and potentials in different parts of the world.

Vocations for Social Change. *No Bosses Here: A Manual on Working Collectively.* Cambridge, Massachusetts: Vocations for Social Change, 1976. How-to-do-it booklet to help people start and sustain their own cooperative workplace.

Walker, Alice. *In Search of Our Mothers' Gardens: Womanist Prose.* New York: Harcourt Brace, 1983. Collection of prose of the award-winning novelist and poet Alice Walker.

Wallace, Paul. *The White Roots of Peace.* Philadelphia: University of Pennsylvania, 1946. An excellent short account of the founding, in 1450, of the Iroquois Confederation, and of Deganwidah, the man who instituted this historic league.

Ward, Colin. *Anarchy in Action.* New York: Harper & Row, 1973. A clear, fresh statement of the traditional vision of an anarchist decentralized community and its practical implications for contemporary society.

"Why Don't We Have Full Employment." *Dollars and Sense* (Sept. 1982): 6. A concise explanation of the systemic sources of unemployment.

Wigutoff, Sharon and Sergiu Herscovia. "Militarism in Textbooks: An Analysis." *Bulletin of the Council on Interracial Books for Children,* vol. 13, nos. 6 and 7 (1982): 15–17. An excellent analysis of contemporary school textbooks with regard to the "hidden curriculum" on militarism, war, conflict resolution and peace.

Williams, William Appleman. *Tragedy of American Diplomacy.* New York: Dial, 1972. In-depth review of American foreign policy with attention to imperialist orientation, despite idealistic rhetoric.

Wycoff, Hogie. *Solving Women's Problems.* New York: Grove, 1977. An excellent account of how, through mutual aid and support, women can cooperate to deal with personal problems.

Zinn, Howard. *A People's History of the United States.* New York: Harper, 1980. A moving account of the American people from the point of view of common people—with an emphasis on their cooperative struggle for change.

CURRICULA AND OTHER MATERIALS FOR ADULTS TO USE WITH YOUNG PEOPLE

Barres, Ellen, Carol Berrigan, and Douglas Bilin. *What's the Difference? Teaching Positive Attitudes About People with Disabilities.* Syracuse, New York: Human Policy Press, 1978. P.O. Box 127, University Station, Syracuse, New York 13210. Excellent classroom activities for teaching students to value those with disabilities.

Bickmore, Kathy. *Alternatives to Violence: A Manual for Teaching Peacemaking Alternatives to Youth and Adults,* 1984. Cleveland Friends Meeting, 10916 Magnolia Drive, Cleveland, Ohio 44106. Useful activities to educate about nonviolence.

Brewer, Linda. *Owakaga: Activities for Learning About the Plains Indians.* United Indians of All-Tribes Foundation, P.O. Box 99253, Seattle, Washington 98199. Excellent activities that accurately depict life of the Plains Indians.

Carpenter, Susan. *A Repetoire of Peacemaking Skills.* Peace Education Network, Center for Peaceful Change, Kent State University, Kent, Ohio 44242. Rationale, strategies, and activities for developing peacemaking skills among people. All ages.

Center for Conflict Resolution. *Building United Judgment: A Handbook for Consensus Decision-Making.* Philadelphia: New Society Publishers, 1985. Describes the philosophy and mechanism for resolving group conflict and for maximizing participation in group decision-making.

Center for Conflict Resolution. *A Manual for Group Facilitators.* Philadelphia: New Society Publishers, 1985. A working manual on communication, planning, and creative problem-solving in groups.

Cloud, Kate, *et al. Watermelons Not War: A Support Book for Parenting in the Nuclear Age.* Philadelphia: New Society Publishers, 1984. A resourcebook with ideas and materials for giving children support in a threatening nuclear age and creative alternatives to fear and violence.

Condon, Camy and James McGinnis. *Puppets for Peace,* 1984. Institute for Peace and Justice, 4144 Lindell #400, St. Louis, Missouri 63108. Use of puppets with young children to teach them peacefulness through varied creative activities.

Cooper, Patricia and Norma Buford. *The Quilters: Women and Domestic Art: An Oral History.* Santa Rosa, California, National Women's History Week Project. Beautifully-illustrated record of art and lives of women quilters in the Southwest.

Cooperative College of Canada. *Cooperation and Community Life,* 1980. Cooperative College of Canada, 141–105th Street W, Saskatoon, Saskatchewan S7N 1M3, Canada. Activity kit for students, ages seven through fourteen, to help them understand themselves and their community and to prepare themselves for cooperative team-learning.

Council on Interracial Books for Children. *Bulletin,* Homophobia and Education Issue, vol. 14, nos. 3 and 4 (1984). A special issue of the *Bulletin* focussing on homophobia and education.

Council on Interracial Books for Children. "Central America: What U.S. Educators Need to Know." Special Issue. C.I.B.C., New York, vol. 13, nos. 2 and 3 (1982). Excellent journal that contains articles analyzing texts, providing teacher background, and offering lesson plans on Central America.

531

Council on Interracial Books for Children. *Guidelines for Selecting Bias-Free Textbooks and Storybooks.* C.I.B.C., 1841 Broadway, New York, New York 10023. Contains guidelines to help educators and students examine books for evidence of individualism and competition.

Council on Interracial Books for Children. *Unlearning Indian Stereotypes.* C.I.B.C., 1841 Broadway, New York, New York 10023. Excellent filmstrip with tape and activity guide that corrects stereotypes about Native Americans and points to some of their cooperative customs.

Council on Interracial Books for Children. "Militarism and Education." Special Issue of the *Bulletin of C.I.B.C.* C.I.B.C., New York, vol. 13, nos. 6 and 7 (1982). An excellent issue of the *Bulletin* with fine articles, activities and curriculum materials that educate about the links between militarism and education.

Department of Cooperation and Cooperative Development. *Working Together: Learning Together.* Saskatchewan Department of Cooperation and Cooperative Development, Stewart Resources Center, Box 1108, Saskatoon, Saskatchewan S7K 3N3, Canada. A very practical resourcebook for teachers that describes steps for implementing cooperative learning—focus on helping students work together in groups.

Dorn, Lois and Martin Eldgredge. *Peace in the Family: A Workbook of Ideas and Actions.* New York: Pantheon Books, 1983. Nonviolent conflict resolution, building community, and developing self-esteem as part of family life.

Educators for Social Responsibility. *Dialogue: A Guide to Teaching Nuclear Issues.* Educators for Social Responsibility, 23 Garden Street, Cambridge, Massachusetts 02138. A resourcebook for teachers K–12 with information for teaching about nuclear issues to students of various ages and creative activities to use in the classroom.

Educators for Social Responsibility. *Perspectives: A Teaching Guide to Concepts of Peace.* Educators for Social Responsibility, 23 Garden Street, Cambridge, Massachusetts 02138. A resourcebook for teachers K–12 with information for teaching about peace, including activities to use in the classroom.

Educators for Social Responsibility, Boston Chapter. *Making History.* Educators for Social Responsibility, 11 Garden Street, Boston, Massachusetts 02138, 1984. Secondary social studies curriculum that helps students work cooperatively to influence the world around them.

Educators for Social Responsibility, Boston Chapter. *Taking Part.* Educators for Social Responsibility, 11 Garden Street, Boston, Massachusetts 02138, 1984. An elementary curriculum that helps students to work cooperatively to influence the world around them.

Goldberg, Susan, ed. *Facing the Nuclear Age: Parents and Children Together.* Annick Press, 5519 Yonge St., Willowdale, Ontario, M2N 5S3, 1984. Booklet which gives reasons for addressing children's nuclear fears and includes peace activities for families of children of all ages. Strong bibliography.

Greenhaven Press. *Opposing Viewpoints Series.* Greenhaven Press, 577 Shoreview Park Road, St. Paul, Minnesota 55112. Series of books on current topics with pro-and-con arguments, for example, The American Military, War and Human Nature. High school level.

Ground Zero Pairing Project, P.O. Box 19049, Portland, Oregon 97219, *Elementary School Educational Package on Soviet Geography, Language, Culture and Children.* Small collection of materials on the land of Russia, Soviet children and their lives, and Russian children's stories and fables. Tape of native of Moscow describing growing up in the Soviet Union. $9.95.

Haessly, Jacqueline. *Peacemaking: Activities for Children. Book 1.* 1984. Milwaukee Peace Education Resource Center, 2437 N. Grant Boulevard, Milwaukee, Wisconsin 53210. Booklet for children to do alone or with adults. Easy, usable format.

Harrison, Marta. *For the Fun of It: Selected Cooperative Games for Children and Adults.* Philadelphia: Friends Peace Committee, 1975. A pamphlet of creative, cooperative games including quiet games that can be played indoors.

Huntly, Alyson, Jim Morin, and Marsha Sfeir. *People Living for Justice.* Dubuque, Iowa: Wm. C. Brown, 1984. An excellent series that focuses on personal, national and international steps that can be taken to create a more cooperative society and world. Five units include: (1) Political and Social Rights and Human Dignity; (2) Militarism and Hope; (3) Work and Co-Creation; (4) Women and Human Wholeness; (5) Economic Rights and Human Development. Written for high school, but can be adapted to lower grades. Christian perspective.

Huntly, Alyson. *Rich World, Poor World.* Dubuque, Iowa: Wm. C. Brown, 1987. Christian perspective; junior high and high school levels.

Jackson, Sid. *Beyond Competition: Six Dynamic New Games for Two or More Players to Win Together.* New York: Pantheon, 1977. Pencil/paper games for two to four players who must cooperate to win.

Jobs with Peace. *Crossroads: The Quality of Life in a Nuclear World.* Jobs with Peace, 10 West Street, Boston, Massachusetts, 1982. Three separate curriculum units—social studies, science, and English—that offer useful and comprehensive lesson plans on issues concerning nuclear war.

Judson, Stephanie. *A Manual on Non-Violence and Children.* New Society Publishers, 4722 Baltimore Avenue, Philadelphia, Pennsylvania 19143. Practical resource for teachers and parents on conflict resolution, affirmation, and cooperation.

Kreidler, William. *Creative Conflict Resolution.* Glenview, Illinois: Scott-Foresman, 1984. A collection of more than two hundred activities for keeping peace in the classroom. K–6.

Larson, Ingrid, *et al. Co-operative Outlooks,* 1983. Cooperative College of Canada, 141–105th Street West, Saskatoon, Saskatchewan S7N 1N3. Handbook of activities for teachers of secondary students about the history of cooperation in Canada, business cooperatives, and cooperation in human behavior.

Leone, Diana. *The Sampler Quilt.* Santa Clara, California: Leone Publications. A good basic book on quilting.

Loescher, Elizabeth. *Conflict Management: A Curriculum for Peace Making.* 940 Emerson Street, Cornerstone, Denver, Colorado 80218. Activities for students at all grade levels for learning peaceful ways of conflict resolution.

Mathers, Sharon, *et al. The Mamook Book: Activities for Learning about the Northwest Coast Indians.* United Indians of All-Tribes Foundation, Day Break Press, Discovery Park, Seattle, Washington 98199. Excellent activities for young children that describe life and customs of Indians of the Northwest.

McGinnis, Jim and Kathy McGinnis. *Educating for Peace and Justice.* St. Louis, Missouri: Institute for Peace and Justice, 1981. Comprehensive resource with numerous learning materials for educating about peace and justice on both domestic and international levels.

McGinnis, Jim and Kathy McGinnis. *Parenting for Peace and Justice.* St. Louis, Missouri: Institute for Peace and Justice, 1981. Valuable book for adults who wish to reinforce cooperative values in children in the home.

McGinnis, James. *Solidarity with the People of Nicaragua and Peru.* 1982. Institute of Peace and Justice, 4144 Lindell #400, St. Louis, Missouri 63108. Booklet that describes six projects for social justice in Nicaragua and Peru and how to develop a pairing project of international support with one of the groups.

Michaelis, Bill and Doris Michaelis. *Learning Through Noncompetitive Activities and Play,* 1977. Learning Handbook, 530 University Avenue, Palo Alto, California 94301. While the activities are not all cooperative, this resourcebook does provide noncompetitive activities for young children.

Moore, Melinda and Laurie Olsen, eds. *Our Future at Stake: A Teenager's Guide to Stopping the Nuclear Arms Race.* Citizens Policy Center, Nuclear Action for Youth Project, 1515 Webster Street #401, Oakland, California 94609. An excellent book describing thoughts, feelings and actions taken by teenagers to help prevent nuclear war.

Nuclear Information and Resource Service. *Teaching Nuclear Issues—Growing Up In a Nuclear World: A Resource Guide for Elementary School Teachers.* Nuclear Information and Resource Service, 1346 Connecticut Ave. NW, Washington, D.C. 20036. An excellent guide for teachers K–8th grade. Includes background reading for teachers, classroom materials, books for children, organizations, and audiovisual materials.

Orlick, Terry. *The Cooperative Sports and Games Book: Challenge Without Competition.* New York: Pantheon, 1978. Excellent collection of active cooperative games and examples of how to make traditional competitive games cooperative.

Orlick, Terry. *The Second Cooperative Sports and Games Book.* New York: Pantheon, 1982. More cooperative games that actively involve people of all ages. Engaging pictures and clear directions.

Palomares, Ulvaldo and Ben Logan. *A Curriculum on Conflict Management: Practical Methods for Helping Children Explore Creative Alternatives for Dealing with Conflict.* San Diego, California: Human Development Institute. Activities to use with kids to help them better resolve conflict.

Peace Child Foundation. *The Peace Child.* Peace Child Foundation, P. O. Box 33168, Washington, D.C. 20030. A play, with curriculum, about how an American boy and Russian girl who become friends brought together other children of the world to persuade their leaders to end the arms race. Videos available plus materials needed to put on the play.

Philadelphia Affective Education Project. *The Interdependence Journal,* 1974. Philadelphia Public Schools, 21st & Parkway, Philadelphia 19104. Excellent teacher-written book about ways to cooperate as teachers in schools.

Philadelphia Affective Education Project. *The Together Book.* Philadelphia Public Schools, 21st and Parkway, Philadelphia 19104. An excellent resourcebook of activities to help students improve group skills. Grades 5–8.

Pogrebin, Letty. "The Secret Fear that Keeps Us from Raising Free Children." *Bulletin,* Council on Interracial Books for Children, vol. 14, nos. 3 and 4: 10–12. An excellent short article describing the ways adults' homophobia keeps us from nonsexist education and childrearing.

Project Adventure, *Teaching Through Adventure: A Practical Approach,* 1976. Project Adventure, Box 157, Hamilton, Massachusetts 01936. Cooperative physical-education activities that use group problem solving and peer assistance.

Prutzman, Priscilla, *et al. Friendly Songs for a Small Planet.* World Around Songs, Burnsville, North Carolina 28714. Pocket-size songbook with a wonderful selection of songs about peace.

Prutzman, Priscilla, *et al. The Friendly Classroom for a Small Planet.* Children's Creative Response to Conflict Program, 15 Rutherford Place, New York, New York 10003. A useful array of activities to use with students that affirm individuals and present strategies for constructive conflict resolution.

Rohnke, Karl. *Cowtails & Cobras: A Guide to Ropes, Cards, Initiative Games and Other Adventure Activities.* Project Adventure, 1977. More fine cooperative physical challenges from Project Adventure.

Rubin, Laurie. *Food First Curriculum: An Integrated Curriculum for Grade 6,* 1984. Institute for Food and Development Policy, 1885 Mission Street, San Francisco, California 19103. An excellent curriculum (adaptive to grades 4–8) to help students learn of the food they eat, the roots of hunger here and abroad, and how students can act locally on global problems.

Salotter, Mary Ruth. *Quilting as a Traditional Women's Art Form: A Kit* (Grades 1–6). National Women's History Week Project, Santa Rosa, California 95402. Complete materials for a very interesting, informative unit on quilting as a traditional art form.

Saskatchewan Department of Cooperation and Cooperative Development. *Working Together: Learning Together,* 1983. Stewart Resource Center, Box 1108, Saskatoon, Saskatchewan S7K 3N3, Canada. A handbook of practical ideas for teachers who wish to begin, or have begun, using cooperative groups in their classrooms.

Schmuck, Richard and Pat Schmuck. *A Humanistic Psychology of Education: Making the Schools Everybody's House.* Palo Alto, California: Mayfield, 1974. A guide to developing a humanistic school environment in which cooperative learning can flourish.

Schniedewind, Nancy and Ellen Davidson. *Open Minds to Equality: Learning Activities to Promote Race, Sex, Class and Age Equity.* Englewood Cliffs, New Jersey: Prentice Hall, 1983. Curriculum materials to build trust and cooperation in the classroom and to enable students to understand and change discrimination based on race, sex, class and age.

Shannon-Thornberry, Milo. *The Alternatives Celebration Catalogue.* New York: Pilgrim, 1982. Ideas and crafts for noncommercial and more cooperative celebration of holidays, alternative gifts that support peoples around the world.

Share, Marjorie. *Quilting Bee/Bee Quilting.* Washington, D.C., Smithsonian Institution Travelling Exhibition Service, 1979. Useful resource for quilt-making.

Silber, Irwin. *Lift Every Voice.* New York: Oak, 1953. Fine songbook of traditional songs about work, struggle, and visions of peace.

Strom, Margot Stern. *Facing History and Ourselves: Holocaust and Human Behavior.* International Education Institute, 51 Spring Street, Watertown, Massachusetts. Excellent curriculum designed for adolescents to promote awareness of the history of the holocaust, an appreciation for justice, and concern for interpersonal understanding.

Union for Concerned Scientists and N.E.A. *Choices: A Unit on Conflict and Nuclear War.* Washington, D.C., 1983. Clear, well-sequenced curriculum unit that presents a practical and thoughtful series of lessons on the arms race, nuclear war, and their alternatives. Geared for 5–8.

U.S. Committee for U.N.I.C.E.F., *Sing Children Sing.* U.S. Committee for U.N.I.C.E.F., 331 E. 38th Street, New York, New York 10016. Series of seven records or tapes of songs from different countries—Italy, Israel, the Congo, Mexico, British Isles, France, Austria.

U.S. Committee for U.N.I.C.E.F., *Sing Children Sing Book.* U.S. Committee for U.N.I.C.E.F., 331 E. 38th Street, New York, New York 10016. Original words and translations for songs and dances of thirty-four countries.

Weinstein, Matt and Joel Goodman. *Everybody's Guide to Non-Competitive Play.* San Luis Obispo, California: Impact, 1980. A fine collection of games and activities that engage people collectively.

Whitmas, Wanda. *Songs That Changed the World.* New York: Crown, 1969. Book of songs that influenced history—including songs for peace and justice.

Winds of the People. From Food for Thought Bookstore, Amherst, Massachusetts 01002. Wonderful collection of songs about cooperation, friendship, and world peace.

MEDIA

Bombs Will Make the Rainbow Break. Films, 8124 N. Central Park, Skokie, Illinois 60076, or Interfaith Center, 132 N. Euclid Avenue, Pasadena, California 91101. School children describe their thoughts and feelings about living in a nuclear age and what they plan to do about it. Fifth grade and up.

Bread and Roses: The Lawrence Strike of 1912. District 1199 Cultural Center, 310 W. 43rd Street, New York, New York, 10036. This slide show includes texts and songs and, using many original photos of workers, presents much factual information about the strike.

Button Button. Carol Duvereck, Fowner Forest Road, Sharon, Vermont 05065. Play written and performed by local Vermont people about the history of war. Mime and singing. Slide show available about how the play was produced.

Caring Work, with Daniel Fader. University of Indiana, Affective Dimension of Reading Series, Bloomington, Indiana. Excellent hour-long documentary by this reading expert that presents an eloquent rationale for cooperative learning.

Children's Creative Response to Conflict. Fellowship of Reconciliation, Box 271 Nyack, New York 10960. Fifteen-minute slide show showing this program in use in classroom.

Circles of Learning. Cooperative Learning Center, 202 Patee Hall, 150 Pillsbury Drive S.E., Minneapolis, Minnesota 55455. Thirty-minute film on cooperatively-structured learning.

Controlling Interest. California Newsreal, San Francisco, California. Available from Pennsylvania State Film Library. A clear, provocative documentary about the power and influence of the multinational corporations in international politics and trade.

Eye of the Storm. University of Connecticut, Film Library, Storrs, Connecticut. Available through many local library systems, this film depicts the classic blue eye/brown eye experiment in which a teacher favors one group and discriminates against another. The effects of competition based on difference is powerfully shown in the children.

Gods of Metal. Wilmington College Peace Resource Center, Wilmington, Ohio. Excellent documentary about people who have taken personal risks and collective action to challenge the arms race.

It's Our Future. STOP Nuclear War, 636 Beacon Street—Room 203, Boston, Massachusetts 02215. A slide-show presentation about the national high school student-teacher organization, S.T.O.P.—Student Teacher Organization to Prevent Nuclear War.

Love Canal: The Issues and Controversies. Media Library, State University of New York at Buffalo, Buffalo, New York 14260. Thirty-five minute slide-audiocassette program about the issues raised by Love Canal.

No Frames, No Boundaries. Creative Initiatives, 222 High Street, Palo Alto, California 94301. Exploration of the frames of reference and artificial human-made boundaries that exist among nations and the interconnectedness of the planet.

Peace Child. Peace Child Foundation, P.O. Box 33168, Washington, D.C. 20030. Videotapes, scripts, and songs from a play about how an American boy and a Russian girl bring together other children of the world to persuade their leaders to end the arms race.

A Place to Begin: An Approach to Nuclear Education. Educators for Social Responsibility, 23 Garden Street, Cambridge, Massachusetts 02138. Examples of classroom discussions, and advise to teachers on how to deal with student fears while developing critical thinking about nuclear issues.

Sadako and the Thousand Paper Cranes. Pax Center, 345 E. 9th Street, Erie, Pennsylvania 16503. Or Institute for Peace and Justice, 4144 Lindell, #400, St. Louis, Missouri 63108. Slide show of the classic story.

Stopping History. Adair Films, 2501 Third Street, San Francisco, California 94107. A documentary presenting reasons why or why not a person decides to act against the nuclear arms race. Traces history of members of a group who took part in nonviolent, civil disobedience in California.

The Time Has Come. American Friends Service Committee, 1501 Cherry St., Philadelphia, Pennsylvania 19102. Uplifting documentary that interviews people participating in the June 1982 March for Disarmament.

Union Maids. New Day Films, Franklin Lakes, New Jersey. Fine documentary combining interviews with three women who were active in labor organizing with footage of those collective efforts, especially in the 1930s and 1940s.

When Women Get to Hurting. WNET-Channel 13, New York. A thirty-minute documentary about the workers' self-managed women's factory, McCaysville Industries.

With Babies and Banners. New Day Films c/o Karol Media, 22 Riverview Drive, Wayne, New Jersey 07470-3191. An excellent documentary of the General Motors Strike in Flint, Michigan in the 1930s focusing on the cooperation among women, cooperation instrumental in winning the strike. Junior High and High School.

Wrath of Grapes. United Farmworkers, P.O. Box 62, Keene, California 93531. A fourteen-minute documentary about the situation of California farmworkers today, especially the effects of pesticide spraying.

PERIODICALS

Children of the Green Earth. P.O. Box 200, Langley, Washington 98260. Newsletter of this international organization dedicated to involving young people in the planting and care of trees and in understanding the significance of that.

Forum. Educators for Social Responsibility, 23 Garden Street, Cambridge, Massachusetts 02135. Newsletter of ESR, that comes with membership, describing current resources and issues regarding nuclear-age education.

The Grapevine. P.O. Box 1319, Ames, Iowa 50010. This is an excellent boycott information newsletter for "Shopping with a Conscience." Published quarterly; $12 a year.

Intercom. 218 E. 18th Street, New York, New York 10003. Journal for educators on worldwide interdependence and how to prepare young people to live in the global village. Each issue includes in-depth lesson plans for a single unit. Three issues per year.

Laser. 168 Bridge Road, Florence, Massachusetts 01060. A children's newsletter about peace. For young people nine through fifteen with information about activities and with quotations on peace.

New Abolishionist. 2521 Guilford Avenue, Baltimore, Maryland 21218. Newsletter of Nuclear Free America, a non-profit international clearinghouse and resource center for nuclear free zones.

Peacemaking for Children. Milwaukee Peace Education Resource Center, 2437 N. Grant Boulevard, Milwaukee, Wisconsin 53210. A newsletter about peace for children and by children—contains useful activities. Available in bulk to schools.

Sharing Space. Children's Creative Response to Conflict Program, Box 271, Nyack, New York 10960. Newsletter of CCRCP full of ideas and resources that encourage cooperation.

Student-Team Learning Newsletter. Johns Hopkins Team Learning Project, Center for Social Organization of Schools, 3505 M. Charles Street, Baltimore, Maryland 21218.

Youthlink. 4835 Avenue S, Minneapolis, Minnesota 55409. A bimonthly newsletter for teachers and parents with information, ideas, book reviews, films, games to help young people envision and work toward a more positive future.

ORGANIZATIONS AND SOURCES OF INFORMATION ON COOPERATIVE LEARNING AND LIVING

Alternatives, P.O. Box 429, 5263 Bouldercrest Road, Ellenwood, Georgia 30049. A source of alternative books and resources. Has a craft shop that carries products made by self-help cooperatives in the U.S. and Third World.

American Friends Service Committee, 1515 Cherry Street, Philadelphia, Pennsylvania and 2160 Lake Street, San Francisco, California. Source of excellent resources and materials for building a peaceful and cooperative nation and world.

Animal Town Game Company, P.O. Box 20002, Santa Barbara, California 93120. Distributor of a variety of cooperative board games. Catalogue available.

Center for the Social Organization of Schools, Johns Hopkins University, 3505 N. Charles Street, Baltimore, Maryland 21218. Source of material for team learning approach of Robert Slavin.

Center for Teaching International Relations, C.T.I.R., University of Denver, Denver, Colorado 80208. Source of materials and curriculum for international and

intercultural studies that enable students to participate more fully in a global society.

Centro de Encuentros y Dialogos, A. C. (CED). Humbold No. 306, Esq. Motolonia, Cuernavaca, Mor. Mexico (Irma Villasenor Salto). Contact organization for cooperatives that make skirts, blouses, baby shirts, scarves.

Children's Creative Response to Conflict Project, Box 271, Nyack, New York 10960. Trains teachers and provides materials to help students find cooperative and nonviolent alternatives to conflict.

Co-op America, 2100 M Street NW Suite 310, Washington, D.C. 20063. Non-profit, member-controlled, worker-managed association linking socially-responsible businesses and consumers in a national network, a new alternative marketplace.

Cooperative Learning Center, 202 Pattee Hall, University of Minnesota, Minneapolis, Minnesota 55455. Source of a variety of materials on cooperative learning from lesson plans to research studies—coordinated by David and Roger Johnson.

Council on Interracial Books for Children, 1841 Broadway, New York, New York 10023. Organization with excellent materials, for teachers and students, that promote educational equity and cooperative values.

Educators for Social Responsibility, 23 Garden Street, Cambridge, Massachusetts 02138. This national alliance of educators and parents work together for nuclear arms reductions through education projects and community action.

Family Pastimes, RR4, Perth, Ontario, Canada K74 3C6. Source of a wide range of cooperative games for all ages. Write for a catalogue.

Food First: Institute for Food and Development Policy, 1885 Mission St., San Francisco, California 94103. A fine resource and research institute with valuable materials on the relationship of world hunger to militarism, U.S. foreign policy, and international economic justice.

Global Education Associates, 552 Park Avenue, E. Orange, New Jersey 07017. Source of educational materials on global interdependence and world order issues.

Global Perspectives in Education, 218 E. 18th Street, New York, New York 10003. Source of materials and curriculum that educate students to global issues.

Ground Zero Pairing Project, P.O. Box 19049, Portland, Oregon 97219. Organization that pairs U.S. communities with Soviet counterparts to enhance information exchanges. Also has educational materials.

Institute for Peace and Justice, 2747 Rutgers, St. Louis, Missouri 63104. Source of material, on domestic and global concerns, that promote cooperation, justice, and peace.

Interaction Book Company, 162 Windsor Lane, New Brighton, Minnesota 55112. Source of books and monographs by the Johnsons and their colleagues.

Interfaith Center for Corporate Responsibility, 475 Riverside Drive, New York, New York 10115. A clearinghouse of information and action for groups and individuals concerned with the impact of policies of businesses on people around the world. Publishes monthly newsletter, "The Corporate Examiner."

Interfaith Center for Economic Justice, 110 Maryland Avenue NE, Washington, D.C. 20002. Cooperative effort of Protestant, Catholic, Jewish and ecumenical agencies to promote policies that help the hungry at home and abroad. Monthly newsletter—"Prepare."

International Association for the Study of Cooperation in Education. c/o Nancy and Ted Graves, 136 Liberty Street, Santa Cruz, California 95660. The international association of researchers and practitioners working in the area of cooperative learning—sponsor of a triennial conference. Newsletter comes with membership.

Kids Meeting Kids Can Make a Difference, Box 8H 380 Riverside Drive, New York, New York 10025. An organization that links young people seven through fifteen with pen pals in the Soviet Union with the goal of opening the lines of communication between young people of these nations.

Lollipop Power, Box 1171, Chapel Hill, North Carolina 27514. Source of children's books with non-sexist, cooperative values.

National Women's History Week Project, P.O. Box 3716, Santa Rosa, California 95402. Source of varied materials at all grade levels documenting women's collective efforts for dignity and social change throughout history.

Nuclear Information and Resource Service, 1346 Connecticut Avenue NW, Washington, D.C. 20036. An information center concerned about nuclear power and nuclear weapons with annotated packets of materials for elementary and secondary school teachers.

Oxfam American, 115 Broadway, Boston, Massachusetts 02116. International group committed to the development of cooperation in disaster assistance through a worldwide network. Emphasis on economic and food self-reliance.

Peacemaking in Education Program. Columbia Teachers College, Columbia University, New York, New York 10027. Materials and workshops to enable educators to promote peacemaking as part of their educational responsibility.

Project on Heterosexism/Homophobia for High School Teachers and Guidance Counsellors, Equity Institute, Box 458, Amherst, Massachusetts 01004. Educational materials and consultants to help educate teachers and students about homophobia in education, as well as other equity issues.

Servas International, Ceresstrasse 23 CH 8008, Zurich, Switzerland. An international organization that promotes international understanding and peace. Its members host foreign visitors in their homes and members similarly live with Servas's families when travelling abroad.

S.T.O.P., Student-Teacher Organization to Prevent Nuclear War, 636 Beacon St., Room 203, Boston, Massachusetts 02215. National student/teacher organization with chapters across the country. Provides media and materials to educate others about nuclear war.

Union of Third World Shoppes, 611 West Wayne Street, Fort Wayne, Indiana 46802. Non-profit, international shop selling handcraft and clothing made by self-help cooperatives in the Third World. Has member shops throughout the U.S.

U.S. Committee for UNICEF, 331 E. 38th Street, New York, New York 10016. Source of materials for global awareness. Write for a catalogue.

Wilmington College Peace Resource Center, Pyle Hall, Wilmington, Ohio 45177. An excellent source of information and inexpensive resources on international cooperation and peace. Periodic newsletter.

Women's International League for Peace and Freedom, 1213 Race Street, Philadelphia, Pennsylvania 19207. Source of general information, media, and peace-education materials.

World Around Songs, Route 5, Burnsville, North Carolina 28714. A source of small, affordable songbooks that contain many songs about international friendship and world peace.

BOOKS FOR YOUNG PEOPLE

Adolf, Arnold. All Colors of the Race. Illustrations by John Steptoe. Lothrop, Lee, Shepard, 1982. Beautifully-illustrated collection of poems giving a view of an interracial family through the daughter's eyes. Age five and up.

Ashabranner, Brent. Gavriel and Jemal: Two Boys of Jerusalem. Dodd. Comparison of lives of a Jewish and

Palestinian boy. Points to the hope for lasting peace coming ultimately through individuals such as these boys. Middle-school age.

Banai, Edward Benton. *The Mishomis Book*. Indian Country Press, 292 Walnut, St. Paul, Minnesota 55102. Stories and legends of Ojibway people—a historical and spiritual odyssey. Middle-school age.

Baylor, Bryd. *And It's All That Way: Legends Told by Anzone Indian Children*. Charles Scribners, 1976. Stories remembered and told by Native American children of the Southwest.

Bentley, Judith. *The Nuclear Freeze Movement*. Watts. A comprehensive look at the history and growth of the nuclear freeze movement. Shows that individual people and groups can make a difference. Middle and High school age.

Brandenberg, Aliki. *Corn Is Maize: The Gift of the Indians*. Account of the Native American's cultivation of corn, showing the cooperation of people with the earth.

Brooks, Cathleen. *The Secret Everyone Knows*. Kroc Foundation, 8939 Villa La Jolla Drive, Suite 203, San Diego, California 92037. Account of feelings of young person in an alcoholic family with suggestions for ways to reach out to others for support.

Cahn, William. *Lawrence 1912: The Bread and Roses Strike*. New York: Pilgrim, 1980. An excellent account of the Lawrence Strike with superb pictures—very readable.

Caraway, Caren. *Beginner's Guide to Quilting*. New York: McKay, 1980. Basic book on quilt making for grades seven and up.

Charlers, Janet and Michael Foreman. *The General*. New York: E. P. Dutton, 1961. A general, who yearned to be the most famous general in the world, unexpectedly discovers the beauty of flowers, fields, forests, and disbanding his army, makes his country the happiest in the world.

Coerr, Eleanor. *Sadako and the Thousand Paper Cranes*. New York: Dell, 1977. Story of Sadako Sasaki who died at twelve of leukemia resulting from the atom bomb. Her courage is symbolized in the paper cranes she and her friends made. Middle-school and up.

Collins, David. *Dorothy Day: Catholic Worker*. St. Anthony-Messenger Press, 1981. Story of this courageous woman who founded the Catholic Worker and fought for peace and justice. Middle-school and Junior High.

Cowley, Joy. *The Duck in the Sun*. New York: Doubleday, 1969. A fable about war brought about when a duck builds its nest in the General's only cannon.

Davis, Andrew. *Conrad's War*. Crown, 1980. An amusing fantasy starring an eleven-year-old boy who is fascinated by war and guns. His views change when he is confronted with the realities of war.

Falcon, Luis Nieves. *Yucayeque*. Bilingual Publications Co., 1966 Broadway, New York, New York 10023, 1980. Daily lives of Taino Indians—food, clothing, ceremonies, politics.

Franchere, Ruth. *Cesar Chavez*. Illustrated by Earl Tholland. New York: Crowell, 1970. A moving biography for the elementary grades of the life of Cesar Chavez and the formation of the United Farm Workers Association.

Green, Paul. *I AM Eskimo—Aknik My Name*. Alaska Northwest Publishing Company, Box 4 EEE, Anchorage, Alaska 99509, 1973. A collection of traditional stories told by an Inuit living in a northern Alaskan village.

Haskins, James. *Resistance: Profiles in Nonviolence*. Doubleday, 1970. An introduction to nonviolent principles followed by biographies of a number of male peacemakers. Upper Elementary.

Hersey, John. *Hiroshima*. New York: Bantam, 1946. True account of six men and women who survived the atomic bombing of Hiroshima. Grades eight and up.

Holman, Felice. *The Blackmail Machine*. Macmillan, 1968. Five children and a woman use their tree house to bargain for community action and world peace. Upper Elementary.

Jones, Toeckey. *Go Well, Stay Well*. New York: Harper & Row, 1980. A South African black girl becomes friends with a white girl amidst apartheid. Upper Elementary and Middle-school.

Jordan, June. *Fannie Lou Hamer*. New York: Thomas Crowell, 1972. An excellent story about the life of the civil rights activist.

Katz, Jane. *I Am the Fire of Time: The Voices of Native American Women*. New York: Dutton, 1977. An anthology of personal accounts and poetry from Native American women today.

Keyes, Ken. *The Hundredth Monkey*. Vision Books, 1982. A visionary book on the impact that individual energy can have to bring about societal change. Upper Elementary-Adult.

Langston, Jane. *The Fragile Flag*. Harper & Row, 1985. Book about Georgie, a young girl who leads a children's march to the White House protesting the President's new Peace Missile. As they walk, many other children join them. Junior high.

Lehn, Cornelia. *Peace Be With You*. Order from Alternatives, P.O. Box 429, Ellenwood, Georgia 30049, 1980. Biographies of peace workers, both known and unknown, throughout history. Middle-school.

Lens, Sidney. *Strikemakers and Strikebreakers*. New York: E. P. Dutton & Company, 1985. Describes origins and history of strikes in U.S. and discusses their purposes and effectiveness.

Levy, Myron. *Alan and Naomi*. New York: Harper and Row, 1977. This story is set in New York City after World War II. Alan needs to work through his dilemma about playing with his friends versus befriending and supporting Naomi who has been traumatized by Nazi brutality in Europe. Upper Elementary.

Leaf, Munro. *Ferdinand*. New York: Viking, 1964. A story of a bull who prefers smelling flowers to fighting in the bull ring. Elementary.

Lobel, Anita. *Potatoes Potatoes*. New York: Bowmar-Noble, 1967. Allegory of two brothers who fight on opposing sides in a war on their own potato patch and about their mother who arranges a peace settlement between the two sides. Elementary.

Maruki, Toshi. *Hiroshima No Pika*. Lothrop, Lee, Shepard. A disturbing and graphically-beautiful account of one family's experience of the atomic bomb. Ages twelve and up.

Meltzer, Milton. *Ain't Gonna Study War No More: The Story of America's Peace Seekers*. New York, 1985. Excellent account of people throughout American history who resisted war and struggled for peace. Junior High and up.

537

Meltzer, Milton. *Bread and Roses: The Struggle of American Labor 1865–1915.* New York: Knopf, 1967. Fine account of the ways working people have acted together to create better working conditions. Middle-School and Junior High.

Meyers, Ruth and Beryl Banfield. *Embers: Stories for a Changing World.* New York: Council on Interracial Books for Children/Feminist Press, 1982. An excellent basal reader containing nonsexist, multiracial stories which often show characters working together cooperatively.

Monjo, F. N. *The Drinking Gourd.* New York: Harper & Row, 1970. A fictional account of how a young boy helps slaves escape on The Underground Railroad.

Olsson, Kari. *Sweden: A Good Life for All.* Minneapolis: Dillon, 1983. A book for young people about Sweden that touches on how cooperation is built into the Swedish nation and way of life.

Ortiz, Simon. *The People Shall Continue.* San Francisco: Children's Book Press, 1977. Epic story of the struggle for Native American survival. Elementary and Middle-School

Osada, Arata. *Children of the A Bomb: The Testament of Boys and Girls of Hiroshima.* G. P. Putnam, 1959. A very personal account of what happened at Hiroshima and Nagasaki. Middle grades.

Petry, Ann. *Harriet Tubman: Conductor on the Underground Railroad.* Archway, 1971. Dramatically-told story of Tubman's life and work. Grades six through nine.

Pomeranz, Charlotte. *The Half Birthday Party.* New York: Clarion, 1984. Story of a boy who organizes a half birthday party for his young sister by asking relatives and friends to contribute—creative, cooperative themes in intergenerational, multiracial story. Lower elementary.

Ringi, Kjell. *The Stranger: A Modern Fable.* New York: Random House, 1968. Story of how people, in fear of a giant stranger, bring out their cannon against him. When they finally get to talk to him they like him a lot and he is invited to stay in their country.

Sarch, Becky. *Fanshen the Magic Bear.* New Seed Press, P.O. Box 3016, Stanford, California 94305, 1973. Story of how Laura, on the advice of Fanshen, stopped collecting rent for the King and encouraged the people to stop paying rent too. They equally share the King's land after that.

Smith, Lucie. *My Mom Got a Job.* New York: Holt Reinhardt, 1979. Account of changes in a girl's life when her mom gets a job—realization that the whole family must cooperate to take care of each other. Elementary–lower.

Smucker, Barbara. *Runaway to Freedom.* Harper & Row, 1979. Two Mississippi girls try to reach Canada and freedom via The Underground Railroad.

Sommer, Joellen and Elyse Sommer. *A Patchwork Applique and Quilting Primer.* New York: Lothrop, 1975. A basic guide to quilting and applique. Grades four and up.

Strasser, Todd. *Friends Till the End.* Delacourt, 1981. An honest story about young people supporting a friend who is dying from leukemia. Grades seven and up. Fiction.

Strickland, Dorothy, ed. *Listen Children.* Toronto: Bantam Skyland, 1982. An excellent collection of stories, poems, plays, and essays by a wide variety of Black Americans. Elementary.

Tehanetorens. *Tales of the Iroquois.* Akwesasne Notes, Mohawk Nation, Rooseveltown, New York, 13683. Traditional stories from the Iroquois nation.

Terzian, James and Kathryn Craner. *Mighty Hard Rock: The Story of Cesar Chavez.* New York: Doubleday, 1970. A biography of Chavez and account of the UFW. Middle-School level.

The Unit at the Fayerweather St. School. *The Kids' Book of Divorce By, For, and About Kids.* Edited by Eric Rofes. New York: Vintage, 1982. A fine example of a cooperative project of 6th, 7th, and 8th graders resulting in an excellent book for kids about divorce. Middle-School and up.

Wahl, Jan. *How the Children Stopped the War.* New York: Avon. Haunting story of a medieval shepherd boy and his army of children. Very descriptive account of collaboration as strength. Middle-School and Junior High.

Watson, Sally. *The Mukhar's Children.* Holt, 1968. The involvement of children of an Arab village leader with children of a nearby Israeli kibbutz beginning to bring about understanding and acceptance of each other's cultures. Upper Elementary.

Weiss, Ann. *Nuclear Arms Race: Can We Survive?* Boston: Houghton Mifflin. A history of the arms race and cause for arms control. Useful glossary and bibliography. Ages ten through fourteen.

Weiss, Malcom E., III. *One Sea, One Law? The Fight for a Law of the Sea.* Harcourt. Story of the seven-year struggle to write a law of the sea treaty covering pollution, overfishing, aquaculture, mining, oil drilling and more. Explores the treaty's future in the face of a U.S. veto. Middle-School to High School.

White, Florence. *First Woman in Congress: Jeanette Rankin.* New York: Julian Messner, 1980. Biography of the woman who was the founder of the Women's International League for Peace and Freedom and a person who voted against U.S. entry into World War I and World War II. Middle-School and Junior High.

Williams, Vera. *A Chair for My Mother.* New York: Greenwillow, 1982. A story of how three generations of women—a grandmother, mother and daughter—cooperate to save coins to buy a comfortable chair to relax in after a hard day's work. Neighbors help too after a destructive house fire. Beautifully told and illustrated. Elementary.

Williams, Vera. *Something Special for Me.* New York: Greenwillow, 1983. Story of a working-class family and especially Rosa who can choose one present for her birthday. She decides on a gift she can share with the whole family. Pre-School through Third.

Wondriska, William. *John, John Twilliger.* New York: Holt, 1966. The Machine Gun Man rules the town and keeps people in fear. John and his dog teach the Machine Gun Man to dance and transform the Machine Gun Man and the town.

Yellow Robe, Rosebud. (retold by) *Tonweya and the Eagles and Other Lakota Indian Tales.* New York: Dial, 1979. Tales and legends of the Lakota Sioux.